A Life of Crime

My Career in Forensic Science

International Forensic Science and Investigation Series

Series Editor

Max Houck

Forensic Examination of Hair
James R. Robertson

Forensic Examination of Fibres, Second Edition
J. Robertson and M. Grieve

Forensic Examination of Glass and Paint: Analysis and Interpretation
B. Caddy

Forensic Speaker Identification
P. Rose

Bitemark Evidence
B. J. Dorion

The Practice of Crime Scene Investigation
J. Horswell

Fire Investigation
N. Nic Daéid

Forensic Computer Crime Investigation
Thomas A. Johnson

Analytical and Practical Aspects of Drug Testing in Hair
Pascal Kintz

Nonhuman DNA Typing: Theory and Casework Applications
Heather M. Coyle

Chemical Analysis of Firearms, Ammunition, and Gunshot Residue
James Smyth Wallace

Forensic Science in Wildlife Investigations
Adrian Linacre

Scientific Method: Applications in Failure Investigation and Forensic Science
Randall K. Noon

Forensic Epidemiology
Steven A. Koehler and Peggy A. Brown

Ethics and the Practice of Forensic Science
Robin T. Bowen

Introduction to Data Analysis with R for Forensic Scientists
James Michael Curran

Forensic Investigation of Explosions, Second Edition
A. Beveridge

Firearms, the Law, and Forensic Ballistics, Third Edition
Tom Warlow

The Neuroscience of Handwriting: Applications for Forensic Document Examination
Michael P. Caligiuri and Linton A. Mohammed

Forensic Metrology: Scientific Measurement and Inference for Lawyers, Judges, and Criminalists
Ted Vosk and Ashley F. Emery

Fingerprints and Other Ridge Skin Impressions, Second Edition
C. Champod, C. Lennard, P. Margot, and M. Stoilovic

Forensic Examination of Fibres, Third Edition
James Robertson, Claude Roux, and Kenneth G. Wiggins

Chemical Analysis of Firearms, Ammunition and Gunshot Residue, Second Edition
James Smyth Wallace

A Life of Crime: My Career in Forensic Science
Douglas M. Lucas

A Life of Crime

My Career in Forensic Science

Douglas M. Lucas

CRC Press
Taylor & Francis Group
Boca Raton London New York

CRC Press is an imprint of the
Taylor & Francis Group, an **informa** business

CRC Press
Taylor & Francis Group
6000 Broken Sound Parkway NW, Suite 300
Boca Raton, FL 33487-2742

First issued in paperback 2020

ISBN-13: 978-1-138-60446-9 (hbk)
ISBN-13: 978-0-367-78752-3 (pbk)

Library of Congress Cataloging-in-Publication Data

Names: Lucas, Douglas M., 1929- author.
Title: A life of crime : my career in forensic science / Douglas M. Lucas.
Description: Boca Raton, FL : CRC Press, [2019] |
Includes bibliographical references and index.
Identifiers: LCCN 2018017261| ISBN 9781138604469 (hardback : alk. paper) |
ISBN 9780429468476 (ebook)
Subjects: LCSH: Lucas, Douglas M., 1929- | Forensic scientists--Canada--Biography. |
Forensic sciences--Canada. | Criminal investigation--Canada.
Classification: LCC HV8073 .L797 2019 | DDC 363.25092 [B] --dc23
LC record available at https://lccn.loc.gov/2018017261

Visit the Taylor & Francis Web site at
http://www.taylorandfrancis.com

and the CRC Press Web site at
http://www.crcpress.com

Contents

Acknowledgments

After a career that spanned thirty-seven years (1957–1994) of public service in the Ontario Centre of Forensic Sciences (CFS)—twenty-seven of them (1967–1994) as the Centre's director—followed by twenty-plus years as a private consultant in forensic science, I have worked with too many wonderful colleagues at CFS and elsewhere, each of whom has had an influence on me, to be able to express my appreciation to each individually. Suffice it to say that the career described in the following pages owes much to a great many exceptional people.

The fact that this memoir exists at all is itself something of a miracle. Since my retirement, a few members of my family and friends or colleagues have periodically suggested that I should write something about my career and some of the cases I worked on. (This usually happened near the end of a social gathering at which a bottle of scotch met its demise and many stories had been exchanged, some of which may even have been true!) I managed without much effort to ignore these suggestions, until 2013. That year, the CFS was preparing to move to a new facility and, in the course of clearing out old "stuff," Jonathon Newman (the deputy director) found my old diaries from the 1957–1983 period. (I have no idea why they were still there or what had become of those for the 1984–1994 years.) Jon kindly delivered them to our home where they prompted a fascinating trip down memory lane filled with many exclamations of, "My God! Did I really do that?" That experience prompted me to reconsider my reluctance to write something about those interesting years.

An even more important contributor to this miracle was His Honor Judge Richard Libman of the Ontario Court of Justice and the "oral history" of my career that he produced for the Oral History Program of the Osgoode Society for Canadian Legal History. Rick has been a good friend since his days in the Crown Law Office of the Ministry of the Attorney General, arguing appeals before the Ontario Court of Appeal. Many of those dealt with breath tests for alcohol and cases of driving after drinking, for which Rick looked to me and other members of the CFS staff for scientific and technical advice. For reasons unknown to me, he decided that he should conduct a series of interviews with me for the Osgoode Program. The 389-page transcript of the nineteen tape recordings Rick made from fifteen interview sessions between April 1995 and November 1996 forms the basis for much of what follows and for which I shall be eternally grateful to Rick and the Osgoode Society.

Figure A.1 Judge Rick Libman.

Since I didn't believe anyone other than my family would have much interest in this story, I never intended to publish it. I therefore had a commercial printer produce about fifty copies, which I distributed to our large family and a few colleagues. Several months later, I was contacted by my friend Max Houck, a highly respected forensic scientist in the United States, who had heard about the book and requested a copy. One of Max's many activities is serving as series editor for the Taylor & Francis International Forensic Science and Investigation Series. Max persuaded me that my story should be published, and this book is the result. He was also very helpful in the preparation for publication.

There would have been no career to write about without the involvement of two extraordinary gentlemen, Dr. H. Ward Smith and Professor L. Joslyn Rogers. I will say more about each of them later, but it was Ward Smith who hired me in the first place and who encouraged me to become active in professional associations such as the Canadian Society of Forensic Sciences and the American Academy of Forensic Sciences, where I was able to develop so many contacts and friendships. "Josh" Rogers became my mentor in forensic science, and it was he who got me involved in such a wide variety of cases and who taught me his forensic science philosophy, which I enthusiastically adopted: "Don't just think or read about it, do an experiment." Many houses were burned, cars were blown up, and a great variety of valuable information was derived from such experiments.

Finally, of course, the greatest contributors to whatever professional success I may have had are my wife, Marie, and our family, Eric, Brian, Kristen, Kelly, and Paul. They gave up their husband and father for many long nights and weekends while he was learning and then performing the forensic science services that made up this career, some of which will be described in the text to follow. The career would never have happened without their enduring support, and this memoir was written primarily for their benefit, to try to describe, at least in part, what I was doing all that time. Hopefully it may also be of interest, in the future, to our grandchildren and great grandchildren and to others with an interest in forensic science.

I apologize in advance to them, and any other readers, for all the "I's" and "We's" used throughout the text. They have not been to indulge an "ego trip" (at least not entirely) but rather because it is easier to record events in the first person than to use a tortuous third-person format.

Doug Lucas

Prologue: Flight 621

July 5, 1970 dawned as a gorgeous midsummer day, the sort we dream all winter about for gardening, golfing, sailing, or just lying about. Unfortunately, the serenity was not to last. At 07:00, Air Canada Flight 621, a DC8-63, the largest jet airliner at the time, departed Dorval International Airport (which did not become Pierre Elliot Trudeau International Airport until 2004) in Montreal en route to Los Angeles, with a brief stop in Toronto. Shortly after 08:00, the plane approached runway 32 at Toronto International Airport (which did not become Lester B. Pearson International Airport until 1984) for a routine landing under ideal weather conditions.

Captain Peter Hamilton had the control, assisted by First Officer Donald Rowland and Second Officer Gordon Hill (four-engine aircraft at that time were required to have a flight deck crew of at least two qualified pilots and an engineer). Their conversation was routine except for an ongoing discussion between Hamilton and Rowland about when was the safest time to deploy the "spoilers," flaps on the upper wing surface that are raised following touchdown to reduce lift and help keep the plane on the ground. Hamilton preferred to deploy them manually after touchdown, but Rowland preferred the flight manual procedure, which required "arming" them "at the flare" so they would automatically deploy as the nose wheel began to roll. Hamilton told Rowland he was tired of the discussion and agreed to allow Rowland to follow his preferred procedure. (Arming the spoilers involved lifting up the handle of a lever, but deploying them required the lever to be pulled straight back.)

At about sixty feet above the runway threshold, the aircraft suddenly dropped, striking the runway with sufficient force to tear off the right outboard engine and part of the lower wing plating. Hamilton instinctively applied full power, even before the momentary touchdown, expecting to perform a normal "go-around" procedure. The aircraft climbed to 3100 feet where, about two and a half minutes after the violent touchdown, a series of explosions in the right wing resulted in the loss of the right inboard engine and much of the wing itself. The aircraft rolled to the right in an uncontrollable descent and crashed at about 220 knots into a farmer's field near what is now Castlemore Road and McVean Drive in Woodbridge, nine miles from the airport. All 109 persons on board (9 crew and 100 passengers) were killed instantly. There was little or no fire.

The Ontario Provincial Police (OPP) was notified, and an officer was on the scene within eight minutes of the crash. In less than one hour, the site was fully secured, and it was abundantly clear that no rescue operation was required. The supervising coroner, Dr. H.B. Cotnam, was notified and took charge of the site. He requested the OPP to organize the recovery of the human remains for identification purposes.

Figure P.1 The crash site.

The Challenge

In 1970, forensic pathology was one of the sections in the Centre of Forensic Sciences (CFS), so as the Centre's director, I was notified and requested to organize and manage the examination of the human remains. Thus began the most intense three weeks of my professional life.

Considering the violence of the impact, the crash site was relatively small, about ninety meters in diameter, centered on a crater about three meters deep. The aircraft wreckage, human remains, baggage, and cargo were haphazardly tangled in bits and pieces across this area. A large portion of the tail assembly, which contained both flight recorders, was found leaning against a fence just outside the farmer's house.

The OPP, following their disaster plan, brought in dozens of officers from all over the province to map the site and search for and recover the human

Figure P.2 The debris field.

remains and any personal property that might assist with the identifications. They did a superb job, as did those who assisted later in the temporary morgue. The bodies of the flight deck crew were quickly recovered and taken to a morgue in the hospital in nearby Brampton for detailed examination.

Two refrigerator trucks were brought to the site for storage and transport of the human remains to the hockey arena in Woodbridge, which was transformed into a temporary morgue. (We had understood that these trailers had been rented, but when they were returned to the supplier we were informed that "no, we won't take them back; we didn't realize what you were going to use them for. You bought them!") The bulk of the human remains (there were no intact bodies) was recovered by July 7, but isolated smaller pieces continued to be found for twelve days. In the end, a total of 806 bags of human remains were recovered and 2,200 bags of personal property were collected, itemized, and cataloged.

My first task was to recruit as many pathologists as possible to assist with what was a critical but unpleasant task. Most whom I contacted readily agreed to cooperate as a matter of professional and civic responsibility. I subsequently received approval from the deputy attorney general to create a small fund to thank them for their contribution by claiming the equivalent of 109 coroner's autopsy fees, about $11,000. Toronto General Hospital provided a portable x-ray unit and staff to operate it; the professor of anatomy at the University of Toronto volunteered his expertise, which proved to be invaluable in identifying small pieces of bone and tissue. By coincidence, the Canadian Dental Association had met in Toronto the previous week, and a small group of interested dentists had formed the new Canadian Society of Forensic Odontology. They quickly volunteered their services, and a majority of the subsequent identifications were based on their examinations of jaws and teeth.

With the human resources in hand, the next challenge was the facility. The ice surface in the arena was suitable for the storage of the remains, and the adjacent dressing rooms could be used for the examinations, but they had no water and only inadequate lighting; excellent lighting was essential. Fortunately, a Woodbridge funeral director offered his local knowledge and personal contacts, and within twenty-four hours, we had water and light in our "examination rooms." I set up my "office" in the arena snack bar.

Figure P.3 My "office."

An important lesson I learned about managing major events such as this was the value of an individual with a particular talent to serve as what I referred to as the "DS," the "designated scrounger," and that funeral director became our DS. Whatever equipment we needed, he was able to somehow come up with, and I quickly learned not to ask him where it came from!

The medical examination of human remains in such a catastrophe has three purposes: to find any evidence that might assist in determining the cause, to develop data that might assist in improved "survivability" in the future, and, of course, for identification purposes so that a certificate of death can be issued and the remains released to the next of kin.

The cause of this crash was quickly established by the Transportation Safety Board investigators based on information from the flight data and cockpit voice recorders. The sudden drop to the runway occurred because "the ground spoilers on the aircraft were inadvertently deployed at an inopportune time with catastrophic consequences." The first officer, rather than arming the spoilers on the flare, had deployed them, causing the loss of lift. His last words, "Sorry, Pete," were clearly heard on the cockpit voice recorder tape. After that initial hard ground contact, the final result was inevitable because of the major damage to the wing. Subsequent analysis at CFS of tissue from the flight crew showed no alcohol or carbon monoxide (ruling out a fire in the cockpit).

The condition of the human remains and the wreckage indicated the impossibility of survival.

The Process

Identification thus remained the sole purpose of the medical examination of the remains. This required two types of information, that obtained from the examination of the remains (sometimes supplemented with information from recovered property, such as wallets and purses) and known information about the people listed on the passenger manifest, such as medical and dental records and descriptions of the clothing they were wearing when they left for the airport. Gathering this known information was the responsibility of Air Canada, which had staff specially trained for this sensitive process using preplanned data collection forms.

A significant challenge for me personally was to develop a procedure that would allow us to rapidly compare the hundreds of bits of known information from the Air Canada forms with the autopsy information derived from the remains. This event occurred before the wide use of computers, which, at the time, were essentially just rapid calculating devices rather than database search engines. I decided that about 100 of the many boxes on the Air Canada form contained information of potential use for identification purposes and modified some "edge punch" cards (on which we normally stored x-ray diffraction analytical data) to contain this information for each person on the manifest. By sticking a knitting needle through the stack of 109 cards for a specific piece of information received from the pathologists (or from the OPP officers who were examining the personal property), I could shake out the cards that had matching information. If several data bits were available, for example, male, dark hair, tweed jacket, only one or two cards for individual passengers would drop out, and any additional information on them could then be looked for. This simple but crude system worked very well but was the source of many chuckles from the participants about "Doug's protein-powered computer."

Since there were passengers on board from seven countries but none from the province of Ontario, the known data took several days to collect and enter onto our cards. For this reason, examination of the remains (except for the cockpit crew) did not begin until July 9. Each examination team consisted of a pathologist, odontologist, fingerprint officer, photographer, and recorder, with the services of a radiologist and the anatomist available as required. Most of the examinations were completed in seven 18-hour days, but a few continued for an additional five days. During this entire time, the odor of the examination rooms competed with that of the typical hockey arena dressing room; in the end, we declared this contest a draw!

When identifications were made by either a fingerprint or dental comparison or a combination of other means, the supervising coroner was advised, and he issued a certificate of death for that person.

The Results

Of the 806 bags of human remains recovered, 560 contained only soft-tissue fragments so distorted as to be of unknown origin and no value for identification. Even many of the larger fragments consisted of only portions of scalp, neck, torso, and buttocks with bits of soft tissue and bone attached. The pathologists quickly learned to label them "NIV" (no identification value) and spent very little time on them. Despite these limitations, our identification teams were able to positively identify 89 of the 109 persons listed on the manifest. Forty-four were identified by dental means, twenty by fingerprints, nineteen by property such as wallets found with the remains, and six by pathologies such as old fractures or other pathological features.

The twenty individuals identified by fingerprints were all from the United States, where fingerprints are required to obtain a passport or, in most states, a driver's license. None of the Canadians on board had their fingerprints on record, due to our somewhat irrational national reluctance to have our fingerprints recorded. It was interesting that all of the persons working in the morgue, including myself, made a point of having the OPP record our fingerprints before we left the arena.

As is often the case in mass disasters, the factor limiting identification of those who remained unidentified was the paucity of known information rather than the amount of information derived from the remains. We were left with fingers and teeth and other bits of useful information that could not be associated with any of the passengers because they had never had their fingerprints recorded or had never been to a dentist. In a few cases, entire families were on board, and there was no one left who could provide the known information. The fact that the flight was an early morning departure also meant that the clothing that many passengers had been wearing was unknown because no one had seen them leave for the airport.

The supervising coroner eventually issued death certificates for the remaining twenty unidentified victims. Although there was no positive medical evidence for identification, there was a considerable amount of documentary information to corroborate the listing of the name on the passenger manifest supplemented by the fact that the people were still reported to be missing.

Three weeks after the crash, the operation was completed; the identified remains (sometimes only a hand, a jaw, or even a single tooth) were placed in individual coffins and either returned to the next of kin or buried with the unidentified remains in a common grave at Mount Pleasant Cemetery in Toronto. The personal property was burned or returned to the agent for the next of kin, the temporary morgue was converted back into a hockey arena, and the farmer's field was returned to him.

As is often the case with major investigations, there was one statistical aberration and bit of serendipity that sticks with me to this day. One of the passengers who we were able to identify was a Dwight Lee Smith. A few fragments of patterned trousers on a leg matched the description we had of what he had been wearing and held a wallet in the pocket that contained a driver's license in the name of Dwight Lee Smith. I felt quite comfortable about that identification until, as we were discussing it with the coroner, I noticed that another bag of remains containing the same patterned cloth in a jacket sleeve included an arm and hand. I asked the fingerprint officer if he had been able to identify the fingerprints. His response was, "I wish you hadn't asked that, Doug, because the FBI sent us the fingerprints of Dwight Lee Smith, and they don't match." We all were incredulous and asked him to go back to the FBI and ask if by any chance they had another Dwight Lee Smith on record. Somewhat reluctantly, another search was made and, much to their surprise (and our relief), there was indeed a second Dwight Lee Smith with the same birth date and born in the same state (although not in the same city) as the one whose prints they had forwarded initially. Fortunately, one was Caucasian and the other was African American; ours was the Caucasian whose fingerprints did indeed match the second set of reference prints.

Three weeks of eighteen-hour days of this type of intense activity was very physically and emotionally draining for everyone. The importance of the findings and conclusions to the families of the victims was such, however, that emotion could not be allowed to impact our deliberations. Sometimes, the team members' compensation for this stress took the form of "morgue humor," which, I must confess, occasionally breached the bounds of good taste.

As a result, after our work was completed, one of the things I made a point of doing was to attend the memorial and interment ceremony at the common grave in Mount Pleasant Cemetery. Air Canada arranged the service and brought the next of kin to it. It helped to restore my thoughts about the entire event to reality and remind me how unbelievably tragic and emotional this had been for those people. (Air Canada also built a memorial at the burial site that, by coincidence, is right beside a memorial tree that my wife, Marie, planted in memory of a favorite uncle of hers who we both had been very close to. It is also close to a similar memorial for the SS *Noronic* fire victims, which will be referred to in Chapter 1.)

The area of the crash is now in the midst of a residential development, but in July 2013, the property developers and the city of Brampton opened a memorial garden in a small park to preserve the actual impact site.

The activities associated with the crash of Air Canada Flight 621 had an enormous impact on me and my professional career. A reader might well wonder (as I often have) how on earth did a guy from Windsor, Ontario, who started out to become a pharmacist ever get into such a position? The answer to that question, and how that career developed, will be described in the rest of this story.

About the Author

Douglas M. Lucas, MSc, DSc (Hon), retired in 1994 from the Centre of Forensic Sciences in Toronto following thirty-seven years of service, twenty-seven as the Centre's Director. His scientific background was in toxicology and chemistry, with particular emphasis on alcohol, fire investigation, and explosives. He has published more than thirty papers and chapters on a variety of forensic science topics.

In 1960, Doug was the first forensic scientist to develop and publish the technique of gas chromatography as a means of identification of petroleum products used as liquid accelerants in suspected cases of arson. This method became a worldwide standard for volatile accelerant identification in forensic arson investigations, as gas chromatography continues to be considered among the most accurate scientific means of identifying flammable or combustible accelerant residues. In addition, Doug authored "Ethical Responsibilities of the Forensic Scientist: Exploring the Limits," published in the *Journal of Forensic Science* in 1989. Doug also has been active with several professional associations and is a past president of the Canadian Society of Forensic Sciences, the American Academy of Forensic Sciences (AAFS), the International Association of Forensic Sciences (IAFS), and the American Society of Crime Laboratory Directors (ASCLD). With ASCLD, he was involved in the development of an international forensic proficiency testing program in the late 1970s and with the establishment of the ASCLD/LAB (Laboratory Accreditation Board) accreditation program in 1982. The Douglas M. Lucas Medal, established in 1999, is presented by the AAFS at each IAFS meeting to a person who has made internationally recognized contributions to forensic science.

Postretirement, Doug continued his association with that proficiency testing program as an advisor and has served as a consultant internationally to many forensic laboratories, primarily with respect to management and/or quality assurance issues. This included serving on a five-member international "Blue Ribbon Scientific Panel" in support of an eighteen-month investigation by the Office of the Inspector General in the U.S. Department of Justice of allegations of misconduct and improper practices by staff of the FBI Laboratory. From December 1998 to December 2003, another major activity involved serving as a member of a three-person international "Peer Review Panel" advising the judicial tribunal for the "Bloody Sunday Inquiry" into the tragic events of January 30, 1972, in Londonderry, Northern Ireland, in which thirteen civilians were killed and fourteen seriously wounded by gunshots during a confrontation with the British Army. From 2003 to 2006, a similar activity was associated with a major investigation by the Northern Ireland Police Service of the Omagh bombing of August 1998, in which twenty-nine people were killed by an IRA bomb. In 2005 and 2006, another important activity was serving as a scientific advisor to the independent investigator examining serious problems in the Houston Police Department Crime Laboratory and Property Room.

The Early Years 1

An oft-repeated (somewhat facetious) piece of advice offered to young people is "Choose your parents wisely!" Fortunately, I did exactly that!

My Family

I was born May 5, 1929, in Windsor, Ontario. Although I don't remember much about that event, I do know that I was born at home, 431 Grove Avenue. (The house is still there, but there is no bronze plaque on the door to commemorate the occasion!) My parents were Melvin Lucas (1901–1977) and Gertrude (nee Fulcher) Lucas (1904–1992), and I was the second child; my sister, Elaine, was four years older than me. My parents had grown up in Watford, Ontario, a small village in Lambton County. Dad was an elementary

Figure 1.1 My family—1934.

school teacher and principal in Windsor; Mother was a stay-at-home mom. I attended Victoria Avenue Public School, followed by Kennedy Collegiate Institute in Windsor. Fortunately, I never attended a school at which my father was a teacher or principal. Nevertheless, I suspect he knew more about my escapades than I would have wished, but he was very good about not repeating tales at home.

A reasonably capable student, I was able to achieve good grades without allowing studies to interfere with my primary interest, sports. I played hockey and football for the high school teams, but my best sport was baseball, which I played at the competitive junior level as a pitcher. Because of the proximity of Windsor to Detroit, I was a fan of the Detroit Tigers and went to many games at what was then Briggs Stadium (later Tiger Stadium), a beautiful traditional old ballpark, famous around the American League for its "ballpark franks" (hot dogs). The walk from the Detroit/Windsor Tunnel exit to the stadium went through what is still known as "Corktown" in Detroit, a district filled with seedy pubs. This was my initial exposure to the seamier side of life that I was to become more familiar with later in my career.

As will appear occasionally as this tale progresses, there were particular events or incidents throughout my early years that, although they went unrecognized at the time, were serendipitous omens of where my life was heading professionally.

Mom and Dad each had close relatives who were active farmers in Lambton County, so each summer in our younger years my sister and I would spend time with wonderful and patient aunts, uncles, and cousins to be exposed to the realities of farm life. We learned that the apparent idyllic image comes at the cost of a 24/7 commitment to the needs of the livestock, dependence on the weather for crop success, and plenty of hard physical labor. Although enjoyable, I never developed a desire to return to the soil. Because Dad had July and August free, we rented a cottage on Lake Huron near Sarnia, and during my teens, he and I worked at a variety of jobs maintaining grounds and painting buildings for wealthy American cottagers or helping local farmers with their crops. I commuted to Windsor by bus on the weekends for my baseball games.

One summer, Dad and I spent time on the Canada Steamship Lines passenger ship *Noronic* working in the galley as it cruised the Great Lakes between Detroit and Duluth. Sarnia, Ontario, was home base for *Noronic*, which coincidentally reentered my life in 1970 during the work on Flight 621. In the early morning of September 17, 1949, *Noronic*, while on a rare cruise into Lake Ontario, caught fire while docked in Toronto and was destroyed with the loss of at least 118 lives (the exact number was never firmly established), the first mass disaster in Ontario. When I was organizing the identification of the victims of Flight 621 twenty-one years later, I read the reports of the identification of the *Noronic* victims, which persuaded me of the value of dental identifications in such tragedies.

Summers working with my father taught me much about having to work for a living. Although he had what were responsible positions, teaching, particularly during the depression years, was not a high-paying profession. He usually had a second part-time job to help provide a better life for his family. For many years, he worked on Saturdays in a retail shoe store where he became one of the most popular and successful salesmen. We were never without a roof over our heads, clothes on our backs, or food on the table. However, my parents never owned their own home until I was in high school, nor did they have a new car until after Elaine and I had both finished school. They sacrificed much to provide an excellent upbringing and education for us, Elaine as a registered nurse and me in pharmacy.

My father loved meeting new people; his gregarious nature resulted in strangers immediately considering him a friend, and vice versa. Later, when he visited our family in Toronto, he would know everyone in the neighborhood within hours, some of whom were unknown to my wife and me. In his professional positions, he earned the respect and affection of both staff and students. As an example, after he retired one of his former students who had been elected mayor of Windsor persuaded Dad to become his part-time executive assistant. There was no job description, which was a good thing, as it allowed Dad to exploit his ability to find creative yet effective solutions to the problems he dealt with as the mayor's personal "Mr. Fixit."

After I started working at the Attorney General's Laboratory, I learned from Windsor Police Department (PD) detectives about another talent he had. They all knew and respected him and loved to regale me with their "Mel Lucas" stories. His final assignment as a principal was in the largest elementary school in Windsor in one of the toughest neighborhoods. Many of his students were well known to the Windsor PD. The detectives told me they never had any problem with investigations in the area because all they had to do was describe the circumstances to Dad. "Leave it with me and come back in a couple of hours," he would tell them. When they returned, they would receive a complete description of what had happened and who was involved. Often, these students would later come back to the school to thank him for setting them on the "straight and narrow."

Although in most of Ontario I eventually became "Doug Lucas, Director of the Centre of Forensic Sciences," in Windsor, I was always simply "Mel Lucas's son."

Dad suffered a stroke in 1975 and died of cancer in 1977; Mom succumbed to Alzheimer's in 1992. My sister, Elaine, remained in Windsor where she married Dr. Jack Prince, and they raised four fine sons. She died in February 2015.

Education

In high school, I did well in science and, although I had no interest in it, Latin. In grade 12, one of my teachers said to me, "Latin and science; you should become a pharmacist." Although I had worked as a bicycle delivery boy for a pharmacy after school and on weekends, it had never occurred to me that pharmacy might be a potential vocation until that chance comment. I had no interest in studying medicine and never even considered law.

Before 1948, pharmacy education in Ontario consisted of a two-year program at the Ontario College of Pharmacy followed by a two-year apprenticeship with a licensed pharmacist. In 1948, the University of Toronto (U of T) and the Ontario College of Pharmacy combined to establish a new Faculty of Pharmacy in the university and introduced a four-year bachelor of science program. The timing was perfect for me and was of great interest because it promised more emphasis on science than had previously been the case. In my final year of high school, I applied for the first class of the new program, which was limited to twenty-five students and, I later learned, I was number twenty-six. The interest had been whetted, however, and since there still was a requirement for a one-year apprenticeship either before or after the academic program, I entered into the apprenticeship program in a pharmacy in Windsor with the assurance of acceptance into the second class in September 1949, the graduating class of 1953.

The apprenticeship was an interesting experience and a good thing for me because it allowed for some maturing to help bridge the gap between high school and university. It also convinced me that retail pharmacy was probably not where I wanted to spend the rest of my life. During the apprenticeship, I was paid just $25 per week, but there was a perquisite in the form of an old-fashioned soda fountain in the pharmacy staffed with young ladies who were an occasional attractive diversion.

The work involved studying a manual to learn about how prescriptions are written and the meaning of the various terms and observing the pharmacists filling prescriptions. Under the pharmacist's direction, I had to make things like ointments and solutions that were not commercially available. It also involved learning something about the business side of pharmacy and, toward the end of the apprenticeship period, actually filling prescriptions, which would be checked by the pharmacist before delivery. A bonus from the apprenticeship was that the experience made part-time work in a pharmacy while at school in Toronto easy to obtain.

Although during the summer before starting my apprenticeship I had worked as a bellhop at a lodge in the Muskoka Lake region, my freshman year in Toronto was the first time I felt that I was truly on my own. I rented a room from an elderly couple in an apartment near the university. Because the Faculty of Pharmacy was still in a building about a mile from the main U of T campus, there was no shortage of exercise as I dashed between the two locations in the ten minutes allowed between classes.

Later that first year, I was invited to join a fraternity, Psi Upsilon, and for the next three years lived in the fraternity house on the campus. That was another valuable experience because many of the members were war veterans completing their university degrees. They were more mature and very motivated to succeed. Some of that motivation rubbed off on us younger members. I subsequently became the fraternity house manager, which taught me a tremendous amount about responsibility. I learned that there is no "They" (as in "Why don't they do something?"); there is only "I" or "We," a valuable lesson that, unfortunately, some people never learn. (Coincidentally, my mentor, Professor Joslyn Rogers, had been a member of the local fraternity that in 1920 became the U of T chapter of Psi Upsilon. It became inactive in 1997.)

Sports were still a compelling interest, and I played on the Faculty of Pharmacy hockey team all four years (the final three as the team captain.) In the second year, however, I started to get excited about chemistry when we were introduced to organic chemistry. It was taught by Professor Fred Lorriman, who was a rarity in universities, an inspiring teacher. Organic chemistry is perhaps the most organized body of scientific knowledge with a completely rational system of nomenclature, and I did very well in it. This interest was enhanced in the third year when in the Faculty of Pharmacy Professor Garnet Patterson taught a course that was a combination of chemistry and pharmacology. He showed how minor changes in the molecular structure of a drug could change its pharmacological effect in a rational and predictable manner. This experience confirmed my original belief that I was going to head in a different direction from retail pharmacy and toward a laboratory environment. Another faculty member, Professor Dan Murray, taught a course in analytical chemistry of drugs. I worked with him on my research project in the fourth year and began to learn something about analytical work in which you didn't do everything with test tubes. There were new analytical instruments, such as spectrophotometers and polarographs, and I became quite fascinated with them.

One of the things I learned in that research project was the importance of safe laboratory practice. While working alone in the lab one night, I did something stupid that resulted in a fire. Fortunately, I was able to extinguish it, but not before it filled the whole lab with smoke and covered everything with black soot. I burned my hands quite badly in the process and had to go to emergency for treatment. Professor Murray never really said anything about my stupidity, but he did make it clear that it was up to me to clean this mess up, which took several days of hard scrubbing.

In the final two years, I took all of the chemistry and pharmacology options rather than the business-related options, which made for a very demanding academic program. (The combination of chemistry and pharmacology, however, would later prove to be a valuable asset to my career.) Nevertheless, at graduation in 1953, I finished second in the class and won several prizes. There was then the question, what next? Fortunately, my timing was again perfect because the Faculty of Pharmacy had decided to offer an MSc program in pharmaceutical chemistry beginning in the fall of 1953; that was for me!

The RCAF

During my undergraduate years, I was able to assist with the costs of education by serving in the Royal Canadian Air Force (RCAF) University Reserve Training Plan (URTP). This service involved training one night a week during the winter and spending three summers at an RCAF base. The first summer was basic training at RCAF Station Crumlin near London, Ontario, where, in addition to lectures and project assignments, we did plenty of foot and small arms drill. Although we were first-year university students (all male), and as cocky as such guys usually are, we enjoyed the discipline that came

Figure 1.2 RCAF Station Crumlin.

with the drill. There was a great sense of satisfaction derived from getting an entire platoon to work with precision in various drills, particularly silent drills, in which we had to execute maneuvers without any verbal order being given. Our rank was "flight cadet," which meant we occupied a no man's land between commissioned officers and enlisted men. Nevertheless, we quickly learned that, in reality, nobody outranks the drill sergeants. They each had their own unique but very effective vocabulary, a few words of which had more than four letters!

This was 1950 and the Korean War had just started. The RCAF committed a transport squadron, 426 Squadron based at RCAF Station Lachine and Dorval Airport, to be the principal means of transport for the military between Canada and South Korea. Our URTP group was assigned a project to develop a plan for the movement of part of the squadron to McCord Air Force Base in Tacoma, Washington, in three days! A huge challenge that we took up with great enthusiasm.

For the second and third summers, 1951 and 1952, I was assigned to the hospital at RCAF Station Rockcliffe in suburban Ottawa. This assignment was another marvelous experience. Because I was billeted in the officer's mess, I became friends with many of the aircrews of the two operational squadrons based there, 408 Squadron, which flew modified WWII Lancaster bombers making an aerial photographic survey of Canada, and 425 Squadron, which was the VIP transport squadron for the government of Canada. They flew mostly DC-3 Dakotas and four-engine Northstars. The Lancaster, with its four Rolls Royce Merlin piston engines, was undoubtedly the noisiest aircraft ever flown. The Northstar was essentially a DC-4 modified with the noisy

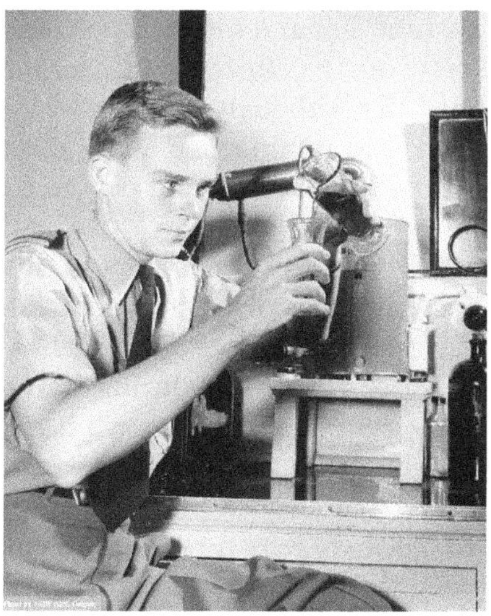

Figure 1.3 RCAF Station Rockliffe.

but highly efficient Merlin engines. (Jet engines did not become common in transport planes until later in the 1950s.) Whenever a Lancaster or Northstar took off, all conversation in the mess, of necessity, ceased.

I was frequently able to fly with 425 Squadron on my days off if there was a flight with room for an extra passenger. One of these flights provided more than just a pleasant diversion. The Grumman Goose, a six-seat amphibian aircraft, was one of the smaller 425 Squadron planes. Its pilot was one of my friends. One Saturday he was flying an air commodore (AC) to his cottage, and there was a spare seat. This was to be my first water landing, and I was cautioned that it would be quite noisy. The AC needed some flying time and so took command. Unfortunately, his landing was unsuccessful. The water was glassy, we hit very hard, flipped over, broke in half, and began to sink in 200 feet of water. I was a bit stunned and thought, "Boy, that really was noisy." It finally dawned on me that something was not quite right because the corporal crewman was yelling, "Get out, get out!" I didn't realize that I was hanging upside down from my seat belt, and when I finally succeeded in unhooking it, I of course fell on my head into a foot of water. However, having been well trained in military etiquette, I sloshed around in the sinking aircraft searching for my cap. I wasn't about to be improperly dressed in the presence of an air commodore! We were rescued (by the AC's wife in their outboard motorboat).

Another interesting experience occurred near the end of my final summer in 1952. By then I had been commissioned with the rank of "pilot officer," the equivalent of a second lieutenant, the lowest officer rank, but at least I was no longer in no man's land. I received orders to report to 426 Squadron at RCAF Station Lachine to travel to Tokyo on one of the Korean War supply flights. On arrival at Lachine, I found myself listed on the flight manifest as the third pilot in the crew of a Northstar. Panic set in but, when I met the other crew and explained that although my rank was pilot officer, I had no piloting skills whatsoever. The captain responded, "We know that. No worry; we have an engineer. This is just a recruiting ploy to try to persuade you to stay in the Air Force."

So I went to Tokyo on the noisy Northstar with flight legs from Dorval to Edmonton, to Vancouver, to Tacoma, to Anchorage, to Shemya (an island at the tip of the Aleutian Islands), to Tokyo. We spent several days in Tokyo at what had been a Japanese naval base during WWII (the showers were designed for much shorter people, and the spray hit at navel level) and then returned. In addition to being noisy, the Northstar was not very fast; the over-ocean legs each took about ten hours. Although we carried military personnel on their way to South Korea, there were no seats for them; they just had to find a place to sit or lie among the mail bags and other cargo. Because the plane wasn't pressurized, when we flew over the Rockies, we had to don oxygen masks. By that time, I had decided I wasn't going to make the military a career, so on my return to Rockliffe, I explained this to my commanding officer (CO); he was not amused! I tried to persuade him that although the military could provide a very comfortable and secure career, as a pharmacist, there was a limit to what rank I could attain. The senior pharmacist in the entire RCAF was a squadron leader, the equivalent of a major. I told the CO that if I joined an organization, I wanted the only thing that might prevent me from reaching the top of the organization to be my ability or lack thereof and not the fact that I was in the wrong profession or trade. (In the RCAF, all the senior officers wore pilot's wings!) He may have recognized this thinking; although he was the most senior medical officer in the RCAF, he was only a wing commander (lieutenant colonel).

Marriage

Another event that was to have a huge impact on my life occurred in the fall of 1952. During the spring term, our class had taken a microbiology course with the household science class. The first day, I noticed a very attractive young woman across the bench from me; she stood out even among her classmates, all of whom were female and almost equally attractive. I thought, "I would sure like to have a date with her," but being somewhat reserved, I did nothing to try to convert this fantasy into reality. Later that year, serendipity again played in my favor when one of the fraternity brothers invited me on a blind date to play bridge with a roommate of his girlfriend. To my great surprise, the blind date was the girl from across the microbiology bench, Marie Michener Macdonald, daughter of Angus J. (1904–1981) and Marion Louise (nee Michener) Macdonald (1904–2005) of Montreal.

Neither of us had played bridge before, so this was a challenging learning experience for us both. (During the evening I persuaded her to try a sip of my beer, and to this day she still accuses me of teaching her to drink.) The following weekend, I invited her to a football game, and things progressed from there, much to my surprise and delight. The rest, as they say, is history.

By the summer of 1953, Marie and I realized that we were destined to get married sometime in the future; however, an unexpected incentive arose. Marie's Grandmother Michener was going to be absent from her apartment for several months and asked Marie if she would look after it for her. We decided that it would be foolish to continue paying for two places to live when there was very pleasant free accommodation available. The social mores of the time frowned on simply living together, so we decided to advance our marriage plans and organized a small family wedding in the chapel in Hart House on the campus.

Figure 1.4 Our wedding day.

Now, after sixty-five years, that decision seems to have worked out well!

Graduate School

During the summer of 1953, I worked in a pharmacy to improve our financial situation in preparation for graduate school in the fall. The MSc program was to be two years, consisting of coursework and, primarily, a research project. We were also expected to serve as instructors in some of the undergraduate labs on a part-time basis, for which we received a small stipend. Every little bit helped!

My major professor was Ross Baxter, whose research interest was the alkaloids of ergot, a fungus that grows on rye and other plants, which has pharmacological properties. My project involved cultivation of a large quantity of the fungus in order to extract a sufficient amount of one of the alkaloids to try to characterize its chemical structure.

Although I did not know it at the time, Professor Baxter's academic interest was to have a major impact on my future. In 1994, there was a murder case in Belleville, Ontario, one of the very rare cases of murder by poison. A Mrs. Bell was charged and subsequently convicted of murdering her husband with strychnine. One of the issues at the trial was how she had masked the taste of the strychnine (which is very bitter); one suggestion was that she had put it into his cocoa. Professor Baxter was asked by Dr. Ward Smith, the director of what was then known as the Attorney General's Laboratory, to examine the stomach contents of Mr. Bell to see if there was any evidence of cocoa. He did, in fact, identify cocoa and in the process developed a close rapport with Ward Smith. (One of those omens referred to earlier.)

Early Married Life

During the fall of 1953, we were both busy. Marie was in her final year in household science, and like every graduate student in a science program, I typically worked in the laboratory fourteen to eighteen hours a day six days a week. We didn't see a lot of each other but must have occasionally met because our first son, Eric, arrived in 1954, calling for another change of plans. As a new father, I began looking for a full-time job. One potential position was in sales with Parke Davis, a large pharmaceutical company. During an interview with the sales manager, I was required to take several hours of aptitude tests. A few days later, he invited me to lunch to outline the results of the tests. The bad news was that they showed I would probably be the world's worst salesman. The good news was that they indicated I should think about a research position. Unfortunately, all such positions with Parke Davis were in the United States. I have been forever grateful that those tests knew more about me than I did!

The dean of the Faculty of Pharmacy then offered to convert my instructor position from part-time to full-time (for eight months a year at $200.00 a month). He also wanted me to continue the MSc program on a part-time basis, which would take four years instead of two. Marie and I made ends almost meet by me working evenings and summers in a pharmacy while she had a lucrative job on weekends as a tour guide at Casa Loma, where the tips for an attractive young co-ed were very generous.

In the spring of 1954, Marie graduated, and in April, her grandmother returned, so we moved to a one-bedroom apartment on the third floor of a house. Marie continued to do occasional weekday tours at Casa Loma, where the other staff enjoyed playing with baby Eric and watching him sleep in the bed of Lady Pellatt, the former mistress of the castle. Our productivity continued (this was before "the pill" after all) and Brian arrived in our cozy ménage in 1955.

By May 1956, we realized we needed more space and moved to a two-bedroom ground floor apartment immediately beside the main Canadian

Pacific Railway (CPR) crosstown line. When Eric and Brian wanted to play with a train, it belonged to the CPR! My future association with the police began there because our next-door neighbor was a woman who ensured that the Liquor Control Board of Ontario was profitable and who "entertained" gentlemen in her apartment at night. Police from 52 Division were quite familiar with her apartment.

Almost Forensic Science

One of the laboratory courses that I instructed involved the analysis of drugs, and it created another of those omens. The Ontario College of Pharmacy (the licensing body for pharmacists) still shared space with the Faculty of Pharmacy, and the OCP inspector, who was responsible for investigating infractions of the Pharmacy Act, was a retired RCMP Drug Squad officer whose office was next door to my lab. Like most retired cops, he loved to tell war stories, and we got to know each other well.

Because of his background, he knew that to get a conviction under the Pharmacy Act, he had to have more than just his word that somebody had sold a drug that they weren't permitted to sell. He therefore asked if I would analyze them for him. It sounded interesting and would contribute a few extra dollars to our kitty. There wasn't any great analytical challenge to the work because the evidence item was usually a package labeled to contain a particular drug.

This work gave me a simple introduction to forensic science, even though at that time I didn't know what forensic science was. I had to testify a couple of times in court, but this was no great challenge since the defense didn't want to deny that their clients had sold the product that they had purported it to be.

Early in 1957, after four years, my research project was nearing completion, and another bit of serendipity came along. I needed an infrared spectrophotometer, a relatively new analytical instrument, to assist in determining the chemical structure of the alkaloid I had been able to extract from the ergot I had grown. The Faculty of Pharmacy didn't have such an instrument, but the Attorney General's Laboratory did. Through the connection that Professor Baxter had with Ward Smith, I was allowed to use their instrument.

In addition to being able to finalize my research, this opportunity led to discussions with Dr. Smith about forensic science and I began to think, "This could be interesting." By that time, we had a third child on the way, so proceeding to a doctorate was not on the table. There was a position available in the Attorney General's Lab, so I applied for it and was hired at the magnificent salary of $4,700 per year. After finishing my MSc, I started in the Attorney General's Lab on May 25, 1957. It was then located in laboratory space of the old Hospital for Sick Children at 67 College Street.

2 The Fledgling Forensic Scientist

Forensic Science in Ontario

Although credit must be given to the medical profession for the first efforts to engage science against crime, not all doctors were on the right side of the law. In April of 1859, Professor Henry Holmes Croft of King's College (now the University of Toronto) testified at the murder trial in Cobourg, Ontario, of Dr. William Henry King that he found eleven grains of arsenic in the stomach of Dr. King's wife, Sarah. This case is the first record of the use of science, other than medicine, in a prosecution in Canada. Professor Croft also testified that he found very little arsenic in Sarah's liver, not sufficient to cause death. Nevertheless, the jury convicted Dr. King. Their finding may have been correct but for the wrong reason, for as Dr. King was led up the gallows steps, he confessed that he had indeed murdered his wife, but with morphine not arsenic.

Professor Croft's laboratory, which I consider to be the first forensic science lab in Canada, was a round appendage that still exists at the southwest corner of University College. The design and location were intended to prevent the transfer of odors to the main building, a wise decision given the lack of refrigeration, the distance some specimens had to travel, and the resultant requirement to often work with "well-seasoned" evidence.

Croft was succeeded in 1873 by Dr. William Hodgson Ellis. A record of his forensic cases survives in his laboratory notebook in the Centre of Forensic Sciences library. An interesting item in it is a newspaper clipping from the Rat Portage (now Kenora—no wonder they changed the name) news dated May 19, 1900. It described a coroner's inquest into the death by morphine overdose of one Oliver Doyle. Mr. Doyle was described as a heavy drinker who lived with a lady friend who was the proprietress of a brothel. Booze, sex, and drugs: it could have been written yesterday!

Professor Ellis retired in 1919, but not before persuading one of his former students, Joslyn Rogers, to take up forensic work in 1911. Rogers, who became professor of analytical chemistry, introduced blood alcohol analysis to the courts of Ontario in 1932 and developed many techniques used in the investigation of a variety of crimes, particularly fires and explosions. Following his retirement from the university in 1954, Professor Rogers continued active practice in the Attorney General's Laboratory until 1967. It was my great good fortune to have this wonderful gentleman as my mentor in forensic science.

During his career at the university, Professor Rogers participated in more than 2,000 cases covering a wide range of crimes; he was essentially a one-man forensic science lab. He was also a much-loved teacher. My first encounter with him was as a student in 1951 seeking his advice on an analytical problem. He didn't know me from Adam but received me graciously, invited me to sit down in his lab, and shared a piece of cake that he had just baked in his laboratory oven, presumably the same one in which he dried stomach contents.

Professor Rogers loved to tell stories about his cases and had a limitless supply of them.

After I described my analytical problem, he talked about a case he had in September 1934 in which he had encountered a similar problem and how he had resolved it. That may or may not have been true, but it was his way of steering me in the necessary direction to solve my problem.

The Attorney General's Laboratory/Centre of Forensic Sciences

Before 1932, aside from the work of Professors Croft, Ellis, and Rogers, the only forensic activities in Ontario were the autopsies performed by a small cadre of hospital pathologists. One of these, Dr. Edgar Frankish, was appointed director of a new Attorney General's Medico-Legal Laboratory in 1932. It was located in an old house at 11 Queen's Park Crescent in Toronto that looked like something from a Charles Adams cartoon. Dr. Frankish traveled the province performing autopsies while his technician, Ms. Verda Vincent, remained in the lab doing tests for blood, semen, hairs, and fibers. In 1941, Dr. Frankish retired, but Ms. Vincent continued doing the lab work on her own until 1950.

In 1951, the attorney general decided to revitalize the laboratory and asked Dr. Noble Sharpe, a pathologist at Grace Hospital, to lead it. Dr. Sharpe recognized that forensic science by then encompassed a much broader range of disciplines and recommended instead that a scientist be the director. Professor H. Ward Smith was recruited from the University of Toronto, Department of Pharmacology, and the modern era of forensic science in Ontario began. The laboratory moved from Queen's Park Crescent to the former Hospital for Sick Children, and Dr. Sharpe continued to serve as medical director on a part-time basis.

When I joined the Attorney General's Laboratory in May 1957, I was the fourteenth person on the staff. The lab was performing examinations in biology (three persons), chemistry (two persons), toxicology (six persons), and

Figure 2.1 Professor H. Ward Smith.

questioned documents/photography (one person), about 800 cases per year. We didn't have a Firearms Section until 1959, when we hired a retired examiner from the Royal Canadian Mounted Police.

One of the early cases that I worked on a few weeks after I started in the lab was a strychnine overdose death from Sudbury, which, unfortunately, was because of a mislabeled bottle in a pharmacist's dispensary. (As I wrote this, I was shocked to be reminded how quickly I began working on my own cases. The formal training program I later put in place after becoming director required up to two years to complete before new staff were assigned their own cases.) The prescription called for sodium sulfate, and the pharmacist filled the prescription from a bottle labeled "sodium sulfate." The patient took the prescribed dose and died almost instantly. The police collected the sodium sulfate bottle and sent it to us. It didn't take long to establish that the white powder in the bottle was not sodium sulfate, but then the question was, "What was it?"

Professor Rogers was working at the next bench and looked at the powder in the jar and announced, "Well, the last time I saw something which looked like that was in 1929, and it turned out to be strychnine." With all the cynicism of youth, I replied, "Oh, sure!" He sampled a bit of the powder, did some color tests with his spot test reagents, and announced, "It's strychnine alright." I was dumbfounded but proceeded to run an infrared spectrum and confirmed that it was indeed strychnine. I never again questioned Professor Rogers's memory!

In July 1957, the lab relocated to 11,000 square feet of space renovated for us at 8 Jarvis Street in what had been a liquor warehouse. (Although we shared the building with the Ontario Provincial Police [OPP] headquarters at 125 Lakeshore Road, Dr. Smith insisted on having our own separate address.)

Figure 2.2 Professor L. Joslyn Rogers.

On moving in, we thought we would be there for the rest of our careers, but by 1966, we had already outgrown that building. We were using the halls as laboratories and had people sitting at desks with an x-ray machine right next to their head. Had there been a Work Place Health and Safety Act in those days, we would have been shut down.

The Breathalyzer

My initial assignment was to train as a toxicologist, which my academic background in chemistry and pharmacology was ideally suited to. Serendipity continued to influence my career; because of the limited space in the lab, the only place for me to work was a small area on a bench in Dr. Smith's office. As a result, I began to learn subliminally about the wide range of cases we received and the challenges associated with managing a forensic science laboratory.

Dr. Smith was in the process of introducing breath testing for alcohol to Ontario using the newly invented Breathalyzer. His PhD thesis had involved developing an improved method for alcohol analysis, and the inventor of the Breathalyzer, Robert Borkenstein, director of the Indiana State Police Laboratory, had consulted with him about the composition of the analytical reagent to be used in it. As a result, in 1955, Dr. Smith received two of the first production models of the Breathalyzer for evaluation.

Figure 2.3 Professor Robert Borkenstein (with the first homemade wooden Breathalyzer).

In the spring of 1956, he trained eight police officers from the OPP and the Toronto Police in the operation of the new instruments. This training was done on a somewhat informal ad hoc basis at night in his cramped office. (The first Breathalyzer test in Canada was subsequently performed by the OPP at Whitby, Ontario, in July 1956.) For the longer term, however, Dr. Smith realized that a more formal Breathalyzer training and operation program was required, and I was assigned the additional responsibility of developing a formalized training course for police officers and the operational protocols they were to follow.

Because I was fresh out of graduate school, I had no practical knowledge about breath testing. To fill this void, I began working with those first Toronto Police Department (PD) officers Dr. Smith had trained to learn the practical challenges of testing drinking drivers. That involved spending many weekend nights (a 19:00 to 03:00 shift was the norm) with them at Regent Street police station, in a very tough section of Toronto. There, it did not take long for me to grasp the differences between the "ivory tower" of academia and the real world of law enforcement. It was a critical learning experience, and I developed a great appreciation for the challenges of police work, the often unsavory people they have to deal with, and the patience required for doing so. As a result of one of the violent confrontations I observed one night, I also learned the dictum "Don't get mad; get even!"

Three months after joining the lab, on August 12, 1957, I began teaching the first formal Breathalyzer training course in Canada to a class of fourteen officers from the OPP and the Toronto, Hamilton, and Windsor PDs.

Figure 2.4 An early Breathalyzer course.

Although the basic principles and operation of the Breathalyzer could be adequately taught in one or two days, a ten-day course was developed to provide the officers with an appropriate background in the theoretical and practical aspects of breath testing. Lectures in the morning covered aspects of the chemistry, physics, and pharmacology of alcohol, and the physiology of breath testing. I was relieved and delighted to learn that although the course was presented as one in science to experienced and sometimes "hard-nosed" police officers who had little or no background in science, they responded very positively to the instruction and to the demands for quality control and quality assurance that were essential to the successful introduction to the courts of Ontario of this new form of evidence.

One of my challenges was to convince the trainees not only that breath tests should and could produce reliable blood alcohol concentrations (BACs), but also that the trainees could do so themselves using the Breathalyzer. To facilitate this, the students conducted practical tests on drinking subjects in the afternoons. The test subjects each day were a few members of the class who were used to drinking alcohol and who volunteered to consume some alcohol over lunch and then be test subjects for the afternoon. An important lesson for me was that, even with police officers, I had to lock up the liquor after the drinking subjects had been prepared for the afternoon's testing.

This practice turned out to be one of the most important learning processes for the students and for myself. When they began, most of the students were quite skeptical about the BAC numbers (e.g., 100 mg/100 mL) that were then considered to be indicative of impairment. As drinking subjects, they learned what the numbers felt like and were invariably surprised to find not only that they could not get to 100 mg/100 mL, but also that at

50 or 60 mg/100 mL they were feeling the "glow," which is the reason most of us drink alcoholic beverages. In addition to the breath tests, blood from the subjects was collected and analyzed, thereby providing the trainees with confirmation that their breath test results agreed closely with actual analytical results of blood.

Having the opportunity to observe, study, and perform physical and mental tests on a large number of drinking subjects (all healthy young males; female officers did not start appearing until the mid-1970s) was also providing me with the opportunity to develop personal knowledge and experience about the effects of alcohol on numbers of subjects much greater than most other "experts" on the topic ever see.

Some of the things I learned were unplanned. One example was that there really is such a thing as alcoholic amnesia. Normally, the students who were drinking would get to the 50–80 mg/100 mL range, which was fine for our testing purposes. What we were lacking was subjects with the higher BACs often seen in impaired driving and homicide cases, that is, in the 200–300 mg/100 mL range. On one course, a Toronto police officer acknowledged that he drank a lot, so we let him loose and got him up to 270 mg/100 mL. I began to get a bit nervous about him, but he seemed to be handling it well. He was one of those atypical people who can get to a high BAC and still appear to be functioning quite well. We finished the day's testing, and his partner drove him home. The next morning, when he arrived at the lab, he drew me aside and asked, "What was I doing yesterday?" Somewhat taken aback I explained to him what he had been doing, and asked, "How are you feeling this morning?" He replied, "Oh, I'm fine physically, but I have no memory of what was going on yesterday. The first thing I remember is that I was in Brantford [about sixty miles away]. I have no idea how I got there or why I was there. Fortunately, I had enough money to get back to Toronto by bus."

He really did have alcoholic amnesia.

In 1957, breath tests were voluntary (but there was no requirement that the suspect be advised of the right to refuse.) For this reason, another part of the course involved instruction in subtle methods for presenting the request for a breath sample in a positive light to a suspected drinking driver. The students had many creative ideas, such as obtaining a fifty-milliliter hypodermic syringe with a four-inch needle and asking, "Which would you prefer sir, blood or breath?" (As a matter of interest, the rate of refusal did not change significantly in 1969 after the tests became mandatory.)

At the end of the course, the students were given oral, written, and practical examinations. Because breath testing was so new, the students were carefully selected by their police chiefs (several went on to become chiefs themselves), which created considerable stress for them. I became aware of this stress when, on each course, one or two would break down and cry while I was giving them the final oral examination.

After each course, I stayed in close contact with these early students to monitor how things were going and, if necessary, to modify the protocols. We also asked them to collect urine samples for analysis as often as they could from their first fifty cases to provide them with support and enhance their confidence in their breath test results. They were not hesitant to seek advice, and it was not unusual for our telephone or doorbell to ring at night with one of them who had a particular question or problem. Many became close friends, and I was pleased to follow their careers as they progressed through the ranks. Some, as they became senior criminal investigators, continued to call me as their first point of contact for forensic science services.

One of these contacts was a call one Sunday afternoon from an OPP officer in Oakville, a town just outside Toronto. He was convinced something was wrong with his Breathalyzer because he had just tested a driver who was on his way home from work and the results were 420 and 430 mg/100 mL. Most people with such a BAC would be in a coma or dead, but this chap barely showed any effects of alcohol. The officer sent a car to pick me up, and I went out to Oakville to see for myself. I confirmed that the instrument was working properly and collected a urine sample that subsequently confirmed the Breathalyzer results. While I could see some effects of alcohol in the driver, they were certainly not what normally would be expected. I remember the incident well because, as mentioned, the driver had been on his way home from work. His job was running the water treatment plant for the town of Oakville. The citizens of Oakville might not have been amused had they known. This was my first experience with such an elevated BAC, and it taught me that although the effects of alcohol on the population follow a normal distribution (bell) curve, there are always a few who are out on the tails of the curve.

Introduction of Breath Test Evidence

Before the introduction of breath testing, the courts had received blood alcohol testimony only from medical doctors or university professors, such as Joslyn Rogers, who had analyzed actual blood samples. Following the introduction of breath testing, judges were being asked to accept such evidence from scientifically unsophisticated police Breathalyzer operators based on their analysis of breath, not blood. As a result, their qualifications to give such evidence and the principles and operation of the Breathalyzer were challenged vigorously in the courts. Nevertheless, as a result of the expert testimony of Dr. Smith, Professor Rogers, and, after I developed sufficient expertise, myself, increasing numbers of criminal courts began to accept the results as a reliable indicator of the BACs of drinking drivers. This produced a great demand for training from the police forces of Ontario and kept me busy for the next few years.

We devoted considerable effort to educating judges, Crown attorneys (prosecutors), and defense lawyers about breath testing. The education was difficult for judges because they believed, quite properly, that they should only make their decisions based on what is presented to them in the courtroom. Our argument was that this should not preclude them from learning outside the courtroom the scientific basis of such tests to help them understand the evidence when it was presented to them in court. To ease their concern, Dr. Smith persuaded the attorney general to host a dinner for judges in Toronto at which we explained this new (for them) area of science. They were very receptive, and that helped to break the ice. After that, we made a point of doing something similar in every jurisdiction when breath tests were introduced.

In the communities in which there was a university, we deliberately involved some local professors so that breath testing would not appear to be just a Crown prosecution tool, but was an academically sound piece of science. At each of these, we would have some volunteer drinkers, local judges or lawyers. A police officer would serve and record the amounts consumed, and the Breathalyzer officers would make their tests. As I look back now, this was a very risky thing to do and was probably pretty dumb on my part because all we needed was for one of these demonstrations to go badly and it would be game over. Fortunately, they always went well, and the participants went home convinced that breath tests work!

I have interesting memories of a few of these events. At one, both the Crown attorney and one of the magistrates (as provincial judges were then known) had agreed to be test subjects. Both had some of their inhibitions reduced as a result, and when I asked the Crown attorney what he weighed, he replied, "One hundred and fifty pounds in the morning, stripped, and ready for gym." This elicited loud laughter from the assembled police and lawyers, which puzzled me until I was reminded that the magistrate's name was Jim Kirkpatrick. Before another in Sarnia, I had a call from the deputy commissioner of the OPP asking me to confirm that the liquor his sergeant in Sarnia had asked permission to purchase was really for legitimate scientific purposes! That taught me, among other things, about the silliness of micromanagement by senior managers.

The first jury trial (*Regina v MacLean*, a case of criminal negligence causing death in October 1957) was a major test of the Breathalyzer. It was presided over by the associate chief justice of what was then called the High Court of Justice of Ontario. The prosecution was led by a senior deputy Crown attorney in Toronto, Arthur Klein, and the defense by the most highly respected defense counsel in the province, G. Arthur Martin QC. As expected, the latter did a superb job for his client and left no legal nit unpicked. The expert witnesses for the prosecution included Dr. Smith and Professors J.K.W. Ferguson and G.H.W. Lucas (no relation) of the Department of Pharmacology in the

University of Toronto. Testifying for the defense was Dr. I.M. Rabinowitch, a retired member of the Department of Metabolism at the Montreal General Hospital. Dr. Rabinowitch's expertise on the subject of alcohol was derived in part from his many years of experience when, before the development of insulin, alcohol had been used in the treatment of diabetics. He was the most prominent Canadian critic of breath testing for alcohol and had written several articles for legal journals on the subject. Dr. Rabinowitch took care of the scientific nitpicking. Although he had many points of criticism, his two main arguments were that breath tests could never be reliable for physiological reasons and that only medical doctors were qualified to interpret the effects of alcohol. (Of the Crown experts, only Professor Ferguson was medically qualified.) The accused was convicted by the jury, which significantly advanced the acceptance of the Breathalyzer in the courts.

The breath test program in Ontario was (and continues to be) successful because the police forces were careful about selecting their members for training, they became well trained, and the operational protocols they were provided with were sound. Dr. Smith and I published the details of the Ontario program in the Proceedings of the 3rd International Conference on Alcohol and Road Traffic in 1962, and it was copied in many other jurisdictions around the world.

The Breathalyzer became the most widely used breath-testing device in the world. Although more modern digital instruments were invented later to replace it, a few Breathalyzers were still in service in Ontario as late as 2009, more than fifty years after its invention.

Point Zero Eight Forensic Science Influences the Law

3

Early Legislation

Driving after drinking is a unique activity for the criminal law to deal with. Unlike most other crimes, it is not unanimously perceived as bad or wrong; otherwise, so many drivers would not engage in it. No one is necessarily injured or loses any property; no one's morals are affected or sense of decency offended. It is a combination of two activities that are each legal, widely practiced, and socially accepted. Even the combination of the two practices is not always something requiring sanction except when one, drinking, is done to the point of adversely affecting that person's ability to safely perform the other.

Nevertheless, since virtually all developed countries have some sort of law(s) to restrict this activity, there must be some universally recognized problem requiring such control.

Canada's Parliament first enacted a law against "driving while intoxicated" in the Criminal Code of Canada (CCC) in 1921. Evidence about "intoxication" was based simply on physical observations. During the 1930s and 1940s, analyses for alcohol in blood began to be used more often but still in only a small minority of intoxicated driving cases. The mandatory minimum penalty for the offense was seven days in jail, and because of what was generally perceived as the undue harshness of this penalty, police were hesitant to charge, or judges to convict, such drivers.

By 1951, Parliament recognized the weaknesses of the "drive while intoxicated" law and added an additional Section, "Driving While the Ability to Do So Is Impaired," to the CCC. Although jail sentences were possible for a first offense, they were not mandatory and were rarely imposed. As a result, this provision was more widely accepted. Determining a subject's blood alcohol concentration (BAC) required blood, but the general North American abhorrence of the hypodermic needle, and the fact that consent was required before blood could be drawn, limited the frequency of chemical tests. When they were used, the courts accepted the results only for the purpose of corroborating the visible symptoms of impairment described by the police and other witnesses.

In 1955, the Royal Canadian Mounted Police Laboratories and the Attorney General's Lab collaborated on a large "closed-course" study of drinking drivers in which they also evaluated the Breathalyzer as a practical tool for police work. This study resulted in the conclusion that all drivers would be impaired by BACs of 150 mg/100 mL or higher.

Such studies, combined with the development and broad adoption of breath testing, made stronger laws feasible and wide-scale enforcement programs practical. Nevertheless, concern about the problem of driving after drinking persisted. In 1962, a committee of the Canadian Medical Association (CMA) issued a report recommending that legislation be enacted making it "unlawful to drive a motor vehicle with a BAC of more than 0.05%" and which "makes submission to a breath test mandatory when requested by law enforcement officers."

This report was reviewed by the Canadian Bar Association (CBA), resulting in the approval of a resolution in 1966 recommending similar legislation, except with a minimum BAC of 0.08%.

Such strong recommendations from the CBA and CMA prompted the Committee on Justice and Legal Affairs of the House of Commons to conduct hearings that resulted in a report later in 1966 recommending legislation that essentially mirrored that recommended by the CBA, except that the BAC limit "should not be less than 0.1%."

The Grand Rapids Study

In 1958, Robert Borkenstein, the inventor of the Breathalyzer, retired from the Indiana State Police and, despite the fact that his only academic degree then was a BA received in 1958 from Indiana University, he was appointed professor and chairman of the Department of Police Administration at Indiana University. (This was a clear demonstration of what a brilliant, self-made individual he was. Bob Borkenstein was the closest to being a genius of anyone I ever knew. I was privileged to work with him on several projects and committees and, in 1999, was proud to be invited to be his biographer. This gave me full access to his office and papers; the result was published in *Forensic Science Review* in 2000.)

In his capacity as a researcher in the field of traffic safety, Borkenstein decided that there was a critical need for a major study on the role that alcohol actually, as opposed to anecdotally, played in traffic accidents. To produce reliable data, he decided to study every traffic accident that occurred in an entire year (1962–1963) in Grand Rapids, Michigan. An innovative aspect of this study was that it included obtaining voluntary breath samples from not only the drivers in these accidents but also drivers passing the same location at about the same time who did *not* have accidents. (Ward Smith had done something similar on a much smaller scale in Toronto in 1952.)

The thoroughness of Borkenstein's preparation for this study is exemplified by the fact that he chose Grand Rapids rather than a more convenient location in Indiana. Grand Rapids was large enough to have a sufficient number of traffic accidents to permit statistical validity; was free of extreme seasonal population fluctuations; had a good balance of heavy and light industry, commerce and educational institutions; and had a good accident records system and a progressive police department. In addition, and not inconsequentially, the population demographics closely reflected those of the entire United States at that time.

Borkenstein also recognized the importance to the study of obtaining the cooperation of the drivers being interviewed. There were a number of sensitive topics in the questionnaire used for the interviews that required subjects to provide information of a personal nature. He identified another organization just down the hall in his own university building that had considerable experience with asking intimate questions of large numbers of people, the Kinsey Institute for Sex Research. Staff members of that institute were therefore asked to train the members of the research team who would conduct the interviews in Grand Rapids. (One of the research team was a member of our staff, Ron Hallett, who we seconded to the study.)

Borkenstein produced a massive report on the results of the study in 1964. It became the most influential epidemiological report ever on the role of alcohol in traffic accidents. The "Grand Rapids Study" included factors such as age, socioeconomic status, and education that interact with alcohol as accident causation factors. It concluded, however, that the contribution of these factors diminishes as the BAC increases and disappears at BACs exceeding 0.08%. The "Relative Risk of Causing an Accident" chart included in the report is one of the most frequently reproduced charts in scientific publications on any subject. The BAC "legal limit" of 0.08%, which became so widely adopted internationally, was derived principally from this study.

A Holiday Message

In spite of the CMA, CBA, and Commons Committee reports and Borkenstein's Grand Rapids Study, Canadian drinking/driving laws were not again changed until 1969. Ironically, it was not these significant studies and reports that had the most influence on Parliament but rather a simple TV "Christmas message" program that focused the public's attention on the effects of alcohol on driving.

On October 24, 1966, Dr. Smith and I were approached by Ed McGibbon, a highly respected freelance TV producer, who had a contract with the Canadian Television Network (CTV) to produce a half-hour public information program on drinking/driving for the Christmas season. He had the grand sum of $5,000 as a budget (even at that time a very small amount to produce a 30-minute prime-time TV program). Ed wanted to film some tests of drinking drivers. Neither Dr. Smith nor I were keen on the idea because there had previously been many such low-speed *gymkhana*-type tests done with drivers on closed courses, backing into garages, driving around pylons, and so on, and we didn't think those were very persuasive. Dr. Smith, somewhat hesitantly, suggested testing drivers operating at "real-world" road and highway speeds, something that had never been done before.

The CTV and government lawyers were not thrilled with this idea for reasons of liability. I suggested that it might be done safely by using professional race car drivers on a race track, which somewhat eased the lawyers' concerns. Such a test group would, I believed, also be more persuasive to the prime target audience, young male drivers.

Ed McGibbon had worked previously on a show about the Ford/Comstock Racing Team, which was managed by Paul Cooke and was able to bring Paul on board, which turned out to be a stroke of genius. Paul arranged for the drivers (four of whom are now in the Canadian Motor Sports Hall of Fame, as is Paul) and the cars, Ford sedans. We did a preliminary test at the Mosport Raceway, but only two laps around the 2.5-mile hilly, twisting Mosport circuit convinced us that it would not be safe to have even highly skilled divers who had consumed some alcohol drive that course.

Paul was familiar with a smaller, flatter course laid out on the runways and taxiways of a former WWII airport, Harewood Acres, near Jarvis, Ontario. We did a test run there and decided that we could safely do what was planned there because it was flat and wide open. (The track belonged to a local farmer, Russell Hare, who used the infields to pasture a flock of sheep, who became a curious audience for our bizarre activities.) With Paul's input, we designed an initial slow, skill-testing area marked with pylons followed by two stretches of the two-mile track, one of which would be driven at typical city speed (30 mph) and the other at highway speed (60 mph). Along the route, we included stop signs, a traffic signal, turns, a U-shaped detour, and a couple of surprise elements simulating a pedestrian appearing suddenly on the road.

Aside from the drivers and the film crew, all the participants on test day were volunteer members of our staff or the Metropolitan Toronto Police Department. Although the finished 30-minute black-and-white film was very professionally produced, all of the budget went into the film crew and production, leaving nothing for the actual test course. As a result, the various course markers (e.g., road markings and pylons) and devices (e.g., pedestrian models) were either "borrowed" or frantically homemade in staff basements, and they looked it!

Figure 3.1 Paul Cook and Dr. Smith Brief, the *Point Zero Eight* test drivers.

On Thursday, November 17, we had a very long, cold, and windy day of testing. The six drivers (four male, two female) drove the course several times as practice and then four laps to establish their "dry" scores based on time, pylons struck, and assessments of their driving performance by other experienced race drivers who rode with them. The drivers then were given an amount of alcohol that they believed they could handle and still drive normally, four to eight ounces of liquor. When their breath tests showed they were in the range of 0.04%–0.08%, they were sent back on the course for their "wet" runs. Most of the drivers felt they would drive just as well as they had before drinking. Indeed, even after completing their wet runs, they still believed they had scored just as well as they had on their dry runs. This was quite consistent with the attitude of many drivers toward the effect alcohol may have on their driving.

All of the drivers showed some deterioration in their performance, even at these relatively low BACs, and for a few, the results were quite dramatic. After the first wet runs, it was considered feasible to give three of the drivers an additional four to eight ounces of liquor to bring their BACs to the 0.10%–0.15% range. The results of these retests were startling, all captured on film.

Everything that was shown in the film actually happened; however, since there wasn't always a camera in position to capture everything, we filmed

Figure 3.2 A "wet" drive.

simulations of some of the events the following Saturday with Paul Cook at the wheel. I took my sons, Eric and Brian, then 12 and 11, with me, and they were given a high-speed run around the track by Paul, which left them with eyes the size of saucers. The rest of the day they played with Farmer Hare's sheep!

The results of all the tests as shown in the film revealed things that surprised even Dr. Smith and me. The most notable of these was the observation by Paul Cooke that there appeared to be a failure on the part of the drivers in their wet runs to sense the attitude or position of the car. This was most noticeable on the curves, when it appeared that the drivers were no longer sensing the car's attitude but only reacting after they could see that it was out of position. Their driving response was therefore late and exaggerated!

There was also a tendency to increase speed, to lose lane control, and to accelerate and brake harder. Most drivers showed poorer judgment of distances; a decreased ability to sense speed, resulting in continued glancing at the speedometer; and a common assertion that things seemed to be happening more rapidly. The one driver who got to 0.15% was so obviously affected that his original observer refused to ride with him. Paul Cooke volunteered for what he later declared was "the scariest ride of my life," and he had been a professional race car driver!

The final film was called *Point Zero Eight*, and it was shown in prime time on the national CTV network on Thursday, December 16, 1966. It resulted in a tremendous impact across the country and was the main topic of much "water cooler" conversation the following day. In response to the demand, CTV reran the program just before Christmas. They also sold something like

3,000 copies of the film all over the world, and it became standard fare in high school driving courses for many years. (In 1994, while I was doing an accreditation inspection of the forensic science lab in Melbourne, Australia, one of the staff members told me that she had seen me [albeit a much younger version] on TV the night before, in the old black-and-white *Point Zero Eight.*)

This simple, very low-budget film, which had started out as nothing more than a typical Christmas public information TV message, had a huge impact on people, including members of Parliament, and was one of the reasons that, when the CCC was amended in 1969, it provided for breath tests on demand and a new offense, driving with a BAC greater than 80 mg of alcohol in 100 mL of blood, i.e., 0.08! A rare example of a piece of legislation that was highly influenced by forensic science.

Surprisingly, this low-budget 1966 film still has relevance. Borkenstein's old department at Indiana University offers an extension course, "The Robert F. Borkenstein Course on Alcohol and Highway Safety: Testing, Research and Litigation," twice a year for international professionals involved in this work. I am regularly invited to the course to show the film and discuss its preparation and effects. The reaction of the students is quite remarkable; most tell me they learned things about the topic that they were previously unaware of, and many request a copy of the film to show to colleagues back home.

The Courtroom "What on Earth Am I Doing Here?" 4

The Search for Truth?

Although in the early years my principal responsibility was developing the breath test program, I did continue doing toxicology cases, searching for drugs and poisons, usually in coroners' cases but also in criminal cases, which required presentation of oral evidence in all three (at that time) levels of the criminal courts. The most frequently detected drug was, of course, alcohol, and the most frequent testimony (in other than impaired driving cases) was about the effect of a particular blood alcohol concentration (BAC) on homicide and sexual assault victims and, occasionally, defendants.

The judicial process in its "search for truth" is quite foreign to someone raised in a scientific environment. The former is adversarial; the latter is collaborative and experimental. All forensic scientists must quickly learn that, in the courtroom, we are playing someone else's game, according to their rules and on their home field. The search for truth is actually just for the "truth" as defined by one side or the other. Unlike most other human endeavors, there are no shades of grey in the judicial process. Indeed, in the criminal courts, grey is simply defined as white. (If guilt is not proven beyond a reasonable doubt, then the individual on trial is not guilty.)

There can be a conflict between scientists and lawyers. As with most conflicts, it usually arises from a lack of understanding by members of each profession of the fundamental principles of the other. Scientists and other nonlawyers have to learn to appreciate a fundamental principle of criminal law: it is better that a hundred guilty people go free than that a single innocent person is convicted. Once the scientist truly accepts that principle and understands that it is the sworn duty of the lawyer to speak for the client as the client would like to speak for himself if he only knew how, regardless of what the lawyer may think about the facts of the case, then she becomes a forensic scientist and understands some of the apparently bizarre things that occur in the courtroom.

On the other side, lawyers have to learn to appreciate that science is very dynamic.

Something in science that is believed to be true today may no longer be true next week. When that occurs, it doesn't mean that the scientist has adjusted his position to suit the facts of the case, it is simply the reality of science. Science can assist in resolving many legal issues, but it may be unable to assist with others. As explained by G.K. Chesterton.

> The moment you step into the world of facts, you step into the world of limits. You can free things from alien or accidental laws, but not from the laws of nature. ——*The Suicide of Thought* (1908)

The differences between the professions can perhaps be summarized thus: it is the duty of the scientist to describe the evidence as it is; it is the duty of the attorney to describe it in the most favorable light for the client.

Having said all that, I can't think of a better system of criminal justice than what we have. Most of the Crown Attorneys I have dealt with were extremely knowledgeable and scrupulously fair. Particularly in my early days, they truly believed in the adage that "the Crown neither wins nor loses." Criminal defense lawyers were highly intelligent and had a broad knowledge of a remarkable array of subject matters. And the vast majority of judges were incredibly patient and strictly focused on ensuring that every trial was fair to the person on trial and that juries were treated with respect. I remember, for example, one Supreme Court judge at a trial in rural Cayuga talking about the need to finish court by 16:30 "so that the jury can get home to do the milking and other chores."

That is not to say that there weren't exceptions. A few Crown Attorneys did function more in the style of the U.S. prosecutor. A few judges tended to be very crusty and impatient with any witness or attorney behaving in a manner they deemed inappropriate. (One chastised me one time for referring to a sample as "blood" because I hadn't tested it to prove that it was indeed blood. The fact that it was red liquid in a tube labeled "blood" didn't cut it with him.) Some defense lawyers could be so aggressive as to be quite obnoxious. I have to confess to occasionally taking subtle revenge on the latter when they asked a foolish question. In one case, after I had described the location of a body found under a set of basement stairs, during a long and tedious cross-examination the lawyer asked me, "And did the stairs go up or down?" Long pause, then a simple "yes" was my response.

The Logistics

In my early years, the first challenge was simply getting to the courts in many parts of Ontario. We could fly to only a few of the major cities. For most locations, the options were a train, bus, or automobile. For example, if going to court in Sudbury, I would get on the train at Union Station in Toronto at 23:00 and get off at 05:30 when it arrived in Sudbury. I would then sit in the station for a couple of hours until it was time for court, hoping that I could give my testimony in time to catch the afternoon train back to Toronto. Otherwise, it was a night in the Empire Hotel, where the fire escape consisted of a rope tied to a radiator by the window.

A private automobile was the default mode of transportation for most locations, often on roads that were not up to the standards of modern multi-lane highways. The lab did not have a car, and before we had our own family car, I relied on the Ontario Provincial Police (OPP), who allowed me to use one of their "pool" cars. (I almost had an accident one time when my foot accidentally slipped onto the siren button, giving me a very loud surprise.)

I also learned quickly that small-town Ontario was no place to expect gourmet dining. In many towns, the only restaurants were operated by Chinese families, and the selection was relatively sparse. For dinner, it was either yesterday's cold roast beef with hot pork gravy or bacon and eggs. One time I asked the local police in Perth, "Where is a good place to eat in Perth?" Their immediate response was "Smith's Falls," a town ten miles away.

Hastings County (and Other) Juries

Juries could be very interesting. In the smaller towns in predominantly rural areas, they were noticeably different from those in Toronto. In giving evidence to a jury in the major centers, the process was not much different from giving lectures at a university. The object was to, in effect, educate the members of the jury about the findings and their significance to the case. However, in some of the rural areas, such as Hastings County, the juries were notorious for being less sophisticated, and the presentation had to be geared to their knowledge and experience.

One example was a case before a grand jury in Belleville, the "county seat" for Hastings County. Grand juries no longer exist; they consisted of seven residents of the county who would hear evidence only from witnesses presented by the Crown Attorney in all the cases to come before that court during that term. Their sole function was to determine if there was sufficient evidence in each case to pass a "true bill" of indictment, which would then place the accused person on trial before a "petit jury" (trial jury) of twelve residents. The grand jury could pass a true bill after hearing only one witness, if they so chose, but they could also pass a "no bill," which meant they didn't believe there was sufficient evidence and the accused would be released without trial; in this case, they had to hear testimony from all of the witnesses listed on the bill of indictment.

This case involved a charge of fraud against a gentleman who owned a restaurant in which there had been a fire. He wasn't charged with arson because there was not sufficient evidence that he had set the fire, but he was charged with fraud because he made insurance claims for restaurant equipment he insisted had been lost in the fire. The insurance company was able to show that this was the same equipment he had been paid for once before as a result of another fire. The Hastings County Crown Attorney had recused himself from the case because he knew the accused, so the Crown Attorney from Kingston, unfamiliar with Hastings County juries, was brought in to present the evidence. The process went on until about noon when the grand jurors told the Crown Attorney, "We have heard enough." The Crown Attorney, assuming that meant they had heard enough for a true bill, said, "Thank you very much," and they adjourned for lunch.

When they returned after lunch, the jurors presented a no bill, which caused much consternation in the courtroom and upset the Crown Attorney to no end. Apparently, what the jurors had meant when they said they had heard enough was that they had heard enough before lunch and noon was their usual lunchtime. That was the end of that case. Leaving the courthouse afterward to go to my car, I happened to follow two of the jurors who were clearly from the northern part of Hastings County, and one said to the other, "You know, that was an interesting case; it sounded to me like he was trying to screw the insurance company!" Which, of course, was what the case was all about! A very fortunate restauranteur.

Even in Toronto, unusual things occasionally happened with juries. In court one day on an arson case, as I stepped into the witness box and looked at the jury while taking the oath, I noticed a man sitting in the first chair—who was probably going to be selected as the foreman of this jury, who I knew very well as a retired fire investigator from the Fire Marshal's Office. The defense counsel must not have been aware of who he had on his jury. After the case was over and the accused was convicted, I ran into the retired investigator and asked, "How on earth did you ever get on that jury?" His reply was, "Well, all it said on my juror's card was 'Retired,' and nobody asked me what I was retired from!"

Women in the Courtroom

A significant change in the justice system during my career was the role of women in it. Until well into the 1970s, there were very few women lawyers, judges, or police officers and women on juries were a rare sight. Interestingly, we had a much greater representation of women on the staff of the Centre of Forensic Sciences than other parts of the justice system. The first time I saw a woman as one of the major players in a trial was one of the first cases Marlys Edwardh, who went on to become one of the most respected criminal defense lawyers in Canada, defended on her own—an accused arsonist.

(Parenthetically, there was an amusing incident during this trial. The detective in charge testified that he could smell gasoline on the accused man's shoes when he arrested him. Marlys thoroughly challenged him about his ability to identify the smell as gasoline, but he was adamant. As the detective and I walked to lunch during the break, there was a noticeable odor in the air, and he exclaimed, "There. That's gasoline. I can smell it!" A bit further on we came across a crew heating asphalt to repair a roof. I quietly said to him, "I didn't know they used gasoline to repair roofs!")

Marlys was, as always, very thorough and had hired a professor of chemical engineering from the University of Toronto to advise her. I gave my evidence, and she cross-examined me; the evidence was quite straightforward. Afterward, I was talking to her in the corridor, and she said, "You know, I got everything from you that I could have gotten from this professor; I don't know why I hired him." I replied, "Well, I hope that you learned something from that." Later, we met each other on many occasions, and she never hesitated to come looking for advice when she thought that it was something we could provide. That was a valuable lesson for her and one we tried to present to all lawyers, that forensic scientists are quite prepared to advise them as best we can regardless of who they represent.

Justice for Indigenous People

Some cases significantly affected my thinking about how the justice system relates to our indigenous population. (Because this is being written in 2017, I will use this description rather than "Indians," even though that was the common nomenclature at the time and was how the ones I came to know described themselves. One of the latter even proudly sported a Cleveland Indians sweatshirt!) One of these cases, *Regina v. Tapawekieschick*, was a murder in 1960 that occurred on the Grassy Narrows Reserve, an isolated reserve with no road access, in the District of Kenora. The residents subsisted on hunting and fishing and had little contact with the rest of Canadian society. John Taipeiweikieschick lived on the reserve in a primitive cabin. He had an adult son who came home drunk one night and proceeded to smash everything in the family home. As I looked at the police photographs, something I will always remember was a photograph of a destroyed battery-powered radio that was the only thing of any dollar value in the cabin. It was obviously an important possession that John had obtained from the Hudson's Bay Company by trading for furs.

John had sent his wife to get the police, which, in those days on the reserves, was the Royal Canadian Mounted Police. It was late, and his wife returned with the message, "They will come tomorrow." Then John sent his wife to get the priest, the other white authority figure on the reserve. After a while, she returned with the same message, "The priest will come tomorrow." John picked up his rifle, went out, hunted down his son, and shot and killed him. That was pretty clearly murder in the legal sense, so John was arrested and charged. I couldn't help but think that John's thought process must have been, "Well, I tried the white man's way, and it didn't work, so I will have to use our traditional way of dealing with this problem."

In October 1960, John was tried for murder in Kenora. My only contribution to the trial was the son's BAC, which confirmed that he had indeed been very drunk. John, I'm sure, understood very little of what was going on in the courtroom, because he didn't speak any English. He was convicted and given the minimum sentence, but the time would have to be served in Kingston Penitentiary. What struck me so much was that for people like John of a different culture and a different philosophy of life, who have tried our way of doing things without success, it didn't seem fair to bring sanctions against them for adopting the traditional ways of their culture, judging them instead by our standards. Also, was it equal punishment for someone like John, who had never left the Grassy Narrows Reserve, where the only people he knew resided, to send him a thousand miles away to serve his sentence in a facility such as a penitentiary in Kingston?

I have never forgotten that case, which made me much more sensitive to the attempts in recent years to bring the indigenous population into the judicial system and to try to adjust the system of criminal justice to recognize the cultural differences.

Another example of the challenge the court system had with this population was what I came to think of as the self-perpetuating homicide cases on the Wikwemikong Reserve on Manitoulin Island (the "largest freshwater island in the world") at the north end of Lake Huron. The circumstances of these cases were almost always the same. The only employment of any significance available to the people was cutting pulpwood in the winter. They would work all winter and in the spring would get paid for the entire season. This would be the excuse for a huge party involving a large amount of alcohol. Almost invariably, this led to a fight, and death would result. In particular, I remember two families, the Roys and the Simons. In 1962, a Simon killed a Roy. The trial brought everyone to the small town of Gore Bay as witnesses in 1963, and after receiving their witness fees at the end of the trial, they returned to the reserve. There was another party, and a Simon was done in by a Roy. The homicides both occurred in the same residence and were so similar that the OPP identification officer told me, I'm sure facetiously, that he just reprinted the photographs from the first case and used them for the second trial.

Gore Bay, My Favorite Court

I always looked forward to these trials each autumn because they took place in Gore Bay, the district seat for Manitoulin. Gore Bay is a fascinating place; just getting there was an adventure. I took the two-hour ferry trip from

Tobermory at the tip of the Bruce Peninsula to South Baymouth on the island and then drove along a narrow gravel road for eighty miles or so to Gore Bay. The tiny old stone courthouse with a small lockup in the basement must have had many stories to tell of murder trials, almost all involving the indigenous population.

One of the reasons I enjoyed Gore Bay was that, ironically, it always seemed to be a very civilized place to have a trial. There was only one place to stay, Gordon's Lodge, and the judge from Toronto, the Crown Attorney, and the defense lawyer, who usually were from Sudbury, and the "expert" witness from Toronto all stayed there. Because it was a lodge, we would sit around the dining table at night for dinner, family style. It was a very pleasant experience because I got to talk to these major players in the judicial process on a much more informal basis than in the courtroom. I often learned that the defense lawyer, who might have given me a withering cross-examination in the afternoon, was a quite charming gentleman across the dinner table at night, and the judge, who appeared so austere in the courtroom, could be a creative storyteller, after a glass of wine or two.

Capital Punishment

One of the sobering aspects of homicide trials during the first five years of my career was that capital punishment was still a reality. Although it was not formally abolished until 1976, the last executions in Canada were in December 1962. One of the final two convicted murderers put to death was Arthur Lucas, a "murder-for-hire" killer from Detroit who slit the throat of a drug dealer in the Waverly Hotel in Toronto. Despite his surname, he was no relation; he was African American.

There were not a lot of people who were executed, but there certainly were some, and a few of the people I testified against were subsequently executed. I always had a queasy feeling in homicide cases to know that the life of the person sitting in the prisoner's dock in front of me was truly at stake. The physical setup of most courtrooms is not designed to ensure the focus on the most concerned individual in the trial, the defendant. The judge sits on a raised bench at the front, and the lawyers are dressed in gowns and have desks and lecterns immediately in front of the judge. The jury sits in an area off to one side, and the witnesses testify from a box just below and to the side of the judge. The person on trial, however, sits in a box behind all the "key players," almost back with the spectators, like a mildly interested bystander. Each time I entered the witness box, I tried to consciously remind myself to look at the accused person to remind myself what the process was all about. And when a life was on the line, this was even more critical.

During the Arthur Lucas trial, I had a conversation with Henry Bull QC, the outstanding hard-nosed Crown Attorney in Toronto at the time, about capital punishment. Somewhat to my surprise, he said,

> You know, if you believe that capital punishment is a deterrent, and that is why we have it, then it makes no sense to do it at midnight behind prison walls. If it is supposed to deter people from killing, then it should be done in public at high noon; unless we are prepared to do it in public, we shouldn't have it at all.

I agreed with him on that issue and was pleased when capital punishment was abolished.

(The actual hangman used the traditional fictional name Arthur Ellis and was supposed to be unknown publicly. However, he was known to a few people as one of the sheriff's court officers who we would pass on the way to the witness box. The only time I ever saw Professor Rogers truly upset was one day when he returned from court and this court officer had said to him as he went by, "Got another one for me, Doc?")

Giving Testimony

There are many important lessons that I learned about giving testimony, sometimes through bitter experience. The most important of all, it may seem trite to say, is to tell the truth. There are obviously many good reasons for doing so: duty, responsibility, reputation, the oath, and so forth. When instructing my staff on the subject, I would finish with, "And if you aren't persuaded by all those good reasons, there is one other; simply, it is easier to tell the truth than it is to lie about something! You don't have to remember what the lie was!"

Another thing I learned was the importance of knowing what my "I don't know" threshold on any topic was. Everybody has one; five-year-old children can quickly bring anyone to their "I don't know" threshold with just one word: "Why?" It is particularly difficult for expert witnesses to acknowledge this reality because our testimony begins with a series of questions detailing all our qualifications as an expert. These are designed by the attorney who is presenting us to make us appear to be the most knowledgeable person on the subject in the country. Having gone through that, there is a real risk of us believing that we are as smart as billed. It can be very difficult psychologically in that context to admit that we don't know the answer to a question. The best words that can be used in answering questions in court are either "Yes," "No," or "I don't know." But it is a tough lesson to learn, and there are some people who, to their peril, never do.

This is analogous to the basic principle lawyers are taught: "Never ask a witness a question you are not sure of the answer to." I saw an excellent example of this in a trial of a man for robbing a convenience store. The detective on the case was Bill McCormack (who later became the Toronto chief of police but was at that time a divisional detective). He testified that the accused man had a distinct Slavic accent that the store owner had described for the robber. The lawyer challenged Bill's ability to identify the accent, finishing with, "You're not a linguist; you don't speak any foreign languages, do you?" To which Bill quietly replied, "Yes, I do. Swahili!" That quickly ended that line of questioning. (Bill's father had been in the British colonial police, and the family had been stationed in Africa for several years.)

Another thing that is difficult for a witness to remember is that the court reporter sitting down in front of you is writing down or recording everything that you say, and it will be available for anyone to read for years to come. It can be a great shock two years hence to be confronted with your own words verbatim from the testimony you gave in another trial. They may even appear inconsistent with what is being said today, hopefully because there has been an advance in science since then.

I developed an acronym that I used in instructing staff about giving evidence. It explains the five most important things to remember about being a good witness:

- Listen—You can't answer a question if you haven't truly heard it.
- Understand—You have to be certain you understand the question.
- Consider—Take a moment to frame your answer.
- Answer.

By then, people would see where this was heading, and I would ask, "What is the fifth thing?" And most would respond, "Shut up" because that started with an S. That certainly is good advice but not what I had in mind. What I was looking for was

- Stick to it.

If you have done the first four things, the answer should be the best answer possible, and you should be prepared to stick to it. One of the most common weaknesses of expert witnesses, who as scientists are trying to be objective and fair, is that they tend to bend over backward to do so and, in effect, reduce the impact of what it was they had said initially.

Broadening Horizons There Is More to This Than Just Alcohol! 5

As the Breathalyzer program became well established, Ward Smith and Professor Rogers encouraged me to broaden my experience with other types of cases. There was always more to learn about the effects of alcohol on people, and I continued to do so, but I realized that I would need more challenges than that to retain my interest in forensic science.

Gas Chromatography and Arson

One triggering factor was a new analytical technique that was just becoming commercially available, gas chromatography (GC). The lab acquired its first gas chromatograph (a Beckman GC-2) in 1958, and because it was initially considered to be an instrument that could be used for alcohol analysis, I was assigned to develop its applications.

I had been fascinated by Professor Rogers's work with fire investigators. When they brought in debris from a suspicious fire and asked if a flammable liquid had been used to start the fire, he would simply sniff the ashes, which was probably the most sensitive technique available at the time. If he smelled anything, then he would steam distill the debris to try to isolate any petroleum product that might be present. I thought, "There must be a more objective method."

GC seemed ideally suited to this challenge since it is a method for separating and detecting the components of volatile mixtures, thus forming a visible pattern for the mixture. Although the earliest GC sensors were not nearly as sensitive as those that became available over the following few years, they nevertheless were adequate for most of the fire debris samples received. The flammable liquids most commonly used to ignite or enhance fires are petroleum products, such as gasoline, kerosene, and mineral spirits, which are mixtures of volatile components. Thus, I reasoned, GC should work well for this application.

During the summer of 1958, I had a very bright young medical student as a summer intern, and we set to work developing a procedure for this purpose. We found that the patterns we could develop from a microliter (μL) or less of these liquids was distinctive for each type of product and permitted the identification of it. We also found distinct differences in the patterns produced by products such as gasoline from different refineries or at different times of the year. These differences, however, could not be used to identify the brand since we also learned that there were widespread commercial exchanges between refineries, and thus we could not say that gasoline we detected in a debris sample that was similar to that produced in July in an Esso refinery necessarily had been purchased at an Esso gas station. In February 1959, I presented the results of this work at the annual scientific meeting of the American Academy of Forensic Sciences (AAFS) in Chicago. Since this was the first GC procedure for this application and was therefore quite revolutionary, it created quite a stir.

The method was published in the *Journal of Forensic Sciences* in 1960, the first publication of this application.

Coincidentally, at that same meeting another forensic scientist from the Orange County Sheriff's Laboratory in Santa Ana, California, Jack Cadman, presented a very similar paper. We had been working quite independently and were unknown to each other, so we each received virtually instantaneous confirmation of our work. As a result, Jack and I became close friends and collaborators for many years after that. He was the first of many such friends developed over the years through contact at scientific meetings. During the time before the Internet and Google, such personal contacts were invaluable.

As better GC sensors and columns were developed, we found that we didn't need actual liquid to identify petroleum products; we could produce distinctive patterns simply by collecting a small sample of the "headspace" vapor from the top of a jar of fire debris using a hypodermic syringe. Modifications of this method became, and remain still, the standard for these types of examinations in forensic science, although the separation powers of GC are now combined with the identification capability of the mass spectrometer to produce an ideal tool for this type of examination.

Fire Investigation

The fire investigators were excited by this new process and were relieved to have something a bit more scientific than Josh Rogers's nose (as good as it had always been) to take to court. This led them to invite me to attend fire scenes with them to assist with the determination of the "origin and cause" of structural fires.

While I learned a lot from some of these investigators, as well as from Professor Rogers, I also learned that some of the guidelines they used in these investigations did not make scientific sense. For example, they considered it a certainty that the place of lowest and deepest burning must be the point of origin of the fire. Such "clues" had developed into a form of mythology that occasionally, unfortunately, led to incorrect conclusions. These practices had developed because most fire investigators learned from other investigators who would simply enter a fire scene after the fact, not knowing what had happened. From their observations, they would develop a scenario that seemed reasonable. In those early days, there had been no experimental work done, which, of course, for scientists was foreign to the way we think and operate.

While individual fires can present very complex challenges and may destroy any evidence of how and where they started, the principles of fire investigation are based on the laws of physics; heat transfers by radiation, convection, and conduction. Application of these principles can help enormously in understanding how a fire progressed. Appreciation of the difference between temperature and heat, and the fact that hot air, left to its natural tendency, will rise, is also important. (At some of our test burns I would win bets with investigators by pouring gasoline down a set of stairs and igniting it at the top of the stairs. Thinking intuitively rather than scientifically, they would bet that the fire would follow the gasoline and burn down the stairs. Of course, it would not because, based on the laws of physics, heat rises and the gasoline underneath the point of ignition, i.e., down the stairs, would therefore not get hot enough to ignite.)

Fortunately, we found an investigator in the Ontario Fire Marshal's Office, Dennis Merkley, who was keen to develop a more scientific evidence-based approach to the examination of fire scenes. Together with local fire departments, we obtained buildings that were slated for destruction on which we could perform full-scale test fires using a variety of scenarios. We would put sensors throughout these buildings to record temperatures and place vacuum bottles to collect air samples for lab analysis. Through many experiments of this type, we disproved much of the preexisting mythology about origin and cause and developed in the fire investigators a much more scientific approach. Similar work was being done about the same time by a few other forensic scientists, such as John Lentini in the United States.

(During one of these test fires, we were studying the absorption of carbon monoxide into the blood using rabbits as test animals. They were confined in a burning room and after an appropriate time were killed instantly with a .22 caliber shot to the head. There was no alternative to using live animals for such research. One of the fire marshal's staff apparently was a PETA supporter and made a complaint to the local police, which made headlines the following day. (These prompted many abusive phone calls from animal activists.) A few days later, I was interviewed by inspectors from the Ministry of Agriculture, whose opening words were a caution under the Criminal Code. They then asked if I had anything to say and, still in some shock, I replied, "No" and they left. I never heard any more about it, but we were much more cautious about dotting i's and crossing t's in such research after that.)

One case (described in Chapter 6) in which we performed a series of test burns will serve as an example of the type of work we were doing. In another,

I heard a very amusing comment during the investigation of a tragedy. There had been a fire in a long-term care facility in which an elderly person had died. We did a full-scale simulation of the fire in a mock-up of the fatality room. In the process, I had a discussion with one of the young firefighters who had attended that fire. He described halls filled with smoke and one patient hobbling toward the exit on crutches. "Get down! Get down!" the firefighter yelled, but there was no response. "So, I kicked the crutches out from under him. I always wanted to do that!" he chuckled.

I had many interesting experiences in fire investigation cases but will describe only two. Both involved fires in restaurants, which seemed to have an unfortunate tendency to catch fire, at night when they were closed and at times when business was slow.

One, in June 1962, involved the Corral restaurant in suburban London, Ontario. The fire started not in the kitchen, where there were multiple sources of ignition, but in an office area. The owner was charged with arson, and in my evidence at the trial, I described my observations, including the fact that I had seen no evidence of an explosion. This last bit seemed to upset the very prominent London defense lawyer because his defense was that the fire had resulted from an explosion of natural gas from a leak in the gas line to the kitchen. His cross-examination went something like this:

Q: Well you are not saying there wasn't an explosion, are you?
A: No sir. What I said was that I saw no evidence of an explosion. I would have expected to see such evidence if there had been an explosion.
Q: I see. Tell me, witness, if I filled a balloon with a gas-air mixture and then ignited it in the restaurant, you wouldn't have seen any explosion damage there, would you?
A: I would expect to see such damage to the balloon, sir.

I was afraid that the lawyer would have a heart attack on the spot. He slammed down his notes, grabbed his briefcase, and announced at the top of his lungs, "Your Honor, this is a contemptuous witness, and I will have nothing further to do with him."

This left me completely dumbfounded and considerably embarrassed; "contemptuous" was not an adjective that had previously been applied to me (at least that I was aware of). Given the opportunity, I would have explained that in a gas-air explosion in the restaurant, the restaurant would have served as the container for the gas, and in his analogy, the balloon was the container; i.e., they served the same purpose and would have experienced similar effects.

Fortunately for me, the judge apparently understood this because his next words were merely "Next witness." I ran into the lawyer at a meeting a few months later and tried to explain this to him. He replied, "I understood that but I had a lousy case," and he apologized for embarrassing me.

The second incident was a fire in another restaurant in Sarnia. When I examined the debris that the fire marshal's investigator had submitted, I found lots of gasoline but was puzzled that I could not smell it. What I could smell very strongly was the odor of vanilla. A simple test, adding some vanilla extract to a small jar of gasoline, showed, much to my surprise, that the vanilla completely masked the odor of gasoline. Apparently, the restaurant owners were somehow aware of this and had placed plastic bags of gasoline and vanilla around the restaurant one night after closing; they believed, quite correctly, that the people living in the upstairs apartment would think nothing of any odor of vanilla coming from the restaurant. The restaurant burned that night, and fortunately, the upstairs tenants escaped safely.

The restaurant owners were charged with arson, and in November 1962, I attended the trial to explain about the gasoline and vanilla. I had to stay overnight in Sarnia and so went to dinner (at another restaurant) with the fire investigator. After we placed our orders, we both happened to look back toward the open kitchen, and there was one of the defendants smiling and waving at us as he cooked our dinners. Our appetites disappeared like coins into a slot machine. If you are reading this, we must have survived!

Screech and Seal Flipper Pie
Fire and Politics in Newfoundland

6

In the early morning of April 26, 1978, a fire occurred in unit 512 of the Elizabeth Towers apartment building in St. John's, Newfoundland. The apartment tenant, Dr. Thomas Farrell, a physician from Cornerbrook, was a member of the Newfoundland House of Assembly and minister of industrial development in the cabinet of Premier Frank Moores. The previous night, Dr. Farrell had been drinking heavily before being helped to his apartment at about 03:00.

About 06:45, the security guard heard Dr. Farrell calling for help. He ran up to the fifth floor, found the corridor full of smoke, and pulled the fire alarm, recorded at 06:48. The first fire truck arrived at 06:50, and by 07:05 the fire was extinguished. The well-documented brief time for the fire, about twenty minutes, became important during the subsequent investigation.

The Initial Investigation and Events

There was considerable smoke damage to unit 512, but the fire had been confined to the master bedroom. Given the prominence of the occupant, the fire department notified the Newfoundland fire commissioner, who responded to the scene immediately. Because of Dr. Farrell's activities the previous evening, it was not surprising that he was unclear about what had occurred. He told the commissioner that he had gone to bed in the bed nearest the window. He woke up and saw flames five to six feet high to his right in the area of the closet. There was not much smoke, and he had no difficulty breathing. He got up and ran out into the hall to turn in the alarm.

The fire commissioner thought that although the fire was confined to the bedroom, the damage was more than he would have expected in a fire of such duration. He therefore asked the Newfoundland Constabulary (the St. John's Police Force) to assist with his investigation.

The bedroom was a typical apartment bedroom, about fifteen by twelve feet. There were two single beds, and Dr. Farrell admitted that he slept in whichever was less cluttered. On the floor was a badly worn wool carpet that only partially covered the floor. He was living as a bachelor when in St. John's and admitted he wasn't much of a housekeeper. Police photographs of the scene confirmed this; clothes, newspapers, books, and so forth, were scattered all over the room.

The carpet was largely destroyed in the fire except for a small area in front of the bureau where there had been a suitcase lying on it. The floor underneath the carpet was wood parquet. It was relatively undamaged except for an area under the window; there was also what was described as a "fishtail pattern" near one of the beds (not the one that Dr. Farrell had been sleeping in) and some charring of the floor in the closet.

Based on these observations, the commissioner, who was one of those fire investigators who believed in mythological guidelines for an origin and cause determination, concluded that there were three points of origin of the fire and that a flammable liquid, probably mineral spirits, had been poured on the floor to set those fires. The fire, in his opinion, was therefore arson. Debris samples were sent to the Royal Canadian Mounted Police Laboratory, but no flammable liquid residue was detected in them. This information became meaningless after we learned that, for reasons unknown to anyone, the samples were not collected until after the commissioner had washed the floor!

The constabulary recommended to the attorney general that Dr. Farrell be charged with arson. The minister sat on that recommendation for several months with the result that, given the strong opinions of Newfoundlanders about politics and politicians, there was much public speculation about a "whitewash." A copy of the police report was leaked to the St. John's newspaper, and Dr. Farrell issued a lawsuit against the newspaper and the Canadian Broadcasting Corporation (CBC). This press coverage all prompted a judicial inquiry into the leak.

Dr. Farrell was eventually charged with arson, but the charge was dismissed at a preliminary hearing. One of the factors in the dismissal was evidence presented by an expert from Montreal, Bernard Peclet, the director of the Quebec Forensic Science Laboratory, who had been retained by Dr. Farrell's lawyer. Mr. Peclet quite correctly cast considerable doubt on the opinion of the fire commissioner about the cause of the fire.

Dismissal of the charge resulted in even more widespread cries of whitewash. The judge conducting the inquiry into the leak of the police report eventually recommended that all the circumstances of the fire be reinvestigated, which added more fuel to the figurative fire. By this time, Frank Moores had resigned as premier and been replaced by Brian Peckford, who appointed another judge to make an inquiry into what had in fact been a small and insignificant fire, except for the person involved.

Ontario Becomes Involved

The inquiry judge appointed Don Mercer, one of the most highly respected lawyers in St. John's, as counsel to the inquiry. He immediately recognized that it would be inappropriate for the fire commissioner or the authorities in Newfoundland to reinvestigate this matter, so he obtained permission from the government of Ontario to have the Ontario Fire Marshal's Office (OFM) perform this second investigation. The OFM assigned Dennis Merkley, the investigator we had worked with in our research, and he asked for assistance from the Centre of Forensic Sciences, myself, Frank McAuley from the Toxicology Section, and Dr. Ray Prime, head of the Chemistry Section.

It was now 1980, unit 512 had long since been repaired and occupied by a different tenant, and there was nothing further that could be done there. All we had were photographs of the scene, which were not of the best quality. Our recommendation to the inquiry was therefore that it would be highly desirable to attempt a full-scale simulation of the fire, which they agreed to fund. This gave us a marvelous opportunity to do some adequately funded full-scale fire simulations and research.

We decided that the simulations should be done based on three different scenarios developed from the condition of the scene and Dr. Farrell's and Mr. Peclet's evidence. We were interested in the burned areas on the floor, the extent of the damage in such a relatively short period, and the fact that Dr. Farrell, although he showed some confusion and had some soot in his nostrils, didn't seem to have suffered any of the toxic effects of carbon monoxide. This would have been expected if the fire had been a smoldering fire of longer duration caused by misuse of smoking materials.

The Simulations

The full-scale fire simulations were performed in October in an old house scheduled for destruction in York Region north of Toronto. A contractor created two separate rooms, identical to the bedroom in St. John's, which were then furnished as closely as possible with the same type of bedroom furniture to present a similar fuel load to what had been in the original fire. We instrumented both test rooms to record temperatures at several places and collect air samples for carbon monoxide determination.

Electrical wiring had been ruled out as a possible source of ignition; there was nothing liable to spontaneous combustion in the room (although Mr. Peclet later suggested this possibility), and thus the most likely initiation of the fire was either a smoldering cigarette or direct ignition with an open flame.

We decided that two of the three burned areas on the bedroom floor could be explained: the one under the window resulted from the fire searching for air and rolling toward the window when it broke, and the burning of the floor in the closet resulted from the clothing in the closet falling and burning on the floor. The burned area we couldn't explain was the fishtail pattern between the closet and the bed, so we decided that was where we would start the fires for the simulations.

Since flaming combustion could be achieved with either a match or a cigarette smoldering for a long period, it didn't matter to the subsequent events how the fire was ignited, so the simulation fires were simply ignited with matches. If the fire had been the result of a dropped smoldering cigarette, it would have to have smoldered from about 03:00 (assuming that Dr. Farrell had gone to sleep around that time) until it reached flaming combustion sometime around 06:45. While smoldering fires can take that long to reach a flaming condition, during that period they would develop an enormous amount of carbon monoxide, which would create a nonsurvivable environment for an occupant of the room.

In the first simulation, we allowed the fire to burn for about fifteen minutes before it was extinguished. As we expected, the burning under the window and in the closet did result, but the carpet remained unburned, unlike the one in St. John's. The second fire we allowed to burn for twenty-three minutes and produced a pattern very similar to what was shown in the St. John's photos except that, again, the carpet hadn't burned.

Figure 6.1 The Newfoundland fire test bedroom.

Figure 6.2 A test burn.

We then decided that we needed to test the possibility of mineral spirits having been used to accelerate the fire. Four liters of the fluid was poured onto the fishtail pattern area of the floor and ignited. As expected, the fire took off very quickly but then rapidly died down and proceeded much the same as the other tests. The only difference in the third fire was that the carpet was destroyed. This we attributed to it being a very windy day and, when the window broke, the wind rushed in and the fire almost got away on us.

We concluded that the destruction of the woolen rug was a red herring, and in fact, the rug had served as protection for the wood floor rather than as fuel for the fire. (Another lesson learned!) The burned fishtail area was probably a result of the original carpet having been very badly worn in that area and thus providing less protection for the floor.

We also learned that there is very little time to escape from bedroom fires such as this. Before the flames were five to six feet high along the walls, as described by Dr. Farrell, temperatures as high as 1,100°C were reached in the doorway and up to 180°C on the bed. This meant that had Dr. Farrell been in that bed and seen such flames, he couldn't have survived, because one or two breaths of 180° air would likely be fatal. The carbon monoxide concentrations were also very interesting. There were quite significant concentrations that, although they varied around the room, would have made survival in the room possible for only a minute or two.

(It has always been somewhat of a surprise to me that otherwise knowledgeable people often speculate about the great hazard presented by toxic gases produced from synthetic materials during a fire. While such gases are produced, their effect on people in fires is insignificant when compared with the more common product of a fire—heat! It gets very hot very quickly in a structural fire, and breathing such hot air is rapidly fatal.)

In November 1980, we went to St. John's to testify at the inquiry and were there for two weeks. Our conclusions and testimony were that the fire probably started on the floor of the bedroom between the unoccupied bed and the closet. It could have started from either a smoldering cigarette or an open flame, but the latter was more likely because it would be very unlikely that anyone could have escaped from a smoldering fire. The fire damage observed could easily have occurred in a fire of twenty minutes' duration. In effect, we ruled out the smoldering cigarette and all other ignition possibilities and concluded that the fire had been started with an open flame.

Mr. Peclet again testified at this inquiry and concurred with most of our evidence. However, he postulated the possibility of spontaneous combustion by developing a theory that a cigarette could begin what he called a "depolymerization" reaction in the cotton bedding. This process would continue for several hours, and even though it would be exothermic, it wouldn't produce smoke or carbon monoxide until flaming combustion resulted. There was nothing in the literature to support this postulation, and we disagreed with it.

Apparently, the judge also disagreed with this theory. The day it was presented, as I was walking back into the courthouse after lunch, he came up behind me and said, "Tell me, son, if I have got this right. If I am at home and me wife is ironing me shirts, and she has got them in her basket and she gets called away on the phone, that eventually those shirts could smolder away and eventually catch fire, is that what Mr. Peclet is trying to tell me?"

I replied, "Yes, Your Honor, that's how I understand it." As the judge then turned away, he muttered, "No goddamn way will that happen," a pretty good hint that he wasn't about to buy this theory.

In the final report of the inquiry, the judge concluded that the fire had been started by an open flame, but there was not enough evidence to bring another charge of arson against Dr. Farrell. Although the report didn't say so, I believed that Dr. Farrell was so drunk that night that he hadn't the foggiest idea what had happened. He may well have lit the fire accidentally.

The political aspects of this case extended even further because counsel representing Dr. Farrell throughout this whole affair was Clyde Wells, who later became the premier of Newfoundland and was a major figure in Canada's constitutional negotiations in the early 1980s. As all Canadians saw during the broadcasts of those discussions, we also saw at the inquiry that Mr. Wells could be very passionate and very emotional about things he feels strongly about. He was a very able and dynamic representative for Dr. Farrell.

By way of a postscript, as Ray Prime and I were at the airport in St. John's on our way home, Bernard Peclet joined us for a beer in the bar. I had known him for many years and had always respected his professional ability. During our conversation, he said, "I guess you didn't think much of my theory?" I replied, "No, Bernie, I didn't." His response was, "Well, it was the best I could come up with." That ended our conversation!

A major benefit from this case was that it confirmed the value of full-scale fire simulations, not only for developing evidence about a specific set of circumstances but also as additions to our general knowledge about fires, how they progress, what sort of environments they produce, and what sort of evidence they leave in the end. This has been extremely useful in training fire investigators, and the quality of fire investigation has increased significantly since the early 1980s as a result.

Our two weeks in Newfoundland also taught us much about the wonderful population of that province and their unique tastes in food and drink. Screech (a powerful Jamaican rum usually blended in Newfoundland) is the popular national drink, and seal flipper pie is a national delicacy. I tried both and can only conclude that they must be an acquired taste!

Carbon Monoxide "Death and the Dark-Haired Maiden" 7

As I became more involved with fire investigations, I began to learn much more about carbon monoxide (CO), the colorless, odorless gas that results from incomplete combustion of any carbon-containing fuel and which is usually the most toxic gas produced in fires. It is also a significant component of automobile exhaust and is frequently associated with improperly adjusted domestic gas appliances and furnaces.

Because CO is a small, light molecule with almost the same density as air, its distribution is subject to the movement of ambient air, such as drafts, wind, and air currents. This property can cause great variations in its concentration over short distances. This, in turn, can create considerable confusion in cases where, for example, two people are found in relative proximity, with one dead from CO poisoning and the other only slightly affected.

We frequently had to attend such scenes to make CO concentration measurements, and I was often surprised at the results. For example, in a case in an old house in Toronto in June 1960, a defective gas furnace had caused the CO death of a previously healthy middle-aged man, but in the room in which his body was found, there was a canary singing merrily away. My measurements showed lethal CO concentrations throughout the room except in the immediate area of the birdcage. Closer examination revealed the reason, a tiny BB-sized hole in the window beside the birdcage that allowed fresh air in at that specific location.

In another case in February 1961, in a small village in southwestern Ontario, a man called the telephone operator (this was long before 911 came on the scene) for assistance because he said he had awakened during the night in bed beside his wife and she was unconscious. When police arrived, they found her dead but the husband apparently quite unaffected. In such a small village, rumors quickly circulated that he had done her in. At the scene, I easily determined the source of the CO, a defective gas water heater, and then began making measurements in the bedroom. Much to my surprise, the air around the pillow on the wife's side of the bed had a high CO concentration, but at his pillow, it was virtually negligible. Measurements of air movement velocities in the room revealed the reason, a current of fresh air from an ill-fitted window drifting over his side of the bed but not hers.

We had many similar cases, but without question, the most complicated was a homicide in Sault Ste. Marie in which CO was the lethal agent. It was the closest thing to a fictional murder mystery that I was ever involved with.

Regina v. Dalton Barber

Although Canada adopted its law and court procedures from England, we did not seem to inherit the British flair for flamboyant murder cases. Indeed, a few days after the end of each year, I would have difficulty remembering details of most of the cases I had worked on during the year. Nevertheless, every forensic scientist has at least one case during their career the details of which remain with them for a lifetime. For me, this was the case of *Regina v. William Dalton Barber* in Sault Ste. Marie, Ontario, in 1965. The trial had all the essential titillating elements—a prominent family, a bizarre murder, and a mysterious "other woman"—which attracted massive media coverage. The defense lawyer became a Member of Parliament (albeit for one term only), and the judge became chief justice of Ontario. The detective in charge became chief of the Sault Ste. Marie Police, and the forensic scientist became director of the Centre of Forensic Sciences (CFS).

Dalton Barber was a member of a very prominent family in the Sault. He was executive assistant to the president of Algoma Steel, and his brother Jack was a vice president. Their father had been a senior executive of both Algoma Steel and the Algoma Central Railroad. The Barber family was very active socially in the close-knit ranks of the executive level of Algoma Steel. The

Figure 7.1 The Barber residence.

Algo Club, a private club for members of this group, was the center of their social activities.

The Dalton Barber residence was an attractive ranch-style bungalow on a large lot on Barber Boulevard, a pleasant cul-de-sac in the east end of Sault Ste. Marie. It had a single-car garage attached to the house by way of a breezeway. The long front lawn, which sported a private swimming pool, sloped down to the beautiful St. Mary's River. The home had been custom-built for Dalton and his wife, who had no children. Presumably, for that reason, it had only a single bedroom, unusual for a home in such a prestigious location.

Mrs. Barber was very active in the community. She and Dalton both drank heavily, and there were obvious, to their friends, conflicts between them. Nevertheless, because of their social prominence, these difficulties were concealed from the rest of the community. One of Dalton's hobbies was writing murder mysteries, and that became a matter of interest as the case developed.

At about 02:30 on December 3, 1965, Dalton telephoned his doctor (rather than the police or an ambulance) and said that he had found his wife naked in the front seat of her Pontiac Acadian station wagon parked in the garage; he didn't know if she was dead or alive. The doctor immediately responded to the Barber residence (doctors still made house calls in those days). He found the front door unlocked, the house full of "fumes" (which he could not further describe), Mrs. Barber dead (her body still warm) in bed, and Dalton, apparently unconscious, lying across the foot of the bed. The doctor called the coroner, the police, and an ambulance for Dalton, who seemed to recover very quickly, almost remarkably so. As he was being removed to the ambulance, he asked for his glasses, pipe, and tobacco to take with him to the hospital.

The coroner noted soot in the nostrils of Mrs. Barber's body, a mucous stain with some lipstick and soot on the pillow, and a large urine stain on the sheet and mattress under the body, indicating that that was where she had died. The skin was cherry pink in color, an indicator of CO poisoning. At the subsequent autopsy, there were no obvious signs of violence or apparent cause of death other than CO. The only sample taken for toxicology was blood. This was sent to CFS, where it was found to contain 110 mg/100 mL of alcohol and to be 50% saturated with carbon monoxide (likely fatal).

There was a vanity and sink on one wall of the bedroom underneath a window, and the police observed soot scattered around this area. Although there was a small fire smoldering in the fireplace in the living room, a source for the fumes could not be located.

The motor of Mrs. Barber's Acadian in the garage was cold. The motor of Dalton's car, a Vanguard station wagon, parked outside the garage, was warm

Figure 7.2 The stain on the bed.

Figure 7.3 Exhaust from the Vanguard.

to the touch. Its interior was full of fumes, and the windows were steamed up. Based on these observations, the police had suspicions about the death from the start, to the point that they considered the possible involvement of a hose to transfer CO into the bedroom from the Vanguard. The only hose they could find on the site, however, was filled with ice; it had not been involved in this event.

At the hospital, the nurses noted some black smudges on the backs of Dalton's hands. A blood sample taken from him showed no alcohol but did reveal about 10% saturation with CO, indicating that he had indeed been exposed to some CO (but not a particularly toxic concentration) that evening. (It was somewhat puzzling that if, as he later said, they had each had their usual few drinks before dinner, their BACs were so different. The lack of alcohol in his blood suggested that he may have lived four or five hours after she had died, plenty of time to accomplish what we later came to believe he had.)

Barber told Inspector Robert McEwan of the Sault Ste. Marie Police that he had arrived home from work and parked his Vanguard in its usual spot outside the garage. His wife and he had their normal few drinks before dinner, after which they had "one of our usual arguments." It was not a happy domestic situation! He said he went to bed about 22:15 and woke around 02:00 to find the house full of fumes. His wife wasn't in bed, so he went looking for her and found her naked and unconscious in her car in the garage. After phoning the doctor, he dragged her into the bedroom and collapsed. Dalton appeared to be toying with questions about any specifics, and according to Inspector McEwan, who knew Dalton and his mystery-writing hobby, he seemed to enjoy the intellectual gamesmanship of the interrogation. McEwan felt that Barber was taking bits from his murder mysteries and injecting them into the conversation, for example, "Well, Bob, if I did it that way, why didn't you find this." It was a very interesting and unusual interview.

One of the things found that evening that was of particular interest was on Mr. Barber's desk, the manuscript for his most recent murder mystery, titled "Death and the Dark-Haired Maiden." As the investigation proceeded, I read this manuscript from cover to cover. It was dreadfully written and, unfortunately, contained nothing that might relate to this real-world mystery.

Within a few days, Dalton left the Sault to "get away from it all and visit friends." As the police later learned, he did go away, but he visited only one friend, a woman in Toronto who was married to another man. This was by prearrangement, and they went off on a trip together. The day before Christmas, they returned to Sault Ste. Marie, where the mystery woman's presence was concealed from all visitors. If anyone visited Dalton, she would remain behind the closed bedroom door and Dalton, who had dismissed the Barbers' long-serving cleaning lady, would explain, "I can't go into the bedroom; it has too many memories."

Over the next month, Inspector McEwan remained suspicious about Mrs. Barber's death. He continued to nose around and kept hearing rumors about the Barbers' relationship from the Peyton Place–like circle at the Algo Club. Dalton had been telling friends that his wife was a "manic depressive" and that he wouldn't be surprised if she killed herself one day. In fact, these friends knew that she was much more robust and healthy than was Dalton. They didn't buy Dalton's stories, and at least three of them told McEwan that Dalton had asked them where he might obtain "knockout drops."

Finally, as so often happens in cases of complex triangles (and quadrangles), in February 1966, a Mr. L-----, another boyfriend of the mystery woman, approached the Ontario Provincial Police (OPP) in Toronto with the information that she was living with Dalton in Sault Ste. Marie. Apparently, she was not very discrete about her various lovers because Dalton obviously knew this informant's name. In Dalton's desk, Bob McEwan later found a poem titled "L----- Is a Prick." The poem went on from there and was of the same literary quality as his murder mystery. The OPP assigned Criminal Investigation Branch Inspector Bob MacGarva to assist the Sault police with the case.

On February 10, 1966, by prearrangement with Dalton, McEwan and MacGarva went to the house. A detective sergeant was stationed outside a door that led out from the bedroom. As Dalton answered the front door, the mystery woman left through this bedroom door but was stopped by the detective sergeant. She and Dalton were "taken downtown" (as they say on all the police TV shows), where they were interrogated separately. After a few minutes of separation, Dalton suddenly stood up and said, "Okay, Bob, I killed her." After considerable discussion with his lawyer and with the local Crown attorney (who was also part of the Algoma social circle), Dalton retracted this statement. Nevertheless, he was charged with murder.

Mrs. Barber's body was exhumed and sent to Toronto for examination. Although some discolored areas were noted externally on the body, they could not be ruled out as postmortem artifacts. One of the reasons for the exhumation was the information about Dalton seeking knockout drops, which I assumed referred to chloral hydrate. Chloral hydrate was rarely encountered anymore, but at one time it was known as a "Mickey Finn" and was quite common. In fact, Joslyn Rogers's master's thesis in 1910 was titled "A Method for the Analysis of Chloral Hydrate in Tissue." Additional tissue samples were taken to analyze for chloroform, the metabolic product of chloral hydrate.

The CFS toxicologist who examined these samples became quite excited when she in fact detected chloroform in them; however, because the samples were from an embalmed body, we needed to confirm that the chloroform was not a result of the embalming process. We were able to get samples of the embalming fluids from the funeral director in Sault Ste. Marie and, much to everyone's chagrin, found that they did indeed contain chloroform, so what might have been quite powerful evidence was no evidence at all.

In March, I went to the Sault to attempt to determine what had taken place on Barber Boulevard that snowy December night. The only likely sources of CO that I could find were the two automobiles. Running the Acadian in the garage did not produce anything significant (fumes or CO) in the house, and the motor became quite warm. This was inconsistent with the police observations on the night of the death that the motor on that car was cold and the house was full of fumes. I also noticed a black soot spot on the inside of the garage door, which could not have come from the Acadian's exhaust pipe, because it was on the opposite side of the car; it could, however, have come from the Vanguard.

When I ran the Vanguard, which was older than the Acadian and not in good condition, in the garage, I could see large volumes of black soot emitting from the tailpipe and could smell exhaust fumes, which quickly filled the house to the point that Bob McEwan and I could not stay inside. (Nevertheless, a toxic concentration of CO in the bedroom, which was at the opposite end of the house from the garage, was not achieved even after one hour. However, the imprudent forensic scientist, who spent more time measuring CO levels in the house and garage than he should have, did experience some toxic effects.) When I returned to the hotel that night, the meal I ordered for dinner went uneaten because I had to go back to my room to be sick, a common effect of CO toxicity.

When I backed the Vanguard out of the garage and parked it outside, it was full of fumes, the windows steamed up, and the motor was hot to touch (i.e., the same condition it was in when the police arrived). Thus, we could show that Dalton's story about finding the body in the Acadian in the garage did not correspond with the evidence. The two cars must have had their locations switched not long before the police arrived, and the Vanguard must have been somehow used to fill the house with fumes to set up the masquerade.

We were convinced that Mrs. Barber had died in the bedroom (the urine stain on the bed), from CO poisoning, probably originating from the Vanguard's exhaust (the soot on the pillow had small amounts of lead in it; gasoline at that time contained tetraethyl lead). Our problem, however, was that we could not establish how, in the absence of any evidence of a hose, Dalton had introduced the CO into the bedroom near her pillow.

Dalton Barber's trial for murder opened on May 3, 1966 (just three months after the event, very speedy by today's standards) before Mr. Justice G.A. Gale and lasted just over two weeks (a long trial in those days, a contrast with today's trials, in which simple preliminary motions can take much more than two weeks). The local Crown attorney recused himself because of his social connections with Dalton and many of the witnesses, so Samuel Caldbick QC, a very experienced Crown attorney from Timmins and Cochrane, took over the prosecution. Because of my close involvement with the investigation, he asked me to attend throughout the entire trial, something we did not normally do.

As we were waiting for the start of proceedings, the Barbers' former cleaning lady, a delightful elderly English lady such as is often seen in old English movies, approached Inspector MacGarva and me in the corridor and said, "I don't know if this is important or not, but on the morning after Mrs. Barber died, I found some burned pieces of garden hose in the fireplace and threw them out on the ash pile in the yard!"

That certainly got our attention! MacGarva, McEwan, and I immediately high-tailed it out to Barber Boulevard. There, still partly covered by the slowly disappearing snow, we found the metal hose fittings and some remaining small bits of hose. "I think we may have solved our problem!" exclaimed McEwan.

Although what we were certain was the final piece of the puzzle had been discovered, Mr. Caldbick was not sure how he could fit it into place at this late date and asked that we keep it to ourselves until he could determine if, or how, it could be used.

Sault Ste. Marie's "trial of the century" proceeded before standing-room-only crowds of local matrons whose bridge games and afternoon teas were sorely neglected for the duration. A challenging problem for Mr. Caldbick, a distinguished gentleman of the old school, was keeping track, in the tight social circle of the Algo Club, of which of his witnesses were related in some way and how! He was quite embarrassed one afternoon when he asked one of his witnesses, "Do you know Mr. K-----?" An audible titter ran through the audience, all of whom knew something Mr. Caldbick didn't: his witness had once been married to Mr. K-----!

The highlight for the spectators was the long-awaited appearance of the mystery woman. She didn't disappoint them with her flamboyant dress, including a matching leopard skin coat and hat. She was, however, somewhat less than attractive, a disappointment for most of the men in the courtroom prompting the unspoken question, "What on earth did Dalton see in her?" She wasn't shy, and her answers to Mr. Caldbick's questions about her various boyfriends were vivid and, in that pre–*Fifty Shades of Gray* era, quite titillating for the society ladies of the Sault.

On Friday of the second week, the evidence (except for the garden hose) had all been entered. Mr. Caldbick then, in the absence of the jury, presented the matter of the recently discovered burned hose to Mr. Justice Gale. After discussion with the defense counsel, the judge ruled that I was to make tests at the house with a hose and if I could show that a hose could have been used to introduce CO into the bedroom, the evidence would be admitted the following day, it then being about five o'clock in the afternoon. This presented a problem since I had no test equipment in the Sault. However, Dalton's brother Jack, who loyally attended the trial each day, volunteered the facilities of the Algoma Steel laboratory, a quite sophisticated lab, to me. This fine gentleman was at that point, I believe, still convinced of his brother's innocence. Later that night at the lab, he told me that his confidence was waning.

What the Toronto *Globe and Mail* (Canada's "national newspaper") headlined the next morning as "Mysterious Midnight Tests at Murder Home" proceeded in the presence of the police, Mr. Caldbick, and the defense counsel, Terry Murphy QC.

We placed the Vanguard in the driveway outside the bedroom window. One end of the garden hose from the garage (the one that had been filled with ice in December) was stuffed into the exhaust pipe with rags, and the other end led into the bedroom through the window and over to the pillow. After starting the car, I collected periodic air samples at the pillow location in vacuum bottles obtained from the Algoma Lab. Within fifteen minutes, the fumes in the bedroom were so thick that we had to terminate the test.

As the hose was pulled from the window, the loose end flopped around spraying soot particles over the sink. Then, as I pulled the other end of the hose out of the exhaust pipe, it was covered with black guck (my technical term), which covered the palms of my hands. Terry Murphy noticed this and insisted that I "make a note that the smudges are on the palms and not the backs of your hands." Having done so, I asked him if it was alright if I washed my hands in a pail of water nearby. He agreed and, of course, as I did so the smudge was transferred to the backs of my hands. I asked, "Would you like me to make a note of that also?" He replied, "I think I'd better go and have a conversation with my client."

The air samples were taken to the Algoma Lab for analysis. Not surprisingly, they showed CO concentrations as high as 8%, which would very quickly (four or five breaths) be fatal. We finished at the lab about 03:00 Saturday morning.

I presented these results to the jury later that morning; they must have wondered why everyone had such bags under their eyes. Mr. Murphy had very few questions for cross-examination. The case was then adjourned until Monday for closing arguments. Sunday morning, I was sitting relaxing in the sunny courtyard of the hotel when, much to my surprise, Justice Gale looked down at me from the balcony of his room and a brief, but for me memorable, conversation took place:

G: Good morning, Doug!
L: Good morning, sir.
G: That was an interesting day yesterday.

L: And an interesting evening also, sir.
G: I rather think that was the *coup de grâce*!
L: Yes sir, it may have been!

Dalton Barber was convicted of noncapital murder on May 18, 1966, and was sentenced to life imprisonment. Although Mr. Murphy consulted some other prominent lawyers, no appeal was filed. Terry later served one term in the House of Commons, following which he was appointed to the High Court of Justice of Ontario. In the late 1970s, I met him by chance at the Sault Ste. Marie airport and, over a pleasant drink, he told me that after serving most of his time in the library at Kingston Penitentiary, Dalton was paroled in 1973 and was living with a daughter from an earlier marriage in another city. If he ever published any of his murder mysteries, neither of us had heard of them. I expressed my disappointment that Terry had lost his seat in Parliament, but he quite contentedly replied, "Well, the good citizens of the Sault kindly voted to keep me in the Sault!"

Nitroglycerine and Explosions

8

Some Things Can't Be Learned in the Laboratory

Nitroglycerine: A Tool for Midnight Withdrawals

As my experience with fire investigations developed, my challenging mentor, Professor Rogers, decided that I should also learn something about explosives. He may have had an ulterior motive because one of the activities that kept him busy, often at night, was dealing with nitroglycerine (NG), remaining after it had been used to blow, or attempt to blow, a safe. During the depression years and into the 1970s, when cash was king and credit cards were rare, there were often substantial amounts of cash stored in the safes that were a common element of the furnishings of most retail businesses.

These were tempting targets for one of the elites of the criminal world, the expert safecracker, some of whom were particularly adept in the use of homemade NG (colloquially known as "soup") for this purpose. Some could open safes with nothing more than a drill and their knowledge of the specific design of a safe's mechanism. Others could introduce a small amount of NG into the mechanism and blow it open. Some, however, were not that skillful but could not resist the temptation to try, often with minimal success. Monday mornings, when businesses opened after the weekend, very often revealed one or more blown safes that had to be dealt with. (In the city, people do not pay much attention to loud bangs. In one case I worked in west Toronto, the explosion was sufficient to rip the door off the safe and blow it through a dry cleaner's shop window out onto Dundas Street; yet no one reported anything odd until the first streetcar the next morning couldn't get past the safe door resting on the tracks.)

Even with the experts who used only small amounts of NG, there was usually some left unexploded. For those with less expertise, there was almost always a significant amount remaining, either inside the safe, if they had managed to introduce it, or, more often, on the floor around the safe. Regardless of the amount, it had to be chemically neutralized before the business could reopen.

Professor Rogers therefore trained me in the intricacies of the neutralization of NG. He had developed a procedure for the chemical neutralization of

NG using a solution of potassium hydroxide in methanol. Because he was such a practical and realistic gentleman, part of the training included us obtaining some old safes to try to blow them ourselves. (We would never have made a living as safecrackers, however, since our efforts usually resulted in either not successfully opening the safe or blowing it and its contents to smithereens.)

NG is produced by the action of a mixture of nitric and sulfuric acids on glycerin. A thermometer is often used to stir the mixture and monitor the temperature since heat is produced in the process. Criminals usually did this in plastic mixing bowls, which would be kept cool by surrounding them with ice. The most important step in the process is ensuring that all the excess acid is washed away; failure to do this efficiently often makes homemade NG much more sensitive than the commercial product. Since the criminals did not have access to a laboratory, as part of my training, Rogers insisted that we make our NG in his kitchen at home using his wife's pots and pans. Marie was not amused when I brought a two-ounce bottle of our product home one night to use at a demonstration in Hamilton the following morning.

Attacks on safes with NG usually left sufficient evidence—detonator leg wires, dry cell batteries, bits of tamping material such as soap, putty, plasticine, tape, cotton, and so forth—that there was no doubt that nitro had been used. Nevertheless, ever a man of practicality, Rogers always did a simple test of any oily liquid remaining at the scene. He would smear a little bit on a hard steel surface and smack it with a hammer (which he always carried for this purpose). If the oily liquid went "pop," that was good enough for him to deal with it as nitro. (Contrary to conventional belief about NG, he often said that he had never heard of a single case where someone had been injured during the production or illicit use of "soup".)

Safecrackers used various methods to insert the NG into a safe. The two most common were by pouring the nitro through a "funnel" made of putty or plasticine into a crack around the door created by pounding with a mallet, or by drilling a hole into the combination box and putting a much smaller amount of nitro, sometimes soaked onto cotton wool, into the box. The latter was a much neater method if the hole was properly placed.

Regardless of the method used to insert the nitro, several situations might be found at the scene: the safe was blown and the door open; the safe was blown but the door still locked, possibly jammed and with the dial removed; or the safe was "souped," the detonator in place, the door closed, and the NG not detonated. This latter was obviously the most hazardous condition. This was the situation I found the first time I had to deal with NG neutralization on my own, in February 1963 at an A&P store in Scarborough.

The first step in the neutralization procedure was an examination for, and treatment of, any drops or smears of NG on the floor around the safe. Then, if the door was open, it was only necessary to neutralize any visible pools or spots inside the safe and the parts of the door and frame that had been attacked. If the door was closed but the detonator had been fired, the additional step of neutralizing all around the crack between the door and frame and in any holes that had been drilled was required. Any putty, plasticine, and so forth, remaining was scraped off with a wooden stick and saved for later disposal by burning.

Once this was done, if the dial was still in place, we would carefully turn it while standing well to the side (the combination wheels are made of brass and therefore nonsparking). If it turned easily, the store owner, or whoever knew the combination, would be asked to approach and dial it to the point where the handle was ready to turn, and then leave. We would then rig some way to turn the handle as remotely as possible with a stick or length of rope from a position as far away from the front of the safe as possible and gently open the door. If the door opened, the owner would be asked to inspect the contents without touching anything, and then any further neutralizing of the interior and contents was completed. If the door did not open after several attempts or if the dial had been removed, it was necessary for the safe manufacturer to be contacted to complete the process.

Each incident was unique, and improvisation of some part of the process was often required. In some incidents, the safe attackers also had to improvise and would make use of materials they found on site. One of the strangest occurrences I had to deal with was on a Sunday night in September 1967 at a high-end butcher shop in the Don Mills Plaza. As noted above, once the NG is inserted, it has to be tamped in place, usually with putty or some other material. In this case, the safecrackers had managed to tip the safe onto its back and placed a complete side of beef on top of the door as tamping. The detonation was successful in doing considerable damage—to the beef!

When I arrived on site, the shop office looked like a battle zone with bits of meat adhering to the walls and ceiling. The safe door, however, had withstood the attack. After I finished neutralizing the NG and was preparing to leave, the shop owner voiced what seemed to be his prime concern: Could he sell the remaining beef? I wasn't about to touch that one (the question was a lot more sensitive than the NG), so I took the classic bureaucrat's exit: "That's not in my mandate. You'll have to contact the Food Inspection Agency!"

Investigating Explosions

Experience in fire investigation and dealing with situations involving NG led inevitably to requests to expand that experience into the investigation of explosions. Again, Professor Rogers was a valued mentor. Initially, there were two types of incidents that I was able to "cut my teeth on": gas/air or vapor/air explosions, and smaller (usually) chemical explosions created by experimenting schoolboys.

The gas explosions invariably resulted in substantial damage, sometimes on a large scale, such as an entire building. One smaller type that I saw multiple times involved acetylene tanks in the vehicles of plumbers who failed to ensure that the tank valve was tightly closed when they parked for the night. Sometime during the night, sufficient acetylene would have leaked out to create an explosive acetylene/air mixture (acetylene has a very wide range of concentrations in air that are explosive), which required only a low-energy spark to set it off, destroying the vehicle and, if it was in a garage, the garage and perhaps the house to which it was attached.

Figure 8.1 Acetylene explosion in a plumber's car.

The first of these that I encountered, in November 1964, presented no challenge as to the nature and source of the fuel, but the origin of the ignition spark was a puzzle. The only thing that might have been operating at the time was the car clock (which had survived the blast), so I removed it to take to the lab. There, I asked our electronics examiner if it could have been the source of the ignition. "No problem," he announced as he hooked it up to a twelve-volt battery and said, "Come with me." We went into a dark closet, where I could instantly see a blue spark emitting periodically when the two electrical contacts in the clock came together. With what could only be described as a smug smile on his face, he asked his electronics-challenged colleague, "Are you OK with that?"

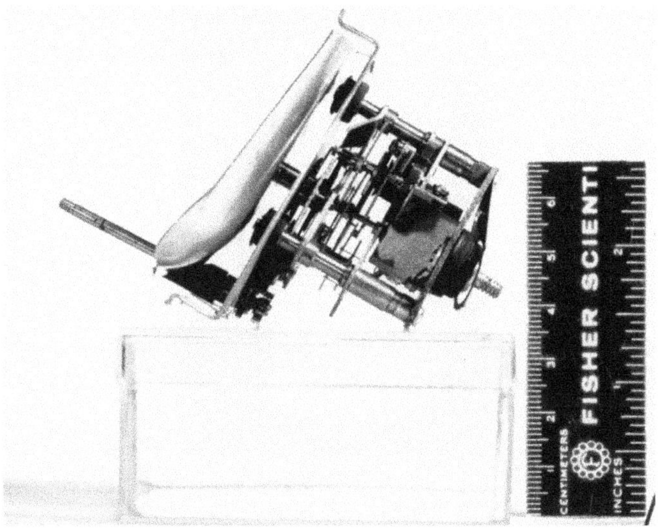

Figure 8.2 The source of the spark.

Another type of gaseous explosion I saw a couple of times occurred in tank trucks that were being filled at the Texaco refinery in Port Credit. Both, one in November 1968 and the other in May 1980, resulted in the death of the driver. They were the result of a static spark developing near the fill opening because of a failure to properly "ground" the tank and the fill pipe.

The experimenting schoolboys presented more of an analytical challenge because of uncertainty about the chemicals they might have access to. They would often start with basic Christmas present chemistry sets but would then progress to whatever they could "borrow" from the high school chemistry lab. For boys of a certain age, chemistry is all about making a stink or a bang, with the latter the much-preferred outcome. Sometimes these incidents were tragic because the boys would seriously injure themselves when things did not go quite as planned.

The preliminary experiments usually involved just mixing a few chemicals (or some common household products) and setting a match to them in the open. The resultant flash (but no bang) would be an incentive to try to modify the process. They quickly learned that to get a bang, the chemicals had to be confined in some container that would allow the pressure to build until the container burst. The container used would progress from aluminum cigar tubes to copper pipe with crimped ends to steel pipe with screw-on end caps. It was when they reached this latter stage and they started improvising homemade fuses that serious problems could develop.

In one tragic case, a teenage boy had somehow learned that the main chemical in blasting caps is lead azide. He discovered that it is quite easily made by reacting sodium azide with lead nitrate and filtering off the

Figure 8.3 Schoolboy's homemade hand grenade.

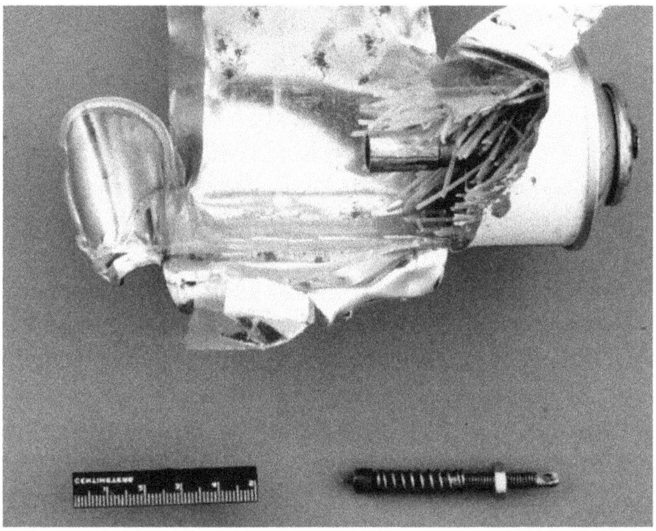

Figure 8.4 Schoolboy's exploded homemade hand grenade.

precipitate. In his high school chemistry lab, he found some sodium azide but no lead nitrate. There was, however, a bottle of silver nitrate, and he reasoned that it would be a good substitute. It was! Having completed the synthesis, he needed to test the product but failed to understand that the very reason lead azide is used in detonators is because it is very sensitive; silver azide has similar properties. He spread some on the curb and struck it with a hammer, and it worked—too well! The hammer was blown out of his hand and struck him in the face, fracturing his skull and removing an eye. Such a waste!

Metallic Sodium

A less serious but interesting, for me, schoolboy prank occurred at Maple Leaf Gardens during a Toronto Maple Leafs hockey game in February 1962. At the start of the second period, a small "explosion" occurred on the ice in front of the Leafs' players' bench, causing great excitement among the players and the 15,000 fans. I was at home watching the game on TV with my sons, Eric and Brian (that was a time when I still watched NHL hockey, a character flaw that I eventually corrected). The referees and paid duty police on hand searched the ice surface, but there was no evidence of a bomb other than a small melted area of the ice. The only thing they could find was a small burned area containing a bit of white powder on Eddie Shack's gloves; he was one of the Leafs' most colorful players. With his trademark grin and cackling laugh, he was flamboyantly pointing at the area. Finally, the game proceeded.

The next morning, a Toronto police detective walked into the lab and presented Eddie's glove to me for examination. I suspected what had happened and quickly identified the white powder as sodium hydroxide, the product of the reaction between metallic sodium and water. One of the first demonstrations that high school chemistry teachers often make for their students is dropping a pea-sized bit of metallic sodium into a beaker of water, producing an instantaneous explosive mixture of hydrogen and air. (Metallic sodium is so reactive it has to be stored in kerosene to prevent it from reacting with water vapor in the air.) Boys are fascinated by the reaction and often develop a scheme to commandeer a bit of this magic metal. One had obviously been successful and managed to throw it onto the ice at the arena.

Gardens management was concerned about possible "copycat" activity and invited me to attend the next three home games in case of a recurrence. There was no repeat, but I enjoyed the games because this was the only way I was likely to be able to afford to see one up close. Before the first game, I returned Eddie's glove to Maple Leaf legend King Clancy, who took me into the dressing room to deliver it in person. Eric and Brian were very impressed!

Disposing of unwanted metallic sodium was a not uncommon event and was a source of mischievous pleasure for myself and Sergeant of Detectives Vic Henderson of the Toronto Police "Bomb Squad," with whom I worked closely. Teachers or lab personnel would find the sodium from some long-forgotten experiment in the back of a cupboard and would call the police to dispose of it. In Toronto, we would choose a sunny summer day, take the jar of sodium in kerosene out beyond Toronto Island's Gibralter Point on one of the police boats, place it on a small wooden raft we had constructed for the purpose, and shoot at it until one of us hit the jar, it broke, and the contents made spectacular contact with Lake Ontario. We were still young boys at heart!

The amount of sodium normally involved in these escapades was usually small, less than 200 g. The largest amount I ever dealt with was about five kilograms in somewhat strange circumstances. A man in North Bay who was an amateur gunsmith had found an old book with a formula for the solution gunsmiths use to treat the barrels of guns to present a shiny bluish surface. The process is known as bluing. As he read down the page, one of the ingredients was shown as 500 g of "sodium," but he failed to turn the page and see "hydroxide" on the other side; i.e., the formula called for sodium hydroxide. He ordered five kilograms of metallic sodium from a chemical supply house (which must have been a bit surprised at the order). When it arrived, he couldn't understand why the container held so much liquid (the kerosene) rather than the powder he expected.

He contacted the supplier, learned what he had on his workbench, and called the Ontario Provincial Police (OPP) for assistance. They, in turn, called me and I drove to North Bay. This was too large an amount to use my preferred treatment (even though Lake Nipissing was inviting), and I decided that we would have to dispose of it in small batches. The OPP got permission to isolate a remote area of the North Bay airport, where we filled a fifty-gallon drum with water, cut the sodium into small pieces, and carefully dropped them bit by bit into the drum using long-handled forceps. It must have presented a puzzling sight to passengers on landing aircraft!

Homemade Explosives

Because of the wide range of chemicals that can be used to produce an explosive mixture, these cases often presented a significant analytical challenge since we had to try to identify any unexploded chemicals remaining, as well as those produced in the explosion. One of the simplest and most common examples would be an exploded pipe bomb, in which we might find both the ingredients of homemade "black powder" (the original form of gunpowder, i.e., carbon, sulfur, and potassium nitrate) and its combustion products, potassium carbonate and potassium sulfate. Others could be much more complex.

An example of this type of case occurred during the evening of September 24, 1968. Pipe bombs made of six-inch lengths of two-inch-diameter galvanized steel pipe fitted with screw-on end caps exploded outside the homes of thirteen executives of the Hawker Siddeley aircraft corporation in Toronto over about a thirty-minute period. (Similar events occurred in Montreal the same night.) "Credit" for the action was claimed by an anti–Viet Nam war group. The "bombs" were small mortars because they each had a "bipod" made from a coat hanger bent around the neck to prop the device at a forty-five-degree angle aimed at the home.

Figure 8.5 A Hawker Siddeley "mortar".

The explosions were not very efficient, and some of the explosive content of the pipe bombs remained. We identified this as a mixture of potassium chlorate and sugar, a well-known homemade explosive substance that is quite sensitive. One device was found almost intact, and we were able to determine the timing/triggering mechanism, which was quite ingenious. It was a small plastic bottle containing sulfuric acid. The perpetrators had experimented and learned how long it would take the acid to burn through the plastic. When the acid contacted the chlorate/sugar contents, the chemical reaction would detonate the mixture. Very little damage resulted, but the chemical analysis was very interesting, and the ingenuity of the device certainly got our attention!

An Embarrassing Case

One of the simplest "kitchen" explosives to make (and by far the most sensitive) is nitrogen triiodide. It is made by mixing iodine with ammonium hydroxide and filtering off the resulting precipitate. The product is quite safe when wet, but after it is dry, it is so sensitive that touching it with a feather will set it off. One case I dealt with involving nitrogen triiodide resulted in considerable embarrassment, for my wife Marie!

After I had become director of the Centre of Forensic Sciences, I didn't often become directly involved in the examination of case materials, except for those involving explosives. One day, S/D Vic Henderson walked into my office carrying a piece of paper bearing some chemical notations. It was part of an extortion note presented to the police by a criminal group demanding the release of two of their members from jail. The note said they had boxes containing 1,000 pounds of an explosive in storage that they would detonate at city hall if their demand was not complied with. The note contained the recipe they claimed to have used to produce the explosive. I quickly recognized that the formula was for nitrogen triiodide and (somewhat rashly, as I think back on it) advised Henderson: "Vic, it's a hoax; you should call their bluff." I reasoned that there was no way these guys, or anyone for that matter, could store that much of this explosive in cardboard boxes because of its extreme sensitivity.

The police told the extortionists to "take a hike" (or words to that effect), and much to my relief, no explosion occurred. That, however, was not the end of the story.

About six months later, Marie received a summons for jury duty. She wondered if she was eligible because of my position and that of our son Eric, who by that time was a member of the Toronto Police Department (PD). I encouraged her to participate because she would find it interesting. Juries are selected randomly from a large panel of citizens, and the chances of being selected are not great. Much to her surprise, Marie was chosen to serve as a juror on a criminal case involving an extortion attempt. She found the experience fascinating until Vic Henderson (who she knew well) started to testify and described taking the extortion note to "Doug Lucas at the crime lab." The juror sitting next to Marie suddenly turned and looked at her while she searched for someplace to hide.

I was out of town, but on my return that night, Marie was agonizing over what she should do. My advice was for her to speak the next morning to the sheriff's officer who attended to the jury and ask to see the judge. She did so and found the judge to be very considerate and understanding of her dilemma. Much to her (and my) surprise, he said that these events would not disqualify her, but if they made her uncomfortable with continuing as a juror, he would certainly understand and excuse her. She quickly accepted the offer with great relief. The odds against Marie being selected for a jury for a criminal case that turned out to have an investigating officer she knew and which was one of the very rare cases that I was then actively involved with were so long that she immediately went to buy a lottery ticket on her way home! It didn't win.

High Explosives

Explosions caused by the detonation of high explosives are easy to differentiate from gas/air explosions. There is usually extreme, but localized, shattering damage, which can produce fragments (missiles) leaving the scene at high velocity and causing secondary damage when they strike. The specific location of the charge can easily be identified by the resultant crater, and the immediate area can be searched in detail for evidence such as bits of the container, burnt fuse, and blasting cap leg wires, which help determine the nature of the device. It is important in these investigations to have the support of someone familiar with the area who can identify objects (or portions of them) and describe their original location. Knowing where such things started from and where they are found helps in locating the "seat" of the explosion.

I had gradually developed experience in these investigations, usually involving car bomb homicides (the first one I worked was on Brock Avenue in Toronto in February 1962, which was never solved) or pipe bombs placed outside houses or retail buildings (one at Honest Ed's, a cut-rate department store in Toronto in June 1962, and others at the Yugoslavian Consulate on Spadina Road during their National Day celebrations in November 1965 and 1967). (The National Day each year seemed to coincide with Grey Cup Day (Canada's football championship), which meant missing most of the game on TV—quite annoying!)

To develop experience about car bombs, I worked with Vic Henderson and others blowing up cars. The police would obtain old clunkers from

Figure 8.6 Experimental car bomb.

wreckers, and we would take them to a worked-out sand pit north of the city, where we would place differing amounts of dynamite in different locations in the cars and blow them up. We could then examine the results and learn the effects of the various amounts and locations of the explosive charges. (Great fun, and we got paid for it!) The first time we did one of these experiments, I watched in awe as the hood from the car rose magnificently into the sky and then gracefully floated back to the floor of the pit. I could barely resist the temptation to run out to try to catch it.

One of these car bomb homicides was in Sarnia in March 1973. A man, whose wife was having an affair with another man, went out to his car parked in the driveway of his home to leave for work. It would not start, but that was of no concern to him because he knew that the main fuse was blown and he had wrapped it in aluminum foil as a temporary repair. He got out, raised the hood, reached in to jiggle the fuse, and a loud explosion occurred. He was seriously injured and died later that day.

I reached the scene that afternoon, and it was readily apparent that a high explosive, likely two or three sticks of dynamite, had exploded under the driver's seat. (Had the man been sitting in the seat, he would have been killed instantly, so the defective fuse had given him a couple extra hours of life.) The method of detonation was also apparent because there were two red leg wires from an electric blasting cap hanging down under the dash. They were very sloppily connected to the turn indicator switch. The police suspected that the perpetrator was the third party in the triangle who did not want the explosion to make a mess in his lover's driveway. He must have thought that the explosion would not occur until the car reached the corner and the driver

Figure 8.7 The Sarnia car bomb homicide.

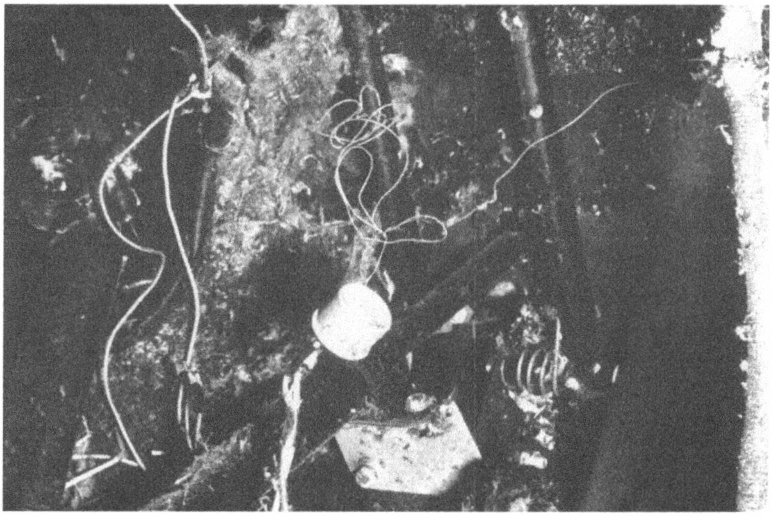

Figure 8.8 Detonator leg wires attached to turn indicator switch.

signaled a turn. He did not realize that the switch is directional rather than on/off, and the power went through the switch to the detonator as soon as the defective fuse was "fixed," completing the circuit from the car battery to the detonator.

The police took me to examine this suspect's home and workbench. It was the neatest, most organized work area I have ever seen, a place for everything and everything in its place! I had great difficulty reconciling the fastidious appearance of this area with the extremely sloppy wiring job of the detonator and asked the detectives how sure they were about this suspect because I had serious doubts. They said they were certain and a few days later told me that he had failed a polygraph test. While that satisfied them, they were unable to develop any other convincing evidence and, since polygraph test results are not admissible in Canadian courts, no charge was ever laid. The suspect had an unshakeable alibi, and I was never convinced he was the right guy.

A Variety of Learning Experiences

Hoggs Hollow

In March 1960, a new wastewater pipe was being installed through the Hoggs Hollow district near Yonge and York Mills in Toronto. Because the pipe tunnel was below the level of a creek running under Yonge Street, the tunneling had to be done under pressure to prevent the creek water from seeping in. Compressed air was therefore pumped through a long hose down into the tunnel. Late one afternoon, an explosion and fire occurred in the tunnel and three workmen were killed.

Labor laws required that to go into a pressurized tunnel, one had to be less than forty years of age. Ward Smith and Professor Rogers were both well over forty, but I was only thirty-one, so I was elected to assist the police with this investigation.

The major issue was the fuel for the fire. There was nothing to burn down there. To get down into the tunnel, we had to enter an air lock where the pressure was raised to that maintained in the tunnel. This process was quite painful to the ears. We then were lowered about fifty feet to a small vestibule where there was a large coil of partially burned two-inch neoprene hose through which the compressed air was pumped from the surface. This hose was covered with heavy oil from the compressor. From the vestibule, we had to bend ourselves around the three-foot-diameter pipe in the two feet of space between the pipe and the concrete tunnel wall and work ourselves out about 100 feet to where the workers had been killed. This experience gave me great respect for the conditions these men had to work under.

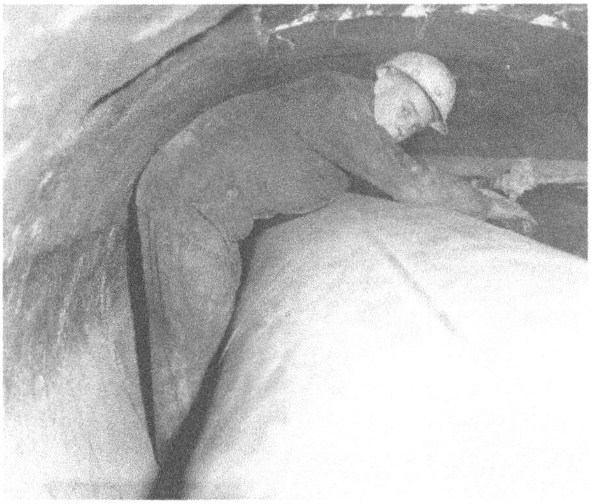

Figure 8.9 Hoggs Hollow explosion.

After a couple of hours, the only potential "fuel" that we could find was the oil-covered hose, which was not considered flammable under normal conditions. After much discussion, Ward Smith, Josh Rogers, and I hypothesized that the flammability characteristics of the compressor oil and neoprene might be different in a high-pressure atmosphere. We therefore consulted with Professor George Wright at the University of Toronto, a real expert on explosives and explosions; he had worked on the development of the major explosive RDX during WWII. He thought we might be correct. Professor Wright assigned one of his graduate students to build an apparatus to test our hypothesis with the result that it was confirmed. The heavy oil-soaked neoprene behaved like gasoline when it was in a high-pressure atmosphere.

Not All Mines Are Explosive

In October 1964, I received a call one afternoon from Sergeant of Detectives Dave Cowan, another member of the Toronto PD Bomb Squad, saying that he was on his way to pick me up to go to Oshawa, where there was a mine in a bank. I assumed it was some land mine or other explosive device and thought, "This could be interesting!" When we got to the bank in the east end of Oshawa, we learned that there had been a failure of communication. The "mine" was in fact an excavated mine that someone had dug under the bank from a neighboring house. Whoever dug it must have been very disappointed (and worn out) because they never got into the bank.

Explosion in an Operating Room

On a very cold January Friday in 1965, an explosion occurred in one of the ORs at St. Michael's Hospital in Toronto. The patient was killed. Cyclopropane was then still in use as an anesthetic, and somehow a spark had developed, causing the explosion. I was impressed with all the safety precautions used to prevent such an occurrence. All the equipment and furniture were well grounded, the floor and footwear of the staff were conductive, and so on. I tested all those things and could find no explanation for the spark. The only thing that appeared unusual was a heavy accumulation of condensation on the windows, a result of the extreme cold outside. Whether this had removed sufficient moisture from the air in the OR to reduce the conductivity to the point that a spark might develop could not be confirmed.

Rush to Sutton Place

Most people feel comfortable and safe in their beds. Whether Myer Rush was one of these or not, I do not know. Mr. Rush was, as they say, "known to police" and had been very successful in his many endeavors, a few of which may have been legal. He lived in the upscale Sutton Place Apartments in Toronto. Overnight on November 10–11, 1967, a bomb exploded under his bed. He was seriously injured but survived. Vic Henderson and I did some more of our experiments, blowing up beds, and concluded that there must have been a stick or two of dynamite placed on the floor under the bed. The bed was destroyed, but the short distance from the floor to the top of the mattress and the mattress itself probably allowed Mr. Rush to survive. He tried to turn a profit from the experience because, with a nephew, he wrote a book, *Bombed in His Bed*, about the event. It never made the bestseller list.

Some Movies Are Truly Explosive

Ontario had a film review board that had been in existence for years classifying (or, if you prefer, censoring) commercial movies. They had a huge collection of old films in their archives, many of which were old enough that the film was celluloid, the principal ingredient of which is nitrocellulose (aka gunpowder). In April 1969, someone at the board realized that their archives could be quite hazardous and asked the Toronto Police for assistance in destroying this material. Vic Henderson and I spent a long Saturday collecting these reels of film, transporting them to our disposal area on the Outer Harbor Spit and creating some very large bonfires, with no hot dogs or marshmallows.

During the 1960s, I had many opportunities to investigate (and learn from) explosions. One of the things that I had learned from Professor Rogers and these experiences was that there was much more to be learned from examining the scene than from the analysis of the debris in the laboratory, a difficult lesson for a scientist. A good example was my most significant learning opportunity about explosions, which came in 1965 with a large explosion at the DuPont explosives plant at Calendar (the birthplace of the famous Dionne quintuplets) near North Bay (see Chapter 9).

An Explosion in a Dynamite Plant "Holy Sh--! This Stuff Is Dangerous!"

9

At about 22:32 on September 21, 1965, an explosion occurred at the DuPont explosives production plant near North Bay, Ontario. It quickly became apparent that two employees were missing and presumed killed. Because of the nature and size of the incident, the newly appointed supervising coroner of Ontario, Dr. H.B. Cotnam, was notified, and he asked the Ontario Provincial Police (OPP) to assign a senior Criminal Investigation Branch (CIB) inspector to the investigation and for me to provide scientific/technical assistance. Inspector Jack Kay (who, when he was a constable in Brantford, had been on my first Breathalyzer training course) was assigned. When we arrived on site the next day, we were curious about a long line of employees outside the personnel office. The plant manager explained that they were resigning because they had previously never truly appreciated the enormous amount of potential energy contained in the products they were making. One of these men exclaimed to us, "Holy sh--! This stuff is dangerous!" None had ever previously seen anything other than the test explosion of one or two sticks of dynamite in an open field.

It soon became apparent that friction was developing between investigators from the various agencies present, including the Provincial Ministry of Labor, the Ontario Fire Marshal's Office, and the Explosives Division of the Federal Department of Mines and Technical Surveys, each of which had specific areas of interest and responsibility. DuPont was somewhat overwhelmed by the number of investigators arriving on the scene, and many of the latter did not understand the reluctance of the company to let them examine the site in detail. A meeting of all concerned was therefore arranged, which proved to be a wise move that saved many work-hours. Company officials stressed that there was still a substantial amount of unexploded material at the site and, until this was disposed of, it was not safe for investigators to enter. At the same time, all the investigators made clear to the company the specific reasons for their attendance. The result was that the authority of the supervising coroner was recognized and an agreement was reached that only one investigation would be made, by his office, i.e., Inspector Kay and me, with the results being accepted by all. The company agreed to cooperate fully by making its experts available, and all the other investigators left the site.

DuPont dispatched the senior explosives expert from its head office in Delaware, and I had the opportunity to work very closely with him and the local technical experts. From them, I learned an enormous amount, not only about the commercial production of nitroglycerine and dynamite but also about the investigation of explosions involving such high explosives.

Safety Elements in Building Design and Production Process

The relatively new DuPont plant, built in 1957, consisted of several buildings and employed about 200 people. The attention to detail and the emphasis on safety was impressive. Buildings that were considered to have a potential explosion risk were about forty to fifty feet square on the inside, constructed of reinforced concrete twenty-four inches thick, and covered with a mound of sand to a minimum depth of eight feet. At one end of each building was a concrete "chimney" running across the entire width of the building and open at the top. This was separated from the work area by a wooden "soft wall." This design was to provide, in the event of an explosion, an easy exit for shock waves and missiles into the chimney and then upward, thus reducing their impact at ground level. Extending through the sand mounds into the buildings were tunnels known as "portals" with reinforced concrete walls and roofs. These provided access for the operators and materials. Where the opening of a portal pointed toward the opening into another building, a "missile screen" was erected. This was a steel shell approximately thirty feet by thirty feet and eighteen inches thick, filled with sand and anchored on concrete posts.

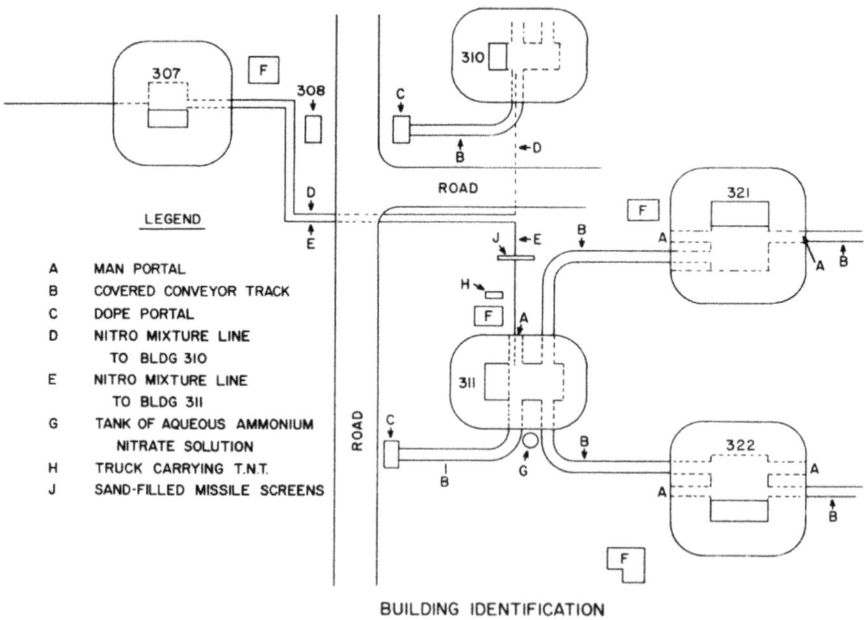

Figure 9.1 Sketch of the production area of the North Bay DuPont explosives plant.

The floors in the work areas were completely covered with a 3/8-inch layer of conductive neoprene. This served as a cushion for any falling objects and, in conjunction with conductive footwear, protected the workers from a buildup of static electricity. All machinery in these buildings was hydraulically operated with motors, pumps, and so forth, located in separate "fan houses." The only electrical power in the buildings was for the lights, which were in sealed units in the walls and ceiling. All removable objects, such as nuts and bolts, were tied to the equipment with nylon thread to prevent them from falling if they became loose.

There were two general types of explosives produced at this plant, nitroglycerine (NG) explosives, commonly known as "dynamite," and "blasting agents," which contain no NG but have ammonium nitrate (AN) as their principal explosive component. Some of the latter also contain TNT. Blasting agents are much less sensitive than dynamite and have largely replaced it for large-scale blasting operations.

The NG was produced in one building with a capacity of up to 2,500 pounds per hour. It was transported, in the form of a temporary emulsion with soda ash solution, through a 650-foot two-inch plastic line with five right-angle bends, to the "separation house" (Building 307). This emulsion was not considered sensitive, and it was believed that an explosion would not propagate through it for any distance.

NG was supplied through plastic lines, in the form of another temporary emulsion, to the two "mix houses" (Buildings 310 and 311), at the rate of about fifty pounds per minute. Inside the mix houses, these lines emptied into large polyethylene separator tanks where the NG sank to the bottom and the water was returned to Building 307. The amount of NG in these tanks was automatically controlled at up to 300 pounds. The NG used in a mix batch flowed by gravity through a rubber hose into a stainless steel drum on a weigh scale.

Mixing was done in approximately 500-pound batches in large copper alloy bowls with a copper alloy rotating paddle. The mixing bowl could be raised and tipped toward the rear to dump a finished batch of mix into an aluminum bucket for transport to a "packaging house" (Buildings 321 and 322). The bucket was attached to a chain-driven cart on heavily greased rails shielded by an aluminum panel on the bucket and a wooden partition between the bucket channel and the cart channel.

There was one mix bowl in Building 310 and two in Building 311. Each mixer required one operator. At the time of the explosion, one of the mixers in Building 311 was being used to mix "Special Gelatin 40%" (a type of dynamite), and the other was being used to mix "Tovex," a blasting agent containing TNT.

The dynamite mixing process required the operator to use a hydraulic hoist to dump the preweighed "dope" (dry materials) into the mixing bowl from an aluminum drum through a wood and plastic chute. Nitrocellulose (to form the gel with the NG) was then added from a preweighed plastic bag, and finally, the preweighed NG was run into the bowl. The mixing time was three minutes and was repeated every ten minutes. After mixing, the operator dumped the mix into the bucket and started it toward the packaging house.

In the Tovex mix process, the dope was added in a similar manner, followed by the TNT pellets, which were delivered in fifty-pound cardboard cartons and stacked along the south wall of the building. Ammonium nitrate liquor (a solution of about 60% AN in water) was added, and it was mixed for about four minutes. Each batch weighed about 600 pounds. The cycle was repeated every six or seven minutes. All dope for both mixers was screened and passed over magnets to remove any iron or steel particles before putting it into the drums for delivery to the mix houses.

The Explosion

The evening was warm and humid; there had been rain early in the evening, but no evidence of thunder or lightning at the time of the explosion. All witnesses agreed that there was only one explosion.

The roof of Building 311 collapsed completely, and some heavy objects from the south portals were blown up to 300 feet in a southerly direction. The missile shield on the north side collapsed, but no heavy missiles from the north portals escaped beyond the shield. The roof and walls of building 307 cracked but did not collapse. Most of the equipment in this building was blown into the chimney area.

The NG transmission line between the NG production building and Building 307 detonated over part of its length. The transmission line between Buildings 307 and 311 detonated over its entire length. The line to Building 310 detonated up to its point of entry into the building. The road was badly damaged at the point where these lines passed under it. Light aluminum panel enclosures on conveyor lines were heavily damaged up to a distance of 200 feet from Building 311, and some building panels 600 feet away were fractured. No blast or seismic damage occurred off the plant site.

The Investigation

The principal issues we were trying to resolve were the source and cause of the explosion and whether the two missing operators were in fact dead. The latter was the easier to establish.

At about 22:19, a worker had seen both operators present in Building 311. At 22:31, one of them spoke on the telephone to someone in the "dope house." From the production records, we learned that at 22:31 the Tovex cart in Building 311 had started toward its packaging house (Building 322), and at 22:32, just as the "Special Gelatin cart" was starting toward its packaging house (Building 321), the explosion occurred. This state of the operations required that two persons must have been present in the building.

A careful search of the entire site over two days located five small pieces of human tissue at distances up to 900 feet from Building 311. The total amount of tissue recovered was just a few ounces, which fit into a brown paper bag that I took back to the lab during the week that it took heavy equipment to excavate the building. Each piece of tissue was identified as human, with some being of ABO blood group A and the rest group B (this was long before DNA analysis). Thus, they must have originated from two different persons. The two operators' blood groups were unknown and could not be established. (One of the subsequent recommendations at the coroner's inquest was that the company record such personal information.) Also, one safety boot toe cap and three boot heels were recovered from the excavation of the building.

At the time of the explosion, production records showed that there were about 105 pounds of NG in the weigh tank in Building 311 and that the operator in Building 310 had just started to fill the weigh tank. When the explosion occurred, he dropped the hose and fled, while the 150 pounds of NG spilled onto the floor. Before any extensive work could be undertaken, it was necessary to neutralize this NG as well as some unexploded NG in the remains of Building 307. DuPont staff accomplished this by collecting and burning it on the site. (I was relieved that I was not expected to try to neutralize such an amount.)

The location of the exact point of an explosion is determined by an examination of the resultant craters and by a careful study of the direction and travel distance of "missiles" as determined by knowledge of their point of origin, the location of their final point of rest, and "missile marks" produced by them, if they can be identified. In the remains of Building 311, several craters were in the floor, and all bits of equipment retrieved were identified by DuPont staff and charted on a "missile map."

At the time of the explosion, production records indicated that about 370 pounds of NG was present in Building 307, and this was the major source of damage to that building. The only parts of the storage tank recovered were from the upper section, which would have contained no NG. Other items that should have contained some NG at the time, such as overflow catch tanks, were recovered undetonated. These were the source of the unexploded NG found in this building. The suction (NG) side of the transmission line eductors had detonated, but the emulsion side had not, indicating that, at this point at least, the transmission emulsion had behaved as expected.

The transmission line between the NG production building and Building 307 behaved as expected and did not detonate completely. The two lines from Building 307 to Buildings 310 and 311 did not behave as expected and were the subject of scrutiny. An undetonated piece of one of these lines was recovered. This indicated that the emulsion was not faulty and that the explosion may have propagated either by jumping from one line to the other or perhaps because pure NG had separated out of the emulsion and settled in low spots as the lines passed under the road. Regardless of the mechanism, it was apparent that any redesign of the system should separate the two lines and eliminate low points.

Because the only human activity at the time of the explosion was occurring in Building 311, major attention was devoted to it. After excavation, a 4½-foot diameter crater was found in the concrete floor behind the Special Gelatin mixer where the cart bucket would have been. This indicated that the bucket had been full and had not moved more than a few inches, if at all. No identifiable remains of the bucket were found, although the remains of the cart were located embedded in the wall in the southeast corner of the building.

A second crater was found in the floor in front of and between the two mix bowl positions, where the weighing drum would have been. This crater indicated that this drum had been full at the time of the explosion and had detonated. This supposition was supported by the fact that no identifiable part of this drum was found and by the heavy and quite symmetrical missile marks found on both mix bowls and their support posts, which could only have come from this tank. There was a third crater in the floor in the position where the TNT cases would have been stacked against the south wall. The DuPont expert estimated that this crater was consistent with the detonation of 200–400 pounds of TNT. Although TNT pellets are very insensitive (large amounts of unexploded TNT were found inside and outside Building 311), they can be detonated by a high-velocity missile. The missile marks on the Tovex mix bowl showed that missiles from the weighing drum were traveling in the direction of the TNT. One of them undoubtedly struck and detonated it.

A fourth smaller crater was found in the floor in the position of the catch tank for the overflow from the NG separator. The NG in the separator must have detonated since no part of it was recovered. There was no corresponding crater in the floor, probably because the separator was eight feet above the floor.

The four support posts for each mixer were found in position. They showed that the Special Gelatin bowl had been in the "dump" position and the Tovex bowl in the "mix" position.

Both mix bowls were found intact in the chimney and showed only minor damage; the Tovex bowl still contained some unexploded mix.

Analysis of this material indicated that at the time of the explosion, ammonium nitrate liquor was being added, which confirmed that the operator must have been present. The Special Gelatin mix paddle was found in two pieces in the west wall, and the Tovex paddle was found intact near the bowl. The cart and bucket from the Tovex mixer were found undamaged and filled with unexploded mix outside the building, about halfway to Building 322.

Possible Causes of the Explosion

No reliable evidence of the direction of propagation or the sequence could be established. Detonation could have originated anywhere from the NG production house to Buildings 307 and 311 to produce the results observed. There were, however, some possibilities that could be eliminated with reasonable certainty.

Tovex is very insensitive, and since some of it was recovered unexploded, it was clear that the explosion did not originate in it. Since there was solid evidence that high-velocity missiles were traveling toward the TNT, its detonation was undoubtedly a secondary event.

The Special Gelatin mixer was in the dump position, and the cart bucket was full of mix. Thus, the explosion was not due to a problem in the mixing process. Special Gelatin 40% can be detonated by shock, excessive heat, or missile impact, but it is not considered particularly sensitive. If the cart bucket had been tilted nine or ten inches off level, it could have contacted the dumped mixer. However, it is highly doubtful that simple sliding contact of the copper alloy bowl with the aluminum bucket would have detonated this mix. NG can be detonated by shock, flame, missile impact, friction, or possibly a spark. Since it was the most sensitive of the explosives involved, it was considered the most likely source of initiation. There was pure NG present at the ends of the transmission lines, in the separator in Building 307 and the separator and weighing drum in Building 311. These were considered the most likely sites for initiation. Of these possibilities, those in Building 311 were thought to be the most likely, as this was the only site where there was any activity at the time.

The possible initiating sources we considered were

- Flame—There was no normal source of flame in any of the buildings. One of the operators was a nonsmoker, and the other's cigarettes were found in his clothes in the change house. Even if there had been a flame from an unknown source, it should have been possible for both men to escape since the NG would have burned for a short period before it detonated.

- Shock—This could have been caused by a dope drum falling from the sling or striking the weighing drum. The status of the operation, however, was such that no dope drums would have been on the hoist. Another possibility, which we considered unlikely, was a fall of the separator or weighing drum onto the floor. Smaller shocks, such as banging the wooden paddles and shovels on the mixers, would not be sufficient to cause detonation.
- Missile impact—No evidence could be found to suggest sabotage or a suicidal act.
- Friction—Initiation by friction would have required a leak or spill of NG. While this was not likely, it had happened in the past. It was most apt to happen during the transfer of NG from the weighing drum to the mixer or from the separator to the weighing drum. Neither of these operations was occurring at the time, but there might have been a previous spill. A flex valve in Building 311 was probably opening at the time of the explosion, and the exposed steel moving parts might have been a source had a leak occurred and contaminated the valve. This was not considered a likely source because of the slow operation of the valve and the curvature of the rubber hose inside the valve. Another source of friction could have been between sand or grit on the floor and the soles of the shoes of the operators, moving parts of the machinery, or the bottom of a dope drum.

Conclusion

Of the two main purposes of the investigation, it was established with reasonable certainty that the two missing persons were dead. Of the search for the cause, however, in spite of all the effort, the broad expertise available, and careful discussion of all the possibilities, the exact cause of this explosion was not determined. Unfortunately, in the real world, as contrasted with TV and novels, such uncertainty is sometimes the only outcome possible! On a more positive note, in spite of the detonation of about 1,500 pounds of explosives, the buildings all behaved as they were designed to do. The transmission lines, however, did not and possible improvements in their design did result.

A coroner's inquest was held, and because the supervising coroner felt it better that the results of the technical investigation not be presented by the experts from DuPont, I was required to present all the technical testimony to the jurors. The DuPont people were reluctant to admit that they did not know what the precise cause of the explosion was, but I had no problem doing so since I had long since learned that "I don't know" is sometimes the best answer to a question. At the end of the inquest, the jurors concluded that the two missing operators (who had never been seen since the explosion) "came to their deaths at 10:30 o'clock in the evening on the 21st day of September 1965, at Building 311, DuPont Plant Nipissing Works, West Ferris Township, and that the death was caused by an explosion which disintegrated the bodies."

A Sequel

In April 1975, another explosion occurred at the DuPont plant. It was déjà vu all over again with many of the same players. Again, we went through the same process and determined that the operation was at the identical point in the production process, but failed again to come up with the specific initiation event. The only satisfaction we could derive was from the fact that because of recommendations made at the first inquest, only one person was killed, not two!

As a result, DuPont decided to stop production of NG explosives at this plant. They have since sold the plant.

Dealing with IEDs "There Has to Be a Better Way" 10

Not all of my adventures with explosives were associated with the aftereffects of their use; sometimes they hadn't yet exploded!

The investigation of explosions had brought me into regular contact with members of the Toronto Police "Bomb Squad." The quotation marks are because, at that time, there was officially no such unit in the Metro Toronto Police Department (MTPD). However, Sergeant of Detectives Vic Henderson of the Holdup Squad and Sergeant of Detectives Dave Cowan of the Break-and-Enter Squad had been sent to New York for a week to work with the New York Police Department (NYPD) Bomb Squad and had this additional function assigned to them. They were equipped with little more than wire cutters, a roll of tape, and a pair of gloves and therefore were quite content to have a young, naive forensic scientist work closely with them. That feeling was mutual because Vic and Dave were both about six feet six and weighed around 250 pounds, so they provided considerable shelter for me when I stood behind them.

Vic Henderson lived not far from our home, so when he received a bomb call, he would pick me up to go to the scene. This often involved a hair-raising ride, including passing streetcars on their left. After such trips, dealing with a suspected bomb was a relief!

One example of these events was a package found behind a tree in the front yard of a home in Agincourt (a Toronto suburb), not far from where we lived. The homeowner was "known to the police" and was involved, among other things, in illegal gambling. He had received numerous threats, so when this package appeared on his lawn in the middle of the night, there was good reason to suspect that it was an improvised explosive device (IED). When we arrived, the divisional detectives had cordoned off the area and advised us that the device had not been touched since its discovery. As we surveyed the package, we realized that it was not a classic fictional ticking time bomb but suspected that it had a pressure-release triggering mechanism designed to explode when the package was opened. A reader may well ask where anyone would find a pressure-release triggering device? Easy—all that is required is a spring of some sort, in this case, a mousetrap.

We had a roll of duct tape so we taped the box tightly and cut a small hole in the side so that we could see inside and confirm our suspicion. There were five sticks of dynamite and detonator wires linking a battery to the trap, which was "armed" with the mouse trap lever held tightly in place by the top of the box. Realizing how the device was triggered, we were comfortable with cutting the wires and opening the box.

Development of New Equipment and Procedures

In May 1963, a military demolition expert was seriously injured while attempting to disarm a bomb in a mailbox in Montreal. Militant FLQ (Front de libération du Québec) separatists had been targeting mailboxes because they bore the symbol of a crown. Dr. Smith realized that such events might not be limited to Montreal and, with some urgency, assigned me to work with Henderson and Cowan to develop equipment and procedures that would be more effective and safer than the traditional wire cutters. There had to be a better way.

We learned that the Montreal PD and the Metropolitan Dade County Sheriff's Office in Miami had developed some items of interest. The former had built a protective shield behind which a person could more safely function, using tools on the end of a long pole. The latter had improvised a suitable (and relatively inexpensive) vehicle to safely transport explosives out of urban areas to a disposal site.

The Montreal PD had also been experimenting with the use of liquid nitrogen to quickly "freeze" batteries, thereby disabling electrically detonated IEDs. We did considerable experimentation with this, but although we found that it did indeed work, we also recognized that it was not a practical tool. Liquid nitrogen is not something that can be conveniently kept on hand, nor can it be readily obtained at short notice in the middle of the night.

Vic and I had rejected the heavy, cumbersome "bomb disposal suits" that were common at the time because they allowed limited visibility and severely restricted mobility and flexibility. (As Vic maintained, "All they will do is make the coroner's job a bit easier!")

The idea of a shield was intriguing, however, so we decided to try to develop one that would be "portable," provide some protection, and allow useful work to be done from behind it. The Montreal PD design, which was about six feet in height, vertical, and therefore vulnerable to blast, did not appeal to us. Our preference was for something that would allow the user to remain as low as possible behind cover. As a result, we developed a shield that was a small platform on wheels that the user could lie on behind a collapsible angled aluminum shield.

Our shield employed the well-established "spaced armor" principle in which two layers of metal are separated by an air gap. The concept is that the first layer removes a lot of energy from a missile and, in the process, seriously distorts its ballistic properties to reduce its penetrating capability. We used two 1/8-inch thicknesses of aluminum separated by a 1 3/8-inch air gap. The aluminum was bent to present a V toward the front and at a forty-five-degree angle from the base. A three-inch by eight-inch window, which was part of the windshield from an F-86 Sabre jet that we scrounged from the Royal Canadian Air Force, was inserted into the shield. Our concept was that this design would permit a user to approach a suspected IED, keeping low yet having some visibility, maneuverability, and a certain amount of protection.

To permit the user to perform some useful functions from behind the shield, there were two holes large enough for the insertion and manipulation of nine-foot-long poles with a variety of attachable tools, which would permit opening or moving suspected IEDs. We chose the nine-foot length because that was the maximum distance at which we found we could perform a reasonable number of tasks (and also avoid wiseacre cracks about not touching anything with a ten-foot pole). The whole unit weighed 185 pounds and cost about $1,000 to build. My work with safes had paid off because Chubb-Mosler, a large safe manufacturer, agreed to produce the shield for us at cost. We therefore named it "The Chubmunk."

Figure 10.1 The Chubmunk–collapsed for transport.

Much of the design work was done on our living room floor, thereby providing much entertainment for Marie and our family with the sight of these two large police officers and me rolling around on the floor trying to come up with the best ergonomic design for the window and the working poles. The purpose of the shield was to protect the operator from injury due to either blast or light shrapnel. The shape, the low position of the operator, and the fact that the Chubmunk was on wheels and could move with the blast proved to be effective. In tests we performed (initially unmanned), it withstood the

Figure 10.2 The Chubmunk–ready for use.

blast effect of at least twelve sticks of 40% dynamite placed six feet in front of it, both at ground level and at three feet above the ground. No damage was done to the shield by any of these blasts. The shape, the material, and the spaced armor also were shown to be effective for protection against shrapnel. Metal cans filled with several sticks of dynamite and two-inch pipe bombs containing 1¼ pounds of smokeless powder exploded six feet in front of the shield did not penetrate even the outer layer of aluminum.

Our new procedures called for transporting the IED to a safe place for disposal. (We were very fortunate that the Toronto Harbour "Outer Spit" was being developed at that time and we were able to arrange an isolated open area for our activities. There must still be many unexplained craters in what is now known as Tommy Thompson Park, which are evidence of our work there.) Transportation required an effective way of doing so for which we copied the Dade County truck. It was a three-ton dump truck modified by the skilled technicians in the Toronto Police garage. At the front of the box, there was added an eight-foot by six-foot deflection plate of ½-inch steel angled at forty-five degrees from the top of the cab to the truck bed. Beneath this plate were storage compartments for our equipment and the Chubmunk.

The principal feature of the truck was a drum forty-eight inches high and forty-two inches in diameter made from ¾-inch cold-rolled steel with a concave bottom made from 1-inch boiler head steel. This drum, which was effectively a forty-two-inch mortar, sat directly over the rear axle of the truck and was surrounded by sand and sand bags. The inside of the drum also contained six to eight inches of sand. The explosives or IED could be remotely placed into the drum using a net on the end of a boom operated from the opposite side of the truck. The boom automatically positioned itself over the center of the drum so that the operator did not have to look at it and could keep himself shielded below the level of the side of the truck.

Figure 10.3 The bomb truck and its crew.

In extensive tests, we found that the truck was well able to contain the explosion of up to ten pounds (twenty sticks) of 40% ammonia/gelatin dynamite and the pipe bombs previously described with no damage to the truck. The blast was directed upward, usually accompanied by a spectacular smoke ring the diameter of the drum rising for about thirty seconds to several hundred feet, accompanied by a loud whistling noise. There was a slight implosion effect around the outside of the drum but little or no effect at the height of six feet immediately beside the truck.

This equipment worked very well for the Toronto PD, but what about all the other police forces in the province and the Ontario Provincial Police? Our next step required the development of training courses to assist them in organizing themselves to deal more safely with suspected explosive devices. Other equipment they could improvise was developed, and we found that a cylinder made of sandbags placed in a dump truck filled with sand could be almost as effective as the Toronto PD truck. Agreements were made with the

Department of Highways to make such trucks available locally as required on an emergency basis.

In October 1964, I was invited to give a presentation about all of this equipment to a group in California, which resulted in many copies being produced.

These projects gave me great satisfaction because, to the best of my knowledge, there has never been a police officer injured in Ontario while trying to disarm an IED. Most of what we developed has since been supplanted with more sophisticated equipment, a very good thing because the IEDs have become much more technical. The modern concept, because of the sophistication of the devices, is to detonate them in place, or at least try to open the package and hope that it doesn't detonate in place, using water cannons and other devices that work very well. It would, however, not be difficult for a reasonably sophisticated IED maker to produce a device that nobody could disarm. I'm very happy that I am no longer doing this type of work!.

Canada's Guy Fawkes* 11

Guy Fawkes, a member of a group of English Catholics who planned the failed Gunpowder Plot of 1605 to blow up the British Houses of Parliament. Guy Fawkes Night, also known as Bonfire Night or Fireworks Night, is an annual commemoration still observed each year on 05 November in Great Britain.

Wikipedia

The vast majority of cases examined in a forensic science laboratory attract little attention from the media or the public. This is a good thing because it means there is no pressure on the staff to produce any results other than those that the evidence material and the techniques of science allow. An exception to this general rule occurred in Ottawa on May 18, 1966, when an event occurred that created initial panic, followed by recriminations, political disputes, and broad national, if not international, interest. It also provided me with one of the queasiest moments of my career.

A Louder than Normal Question Period

At 14:58 that day, during Question Period in the House of Commons in Ottawa, a time when a majority of the Members of Parliament (MPs), including Prime Minister Lester Pearson and opposition leader John Diefenbaker, were present, there was a loud boom and a disturbing quiver to the old stone walls of the magnificent Centre Block of the Parliament buildings. Smoke and acrid fumes quickly filled the chamber and galleries. Some of the members who were war veterans quickly recognized the odor as something they had hoped they would never smell again, from a blast of high explosive. The source was easily traced to a men's washroom on the third floor, just a few steps from the entrance to what was then known as the "Ladies Gallery." Two members who were physicians raced up the stairs to the washroom,

* Many of the details about the Ottawa portion of this case are from a book, *The Mad Bomber of Parliament Hill*, by James Fontana, a retired provincial court judge and former assistant Crown attorney in Ottawa who I knew very well. It was published in 2005 by Borealis Press in Ottawa.

where, through the dense smoke, they discovered the dismembered body of a male who gasped his final breath as they arrived. It was obvious that there was nothing they could do for him, so they left the washroom in charge of a security guard.

Figure 11.1 The washroom.

Figure 11.2 The House of Commons (from the Ladies Gallery).

Back in the House, as the realization of what had occurred took hold, the speaker temporarily adjourned the session, and many of the members left the building while speculating whether this was the opening shot of something much larger. Within the first hour, confusion reigned about who was in charge. The interior of the main Parliament building is the responsibility of the speakers of the House of Commons and the Senate. Parliament Hill is federal property and is policed by the Royal Canadian Mounted Police (RCMP). The surrounding area is the jurisdiction of the Ottawa Police Department (PD). Sudden deaths in Ontario are investigated by a coroner under the authority of the Ontario Coroner's Act. However, because it is a Provincial Act, it does not apply in the federal Parliament buildings.

The Crown attorney quickly assembled a meeting of all the players and, after much heated discussion, the speaker of the Commons agreed to "delegate" his responsibility to the Ontario coroner, with the proviso that the security precautions in the House of Commons must not be part of the coroner's investigation, thus removing a critical issue from the process. The coroner, in turn, requested that the Ottawa PD assist him with the investigation.

By this time, the media were already speculating about who, what, and why; somebody must be to blame for such a spectacular breach of security. Over the next few days, there were constant calls for "beefed up" security on Parliament Hill. (If this sounds familiar, it should; the same shrill calls were made in October 2014 following the shooting of a military guard at the National War Memorial in Ottawa and an attack on the Centre Block of Parliament. "*Plus ça change ...*")

When the coroner made a preliminary examination of the remains in the washroom, he recovered a wallet in which there was a Toronto Public Library card in the name of Paul Chartier with an address at 271 Major Street in Toronto. About 18:30, the Ottawa detective in charge of the investigation received a call from the manager of the St. Louis Hotel across the river in Hull (now Gatineau), Quebec. The manager, having heard the news of something serious happening in the Parliament buildings, wanted to report his suspicions about one of his guests who had checked in early the previous day. A detective sent to interview him found the name of the suspicious guest in the hotel register, "Paul Chartier, 271 Major Street, Toronto." He had left the hotel late in the morning but, before doing so, had paid for an additional night's stay ($3; this was not a luxury hotel) and said he would be back.

A Rooming House in Toronto

To follow up this lead, about 19:30 the senior investigating officer called the Toronto PD and requested the duty inspector (that night it was Inspector

Maurice Richardson of the Holdup Squad) to have 271 Major Street checked out. Richardson sent two detectives to the address, a quiet street of older houses, many of which had been converted to rooming houses occupied primarily by students from the nearby University of Toronto. The landlady at 271 Major confirmed that one of her five roomers was indeed a man known as Paul Chartier, who had been renting the front room on the second floor for $10 a week for about five weeks. He was, she said, away for two days "on business in Ottawa."

She showed the detectives the room (the door to which had an extra padlock that Chartier had added but for which she had a key). The room was a mess, but the detectives did not stay in it long because, in the bureau drawer, they found four sticks of 40% Forcite (a brand of dynamite made by CIL Explosives) and two cardboard cylinder "bombs"!

About 20:00, I received a call from Inspector Richardson: "We have a situation at 271 Major, and we need your help. I've sent a car to pick you up." Thus began a most interesting evening and late night.

On arrival at the site, I found that one of the detectives was Detective Sergeant John Holm, who had recently shown an interest in the "Bomb Squad" and had received some training from Vic Henderson (who was on vacation).

I quickly confirmed that the Forcite was genuine (there were also two half sticks) and not of any great concern since they were not "fused." The two bombs were toilet paper rolls filled with black powder and taped shut at both ends. (Some of the newspaper wadding in these was from the *Toronto Star*, dated May 9, 1966, so these bombs were of relatively recent origin.) These also were of minimal concern but would have to eventually be taken to our destruction area at the Outer Harbour Spit. We also found an almost five-foot length of safety fuse and three blasting caps. Our real concern was about what else might be hidden in the general mess of the room.

Included in the debris were pages and pages of writing paper filled with handwritten ravings that were almost incoherent and quite irrational rants about the failures of the government. One set was titled "If I Was President of Canada." Another was "Young Years," describing how life, and politicians, were responsible for Chartier's current unhappy status. This was just three years after we had seen so much about the written diatribes of Lee Harvey Oswald in Dallas and I thought we must have the same type of deranged individual here. He could be dangerous.

There also was a tape recorder and tape of someone (presumably Chartier) singing the well-known Mario Lanza hit from a 1950 movie, *Be My Love*. The singing was of the same quality as the writing.

The "queasy moment" I referred to occurred as I searched under the bed. I felt something round and hard stuffed inside a wool sock. As I gently slid my hand (rubber gloves were rarely worn in those days) down into the sock, it came into contact with something hairy that (given the circumstances) I was afraid might be a human scalp. "Ugh." I slowly extracted it and found a male toupee wrapped around a microphone. Now, what sort of person keeps a microphone wrapped in a wig inside a sock?

The only really useful information we found that evening came as I sat at the small table in the room. It was covered with writings and papers of all kinds, which I casually was scanning when I came across the cardboard backing from a writing pad. On it was written what appeared to be some arithmetic calculations. The first bit that caught my attention was "sixty seconds per foot." "Oh, oh," I thought; the burning rate of safety fuse is nominally forty seconds per foot. Could these be his calculations for the length of fuse he thought he would need in Ottawa?

As I worked my way through the numbers, it became clear that these were indeed his calculations for the length of fuse he estimated would be required to give him the time required to throw his bomb and escape. About two lines further down I exclaimed, "Oops!" There was a mistake in arithmetic. Instead of what should have been 36, he had 3.6 for the number of inches of fuse required. This would make the actual time from ignition of the fuse to the detonation of the charge about ten seconds rather than the 180 seconds he was aiming for!

Our work was finished for the night.

The next day, the Toronto detectives visited a well-drilling company north of Toronto, the only retail source of dynamite in the area. (It is where we obtained the dynamite and detonators we used in all our tests.) The detectives had a photo of Chartier that we had found in his room and the landlady had confirmed was him. The salesperson immediately recognized the man in the photo and confirmed that she had sold him six sticks of Forcite, six feet of safety fuse, and six blasting caps on May 13, 1966. He had used a different name and address for the purchase and said he was going to use it to "blow some stumps up north." She also mentioned that she had told him that the fuse burned at "one foot a minute" because he seemed uncertain about that. Even with accurate arithmetic that mistake would have produced a 33% error in the burn time!

Meanwhile, Back in Ottawa

Late in the afternoon of May 18, an autopsy was performed on the remains. There were more than thirty areas of traumatic blast injuries centered on the right forearm and upper trunk; he must have been holding the bomb in his right hand close to his body when it detonated. The body was also peppered with fragments of copper pipe, including one jagged piece that had pierced his aorta. His blood alcohol concentration was later determined to be 62 mg/100 mL.

Ottawa PD investigators performed a detailed crime scene search of the severely damaged washroom and the hotel room. They collected a large number of items that were taken to the RCMP Forensic Laboratory in Ottawa. Included in these were three pieces of safety fuse, eight, four, and two inches in length. Only the two-inch piece had burned. Other significant items were a book of matches (presumably used to light the fuse), some bits of an Ottawa newspaper (indicating that the bomb had probably been assembled in Ottawa, not Toronto), and many fragments of copper pipe of two different diameters. The brisant nature of the pipe fragmentation suggested that one stick of dynamite had been inserted into a length of copper pipe, which in turn had been inserted into a slightly larger diameter length of pipe. This, in combination with some nuts, bolts, and screws, indicated that Mr. Chartier wanted more than just blast damage; he also wanted flying shrapnel, which would kill or seriously injure more people. This was not a prank!

The military ordnance expert who assisted the Ottawa police in the examination of the washroom and the recovered debris concluded that Chartier had lit the two-inch fuse while standing in the cubicle nearest the washroom exit and had just started to leave the cubicle holding the bomb close to his body (probably under his jacket to conceal it) when it detonated. He also opined that had the bomb been dropped onto the floor of the House of Commons from the Ladies Gallery, the explosion at floor level would have killed at least a dozen MPs! (I am unclear about how he arrived at such a conclusion based on the information available!)

Additional evidence was gradually developed from witnesses coming forward as a result of the massive news coverage. A housekeeper at the St. Louis Hotel remembered that Chartier had stayed there previously, and the register showed this stay to have been on April 21–22 that year.

Another man volunteered that he had struck up a casual conversation with Chartier as they explored the grounds of Parliament Hill on April 22. This witness was very upset because he thought he had put the idea of a bomb into Chartier's head. In the course of their conversation about Parliament, he had told Paul that anyone could go into the building to observe the proceedings and, what was really disturbing him, he had facetiously and unfortunately presciently added that "some fool could go in there with a bomb and toss it right down in the Commons before anyone caught him." (The detectives tried unsuccessfully to persuade him that, based on his writings, Chartier had planned this action long before that day on the Hill.)

Chartier left that conversation and walked into the Centre Block, where he wandered the halls freely (anyone could in those days) but was stopped when he inadvertently started to walk up a stairway reserved for MPs. He was directed to a public stairway that took him up to the third floor and the entrance to the Public Gallery. He entered and took a seat, which must have been a surprise for him because he could look down and see the prime minister not more than a short baseball lob away.

Chartier returned to Toronto on the evening bus.

When he got back to Toronto, Chartier wrote a letter to the House of Commons requesting permission to address the members on an important matter of urgent public business. He received a reply from the Clerk of the Commons dated May 2 advising him that only elected members were permitted to speak. This infuriated him, and he ranted and raved to anyone who would listen about the arrogance of those guys who just did what they felt like and wouldn't listen to the ordinary taxpayers who were their bosses.

Another witness who had ridden the overnight bus from Toronto to Ottawa on May 16–17 remembered sitting beside someone who he was certain was Chartier.

The night of May 17–18 was spent in the St. Louis, and sometime during the morning of May 18, the bomb must have been assembled. At this time, Chartier had no idea how far he would have to walk from some secluded place where he could surreptitiously light the fuse to a seat in the Public Gallery and, therefore, how long he would have to allow for the fuse to burn. For that reason, he prepared three fuses, eight, four, and two inches long, and attached a blasting cap to each. These were inserted into the stick of dynamite with the free ends sticking out, permitting one of them to be lit. Because of the incorrect burning rate he had received and his faulty arithmetic, even the longest of these would provide only 26 seconds, at most. Hardly enough time!

A security guard remembered Chartier arriving at the entrance to the Public Gallery at the north end of the Commons shortly after 14:00 on May 18, but the Gallery was full. He advised Chartier that he would have to wait until a seat became vacant. This caused great upset, and some heated words were exchanged, but the entrance was denied. Paul left the Public Gallery entrance and wandered around the hall until he arrived at the Ladies Gallery at the south end of the Commons, where another security guard told him there were seats inside and that men were permitted to enter when the Public Gallery was filled. In response to a question about a washroom, the guard pointed to a door just across the hall from where they were standing. Chartier entered the gallery and took a seat in the front row, looking directly down onto the Members on the floor.

At about 14:35, Chartier left his seat and asked the guard if he would save it for him. This request was denied, and again there were words, but he left and entered the washroom where, at just a few seconds before 14:58, he lit the two-inch length of fuse. At 14:58, the explosion occurred in the washroom, a mere fourteen steps from the entrance to the Ladies Gallery.

All of this and other evidence was presented to a coroner's inquest in September in Ottawa. I attended and provided the evidence about what we had found in Toronto. Unlike most inquests in those days, which lasted perhaps a couple of hours in the evening and received little or no media coverage, this one lasted three days and was covered by members of the Parliamentary Press Gallery.

The who, what, when, and where were quite straightforward and unambiguous. The why not so clear.

Paul Chartier was born in a small town in Alberta in 1922. His father owned a local hotel and was quite successful, as was Paul's brother, who owned hotels in the United States. Paul was not so successful. He had not done well in school (arithmetic was obviously not a strong point) and left before graduating from high school. He had tried several businesses with little success and drifted around Canada and the United States performing short-term jobs as a truck driver, security guard, or casual laborer. He even spent a short time at a gold mine in Yellowknife, where he worked as a kitchen helper and, briefly, as a blaster's assistant (he apparently didn't learn much in that position).

By the time he reached his early forties, Chartier was a disillusioned, frustrated, suspicious, and depressed man who blamed "The System" and those who run it for the lack of the success he believed he so richly deserved. This was manifested in his writings and his rants to his brother and casual acquaintances. He had been married, but that too was a failure, blamed on everything and everyone, except Paul.

Figure 11.3 Guy Fawkes (logo used by many police bomb squads).

Why did he plan to set off a bomb in the House of Commons? With such a twisted mind, who can say? One of Lucas's laws is "Don't waste a lot of effort seeking a rational explanation for an irrational act!"

Unlike Guy Fawkes, who was unsuccessful but is still remembered, Paul Chartier was at least partially successful but is almost completely forgotten. Perhaps we should establish a "Paul Chartier Day" when we could all get together and practice our multiplication and division tables.

Mr. Miscellaneous "Can You Do Something with This?" 12

Because I had shown an interest in handling cases other than alcohol and toxicology, and had advised Ward Smith that I would not be content just managing the Breathalyzer program once it had matured, he was more than happy to assign me the oddball "one-off" types of cases that are part of the input to every full-service forensic science lab. He therefore created a new section in the lab, the Organic Chemistry Section (a Chemistry Section already existed), and appointed me section head. This was, in part, a tactic on his part to get me a promotion in the civil service, the promotion being the only way an increase in pay was possible. I was very grateful.

The "section" consisted of myself, Professor Rogers, and Rita Charlebois, who did the blood alcohols, and a technician who assisted me with the other cases. Ron Hallett later joined us, mainly to look after the Breathalyzer program. Fire and explosion investigations were our principal additional activity, but other things that had the potential to produce some laboratory evidence also came in our door. I was always impressed with the curiosity of some of the detectives who would come in and ask, "I've got this case and wonder if you might be able to do something with this?" I became known as "Mr. Miscellaneous" around the lab.

Dr. Smith had a friend, Dr. Briggs White, who was the head of the Scientific Analysis Section in the FBI Laboratory (he later became the director of the

Figure 12.1 Dr. Briggs White.

entire lab) in Washington, D.C., and arranged with him for me to spend a week there learning more about the wide variety of examinations they performed. Although explosive residues were the largest component of the cases that section received, because they served police departments across the entire United States, they also received large numbers of the oddball types of cases that I was destined to handle in Ontario. Two of Briggs's staff, Jack Gallagher and Bill Heilman, were wonderful mentors who spared no effort demonstrating to me how they handled these cases. They were both excellent chemists, although both had spent a few years as investigative special agents in FBI field offices (the normal practice at the time for all FBI Lab staff).

This experience was invaluable and created strong relationships, both personally for me with Gallagher and Heilman and institutionally between our two labs. In those years, for historical reasons, the FBI chose not to have close involvement with state and local labs in the United States. The staff of the lab was therefore somewhat isolated from other forensic science agencies. To fill this gap, they were quite pleased to establish closer working relationships with our lab and also with the Royal Canadian Mounted Police Labs. We all benefited from this association.

Criminal Abortions

One of the miscellaneous types of cases was criminal abortions, which were quite common in those days when birth control was not a widely discussed topic and before the "pill" was developed. Condoms were not openly displayed in pharmacies as they are now; you had to sidle up to the back counter and quietly ask the pharmacist for them. The inevitable result was unwanted pregnancies with no provision for proper medical abortions. As with many such problems, the solution that developed, criminal abortion, was not a desirable one.

A few laypeople developed "expertise" in this procedure, using some very crude techniques. The most common of these was to inject a soap or detergent solution into the vagina of the pregnant woman and hopefully somehow free the fetus from the uterus and abort it. One of the problems was that sometimes the soap went where it shouldn't and produced air bubbles in the bloodstream, which can kill very quickly. Other methods involved mechanical manipulation with things like coat hangers, knitting needles, and some other truly gross tools. Often these procedures had tragic consequences, such as serious trauma, infection, and sometimes death, which would bring in the police.

I got involved with these cases when a detective sergeant in the Toronto Police Morality Squad began to specialize in their investigation. (To no one's surprise, given police humor, his colleagues began referring to him facetiously as Dr. Fetus.) He came into the lab one day with some samples from an abortion death and asked if I could examine the vaginal contents from the victim to see if there was any soap. If there was, could it be compared with soap he had recovered from the scene?

This had not been done before, and I had no idea whether it was possible, but told him I would give it a try. My technician and I were able, somewhat to our surprise, to develop a method for extracting soap from the vaginal contents. Then, using the same gas chromatograph we used for the arson cases, we found that we could not only identify the fatty acids that made up the soap but also produce a pattern of them, which differed from one soap to another. This allowed a reasonable comparison to be made between the soap recovered from the victim and that collected at the crime scene. That case went to court, and the evidence was accepted.

There is nothing that produces a demand for a forensic science service more quickly than a detective having a case using that service which reaches a positive conclusion. So, the fact that soap could be identified and compared in abortion cases became known in the Ontario law enforcement community and developed into another "routine" service that the lab had to offer. Dr. Noble Sharpe and I formed a team; he would examine the devices used from a medical point of view, and I would do the chemistry. Some of the cases were truly sad. There is little more tragic than a young healthy female who may have made an unfortunate mistake and died in some very desperate circumstances as a result.

One such case I remember clearly because it occurred in Windsor, Ontario, on the street immediately behind where I had been raised. The abortionist was a woman whose husband was a burglar, and both were well known to the Windsor Police Department (PD). He was in and out of jail regularly, so she had developed this business as a way of financing herself during the periods when he was locked up. In this case, she had done her best to clean up the scene after her "patient" had died and then called an ambulance. She told the police that the victim was a friend who was visiting and had died suddenly in her bedroom.

The police collected the bedspread and brought it to the lab, where I found one tiny spot that I was able to identify as a liquid detergent. They went back and collected all the liquid detergents from the house, and I found one that had the same composition as the spot on the bedspread. That, together with what the police knew about her activities, was sufficient to charge her and bring her to court, where she was eventually convicted of manslaughter.

She was a very attractive woman, and when I saw her outside the courtroom before I knew she was the accused person in the case, I thought she must be one of the doctors or nurses from the hospital or at least the proprietor of an upscale beauty salon. I was astonished when she began a conversation with the detective and demonstrated a vocabulary that might be expected from a drunken sailor!

I remember another of these cases for a quite different reason. It was a murder charge resulting from an abortion in Bancroft in which the soap injector was a French's mustard plastic squeeze bottle. I had compared the soap contained in it with the soap from the vaginal contents from the victim. A pathologist from Belleville had performed the autopsy, and we were both at the preliminary hearing in Bancroft to testify about our evidence. The defense lawyer was Terry Kelly, a larger than life character from Oshawa.

Terry knew he had a terrible case. However, his cross-examination of the pathologist and me was one of the cleverest I ever experienced. He asked the pathologist many questions about the chemistry of soap but none about the medical aspects of abortion. Of course, the pathologist quite properly said that he couldn't answer any of those questions. Terry then asked me all kinds of questions about the medical aspects of abortion, which I couldn't answer, but none about the chemistry of the soap. As a result, he made it look to the court in Bancroft that these two "experts" from down south must be a couple of dummies because all they could say was "I don't know" or "I'm not qualified to answer that." The accused woman was discharged.

Fortunately, most of the abortion cases stopped occurring in 1988 when the Supreme Court of Canada ruled that the law against abortion was unconstitutional and legal medical abortions in proper clinical settings became available.

Illegal Gambling

Another type of case I became involved with because an investigator asked an unusual question was illegal gambling and bookmaking. Illegal gambling was a problem primarily only because, in specific circumstances, it was illegal. However, it unfortunately also had the potential for abuse by a few police officers. In fact, in the early 1960s, there was a major scandal in Ontario about alleged complicity of a senior officer of the Ontario Provincial Police (OPP) with gamblers. He testified before a Royal Commission inquiring into the existence of organized crime in the province that he had just happened to find a peanut butter jar filled with $100 bills buried in his garden.

There were two notorious gamblers, Joseph McDermott and Vincent Feeley, who ran gambling houses, one on the #10 Highway (Hurontario Street) in Cooksville and another in Niagara Falls. My first experience with this type of case occurred when members of the OPP Anti-Gambling Squad came into the lab one day after a raid on the house in Niagara Falls. They had received information that only American currency was used in this gaming house and the bills all were coated with paraffin wax, so as the money moved quickly back and forth across the tables, there was less risk of bills sticking together. The police had seized the cash from the tables and were seeking corroboration of this tip. "Is there any paraffin wax on these bills?" was the question put to me by the sergeant in charge of the squad, John Anderson. (John was a very decent honorable man who looked more like a suburban school principal than an undercover cop. Unfortunately, through no fault of his own, he became peripherally involved in the scandal involving the senior officer with McDermott and Feeley, and his career was sidelined.)

Sergeant Anderson plopped a total of $10,000 in US$100 bills down in front of the young forensic scientist, who had a growing family and little money. I must confess there was a momentary temptation since I had never seen that kind of money in my life before. That night at dinner, I described all this to Marie, and we fantasized about things that might be done with $10,000 (as we still do occasionally about winning a million dollars in the lottery). Finally, Marie announced, "Well that's all very well, but what would we do on the second day?" That ended that line of speculation.

I extracted the wax from some of the bills and, using infrared spectroscopy, I was able to identify paraffin in the extracts. Paraffin wax is a mixture of hydrocarbons of varying carbon numbers, and it produces a beautiful infrared spectrum that leaves no doubt about its identification. I realized that I needed to run a blank test to show that normal U.S. currency does not contain paraffin, so I went to my bank and explained to the manager why I needed some American $100 bills (I didn't have that much in my bank account). My story was so unusual that he was prepared to float me a short-term (one-day) loan of several hundred U.S. dollars for the experiment. I found no paraffin in this currency, and the bank manager got back the cleanest currency he had ever seen.

When I testified about these results in Niagara Falls, McDermott and Feeley both seemed quite amused by all the fuss. They couldn't believe that the police and this naive young chemist would devote all this effort to prove something they would have been quite prepared to concede. A couple of years later, both McDermott and Feeley were also convicted of conspiring with a constable on the Anti-Gambling Squad to bribe another young member of that squad.

One final note about Mr. Feeley. At that time, the lab shared a building with the OPP headquarters, although we had separate entrances. One Friday afternoon, we had a group of coroners in for a tour of the lab. As they were leaving at about 16:30, Sergeant Anderson happened to be walking past our entrance on the way to his car. He saw something odd and came into the lab to speak with me. "Who were those people who just came out?" he asked. When I told him they were a group of coroners, he replied, "Well, one of them was Vincent Feeley!" (This was before I had seen him in court.) He had, as they say, the nerve of a gambler and must have enjoyed his stroll around the lab.

The waxed money case initiated my relationship with the OPP Anti-Gambling Squad, which soon extended to the Toronto PD Morality Squad's Anti-Gambling Unit. Two of their very bright detectives, John Leybourne and Tom Stewart (both of whom later were promoted to the Homicide Squad), came in one day with a question of their own. This was before there was any possibility of legal wiretapping. One of the challenges they had in investigating bookmaking cases was that bets would be called into a phone number that was known to the bettors, the "front end," at a location well known to the police. The bet would then be immediately relayed by the bookmaker to another number, the "back end," at a different location unknown to the police. As a result, there were no records retained at the front end and thus no evidence. The records were at the back end, and the challenge for the detectives was to locate it.

One of the techniques they developed to accomplish this was to obtain a search warrant for the location of the front end, execute it, and, in the course of the commotion, hide a tape recorder. Thirty minutes later, they would execute a second search warrant and recover the tape recorder. This gave them a thirty-minute recording of the sounds at the front end. Some of these sounds would be of the telephone being dialed. (There were no push-button phones in those days.)

The detectives' question to me was, "Can you tell us what is the number that is being dialed?" Again, I had no idea whether we could do this or not, but I had a good friend (Bill Hayman, a sales engineer with an analytical instrument company) who was an electronic genius. I spoke with him, and he was intrigued by the question. We spent the weekend in the lab while Bill designed and put together a simple rectifying circuit that allowed us to translate the output from the tape recorder into a signal that we could transfer to a standard DC strip chart recorder. (We used the recorder attached to the gas chromatograph that Bill had sold us, the same one we used for our arson work.) This allowed us to see as well as hear the signal.

During our preliminary experiments, we noticed that the time for the dial to return to rest was quite constant for each digit. If we could measure that time for known digits for that phone, it should allow us to determine the seven digits in a telephone number. Fortunately, the bookmaker had called someone who the detectives recognized and whose telephone number they knew so we had a "control" number to work with. Once the conditions were established, we found it quite easy to mark on the strip chart the peak that corresponded to the dial reaching the stop and the one representing its return to rest. The distance between these was then compared with those for our control digits. When we tried this in the lab, it seemed to work.

Finally, with great trepidation, we advised the detectives what we believed the number was for the telephone of interest. They were able to use that information to get the address for that phone from the telephone company and obtain a search warrant for that address. They crashed the door with a sledgehammer and, to the great relief of Bill and me, it was the right place, and the police were able to gather the betting records. These indicated that this one location was doing about $220,000 (early 1960s dollars) of business per week!

The same technique was used several times until word got around in the gambling community and they changed their practice. There was one instance where our predicted number was off by one digit, and the Toronto Police had to buy a new door for a terrified elderly lady.

Following this success, the more progressive bookmakers realized that the reason they had this complicated arrangement of front and back ends was that the most incriminating evidence was obviously the records of the bets. One of them found something called "flash paper" in a novelty store and began using it to record the bets. This paper got its name from the fact that it would disappear in a flash when touched with a cigarette or burning match. For a while, whenever the police knocked down his door, all they would see would be a bright yellow flash and a puff of smoke. No records.

The same two detectives brought a sample of the paper into the lab and asked if I could tell them what it was. I had never heard of it but was able to obtain an infrared spectrum from it that identified the flash paper as nitrocellulose, ordinary paper (cellulose) that had been nitrated (analogous to the nitrating of glycerin to make nitroglycerine).

As I was explaining this bit of chemistry to the detectives, I mentioned that nitrocellulose is what gunpowder is made of and is therefore an explosive substance. I pulled my copy of the Criminal Code down from a bookshelf to look up the definition of "explosive substance" and found that it "includes anything intended to be used to make an explosive substance." We then looked at the sections dealing with offenses involving explosives and found that it was an offense for a person to have possession of an explosive substance "without lawful excuse, the proof of which lies upon the person." Obviously, the section was intended to prevent people from using things such as dynamite to blow up a car, but as we talked about it, we realized that the bookmaker did not have a lawful excuse for possessing this explosive substance; he had it for bookmaking!

The detectives therefore went and seized some flash paper from the bookmaker, who, I'm certain, was the most surprised guy in the world when he was charged with illegal possession of an explosive substance. As we prepared for court, we all realized that a judge might be hesitant to accept the evidence that flash paper was an explosive substance based solely on its identification by an infrared spectrum. So I had our Firearms Section empty the powder out of a .38 caliber bullet and reload it with the same weight of flash paper. When I fired this bullet, even I was surprised that it penetrated a two-inch pine board! The detectives thought this was marvelous. I wasn't as excited as they were; I was more persuaded by the infrared spectrum.

We went to court with this type of evidence in several cases. Some judges saw through it immediately, "This is not what this section of the Criminal Code was intended for," and would dismiss the charge, while others would also recognize it as a tactic but think "how clever" and convict the accused bookmaker.

One of these flash paper cases involved a notorious Toronto bookmaker by the name of Max Bluestein. (Max looked exactly like someone Hollywood would cast to play a bookmaker/gambler.) He was not a small-time bookmaker but ran a large gambling operation that was a target for takeover by organized crime. He resisted and became a *cause célèbre* when, in 1961, he was beaten up horribly in a tavern in Toronto. When I went to court in the case, I met Max and some of his hangers-on, all of whom looked like the cast of a *Guys and Dolls* production. While we sat in the witness room waiting to testify, one of these characters was describing a poker game he had been in the night before and someone had broken in and robbed the players. "These three guys that broke in had guns and baseball bats," he said. "I can take my chances with the guns, but I didn't want to mess with those baseball bats!" Being young and foolish, I replied, "Yeah, the guy might not remember to keep the label up." He didn't see anything amusing in my comment, and I quickly realized I should go for a walk down the corridor.

The gambling cases were mostly fun because, in contrast to the abortion cases and most of the other work we did, there was nobody seriously harmed in most of them. Both the accused people and the police investigators were very interesting. One of the detectives with the Toronto Police Gambling Unit, Anatoli Wozniak, was perhaps the most colorful person I ever met. He had been assigned to the unit because he was known to be an excellent "phone man." Initially, I didn't know what that meant, but I subsequently learned that when they hit a bookmaker's place, they would continue to answer the phone for a while to get evidence. This was Anatoli's job because he was exceptionally quick-witted and he could talk like a bookmaker perfectly. He developed this specialty and was recognized far and wide as the number one "phone man" in the province.

One very unusual case involved a suitcase the police seized from a professional gambler who made a very good living attending private high-stakes crap games. (When I lived in the fraternity house, we used to run one of these games on our pool table each year, and I was amazed at the players who would turn up with large amounts of cash. They certainly weren't university students.)

This suitcase was filled with dice of every color, size, and design, including those of Las Vegas casinos, that one could think of. They also were not legitimate dice. The greatest number would not have all the spot patterns representing digits one to six. They would instead have a spot pattern representing duplicate digits on opposite sides. (Since the players could only see three of the six sides of the dice when they lay on the table, they would not be aware of these aberrations unless they picked the dice up and examined them closely. In a normal fast-moving game, that would rarely occur!) The result was that the user would have a pair of dice that could not produce a seven or another pair that would always come up with a seven or eleven.

Figure 12.2 Gambler's dice collection.

Other dice in his collection were less obviously "fixed" by being not quite even on all six sides or having lead inserted below the dots. (I could see this using a fluoroscope.) This gambler's technique was to watch the game for a while to see what the dice looked like and then go out to the suitcase in his car and select dice of the same type. When his turn to roll came, he would substitute his dice with a bit of sleight of hand and would bet based on the dice he had chosen. I never heard what happened to him. Perhaps he became CEO of the Lottery Corp.

Another learning experience resulted from the fact that, in downtown Toronto, the gambling cases were held in the same courtroom on the ground floor of the old city hall as the prostitution cases. While we sat waiting for our gambling cases to come up, there would be a steady procession of "professional women" passing through. Their cases didn't take long. I found the rapport that existed between the police officers who were arresting these young women and the women themselves very interesting. There was no animosity; it was simply, "You do your job, and I'll do mine." The conversation between them was easy, and I learned that, far from being exploited by vicious pimps (at least in those days), most of them thought they had a great job; they couldn't believe they were being paid for it.

Another function of the Toronto PD Morality Squad, which thankfully I never had to deal personally with, was the investigation of bawdy houses and body rub parlors. When the squad raided these establishments, they would seize all of the towels that were there, presumably for cleaning up after the activity. They would arrive in the lab with several garbage bags filled with towels, and all the members of our Biology Section would try to hide. The request would be to (a) find semen on them and (b) show that the semen was of more than one blood group, proving that more than one male was involved. Those types of cases eventually petered out as society became more accepting and enforcement of these laws became a much lower priority. No one in the lab was unhappy about that because those cases were a logistical nightmare. Over and above all the examination work, the record keeping for the large numbers of items took an enormous amount of time, and the staff were not convinced that this type of examination was an appropriate use of their time.

The bookmaking and gambling cases went on for several years until the ability to obtain orders for wiretaps arrived, legal off-track betting was introduced, and lotteries and casinos became magnets for the vast majority of small-time bettors. As a result, some of the fun went out of my job.

13 Missing Person or Homicide? *Regina v. Arthur Kendall*

Although by 1961 I had expanded my forensic science activities into cases other than just alcohol analysis, other sections in the lab dealt with a wide variety of other types of cases. One of these, the Biology Section of which John Funk was the head, examined evidence items such as body fluid stains, hairs, and fibers. The vast majority of these cases were sexual assaults and homicides. Nevertheless, we were still a small group and sometimes, when an unusual case cropped up, we all pitched in to help.

Such a case involved one Arthur Kendall. He was suspected of killing his wife, but her body had never been located. Can someone be convicted of a homicide in the absence of a body? There had never previously been such a case in Ontario.

In the spring of 1952, Arthur Kendall, his wife, and five children, aged 2–12, moved into a small cabin in a very remote location between Highway #6 and Lake Huron near the tip of the Bruce Peninsula. Kendall, an itinerant farmhand, had obtained summer employment at a nearby sawmill and the cabin belonged to the sawmill owner. At the end of July, Kendall moved his children out of the cabin and back to the farm in Grey County, from whence they had come. There, they moved in with the farm lady, who was separated from her husband, and her children. Kendall's wife was no longer with the family, and when questioned by neighbors and friends as to her whereabouts, he told various stories about her leaving him for another man.

Since this story was inconsistent with Mrs. Kendall's reputation as a wife and mother, her disappearance came to the attention of the Ontario Provincial Police (OPP). A thorough investigation, including an extensive search for her body, was made under the direction of Criminal Investigation Branch (CIB) Inspector Harold Graham (who later became the OPP Commissioner). Graham was very skeptical about Kendall's story and suspected the worst. However, since no real evidence was found and the children either said nothing or gave variations of their father's story, the intensity of the investigation gradually diminished.

Graham was a dogged investigator, who would never give up and, periodically over the ensuing years, he would make contact with the children as they grew older, "just to keep in touch." These contacts paid off eventually in early 1961 after three of the Kendall children had either married or moved away from their father. One of the girls decided to tell Graham what she knew about the disappearance of her mother. Her story was subsequently independently corroborated by her sister and a brother.

The reason they each gave for their prolonged silence was their mortal fear of their father. They told Inspector Graham of being awakened at the break of day one morning in July 1952 by a commotion in the cabin. They heard their mother screaming, "No, Art, please don't; please don't!" and then watched their father place a bloody butcher knife on a counter. They then saw the limp body of their mother being dragged out of the cabin by their father. He returned about a half hour later, wearing hip boots, gathered some bed clothing, garments, and the knife, and left again for a similar length of time. On his second return, he used some rainwater to wash the cabin floor, a rare activity for him they said. Their father then told the children to get up, that their mother had left during the night and would never be back; they must not mention her departure to anyone. Later that day, they moved out of the cabin and back to the farm.

Based on this information, Graham again interviewed Kendall, but he persisted with his original story. He was charged with murder, and another extensive search of the area around the cabin was conducted with negative results. The entire area was very swampy, and it would be quite possible to dispose of a body there that would never be found.

Inspector Graham asked the lab to examine the cabin, and John Funk was assigned the task.

Because John and I had become close friends and commuted to work together, he asked me to assist him. The cabin had not been lived in since Mrs. Kendall's disappearance but had been used for storage purposes by the mill owner. When we arrived, we found it to be housing odds and ends of hardware and other such items related to the mill. The floor was littered with an accumulation of dirt, some of it the deposits of birds and rodents during the previous nine years. We used a screening test for blood and found many positive indications all over the floor. These tests, however, could not differentiate between animal and human blood, and the possibility of it being animal in this location was quite real. We decided that to do a proper examination, it would be necessary to dismantle the entire floor and take it back to the lab for detailed examination.

After the floor was reassembled in the lab, John was able to confirm that the spots were human blood and marked the location of about three dozen stains, one of which appeared to have been swabbed. When photos of the floor with these locations marked were shown to the children, the pattern of where there was blood and where there wasn't corresponded with locations they described of the events of the night of their mother's death. For example, of one area with no stains, they said, "That's where our bed was; that area would have been under our bed." In another area where there was what appeared to be a trail of blood they said, "That's where Dad dragged Mom across the floor and out the door."

At Kendall's trial, the testimony of the now adult children, corroborated by John Funk's evidence about specific locations of bloodstains on the floor, was sufficient to convict Mr. Kendall of murder despite the fact that Mrs. Kendall's body had never been found. Arthur Kendall was sentenced to death in 1962; however, probably because of the absence of the body, his sentence was commuted to life imprisonment.

There was an interesting postscript to this case. Kendall was transferred to a prison in British Columbia to serve his sentence. A few years after I became director of the Centre of Forensic Sciences (CFS), I began receiving letters from him. This correspondence went on for several months. He was asking for details about the examinations we had made, how they were done, and what our findings meant. It was never entirely clear to me what his purpose was since it was long past the time when there was any chance of an appeal. My only thought was that, as he now had plenty of time on his hands, he might be writing a book about the death of his wife. I mentioned this to Commissioner Graham and learned that he had received similar correspondence and had reached the same conclusion.

The last I heard of Arthur Kendall was shortly before I retired in 1994; he had finally been granted parole. I never saw any book that he may have written; it might have been a fascinating read!

How to Get a New Lab? *Regina v. Wayne Ford* 14

By 1966, we had seriously outgrown the laboratory at 8 Jarvis Street. The Questioned Documents Section had been relocated to another building, and we were using the corridors as labs and offices. Ward Smith made regular submissions to the Attorney General's Department and a strong "business case" for a new larger building. These were always met with "yes, we certainly agree that you need much more space," but nothing ever came of those agreements.

It was the unintended consequence of a very unusual case and the serendipitous result of a casual invitation to the Justice Committee of the Legislature in 1967 that eventually led to the government decision to approve plans for a new building for the Centre of Forensic Sciences (CFS) (the lab's name had been changed in 1966).

The strange case of the disappearance of Mrs. Minnie Ford began on Wednesday, May 22, 1963. At about 20:00 that day, a close friend called Mrs. Ford at her home in Willowdale, a suburb of Toronto. The phone was answered by Wayne Ford, Mrs. Ford's sixteen-year-old son, who told the caller that his mother was out of the city. The friend was aware that Wayne had caused his mother considerable anxiety since her husband, who had operated a prosperous service station, died and she was concerned about his evasive attitude during the call. She therefore contacted Minnie's sister, who told her that she had not heard from her sister since May 12 and that she had not shown up for a trip they had planned to Niagara Falls on May 16. The following day, Mrs. Ford was reported missing to the Toronto Police.

Detectives questioned Wayne and a friend, Ron Walli, at the Ford home and were told that they had not seen Mrs. Ford since 09:30 on Saturday, May 18. They said she had told them that she was going to see some friends and suggested that they go up to the family cottage on Lake Couchiching in her car, a 1959 Cadillac. She would join them there the following Monday or Tuesday. They told the detectives that they had done as suggested and had picked up another friend, Larry Metcalf, on the way. Mrs. Ford never showed up at the cottage, and they had not heard from her.

The detectives began to suspect that something untoward had happened to Mrs. Ford.

She was a widow with a significant estate and a son who was not the least bit concerned about his mother's whereabouts. After Mrs. Ford's disappearance, the Ford home became the scene of wild, drunken parties and many of Wayne's friends, some of whom were "known to the police," became constant occupants of the house.

Searches were conducted at the Ford cottage, where one detective noted a child's wagon in front of the cottage, the wheels heavily coated with dried mud and two-wheel marks leading down to the dock. Detectives also learned that the owner of the neighboring cottage had discovered that his boat had been moved, an anchor was missing from it, and his cottage had been broken into.

Although Wayne was periodically questioned about his mother's disappearance over the ensuing three years, he continued to deny any knowledge of her whereabouts and repeated the same story he had told originally.

In 1966, Wayne was convicted of carrying a concealed weapon and possession of stolen goods and sentenced to reformatory. He escaped from there, was caught, and on July 5, 1966, was convicted of "escape lawful custody" and transferred to Kingston Penitentiary.

On Sunday, October 16, 1966, about 10:00, a cottager on Lake Couchiching discovered an object on the shoreline that he initially thought to be a mannequin. On closer examination, however, he realized that it was the decomposed body of an adult female.

Local Ontario Provincial Police (OPP) officers were called and observed that the body was lying on its side in a crouched position and appeared to be covered with a plaster-like material. It had portions of clothing adhering to it, and a white plastic band was loosely bound around the neck. Floating nearby in the water was a blue and white beach bag with the name "Hotel Algiers, Miami Beach, 25th, 26th Street" on the side; the band around the neck appeared to have come from this bag. These officers thought that the plaster-like material and the crouched position of the body suggested that it had probably been encased in plaster in a trunk or crate.

The body was taken to the CFS for a postmortem examination by Dr. Fred Jaffe. The skull showed almost complete fragmentation of the facial bones, and there was external evidence of ligature strangulation. Two separate two-inch-long pieces of a spindle-shaped metallic foreign object were embedded in the right side of the skull.

Dr. Jaffe concluded that the body was that of an adult, white female, approximately five feet six inches in height. It could not be further identified and appeared to have been in the water at least two years. The fragmentation of the face and skull, if inflicted during life, would have caused death very rapidly. The presence of a deep groove encircling the neck indicated that a broad ligature had been tightly applied around the neck, but whether this occurred before or after death could not be determined.

I received the plaster-like material (one of my miscellaneous cases) and determined that it was not plaster but was composed of some saponified fatty acids; i.e., it was a form of soap. This particular soap is known as adipocere, sometimes referred to as "grave wax." It is not common but is known to be formed slowly during bacterial decomposition of a body in the absence of air and in a wet environment. It can take many months to form. In this case, almost the entire body had been converted to adipocere.

OPP divers searched the lake and raked the shoreline, finding numerous articles, including a slipper sock that was identified as a type Mrs. Ford was known to have had and many pieces of clothing still bearing blood stains. This suggested that they had been dry when the body entered the lake. Pieces of the adipocere were found on the shore near the body, as was a pair of men's suede loafers. One of these had green tape on the inside, and a paint stain on the shoes appeared similar to that on the floor of the late Mr. Ford's service station. Numerous pieces of plywood with printing on the side that matched a crate known to have been in the Ford basement at one time were recovered, as was a piece of canvas with white lettering, RCASC and the initial F, which appeared to be part of a kit bag similar to one Mr. Ford had owned. Also found was a sawed-off baseball bat bound with green and black tape.

As a result of these findings, Wayne was again interviewed at Kingston Penitentiary, but he repeated the same story. Lengthy interviews with his associates, however, began to reveal that during these three years, Wayne had made utterances that tended to support the theory that he had murdered his mother and that his two friends, Ron Walli and Larry Metcalf, knew much more than they were admitting.

On November 9, the detectives interviewed Walli and Metcalf separately. After lengthy questioning, Metcalf suddenly stood up and said he "would now like to tell the truth." He stated that Wayne had told him how he had an argument with his mother on Friday, May 17, 1963, and in the course of this argument, he had stabbed her several times in the head with an ice pick. Wayne also described how he and Walli had dragged Mrs. Ford's body from the kitchen into the basement, where they jammed it into a wooden crate containing household effects. They had then scrubbed the floors to clean up all the blood. The crate was carried out to the garage and placed in the trunk of Mrs. Ford's Cadillac, which they drove to Lake Couchiching. There, they deposited the crate in the garage at the Ford cottage and returned to Toronto.

Metcalf continued that, the next day, Wayne and Walli picked him up and drove back to the cottage to show him the body in the crate. He told how Wayne had a handgun in his belt with which he threatened him and Walli if they didn't do as he ordered. They placed the crate on a child's wagon and pulled it down to the dock, where it was loaded onto a small boat that they began rowing out into the lake. After some distance, Wayne told them to stop, and they pushed the crate overboard. During this process, the transom of the boat gave way, and the boat began to sink. Wayne swam to the crate and forced it under until it sank. Walli swam back to shore to get the neighbor's boat and came back for Larry and Wayne, who were clinging to the sinking boat. (The image of Wayne trying to hold a gun to threaten Larry while trying to keep the boat afloat and hold on to it has always been, despite the tragic circumstances, a source of amusement for me.)

Questioning of Walli in the presence of his lawyer corroborated Metcalf's statement. As a result, on November 23, 1966, Wayne was returned from Kingston Penitentiary and charged with the murder of his mother.

Because the body had been found in OPP jurisdiction, but the murder was believed to have occurred in Toronto, investigators from both agencies worked closely to build their case. They were satisfied that the evidence showed that if the body from Lake Couchiching was indeed that of Mrs. Ford, then Wayne had killed her. They were not satisfied, however, that they could convince a jury "beyond a reasonable doubt" that the body was, in fact, that of Mrs. Ford. They needed more forensic evidence to do so.

The condition of the body was such that the autopsy had not produced any evidence of value for identification. Some of the items recovered from the lake, such as the wood crate, the plastic bag, the shoes, and the duffle bag, could be identified as having come from the Ford home, so if they could be connected with the body, then the body could also be associated with the Ford home. Mrs. Ford was the only female missing from the home.

John Funk established that the green tape in the suede loafer was the same type of duct tape as that on the sawed-off baseball bat, and one end of the tape on the bat made a "physical fit" with a roll of green tape recovered from Mrs. Ford's possessions. The two pieces of metal from the skull were shown to form an ice pick.

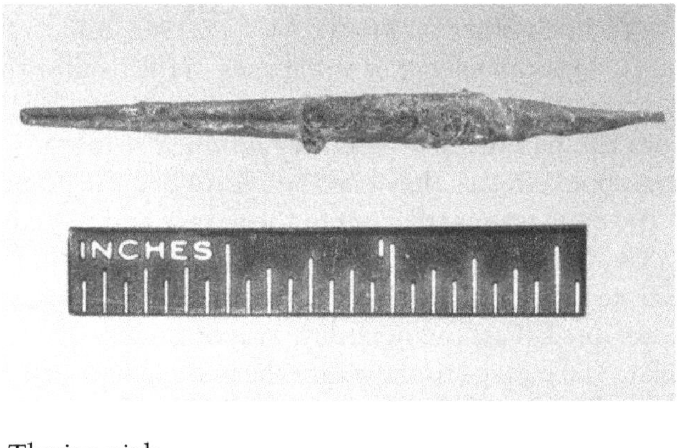

Figure 14.1 The ice pick.

I analyzed and compared bits of adipocere adhering to items from the lake, such as pieces of clothing, the duffle bag, and wood from the crate, with samples of adipocere removed from the body and found them to all have the same composition of fatty acids.

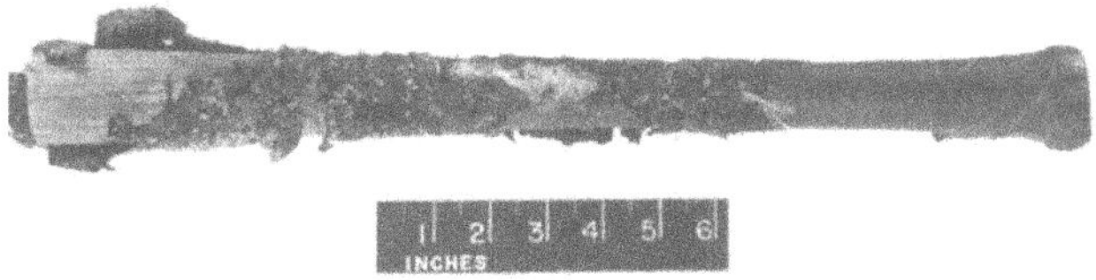

Figure 14.2 The sawed-off baseball bat.

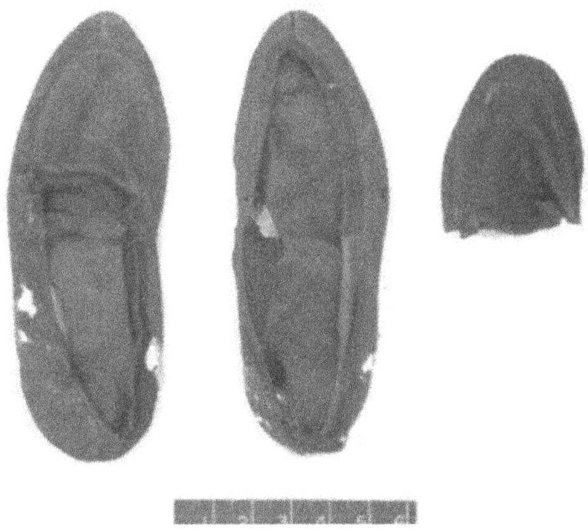

Figure 14.3 Adipocere and tape on the loafers.

Wayne Ford's trial in May 1967 was presided over by the Honorable Justice Donald Morand (who was originally from Windsor and knew my father very well). All the evidence was presented, and the jury was convinced that the body was indeed that of Mrs. Ford and that Wayne had killed her. He was convicted of noncapital murder and sentenced to life in Kingston Penitentiary, where, in 1971, he was a central figure in the notorious Kingston Penitentiary riot. Wayne was eventually paroled and, in 2013, was known to be living in a trailer park in British Columbia.

I sat next to Justice Morand at a Medico-Legal Society dinner some months after the trial, and we had a brief discussion about the case. He asked if I had noticed that when Wayne was in the witness box and the Crown attorney was showing him the sawed-off baseball bat "I moved as far over to the other side of the bench as I could. There was no way I wanted to be anywhere near that guy when there was a weapon close at hand!"

Returning to the opening paragraphs of this chapter, because it was known that a major issue at trial would be whether the body was in fact that of Mrs. Ford, the coroner had refused to release it for burial. It therefore remained in residence at CFS wrapped in plastic on a gurney in the walk-in fridge of our small morgue. During the trial in 1967, by coincidence, we had arranged a tour of the lab for members of the Justice Committee of the Legislature.

Like every other tour group, they were keen to see inside the morgue and autopsy room. When we opened the fridge door, there were the remains of Mrs. Ford wrapped in plastic on a gurney. The committee members were shocked, to say the least, with the nature of her resting place. Shortly after that, the Justice Committee recommended approval for a new building for the CFS and the legislature eventually agreed!

A lesson I learned from this experience was that although submissions for additional resources must thoroughly document demand and need, they are not, in and of themselves, likely to meet with much success. There must also be something that attracts the eye of the political players. This was an important lesson for me as I went on to become the Director of the Centre of Forensic Sciences.

15 The Attorney General's Lab Gets a New Name and a New Director

In July 1966, as part of Dr. Smith's drive to broaden the lab's relationship with the University of Toronto and to enhance its commitment to research and independence from the police, he persuaded the attorney general to approve an order in council changing the name of the lab from the Attorney General's Laboratory to the Centre of Forensic Sciences (CFS). The center's mandate was to serve the entire law enforcement and justice systems and to conduct research and training in the forensic sciences.

In early 1967, Dr. Smith became seriously ill and was forced to take several months off. During his absence, John Funk and I shared his responsibilities in addition to our regular jobs. Although Ward was able to return to work briefly in late spring, he died on July 14, 1967, at the age of fifty-two. Sadly, he hadn't lived to see the ongoing impact of many of his initiatives, the continuing use of the Breathalyzer in Canada for more than fifty years, the remarkable acceptance of the 0.08 legislation, the continued growth in size and stature of the Centre of Forensic Sciences, the success of an international meeting in Toronto in 1969, the new laboratory at 25 Grosvenor Street, and the professional achievements of many of the staff he had recruited, trained, and mentored.

Perhaps the most fitting epitaph for such an accomplished man is the thought contained in a note in his handwriting that I found on his desk after his death. I was never able to identify the source but have always believed that it expressed his philosophy: "A man will be remembered not by the hole he has left but by the mountain he has conquered."

John and I continued to share the director's duties until October 13, 1967, when the deputy attorney general announced that I had been appointed director. With just slightly more than ten years of experience in forensic science, and virtually none in management, I realized that my life, and that of our family, was going to be significantly altered.

In addition to the primary responsibility of directing the activities of what was becoming a large, full-service forensic science laboratory with a growing international reputation for excellence, I had inherited two additional responsibilities from Ward Smith that were going to make significant demands on my time. One of these was the planning for, and development of, a new laboratory, and the second was the organization of a major international scientific meeting in Toronto in June 1969.

Figure 15.1 The new director.

Directing CFS

My earliest decision was that I wasn't going to follow one of the examples of my predecessor who, although he was a brilliant scientist who had provided excellent scientific leadership and personally examined many of the cases during his first ten years as director, in later years had devoted the majority of his time to administrative matters, which he also managed very well. My interest was much more in the forensic science operations. I therefore decided to delegate as much of the administration, for example, personnel, finance, and dealing with the government bureaucracy, as I could. Fortunately, I always had excellent secretaries who could do much of this work far better than I could.

The delegation was also made much easier for me by one of the final things Dr. Smith had accomplished, obtaining approval to establish the position of executive officer. He recruited a retired Royal Canadian Navy lieutenant commander, Bill Mitchell, who proved to be extremely capable of managing the administrative affairs of CFS and dealing with the bureaucracy.

Directing the scientific operations was in itself a very demanding responsibility. John Funk and I had served Ward Smith in the role of de facto (but informal and unpaid) deputy directors. I was therefore relieved when I secured approval to formally establish the position of deputy director and appointed John Funk to it. Essentially, I directed the casework and John managed research and training, and we worked very comfortably together. Sadly, John died in 1980.

I also made some changes in the structure of the sections. The Organic Chemistry Section, which had always been an aberration created for me personally, was dissolved, with the alcohol analysis and Breathalyzer functions being restored to the Toxicology Section, where they properly belonged, and the arson, explosives, and miscellaneous cases transferred to the Chemistry Section.

Another early decision was a major review of a research program we had been devoting significant resources to for several years. A professor of chemical engineering at the University of Toronto had developed a technique known as neutron activation analysis (NAA), which was a highly sensitive method for the analysis of chemical elements. It involved irradiating small samples in a nuclear reactor (we used the one at McMaster University), making the elements radioactive and then detecting the radiation emitted by them. He had applied this technique to the analysis of trace elements in hair, a common evidential item for which forensic science had only limited ability (using microscopy) to compare samples.

Both the Royal Canadian Mounted Police (RCMP) and CFS were very interested in this application and had funded students through their PhD programs to evaluate it. Their work demonstrated that the trace element composition of hair could be readily established using NAA, and the professor took a few of these cases to court. Unfortunately, he was a bit premature, and his testimony resulted in some controversy about this technique. I therefore assigned one of our staff, Norm Erickson, to spend a year making a detailed evaluation of the capability of NAA of hairs for comparison purposes. Essentially, he found that with clumps of hairs, there was considerable variation in the trace element composition between individuals, but with single hairs, there was more variation in the elemental composition of hairs across a single scalp in some individuals than there was between different individuals. Since the vast majority of hair cases involve single hairs, the technique therefore had very limited practical value, and I decided to cancel that program.

During my first few years as director, our Biology Section, and most other forensic labs, was devoting considerable time and effort to validating and introducing additional genetic markers to our blood typing capability. As a result, the significance of such evidence from bloodstains was being increased considerably, but at a cost to timely reporting. One result was that the backlog of such cases was becoming unmanageable and delays in reporting results unconscionable.

I took the time to review all of the homicide cases we had examined in the previous year. Much to my surprise, I found that although there certainly were cases in which such additional evidence was valuable in establishing the source of the blood, in the majority of the homicides the source of the blood was not a major issue since there was only one of the parties bleeding. What was an issue, however, was how the blood got there. For example, did it get there because the suspect had stabbed the victim and it sprayed onto him, or could it have gotten there because the suspect discovered a bleeding body and brushed against the blood while trying to assist? As a result, we started becoming much more selective in the cases in which we would use all the genetic marker systems available for identification purposes and began devoting much more time to enhancing our ability to interpret the significance of bloodstain patterns.

As our staff increased, I realized that we had to become much more diligent and consistent in their training, and so under the leadership of Elgin Brown, the Biology Section head, we developed a standardized two-year training program that had incentives and hurdles built into it that could be very thoroughly documented. We also managed to devise, and sell to the bureaucracy, a rational staff classification system and salary scale that was uniquely designed for our forensic scientists rather than the much more general system that applied to all other scientists in government.

Another change I made was purely symbolic, but it did have an impact on the staff. Dr. Smith rarely wore a lab coat, and it had become a bit of a status symbol for staff not to wear a lab coat. I was old-fashioned and didn't think that was appropriate in a laboratory; lab coats were symbols of science, and I wanted science to be the principal culture of the CFS. I tried to make this point subliminally by always wearing a lab coat myself. Most of the staff eventually picked up on this and lab coats became more common dress in the lab. (There was also a practical reason I wore a lab coat; the extra pockets were very useful.) Toward my later years, this trend was reversed because the lab work had changed substantially; much less was being done at the laboratory bench and much more at computer terminals on staff desks.

I was very fortunate that CFS was in the Department of the Attorney General, where all the senior managers were lawyers. They knew little if anything of science and were somewhat intimidated by it. As a result, they were content to let me manage on my own, and I had much more independence than I would have had in a different department. I usually only saw the assistant deputy attorney general who was my boss on social occasions!

In 1967, another event of historical significance to forensic science in Ontario occurred.

Following Ward Smith's death, Professor Rogers and Dr. Noble Sharpe decided it was time for them to retire. Both were about eighty years of age and had been active in forensic science for well over fifty years.

I missed them both enormously, in particular, Professor Rogers, who had provided me with so much advice and encouragement. He was one of those memorable characters deserving of enormous gratitude from everyone whose lives he touched. Unfortunately, he operated from his hip pocket and never wrote anything. Over and above his interests in chemistry and forensic science, Joslyn Rogers was also an active fisherman, a businessman who was part owner of a small chemical supply company, an avid student of history and religion, a tolerably good cook, and a gardener par excellence. I'm certain he was the only resident of North Rosedale who kept a slingshot in his basement to shoot through the window at the squirrels who were enjoying his garden.

Following his wife's death, he had also become part of our family and a third "grandpa" to our children. In his later years at CFS, he had purchased a small farm in King Township, where he developed a massive vegetable garden. On many Sunday afternoons, our entire family would visit the farm to help with the weeding, and our boys would delight in the opportunity to drive the small garden tractor to cut the grass. While the main beneficiaries of the garden were the local crows, raccoons, and other wildlife, on Monday mornings in late summer and early fall he would arrive in the laboratory with baskets of beautiful fresh vegetables for the staff.

My final story about Professor Rogers exemplifies how he planned and thought about his colleagues and friends. In the early 1960s, he came into my lab one morning with a bag containing a forty-ounce bottle of Hudson Bay Rum. He had purchased it the year he was appointed to the university staff in 1911 and had saved it in the attic of his home all those years. My instructions were to store it until after he died and then share it with some of his friends in the lab and the police. I accepted this responsibility and, when the time came in 1972, I followed his instructions. We gathered in his old lab, got out clean beakers (the only appropriate vessel for drinking in a laboratory), removed the cork from the ancient Hudson Bay Rum bottle (which crumbled at the first stab), and poured special drinks for all. It tasted awful! We persisted, however, and told lots of Josh Rogers stories; somewhere we were certain we could hear a jolly chuckle and a "Thank you, guys." Linnaeus Joslyn Rogers, a wonderful, gentle, brilliant man; a patient mentor; a loyal friend!

Dr. Sharpe was also a great loss, but fortunately, I was able to recruit Dr. Fred Jaffe from one of the hospitals, and he took over the position of medical director on a full-time basis, which was a great relief for me.

The International Meeting in 1969

In the summer of 1966, Ward Smith had attended the Fourth International Meeting in Forensic Medicine in Copenhagen. At that meeting, a decision was made to formally establish an International Association of Forensic Sciences (IAFS). During these discussions, Ward agreed to host the 1969 meeting in Toronto and was elected president.

On his return to Toronto, he advised the attorney general of what he had done and received assurance that the Ontario government would provide some support in the form of a luncheon for the delegates. He also received assurance from the Canadian Society of Forensic Science (CSFS) that they would act as co-sponsor (although they had very little money). Shortly after that, Ward's health began to deteriorate, and he was unable to do anything further about the meeting.

After becoming director, I suddenly realized that the clock was ticking on this responsibility and I had better start doing something about it. The new IAFS did not yet have a constitution, so there was no provision for succession in the presidency. Because I was the incoming president of CSFS, the society proposed to the past presidents of the four previous international meetings (in Ghent, New York, London, and Copenhagen) that I should succeed Ward Smith as IAFS president. They were only too happy to agree since they had all been through one of these meetings and were aware of how much work was involved. Thus, I became president of IAFS for the 1967–1969 period.

A planning committee was assembled with members of our staff and senior members of the RCMP Labs, the Federal Food and Drug Labs, and the University of Toronto. The RCMP agreed to provide funding in the form of a formal banquet at which the RCMP concert orchestra would provide entertainment. The University of Toronto provided the venue, which meant the cost was minimal but our staff would have to look after all the details of the arrangements (signs, room assignments, projection equipment, etc. Bill Mitchell took on the responsibility of managing all of that and did a superb job). A major function of the committee was fund-raising. We all spent many hours trying to call in favors with only limited success.

We had to create a mailing list of potential delegates (a major challenge in the days before computers and the Internet) and then realized that mailings to all those on the list would be expensive. Since revenue would not be coming in until people registered for the meeting, we had no money for postage and I had to take out a personal loan of $1,000 as "seed money." (Fortunately, the son of Francis Camps, one of the past presidents from London, England, had a senior position with one of the banks in Toronto and arranged the loan for me.)

Fred Jaffe organized the scientific program, an enormous job, and it was a great success. Although these programs are the raison d'être for such meetings, social events are also critical and what delegates remember, particularly if they don't go well. We were blessed. The weather in June 1969 was spectacular, the campus provided a comfortable venue for the scientific program, and the delegates loved the social activities, an evening ferry ride in Toronto Harbour with a Dixieland band, a day trip to Niagara Falls, an evening reception provided by the city at the spectacular then-new city hall, an outdoor moose BBQ at Mark Kenney's Ranch, and the gala formal banquet and dance at the Royal York Hotel.

(The moose for the BBQ was the major logistical challenge of the entire meeting. It was provided by the RCMP in Saskatchewan, out of season, and traveled to Toronto on the governor general's airplane because commercial carriers were not allowed to transport uninspected meat. By fortunate coincidence, the governor general at the time was Marie's uncle.)

The program for the ladies (accompanying persons) was organized by Pam Newall and included a day at the Woodbine horse races, lunch at the Royal Canadian Yacht Club, and sherry parties at the homes of members of our staff.

In the end, we were all exhausted but also exhilarated because the feedback from the delegates was outstanding. Attendance at the Fifth International Meeting of the Forensic Sciences was more than 500 delegates from all over the world, and a constitution for IAFS was adopted. Our budget ended up at about $50,000, and much to Marie's relief, I was able to pay back the bank loan. We even had a small surplus, which was turned over to the president of the sixth meeting, Dr. Thomas Marshall from Belfast, to help him avoid the necessity for a personal loan.

The New Laboratory Building

As described in Chapter 14, when we received approval to plan a new laboratory in early 1967, we were desperate for space at 8 Jarvis. The staff was ecstatic when I informed them about the approval; little did we know that it would be eight years before we could actually occupy the new space!

The first step was the appointment of contract architects. We were very fortunate in the appointment of a well-respected Toronto firm, Ludlow & Fleury. Their experience in building labs for industry and hospitals was an enormous asset and very much simplified their "learning curve." Basil Ludlow and Bill Fleury were perfectly matched partners, Ludlow was a practical, pragmatic, hard-nosed businessman/architect, and Fleury was his artistic and creative partner. They hired an engineer, Bill Kitchen, to design all the mechanical systems, which are critical for a laboratory. Bill was a somewhat eccentric genius who did not believe in using a one-inch pipe if there was room for a two-inch one. We developed a wonderful close working relationship with them over the next few years and experienced very little interference from the government architect, who was nominally in charge.

To identify a site, we looked at several in the Queen's Park area and at the then-developing Sheridan Park Science and Technology Centre in Clarkson. Fortunately, a site at 25 Grosvenor Street, a vacant lot owned by the Liquor Control Board of Ontario (LCBO), became available. The government decided that this land was too valuable for just a liquor store and that they should build a nineteen-story building on it. We were assigned the lower six floors plus two basements for a total of about 80,000 square feet. A separate, but attached below grade, building for the Pathology Section and morgue was to be built at 26 Grenville Street as part of the complex.

Since the lot was owned by the LCBO, the initial plan was to have a liquor store at street level; however, when this was announced, several editorials appeared in the daily papers pointing out the irony of having a liquor store and morgue in such close juxtaposition. A decision was quickly made at the political level to remove the liquor store and replace it with the coroner's courts.

Over the next eighteen months, plans were developed. We involved the CFS staff in the planning process with great success. They enjoyed it and contributed significantly to the final design. Because of the absence of interference, we were able to include virtually everything we needed. We even were allowed, because laboratory space is so expensive to build, to plan for sufficient space to comfortably double the size of the staff, something unheard of in government. (This was fortunate because, by the time CFS moved to its current location in suburban Downsview in 2013, the staff had more than tripled in size.)

Unfortunately, other government priorities intruded in 1969, and the start of construction was deferred. We continued to struggle with what was now an embarrassing lack of space at Jarvis Street. Finally, in 1972 we received authorization to proceed with construction. The day the shovels went into the ground was a day of much celebration around CFS.

We were fortunate to be able to monitor the construction process quite closely, which permitted us to develop a good rapport with many of the tradesmen. Bill Mitchell was on site almost daily. We quickly learned to distinguish between those wearing white hard hats and those wearing blue ones. The former were senior people who had authority but always pointed out how expensive it would be to make any changes we requested. The blue hats had no authority, but they did have big hammers and were not concerned about costs. For example, one day I realized that it would be nice to have a door between my office and the adjacent boardroom. The white hat explained how much that would cost. I waited a while and asked a blue hat what would be involved. "You want a door there?" he asked. "Yes," I replied. He immediately took a sledge hammer and knocked a hole in the wall. "There's your door; we'll finish it up tomorrow!" So far as I know, the white hats never noticed.

Watching the building transition from lines on blueprints to "bricks and mortar" was very exciting and satisfying. My major concern throughout was not that there might be some things that didn't work well; I just assumed there would be. Instead, I worried that we had forgotten something critical, like a front door or washrooms. It was a great relief when we moved in to find that everything critical was there.

Before the actual move, I told the staff that they would find this to be a major change in how they did things, some of which they might not care for, and said they would each be allowed one bitch but with the additional caution, "Don't waste it!" A few never did use theirs.

An example of a major change in procedures required by the new building was the establishment of the Centre Receiving Office (CRO). When we were at Jarvis Street, all of the operational labs were on one floor. Police officers bringing in cases would stroll around the corridor, often looking for a specific examiner to accept their case. The items to be examined were transferred directly to that person along with verbal information about the case. While this process simplified the "chain of continuity," it was very time-consuming for both parties (detectives love to tell "war stories") and sometimes meant that the examiner received more information than really necessary.

As we were planning the move to Grosvenor Street, I realized the complications that investigators would encounter wandering around six floors trying to find someone to receive their items. I therefore developed the concept of a central case receiving office staffed with senior examiners and a retired police identification officer who would serve as a liaison officer making follow-up contacts with investigators. This meant that police delivering cases had only to go to one location to accomplish their task. At the same time, we introduced a "Case Submission Form," which the police had to complete before they arrived; it included space for all the information we needed and saved a lot of paperwork for our staff. It also documented the information we had received about the case in the event there were later allegations that we might be biased by too much irrelevant (to us) information.

Initially, most staff did not like the CRO because they lost direct contact with the police, which was often quite enjoyable and did have some value. Although I was sympathetic to their concerns, I decided that direct communication was not a critical issue. The majority of our cases arrived from around the province by mail or common carrier, and there was no direct communication with the investigators. Staff also were not pleased that they would occasionally have to take their turn in the CRO, which took them away from their labs. Otherwise, the system worked very well and eventually became accepted by all as the best way to manage case submissions at 25 Grosvenor. Finally, in July 1975, CFS moved into its new facility, and it was magnificent. We received many visitors from other labs who would be awestruck when they saw what we had developed. This venue served the CFS well until 2013.

As the staff grew larger and busier at 25 Grosvenor, I began to develop plans for a system of four or five regional labs around the province. The first would be located in Sudbury to serve northeastern Ontario. Again, detailed submissions came to naught until a policy was adopted by the government to relocate jobs from Toronto to the northern Ontario cities of North Bay, Sudbury, Sault Ste. Marie, and Thunder Bay. The Ontario Lottery Corporation

Figure 15.2 25 Grosvenor Street.

was to be the prime job provider in the Sault, but they fell fourteen persons short of the government's objective. By coincidence, my planned staffing for this lab was fourteen. That got us into the project, and we received approval to develop laboratory space in what was to become the Roberta Bondar Building on a site in downtown Sault Ste. Marie on the shore of the beautiful St. Mary's River.

Although operationally Sudbury would have been a more central location, I wasn't about to turn down this opportunity. John Wells, head of the Chemistry Section, agreed to become the director of this Northern Regional Forensic Laboratory, and he worked closely with the local Sault architects on the design. In 1992, the staff moved into the 16,000-square-foot facility, and it has served the north well since then.

Ministry of the Solicitor General

In 1972, during one of government's periodic reorganizations, a decision was made to create a new Ministry of the Solicitor General by splitting off the law enforcement and other investigative functions from the Ministry of the Attorney General. Despite our lobbying, and that of the deputy attorney general, to maintain forensic science within the Attorney General's

Figure 15.3 Sault Ste. Marie lab (The top floor).

Ministry, the Center became part of the new ministry. As part of the reorganization, the Pathology Section was split off from CFS to become a separate branch. I was also opposed to this change but lost that battle because the new chief pathologist (Dr. Jaffe had previously decided to return to hospital work) recruited from the United Kingdom would not accept the position on any other basis.

The new solicitor general was a career politician and longtime cabinet member. He had a personal staff of four or five—a secretary, executive assistant, constituency assistant, and chauffeur. He impressed me at his first meeting with the senior staff of the new ministry when he announced, "You fellows run the ministry, and I'll make the speeches." For one of his successors in office who stayed in a hotel when in Toronto, I learned that the key support person was the chauffeur. If there were a document I was anxious for the minister to read, I would give it to the chauffeur because he packed the minister's briefcase with the papers the minister would read that night at his hotel!

That arrangement worked very well until around 1985, when the structure of the cabinet was changed, and the minister's office staff was increased dramatically with bright, young, totally inexperienced staffers as policy advisers, communication advisers, and so forth. The solicitor general's political staff increased to about thirty. They saw their principal responsibility to be ensuring that the minister looked good and got reelected, whereas regular public servants saw ours as delivering services to the public as efficiently and effectively as possible. The political staff seemed to believe that direct service providers were there to support them rather than the other way around. I did not enamor myself with some of these advisers when, at one point in a moment of exasperation, I exclaimed, "We don't need any more advisers; what we need are more doers."

"Get Involved" They Told Me, So I Did Professional Associations

16

Early in my career, Ward Smith and Professor Rogers both encouraged me to become active in professional organizations. Both were founding members and past presidents of the Canadian Society of Forensic Science (CSFS), and Ward had been chairman of the Toxicology Section of the American Academy of Forensic Sciences (AAFS) and the National Safety Council (United States) Committee on Tests for Intoxication (now the Alcohol, Drugs, and Impairment Division). I eagerly followed their advice, which resulted in many positive impacts on my career.

Canadian Society of Forensic Science

I became a member of CSFS in 1958 and attended my first meeting in Montreal that same year. It was exciting for a neophyte forensic scientist to have the opportunity to personally meet some of the very prominent members of the Royal Canadian Mounted Police Labs, the Quebec Lab, and the Food and Drug Labs. Dr. Smith ensured that I would become actively involved when, during his presidency in 1959, he got me elected as the society's secretary. As with many small professional organizations, the secretary was responsible for managing the administrative affairs of the society, so I had to learn much about CSFS and its activities.

In 1967, members of CSFS recognized that the changes dealing with drunk driving being planned for the Criminal Code of Canada, as described in Chapter 3, would require enormous, rapid expansion of existing breath test programs. We had great concern that, in the absence of nationwide science-based standards for equipment, training, and operations, enforcement of the legislation would be left to individual police forces with a resultant wide variability in the quality of breath test evidence. The society therefore established a Special Committee on Breath Testing (now the Alcohol Test Committee [ATC]) to develop recommendations on standards and procedures. This committee provided advice to the Department of Justice (DOJ) officials drafting the amendments, to the members of Parliament who would have to consider them, and to the police forces who would be required to enforce the law. I was one of the original members of the committee, served as its chairman from 1980 to 1984, remained an active member of it until 2000, and served as the committee's archivist providing ongoing "institutional memory" until 2008.

The committee had the good fortune to be consulted during the early stages of the drafting of the legislation and, on the recommendation of the director of the Criminal Law Section of the DOJ, became the official scientific adviser to the minister of justice on these matters. This relationship continues to this day. A major responsibility of the ATC is the evaluation of equipment submitted to DOJ by manufacturers for approval by the attorney general of Canada as "suitable for use" in the enforcement of the relevant sections of the Criminal Code.

In 1968, I was elected president of CSFS, which, in addition to broadening my knowledge of forensic science in Canada, led to my becoming president of the International Association of Forensic Sciences (IAFS), as described in Chapter 15.

Following my retirement from CFS, the CSFS did me the great honor of establishing the Douglas M. Lucas Award in 1995. This award is granted occasionally to a respected member of the society who "through his or her professional activities has demonstrated genuine leadership both within the Society and in a particular field of Forensic Science in Canada and internationally." This honor was exceeded in 1996 when the society awarded me its highest award, the Derôme Medal, "for outstanding contributions to the field of forensic sciences and the Canadian Society of Forensic Science." The award is named for Dr. Wilfred Derôme, a pioneer in the forensic sciences who established the first forensic science laboratory in North America (and one of the first anywhere in the world) in Montreal in 1914. Part of my sense of honor came from the fact that an earlier recipient had been Professor Joslyn Rogers!

American Academy of Forensic Sciences

Ward Smith encouraged me to attend my first meeting of AAFS in Cleveland in 1958. I was awestruck in the presence of so many distinguished forensic scientists who had previously been simply names in books and on scientific papers. I recognized what a privilege I had been granted and determined to try to merit this by contributing as much as I could to the organization. Initially, I did this by presenting papers to the academy's Criminalistics Section and by publishing in the academy's *Journal of Forensic Sciences*.

These activities allowed me to meet, and develop friendships with, many other members and to begin to develop a professional reputation in the academy that resulted in my election as secretary of the Criminalistics Section in 1961 and chairman in 1962. Once I had served in those positions, I assumed that my leadership role in the academy had been completed. Little did I know what the future had in store!

AAFS was founded in 1948 by a relatively small group of eminent forensic scientists led by Dr. R.B.H. Gradwohl of St. Louis, who became its first president. In the early years, the academy's affairs were managed by a few of these pioneers. They were conservative in their views about the role of the academy and who should be eligible for membership. By 1970, however, the membership had increased from the original 100 or so to more than 900 and, understandably, many of the newer members began to believe they should have some input into the academy's management, something the "old guard" was reluctant to recognize. They did not truly appreciate the profound changes that were occurring as AAFS grew from a small, somewhat parochial club to a large, multidisciplinary, geographically dispersed scientific organization with a significant proportion of "next-generation" members. These differences came to a head at the February 1970 meeting at the Drake Hotel in Chicago over issues that, from today's perspective, appear somewhat trivial but which were anything but to some of the members in the context of 1970.

Before 1970, the three-day academy meetings were devoted almost exclusively to the delivery of papers and other scientific exchanges of information; whatever "business" that needed discussion or approval was typically dealt with summarily in less than an hour at a "business meeting." The 1970 business meeting was therefore scheduled for 17:00 on the second day of the gathering in the full expectation that everyone would be free for preprandial activities by 18:00. Instead, the meeting became very fractious, and by 20:00, only a small portion of the agenda had been covered. Tempers were running almost as high as the members' desperation for food and drink. The debate became so intense and so emotional that, at one point, I was concerned a few participants might come to blows. The president, James Osterberg, wisely decided things needed to cool down and adjourned the meeting until 08:00 the following day.

Since, like the majority of the membership, I had previously paid only minimal attention to academy business matters, I did not understand what all the fuss was about. There seemed to be several issues, but two, in particular, dominated the debate. The first was whether the academy should be inclusive (i.e., accept members with qualifications other than in the physical/medical sciences) or exclusive (and in particular not accept members from the social sciences). The second was about what should be the academy's role, if any, with the recently established Forensic Sciences Foundation Inc. (FSF). The latter was the more contentious issue.

FSF had been established by a few "activist" members of the academy's board of directors without any discussion with the overall academy membership. It was to serve as the research and education arm of the academy and would be able to accept and manage grants, something the AAFS tax status precluded. A major concern of many members, including myself once I learned of it, was the fact that the bylaws of the foundation had been written in such a way that the founding board of directors would have the exclusive right to nominate and elect future boards of directors; that is, they could be self-perpetuating. The opposition faction perceived this to be a boondoggle that would be used to fund research grants for only the members of the FSF board.

When the meeting resumed the following morning, there had obviously been much discussion in the rooms, hallways, restaurants, and bars overnight. Professor Rolla Harger of Indiana University, one of the leaders of the opposition faction, presented a motion to refer the contentious issues to an ad hoc Committee of Past Presidents to prepare a report and recommendations for discussion by the entire academy membership at the 1971 meeting. This was approved, and the cease-fire allowed the members to get back to their scientific interests. Unfortunately, the weapons were only temporarily holstered and would soon be drawn again!

Figure 16.1 Professor Rolla Harger.

The Past Presidents Committee was chaired by Professor Oliver Schroeder of Case Western Reserve University, a brilliant professor of law and a superb writer who I later was privileged to have as my mentor on professional ethics. He wrote the committee report, which was circulated to the academy membership in the summer of 1970. On the key issue of the foundation, it recommended a series of principles to serve as guidelines in structuring any foundation that could be affiliated with the academy. These would require significant changes to the FSF bylaws, including the manner of nominating and electing its board.

The dispute continued at the February 1971 academy meeting in Phoenix, Arizona. Fortunately (as it turned out), Marie attended this meeting with

Figure 16.2 Professor Oliver Schroder.

me, just the second time for her (the first had been in Honolulu in 1967, for obvious geographic reasons). The report of the Past Presidents Committee had resolved the exclusive/inclusive issue, but the group who were referred to as "That Foundation Bunch" by the opposition had not reacted well to the recommendations about FSF. The entire meeting was dominated more by backroom politicking than scientific exchange. The opposition faction decided that, for the first time in AAFS history, they would not accept the nominating committee's slate of officers and would instead present nominations from the floor. Unheard of! But who should they nominate for president? (Actually president-elect since the Academy president's responsibilities were so all-demanding in the absence at that time of any permanent academy office or staff. A year as president-elect was necessary to prepare for the presidential term.)

I was not involved in any of these discussions as I tried to focus on the scientific presentations. Much to my surprise, at lunch on day two of the meeting I was greeted by a group led by a good friend, Bob Cravey, the chief toxicologist in the Orange County, California, Sheriff/Coroner's Lab, and Dr. Lemoyne Snyder, one of the academy's founding members (who had created the academy's name. He later told me that he intended "American" to be interpreted in the continental rather than just the national sense). Bob's opening line to me was, "Doug, we would like to nominate you for the position of president-elect. We believe you are someone who is admired and respected by the entire membership and who can restore common sense and bring peace to the AAFS."

Wow! Who Knew?

When I regained some semblance of rationality, I realized that I was not at all certain that I wanted the position in the current circumstances. I even had some doubt that the academy would still exist in another year, let alone continue into the future. So I thanked them for their confidence and asked for a few hours to consider the proposal and to discuss its implications with Marie. She, of course, was supportive, but it was another serendipitous event that made the final decision for me.

Before lunch, Marie and I were enjoying a beer beside the pool at the hotel discussing the situation and, by chance, a few of That Foundation Bunch were sitting at the next table. I could not help but overhear their conversation, which had nothing to do with nominations or elections; at that point, they were not aware of what the opposition had in mind. Their discussion was about Dr. Tom Marshall, the chief pathologist for Northern Ireland who had succeeded me as president of the IAFS and was planning the 1972 international meeting in Belfast. This was a very intense time of "The Troubles" in Northern Ireland, and many academy members had expressed reluctance to attend a meeting in Belfast because they considered it unsafe. (In fact, in January 1972, following the "Bloody Sunday" killings in Londonderry described in Chapter 25, Tom did have to relocate the meeting on very short notice to Edinburgh, where it was still a great success.)

Back to poolside in Phoenix. We overheard one of the group announce to the others that he had just managed to "set up" Tom Marshall with a member of the media who "would do a real number on him." That did it. If that was the way this group thought and acted, I didn't want them running the academy or the foundation. Such thinking would be destructive of the academy. So, I called Bob Cravey and advised him that if they still wanted to nominate me, I would accept.

At the business meeting the next day, when the routine call was made for nominations from the floor, most of the people in the room were stunned when Bob stood up and nominated me for president-elect. Confusion reigned because this had never happened before and no one was sure how to proceed. Ballots were finally prepared and distributed, and the secret vote took place.

The candidate proposed by the nominating committee was Robert Joling, a lawyer from Kenosha, Wisconsin, who had been very active in the academy and with the foundation. When the results were announced, much to my (and I suspect many others') surprise, I was elected, the first member from outside the United States to hold this office.

Fortunately for me, and for the academy, two additional nominations were made from the floor, for the positions of academy secretary and member of the Executive Committee. Dr. James Weston, chief medical examiner of New Mexico, was nominated as secretary, a key position in the academy at that time because the secretary's office became the academy office and the secretary managed most of the administrative matters of AAFS. Dr. Don Harper Mills, a pathologist/lawyer from Long Beach, California, was nominated as member of the Executive Committee. Both were elected and became towers of strength for me and the academy. Each later became AAFS president in his own right (as did Bob Joling).

During the remainder of 1971, the foundation board recognized the setback they had received with the election of the new group of academy officers. They therefore presented a plan to the AAFS Executive Committee outlining a way for the two organizations to coordinate. Unfortunately, it failed to address the critical issue of the self-perpetuating board and was rejected.

At the February 1972 academy meeting in Atlanta, another long (four-hour) business meeting dealt with the foundation issue. The membership approved a resolution drafted by Jim Weston directing me as the incoming president to appoint a committee to attempt to negotiate with the board of FSF a way to bring the foundation under the direct control of the academy and, if that was successful, to draft revised bylaws for the foundation. These would be submitted for approval by the full academy membership at the 1973 academy meeting. I appointed Don Mills as chairman of the committee, of which I would be a member, to accomplish that task. Don did a superlative job over the following year, and after many meetings and discussions with a great many AAFS members, we finally persuaded the FSF board of trustees to agree to resign their positions immediately before the academy meeting.

At the business meeting, I was determined to have the foundation business resolved quickly once and for all. Don Mills presented his committee report and responded to a few questions. I had persuaded Professor Rolla Harger, an influential leader of the faction opposed to the Foundation Bunch, to present the motion for the academy to take over FSF. It passed without discussion. Whew!

Harmony was finally restored to AAFS, and there has never since been an issue that divided the academy to a similar extent. The precedent for nominations for officers from the floor occurred once or twice afterward but has not recurred for many years now. The final decision at the 1973 meeting was to establish a permanent office in Rockville, Maryland, staffed with a

Figure 16.3 Ken Field.

full-time executive director of both AAFS and FSF. We were very fortunate to recruit Ken Field, a very experienced researcher to fill this position as, over the next few years, the position was funded largely from research grants managed by the foundation. This move significantly reduced the enormous responsibilities that had previously been shouldered by the AAFS president and secretary. In 1979, the office was moved to Colorado Springs, where it now occupies a building owned by the academy. Today, the staff consists of thirteen full-time positions and academy meetings go on for a full week.

(Once again, I was unaware of what the future held for me because, in 1986, I was elected chairman of FSF and remained in that position until 1991. During that period, the foundation established an endowment fund, the interest from which now funds research projects through "Lucas Research Grants" and other means.)

During my year as president of AAFS, in addition to the foundation matter and the normal responsibility of organizing a scientific meeting, the 1973 meeting would also be the silver anniversary meeting of AAFS, which would have to be appropriately celebrated. An unforeseen challenge for me was that the meeting was to be held in Las Vegas, Nevada, and some of the older, more conservative members planned to boycott it because of the location. They believed Las Vegas to be a den of iniquity that members of a law enforcement–oriented profession should have nothing to do with. I spent many hours on the phone with members for whom I had the utmost respect trying to convince them that yes, although it is a center for gambling, it is also a place where the gambling is as honest as it is possible to be. I was successful with a few of these members.

In recognition of the silver anniversary, we organized a gala black-tie, seven-course dinner and invited all the surviving founding members of the

Figure 16.4 AAFS silver anniversary banquet.

academy to attend. At previous banquets, the guest speakers had been lawyers, judges, police chiefs, and even gossip columnist Ann Landers. I had seen as part of my mandate the restoration of more science to our meetings and had scored a bit of a coup, in that period when space exploration was a matter of keen public interest, in getting the director of the Pasadena Jet Propulsion Laboratory to be our guest speaker. Unfortunately, I had also invited our oldest living past president, Rolla Harger, to spend five minutes discussing the founding of the academy. I should have known better because I had never heard Professor Harger speak for only five minutes anywhere anytime on any topic. Despite my subtle (and some not so subtle) attempts to encourage him to wind it up, by the time he finally sat down, people's bladders were dictating that they politely (or not so politely) leave the room, and our distinguished space pioneer guest speaker finally rose to speak to a half-empty banquet hall. So much for best-laid plans!

Despite that hiccup, the meeting at the Las Vegas Hilton was a great success in part because the hotel staff was so professional that any glitch would be corrected in minutes after just one phone call. I met the issue of gambling head on by arranging a "behind the scenes" tour of the casino for any members who were interested. It was led by a "pit boss" named Sherlock Feldman (I kid you not; that was his real name). He looked and acted exactly like someone Hollywood might cast for the part. The security features were extremely impressive. I later learned that the Hilton was disappointed with our meeting because revenue in the casino was well down that week. I could have warned them about that because I knew from previous experience that our members would go to scientific presentations from 07:00 to 22:00 and then go back to someone's room to look at another slide or two.

Elvis Presley was the featured entertainer at the Hilton that week, and his shows were well attended.

As president of the academy, I shared with Marie the presidential suite in the Hilton, which included every luxury and service we could imagine. When the meeting ended, we had decided to spend an additional night in Las Vegas before making a trip to the Grand Canyon. The Hilton was pleased to oblige us—with a regular room. That restored us quickly to reality!

Most academy past presidents tend to back off or disappear entirely after their term; I seem to have been one of the exceptions. In 1976, Don Mills and I were co-chairs of a committee that developed a code of ethics for the academy. Once it was accepted in 1977, I was appointed a member of the new Ethics Committee and served on it until 1994. From 1982 until 1994, I was its chair, which required many hours investigating and presiding over hearings of allegations of nonethical behavior by members of AAFS. (This included one involving a pathologist from Texas who wrote autopsy reports without the bother of actually performing the procedure. The local funeral directors were quite content with this, as it made their work so much easier.)

In 1986, Don Mills was academy president when the Ministry of Public Security in China invited the academy to participate in an international scientific exchange. Don asked me to serve with him as co-leader. He and his wife led half the group of about sixty-five that traveled to Beijing, Shenyang, Guilin, and Guangzhou, while Marie and I led the other half to Beijing,

Figure 16.5 AAFS China tour 1986.

Shanghai, Hangzhou, and Guangzhou. In addition to lectures at each location, we had the opportunity to visit the forensic labs and have discussions, through interpreters, with the staff. We found some of the labs, for example, Beijing and Guangzhou, to be well equipped and staffed with well-educated people, while others were quite basic. What was lacking in all of them was experience with actual cases. Forensic science evidence is hardly required in a country where the population is so large and crowded that there are twenty eyewitnesses to virtually every crime! At the conclusion of our visit, we recommended that they send people to North America where they could get experience with real cases, a recommendation that does not reflect well on North American society.

Our groups did have some time for sightseeing and found many impressive and attractive sights. We also visited with many members of the population at large, who seemed happy with their lot and anxious to practice their English with us. The Great Wall was undoubtedly the highlight of our tour and exemplified what we concluded about China; if they decide to do something, even if it may not be the wisest thing to do, they have the population to do it. The Great Wall was built to keep out invading hordes from the north. However, it was built through mountains that were already serving that purpose. Its design was to permit horses and riders to ride eight abreast across its entire length, despite the fact that many of the inclines are so steep that steps were required, steps that would preclude the passage of any horse!

I also served as a member, again with Ken Field, of the Strategic/Long Term Planning Committee from 1989 to 2009 and, as its chair in 2007–2008, co-chaired a review and update of the code of ethics and its procedures. Having been president for the silver anniversary meeting, I was asked to chair a committee to plan celebrations for the golden anniversary meeting in San Francisco in 1998. In this role, I learned something about the cost of entertainment.

I had the grand idea that a golden anniversary celebration in San Francisco in the Golden State should have as its banquet entertainer Tony Bennett, who "left his heart in San Francisco." We found that he was available, but his fee would have been many multiples of the total budget for the entire meeting. On top of the fee, he required first-class airfare from New York for the members of his entourage. We decided that if he wanted to get his heart back, he would have to do so on his own.

In the end, I was quite pleased that the academy board agreed to confer an honorary membership on Professor Alec Jeffreys (now Professor Sir Alec), the developer of forensic applications of DNA, from the University of Leicester. He agreed to be our banquet speaker, and we were all enthralled. We learned that his research had nothing to do with forensic science; he was looking for the human copy of the myoglobin gene in grey seals when one Monday morning he noticed large variations in patterns on an autorad and almost immediately recognized their potential for what for him was a foreign field, forensic science. The paper he published in 1985 about his discovery included a massive understatement: "We anticipate that these DNA 'fingerprints' can be used in forensic applications."

As part of the golden anniversary celebrations, Ken Field, with the help of a few others, including me, produced a book describing significant events in the first fifty years of the academy's existence. My chapter was a review of the scientific programs during those years, and one of the things that struck me as I went through the old programs was how quickly after a new scientific discovery was made that papers describing forensic applications of it appeared on the AAFS scientific program. For example, Alec Jeffreys's DNA discovery was published in *Nature* in March 1985, and the first paper describing a forensic application was presented at the February 1987 academy meeting. Also, in a section of the chapter I titled "Gee, I Wish I Had Heard That One" I outlined some of the creative titles some authors came up with, such as "Suicide by Clamshell: A Case Study of Shell Shock," "Killer Piano: Who Needs a High Note?" or my favorite,

"Three Strikes and the Seven Dwarfs: Feces, Bugs, and Little Green Men in the Land of Snow White." I have no idea what they were about.

One of the developments I took great pleasure in was something Ken Field and I came up with in 1980, "The Last Word Society," which would be devoted to presentations on unusual historical cases for which there probably can be no last word. It began in a small room one afternoon with Ken presenting his research on the mystery of whether the body under the statue of John Paul Jones in the U.S. Naval Academy Library in Annapolis is, in fact, that of John Paul Jones. That prompted me to present the following year my story about the whereabouts of Canadian artist Tom Thomson's remains. These seemed to inspire interest in others, and within a couple of years, the Last Word Society became a regular evening session at AAFS meetings, held in the largest meeting room available with standing-room-only crowds. Many of these presentations are the most scholarly presented at the meetings. Three of my contributions will appear in Chapters 17 through 19.

AAFS has been an important part of my professional life for almost sixty years. Although I have continued to attend the annual meetings (usually accompanied by Marie) and am occasionally invited to make presentations, the meetings are now mostly just social occasions for me since the science has pretty much passed me by. My only professional commitment is as a member of the foundation's "Think Tank" Committee, which tries to identify emerging technology that may have specific applications in forensic science sometime in the future.

Committee on Alcohol and Other Drugs, National Safety Council

This committee (originally the Committee on Tests for Intoxication) was established in the mid-1930s to bring together prominent researchers in the field of alcohol and traffic safety to discuss and provide advice on a critical issue for the Traffic Division of the National Safety Council (NSC). This committee became the premier source of standards for the use of chemical tests for alcohol, both blood and breath, in the enforcement of driving while impaired (DWI) laws in the United States and Canada. It (in cooperation with a committee of the American Medical Association) was the source of the legal limit of 0.15% blood alcohol concentration (BAC) that became widely recognized in the 1940s and 1950s.

At my first academy meeting in 1958, I also attended the NSC committee meeting (which was held at the same time and place) and became a member in 1960. At these meetings, I had the good fortune to become associated with some remarkable leaders in this field, including Professor Rolla Harger of Indiana University (IU), who had invented the first practical breath-testing device, the Drunkometer, in 1937; Professor Robert Forney Sr., also of IU; Dr. Herman Heise; Dr. Irving Sunshine; Professor Kurt Dubowski; Dr. Morton Mason; and particularly Professor Robert F. Borkenstein, the inventor of the Breathalyzer.

I became very involved with the activities of the committee, including chairing a special subcommittee that drafted performance and operational standards for roadside screening devices when they were first introduced around 1974 and serving as chair of the committee itself from 1977 to 1979. In recognition of this and other activities, I was awarded the NSC's Robert F. Borkenstein Award in 1997. This award recognizes individuals "who, through a lifetime of service, have made outstanding contributions to the field of alcohol/drugs about traffic and transportation safety."

American Society of Crime Laboratory Directors

As noted in Chapter 12, until Briggs White became assistant director of the FBI in charge of the entire FBI Laboratory, they chose to not have close involvement with state and local labs in the United States. The staff of the lab was therefore somewhat professionally isolated. Dr. White recognized that this was not a desirable situation and, in 1973, he persuaded the then director of the FBI, Clarence Kelly, to invite about fifty lab directors from around the United States and Canada to attend a meeting at the FBI Academy in Quantico, Virginia.

The purpose of the meeting was to open channels of communication between crime laboratories around the country and the FBI. The meeting was well received and led to an agreement that an association of crime laboratory directors should be created. The primary focus would be on matters related to organization and management. A steering committee was formed that drafted a constitution and, in the fall of 1974, the American Society of Crime Laboratory Directors (ASCLD) was born. It held its first meeting at Quantico, and Briggs White was elected the first president.

All of the early meetings were subsidized by the FBI and were held at Quantico, where we shared rooms in a dormitory, made our own beds, and dined in the cafeteria. During our times there, the normal training activities of the academy would continue, so our discussions were constantly punctuated with gunfire from the multiple shooting ranges or our sleep might be interrupted when we became unknowing subjects of a surprise nighttime raid exercise. I also became aware of how protective state organizations are of their independence from federal agencies. When it came time to nominate members for the board of directors of ASCLD, the members were very careful to ensure that state and local lab directors formed a majority and no more than one or two federal lab directors would be elected. Fortunately, as the organization matured those battles were forgotten. (I was never aware of what, if any, discussions took place about the election of the first non–U.S. citizen, me, as president in 1977.)

ASCLD became a very influential organization in the United States because its members recognized the importance of political action and were quite prepared to sponsor or encourage political contacts on issues that were of concern to forensic science, usually related to federal funding. It also introduced two programs that have had a huge impact on quality assurance in forensic labs, proficiency testing, and laboratory accreditation.

In the 1960s and 1970s, if a lab director was asked about the quality of the work in his lab, the response would be something like, "Well, we have never had a problem!" If then asked, "Have you ever looked for one?" there would be a pause followed by, "Uh, well not really." Routine proficiency testing was not widespread. In 1974, the Forensic Sciences Foundation Inc. initiated a research project "to determine the feasibility of proficiency testing as a tool to uncover problem areas in laboratory performance." Collaborative Testing Services Inc. (CTS) was retained as the contractor, and a group of eight forensic scientists, most of whom were members of ASCLD, was appointed as the Project Advisory Committee (PAC). Unfortunately, before the final report of the project, which was generally positive, was published in 1978, the federal agency that had funded it, the Law Enforcement Assistance Administration (LEAA), issued a press release that was highly critical of crime lab performance.

Despite the resultant furor, most ASCLD members recognized the value of regular laboratory proficiency testing and asked CTS to continue the program on a subscription basis. ASCLD appointed another PAC to oversee the program. In the early years, the PAC members produced the tests that CTS distributed. That program grew rapidly both nationally and internationally and resulted in a very significant improvement in lab performance over the years. Because of my strong belief in the value of proficiency testing, I served as a member of the PAC from 1978 to 2000 and as its chair from 1981 to 1991. Following my retirement from CFS in 1994, I have continued my association with CTS by serving as an adviser on its internal quality assurance practices.

As mentioned, in the early years members of the PAC produced the tests that, in my case at least, meant involving members of our family. For footwear impression tests, I would show the samples to some of our grandchildren, and if they could get the right answer, I would decide that the test was too easy. Marie was my adviser on textile fiber tests, and in one DNA test, I "volunteered" the entire family. It was a "reverse paternity" test, such as would be used in cases where there is DNA from a crime scene but no body was located to obtain known DNA samples from. In such cases, samples are requested from parents and siblings of the suspected victim and used to "create" the DNA profile of the missing person. For this proficiency test, we therefore needed a family to provide all the test samples and our family agreed to donate their blood. The test worked very well, but when I described to a colleague how it was produced, his reaction was "You did what? Did you even think about it?" No, I hadn't, but our family now is one of the few that has DNA proof that all of our familial relationships have been confirmed scientifically!

If that hypothetical lab director who was asked about proficiency was also asked, "Is your laboratory a good laboratory?" his immediate response would be, "Of course." If then asked, "Who says so?" there would be some hesitation followed by, "Well, I guess I do," and then a sudden recognition that perhaps that wasn't quite good enough. In the mid-1970s, partly as a result of what was being revealed by proficiency testing, ASCLD recognized that action was needed to establish standards of operation for crime laboratories to enhance public confidence in their work. As a result, one of the early ASCLD committees was assigned this task. For approximately four years, it worked on various programs that could be used to evaluate and improve the quality of laboratory operations. It eventually decided that an accreditation program based on external peer review would be the best possible means of achieving that goal.

Each year the committee presented the results of its research and development for that year to the ASCLD membership for input and approval. Finally, in the fall of 1980, the concept of a program of laboratory accreditation was approved by the membership. In June 1981, the committee was expanded to include representatives from the National Association of Chiefs of Police and the National District Attorneys Association and was transformed into the first board of directors of the American Society of Crime Laboratory Directors/Laboratory Accreditation Board (ASCLD/LAB).

Despite the overlap in their names, ASCLD and ASCLD/LAB were separate and independent organizations. [In 2016, ASCLD/LAB became affiliated with ANSI-ASQ National Accreditation Board (ANAB)].

The accreditation process involves a laboratory having written documentation of its policies and processes, a quality control/quality assurance program, health and safety requirements, security, and evidence-handling procedures. These are inspected on site by a team of trained accreditation inspectors who search to see that the lab is doing what it says it does. A major part of the inspection is a review of case files and interviews with all staff members. The process is very rigorous, and many labs are unable to pass the inspection the first time around. They are then required to make corrections or changes to their procedures.

The first labs to go through the process were the eight labs of the Illinois State Police (ISP) system in April 1982. I was a member of that inspection team and have always admired ISP for leading the way since neither they nor our inspection team knew quite what to expect. At the first few labs, there were many disagreements that somehow would get resolved, and when we reached the next lab in the system, what had been a problem earlier had been corrected, literally overnight. Since those early inspections, we have seen good labs become even better and poor labs become good, as a result of the accreditation process.

The ASCLD/LAB program became so successful that it achieved international recognition with requests for accreditation from Australia, Canada (the Centre of Forensic Sciences in 1993 and the Northern Regional Lab in 1994), Hong Kong, Malaysia, New Zealand, and Singapore. In 2003, it adopted the internationally recognized standards of ISO 17025, supplemented with its own forensic science additional requirements.

I remained an accreditation inspector from 1982 to 2003 and led inspections of more than thirty labs, from Miami to Oregon, Chicago to Texas, and New York to Los Angeles and Melbourne, Australia. Some of these were done several times since labs had to go through the process every five years. I had no difficulty justifying (to myself, if not to some of the bureaucrats) the time spent on these inspections since I learned something in every lab I ever went into, sometimes if only how not to do something.

The ASCLD/LAB policy was that inspectors had to retire when they left their laboratory director's position. However, Bud Keaton, the executive director of ASCLD/LAB, a good friend who is the only person I know who was active in forensic science longer than I was, ignored that policy in my case and kept me active to lead inspections in "problem situations" until 2003 when I no longer felt comfortable doing so, because of the length of time I had been away from active practice.

I have always been grateful for the learning opportunities I gained from my involvement with both ASCLD and ASCLD/LAB and for the many good friends I made. Both organizations expressed their appreciation for my contributions with honors that are very special to me. In 1993, ASCLD/LAB established the Douglas M. Lucas Distinguished Service Award "for exemplary and untiring efforts to improving the quality of forensic science laboratories and for dedication to the ideals and goals of the American Society of Crime Laboratory Directors Laboratory Accreditation Board." I was the first recipient of the award. Since 1993, fourteen others have received it (it is not given every year), twelve of whom I have known very well and have been delighted to have my name associated with.

In 1999, ASCLD bestowed its highest award on me, the Briggs J. White Award for Leadership Excellence. I have truly been blessed.

International Association of Forensic Sciences

As discussed in Chapter 16, the IAFS was formally established at the international meeting in Toronto in June 1969. Credit for the conception of an

English-language meeting of forensic scientists must be given to a wonderful gentleman, Professor Frederic Thomas of the University of Ghent, Belgium, whose original idea was to provide an opportunity for pathologists interested in forensic pathology and the pathology of trauma to meet and discuss matters of mutual interest. He successfully proposed that such a meeting be held in Ghent in July 1957. The meeting was a great success, and one of the active participants, Professor Milton Helpern, chief medical examiner of New York City, volunteered to organize a second meeting in New York three years hence. His meeting added toxicology, forensic biology, and criminalistics to the program. A third meeting was organized by Professor Francis Camps in London in 1963 (the first one I attended) and a fourth by Professor Harold Gormsen in Copenhagen in 1966. It was at this meeting that it was decided that a more formal structure should be established, and this led to the founding of IAFS in Toronto in 1969.

Since 1969, international meetings have continued to be held (in English) every three years, in Edinburgh (1972), Zurich (1975), Wichita (1978), Bergen (1981), Oxford (1984), Vancouver (1987), Adelaide (1990), Dusseldorf (1993), Tokyo (1996), Los Angeles (1999), Montpellier (2002), Hong Kong (2005), New Orleans (2008), Madeira (2011), Seoul (2014), and most recently, Toronto (2017). As a past president and member of the council, one of the benefits is that my travel expenses are paid by the meeting organizers, and I have had the privilege of attending all except Zurich and Bergen.

IAFS is a unique organization; it is an association virtually in name only. It has no members, no membership fees, no budget, and no permanent secretariat, and it allows anyone registered at one of its meetings to vote on any matter raised at a business meeting; matters are rarely raised at the business meetings, which are held only infrequently. The association does have a constitution, approved in Toronto in 1969, which may be the shortest of any professional association. It simply states the aims and objectives of the association to be

- To develop the forensic sciences
- To assist forensic scientists and others to exchange scientific and technical information
- To organize meetings

IAFS accomplishes these objectives through its only activity, which is the selection of an individual to preside over the meeting and thus the choice of the venue. Its continuing success may be a result, at least in part, of the fact that it is the only worldwide organization that brings together both academics and practitioners of all the various disciplines involved in forensic science.

The governance of IAFS is quite undemocratic; a Council of Past Presidents selects the president, who determines the venue. The president, on completion of his or her meeting, automatically becomes a member of the council for life.

Each meeting is the total responsibility of the president. It must be self-financing since IAFS has no funds. The most that an incoming president can expect is some seed money from the previous meeting to cover initial start-up expenses. This amount grew from the $5,000 transferred between the Toronto and Edinburgh meetings to more than $75,000 following the Adelaide meeting. Budgets have also increased and are now close to US$1.6 million, which must be raised from grants, donations, exhibitor fees, workshops, and delegate registration fees. The president is required to submit an audited financial accounting to the council before the next meeting and transfer any resultant surplus to the succeeding president.

This is a daunting responsibility for the president, and until the 1981 meeting in Bergen, it was necessary for the council to twist arms to persuade someone to agree to take it on. In Bergen, for the first time, we had two groups competing for the presidency and had to make a choice. That has since become the norm, and the council now must review mammoth bid documents, videos, and so forth, from several bidders for each meeting and choose one that it believes has a presidential nominee with appropriate international professional stature, has the infrastructure and funding sources to successfully produce the meeting, and will involve forensic scientists from differing parts of the world.

A wonderful feature of these meetings is that each develops a unique character, representative of its location, funding, and president. Most have been roaring successes. Some personal highlights have been Oxford University in 1984, where we stayed in college residences, some of which, as the brochures described with tongue only partially in cheek, "had been modernized as recently as the late 1700s." I fantasized about who over the past 300 years might have occupied my room up under the eaves at Queen's College and had to make the same hike four floors down to the basement for hygienic necessities. Vancouver in August 1987 was incredible simply because it turned on the type of weather that, when it does occur, makes Vancouver one of the most beautiful cities in the world. Delegates wondered how much one had to pay to get a job there.

We were nervous about leaving Europe and North America for the first time and going "down under" to Adelaide. Our concern was unwarranted. The meeting there under Bill Tilston's leadership was a huge success and was memorable for Marie and I because we had a chance to go sailing in the Murray River Estuary and out to have a look at the daunting Southern Ocean. I had spent a week before the meeting doing some work for the South Australia Lab, and the SA police were very good about taking Marie with them if they had room in one of their small planes when they were flying somewhere in the state. The assistant commissioner who asked me if she would like to do this rather hesitantly asked, "How much does she weigh?" These were really small planes! As a result, Marie saw more of South Australia than most South Australians ever do, including aboriginal lands, because many of her fellow passengers were aboriginal police being flown to their bases. She and her police pilot (who took her sightseeing locally while they waited for whatever business had taken them to a site to be completed) stumbled upon a homicide scene at Bordertown, which he quickly whisked her away from.

Dusseldorf in 1993 was one of the few disasters. It was held at the University of Dusseldorf, which we had been looking forward to but which proved to be quite inadequate. The most memorable problem was that there was no auditorium large enough to hold all the delegates. However, we had been persuaded that they had found a creative solution to this problem, an enormous circus tent. It seemed a great idea until the first speaker turned on the projector to show the slides which are an essential component of virtually every science presentation. Unfortunately, the tent was waterproof but not sunproof. It could not be darkened, and the slides were impossible to see.

On the other hand, the 1999 meeting at the University of California in Los Angeles was highlighted by an outdoor gala banquet under a full moon and stars that shone magnificently on the beautiful campus surrounded by imposing buildings. A backup plan in case of inclement weather had not even been considered. In Montpellier, in 2002 the ancient university in its picturesque Mediterranean setting was a highlight on its own but was topped by an elegant medieval banquet in an ancient monastery that had been converted into a winery. Hong Kong in 2005 is hard to top, but for me the highlight was the large number of delegates from mainland China who we met for the first time.

At the Hong Kong meeting, on August 26, 2005, the council awarded the 2008 meeting to New Orleans. Three days later, on August 29, Hurricane Katrina struck New Orleans, wiping out large parts of the city, including the Superdome Hyatt Regency Hotel where President Ron Singer had planned to hold the meeting. Nevertheless, he pulled it off at the Marriott on the Mississippi River, and Marie and I enjoyed a New Orleans tradition, breakfast at Brennan's, the most delicious (and expensive) breakfast (or meal of any kind) we have ever had.

In 2011, the nineteenth IAFS meeting was held in Funchal, the capital of the Portuguese island of Madeira. The venue was the Pestana Casino Park Hotel and Congress Centre, a beautiful modern facility on the harbor. This was the first time IAFS had ever held its meeting at a resort-type venue, near a casino (by sheer coincidence, delegates had to walk past the casino to get from the hotel to the Congress Centre), and at a location quite so remote. Madeira, although part of Portugal, is located about 650 km off the northwest coast of Africa about one and a half-hour's flying time from Lisbon. Despite (or perhaps because of) the location, this was the largest and perhaps most successful IAFS meeting, ever with approximately 1,700 delegates from 109 countries registered. Every continent except Antarctica was represented. A display of the flags of all the countries was prominent in the venue, on the literature and scrolling across the projector screens, prompting informal contests of "name that country."

The highlight of the 2014 meeting was its president, Dr. Heesun Chung, the first female president of IAFS. She was the most elegant, charming, and gracious of all the presidents, in addition to being a very effective organizer and leader. For the first time, the budget for the Meeting exceeded $1 million, so she was also an excellent fund-raiser. Seoul is a modern, very dynamic city in marked contrast to its northern neighbor just fifty kilometers away.

The twenty-first meeting returned to Toronto, the first time for a repeat location. Professor Michael Pollanen, Ontario's chief forensic pathologist, ran a highly successful meeting in the Sheraton Centre Hotel. One of several unique features at this meeting was the presentation of the thirty-nine preconference workshops off-site in the beautiful new Forensic Services and Coroner's Complex (FSCC). Although this required transporting the participants about fifteen kilometers each way, this did not deter participants as the workshops "sold out." This location permitted "hands-on" activities for some of the workshops in actual laboratory facilities. During the conference itself, 1,440 registrants from eighty-six countries attended.

At the Adelaide meeting in 1990, to recognize the occasion of the first gathering of IAFS outside Europe and North America, the organizing committee established the Adelaide Medal to be awarded to a "distinguished international forensic scientist." I was honored to be the first recipient "for scientific achievements that have had a marked influence on the forensic sciences from an international perspective." Other recipients since then have included Dr. Ray Williams, director of the Metropolitan London Police (Scotland Yard) Lab, in 1993; Brian Culliford, an outstanding British forensic serologist and developer of many of the genetic markers used before DNA came on the scene, in 1996; Dr. Ian Evett, a forensic statistician with the UK Forensic Science Service, in 1999; Alastair Ross, head of the National Institute of Forensic Science in Australia, in 2002; Professor Sir Alec Jeffreys, of the University of Leicester and developer of DNA profiling, in 2005; Professor William Bass, renowned forensic anthropologist at the University of Tennessee and developer of the "Body Farm," in 2008; Professor Angel Carracedo, of the Institute of Legal Medicine in the University of Santiago de Compostela in Spain, in 2011; Dr. Tony Raymond, manager of the Strategic Forensic Sciences Branch and chief scientist of the Forensic Services Group of the New South Wales Police Force in Australia, in 2014; and Professor Cristina Cattaneo of the University of Milan, in 2017.

17 Last Word Society Stories No. 1 (1979) "Was Tom Thomson Murdered?" or "Whose Bones Are Buried under That Spruce Tree?

As mentioned in Chapter 16, one of the initiatives for the American Academy of Forensic Sciences (AAFS) I took the greatest pleasure in was something Ken Field and I came up with in 1979, which we named "The Last Word Society." It was devoted to descriptions of unusual cases, usually historical, in which the presenter had a personal involvement or had done extensive research, stories for which there probably could be no "last word." We emphasized that such presentations were "stories" and not formal "papers." What follows in the next three chapters are three of the stories I told. They have been edited somewhat from the original to include relevant new information that has developed since these stories were presented. The first was about Canada's most famous artist, Tom Thomson.

Any list of things uniquely Canadian would be relatively short. Although it might include Hudson's Bay blankets and custom-built lacrosse sticks, it is unlikely that most people's lists would include art. There is, however, a readily identifiable Canadian art form, other than Eskimo carvings. Most Canadians know there once was something called the "Group of Seven."[1] Almost every elementary school art room has a print of *West Wind* or *Jack Pine* hanging prominently, and virtually every Canadian knows they were painted by someone named Tom Thomson.

This is a story about this unique Canadian artist, about his death and the ongoing speculation about where he is buried. Because mysteries make the best stories, there is an element of mystery about this story, and probably always will be. It is based fundamentally on the recollections of just three or four people, recollections that, with only a few exceptions, did not begin to be recorded until at least thirteen years and, in some cases, almost forty years after Thomson's death in 1917.

Tom Thomson was born in Claremont, Ontario, in 1877 and raised on a small farm at Leith near Owen Sound. He never received any formal training in art, and his very early work reflects this. In 1904, he joined an engraving firm in Toronto, which brought him into association with a group of weekend artists.

A trip in 1912 to Algonquin Park was the catalyst for his metamorphosis from tentative dauber to a remarkable intuitive artist, well ahead of his colleagues, who were probably more hindered than helped by their academic training. Canadian painting at the time consisted almost entirely of landscapes, pastel views of bucolic scenes invariably showing a tree, a stream, and a cow or horse. Structure outshone color, and the north was ignored; after all, no one lived there! Thomson's genius was in discovering the ruggedness of the reality and in introducing real color to his work.

In the spring of 1913, Tom quit his job in Toronto and returned to Algonquin, where he quickly became a fixture in the small lumbering community of Mowat on Canoe Lake. For the next four years, his pattern was to sketch in the park in spring and fall, accept what work he could get as a fishing guide or park ranger in the summer, and return to Toronto in the winter to live in an old construction shack behind the Studio Building in the Rosedale ravine in downtown Toronto. There he would develop some of his sketches into major canvasses. The first of these, *Northern Lake*, was sold to the Ontario government in 1913 for $250. The National Gallery of Canada bought its first Thomson, *Northern River*, for $500 in 1915. His two accepted masterpieces, *Jack Pine* and *West Wind*, were painted in the winter of 1916–1917 from sketches made at Grand Lake in the park. The former went to the National Gallery for $750 in 1918, and the latter to the Art Gallery of Ontario in 1926 for $1,500.[2] These, at the time, substantial prices for the work of a previously unknown artist were quite remarkable and indicated that his work was becoming well recognized.

Figure 17.1 Thomson the artist.

Figure 17.2 Thomson the fishing guide.

July 1917

The mystery began on the evening of July 7, 1917. Most of the players in the story agreed (although not until years later) that there was a party, at which considerable alcohol was consumed, in a cabin on Canoe Lake. From that point on, discrepancies develop between the stories told over the years, by the various participants, and also between those told at different times by individual participants. A quarrel developed, either between Thomson and Martin Blecher Jr., a young American cottager, or between Thomson and Shannon Fraser, the proprietor of Mowat Lodge where Thomson usually stayed when at Canoe Lake. If the quarrel was with Fraser, it was about money that Fraser was alleged to owe Tom, and blows were struck. If it was with Blecher, it was likely over a woman, Winnifred (Winnie) Trainor, and a threat was made by Blecher against Thomson.

In 1917, Ms. Trainor was thirty-seven years of age and living with her parents in Huntsville. They had a cottage on Canoe Lake, next door to the Blechers. Thomson and Winnie were known to be good friends, he often stayed in the Trainor cottage when the family was absent, and he stored some of his belongings and sketches there. Some residents claimed that Tom and Winnie were engaged to be married; others denied this. The evidence is at best conflicted.

Although memories of the events of the evening of July 7 differ, the story about a quarrel became the source of much speculation in the ensuing days, weeks, months, and years.

Figure 17.3 Winnie Trainor.

Sunday, July 8 dawned with brisk easterly winds bringing light rain. By noon, the rain had stopped and, shortly before one o'clock (according to Fraser), Thomson set out in his canoe from Mowat Lodge bound for Gill Lake to catch a big trout. Fraser said he watched him head south down the lake until he rounded Big Wapomeo Island about 3/4 of a mile away. (See the map sketch Figure 17.5.) No known person saw (or admits to having seen) Thomson alive again.

Figure 17.4 Mark Robinson.

Later that afternoon, Blecher and his sister are said to have seen an overturned canoe floating near Big Wapomeo. They didn't, however, investigate or mention it to anyone until the following day. Whether this was Tom's distinctively colored canoe or one previously reported missing from another lodge depends on whose recollections are to be believed. Regardless, Tom's canoe was recovered on July 10 behind Big Wapomeo. Some said a small packet of food was still in the bow and the portaging paddle was lashed in position. Tom's working paddle and fishing gear were never found.

Despite an intensive search organized by the park ranger, Mark Robinson, whose diary contains the only contemporaneous notes of events, nothing further was found until the morning of July 16, when Dr. G.W. Howland, a professor of neurology at the University of Toronto, spotted something in the water just out from the cottage he was staying at on Little Wapomeo Island. Two fishermen passing in a canoe identified it as Tom's body and took it to shore on Big Wapomeo, where it was tied to some tree roots at the water's edge. Because of its condition, they did not want to remove it from the water.

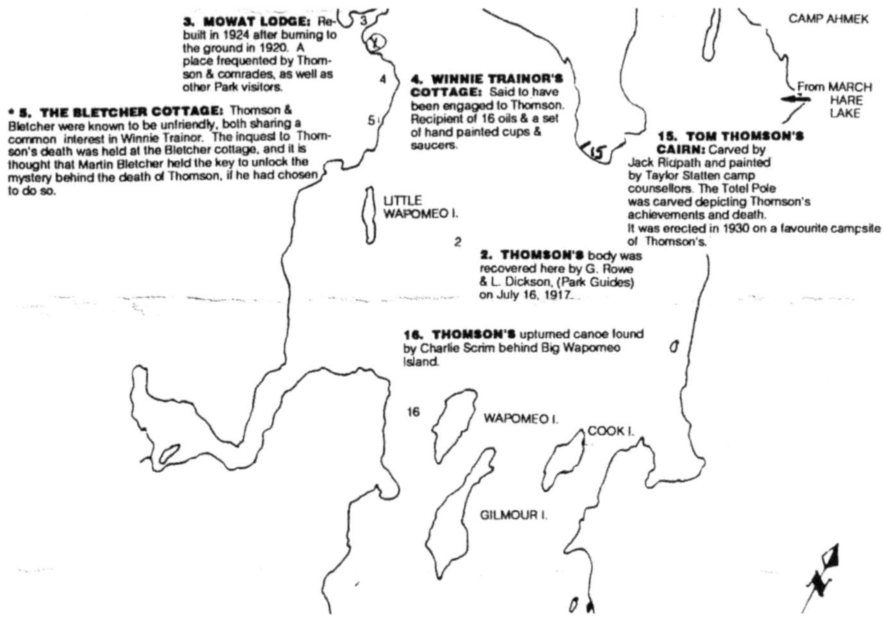

Figure 17.5 The Canoe Lake area of Thomson's death.

The nearest coroner, Dr. A.E. Ranney of North Bay, was notified and the depressing wait for him began. He did not arrive on the evening train as expected, and by the morning of July 17, Robinson could not abide the thought of the effect of another July day's sun on the already badly decomposed body of his friend. He was instructed by his superior, G.W. Bartlett, the Algonquin Park superintendent, to have Dr. Howland examine the body and then proceed with its burial. Thus, another log was added to the fires of future speculation. (It must be remembered that this was 1917; law enforcement resources as we know them today did not exist. Although the Ontario Provincial Police (OPP) had been established in 1909—with only forty-five members—by 1917 its complement was still probably less than 100, dispersed across the entire province of Ontario. Superintendent Bartlett was therefore the supreme authority in the park.)

Dr. Howland removed the clothes from the body and—given the conditions—made only an external examination of it. He noted a "four-inch linear bruise" on the right temple as the only mark of violence. Air was issuing from the mouth, and there was some "bleeding" from the right ear. Another complication was added when Robinson recorded in his diary that the bruise was on the left temple.

Two undertakers arrived by train from nearby Kearney. They cleaned and embalmed the body, wrapped it in a shroud, and placed it in an oak casket inside a rough cedar box. That afternoon, the coffin was carried in Fraser's horse-drawn cart (which, ironically, had originally been a hearse) up the hill behind Mowat Lodge to a tiny cemetery where two earlier graves were marked and enclosed with a picket fence. There, a small, hastily assembled group attended the burial; Martin Blecher Sr. read the service.

Figure 17.6 The Canoe Lake grave site ca. 1930.

The coroner arrived on that evening train—too late to examine the body. He was served dinner by Mrs. Blecher and then convened an informal inquiry (it was not a formal coroner's inquest since there was no jury) in the Blecher cottage about 22:30. He heard testimony from Dr. Howland and five others. Dr. Howland said the blow causing the bruise on the temple was not enough to cause death, and by midnight the coroner reached the only possible conclusion: "accidental death due to drowning." He returned to North Bay on the morning train on July 18 and remained content with his verdict for the next thirty-nine years. Again, we must remember that this was 1917 in a remote area. The informality of the proceedings was the norm for the time and place. Roy MacGregor in his 2010 book (see below) thought it suspicious that the coroner's report could never be found. In fact, there probably never was a formal report other than the two simple forms, "Coroner's Warrant to Take Possession of Body" and "Warrant to Bury After a View," required by the provincial registrar general. There was no centralized chief coroner's office or record depository in Ontario until the mid-1960s.

The evening train on July 18 arrived with the foundation for another mystery. H.W. Churchill, an undertaker from Huntsville, got off the train with a metal casket and instructions to exhume the body and send it to Leith for burial in the Thomson family plot. His services had been arranged by Winnie Trainor on behalf of the Thomsons. She was very upset that Robinson had refused to allow her to see the body and that he had ordered its burial before the coroner had the opportunity to examine it.

In 1956 (i.e., thirty-nine years later), a prominent resident of Canoe Lake, Taylor Statten, recorded notes that included one stating that Shannon Fraser (who people at Canoe Lake described as an unreliable source of information) had claimed that "Churchill asked to be left alone at the grave on the hillside with instructions to be picked up at midnight." At the station the next morning, as the sealed casket was loaded on the train, Mark Robinson, according to an interview he gave in 1953, noted that the weight distribution didn't feel right. (There is nothing about this in his diary notes.) When he went back to the grave to inspect it, "there was only a hole such as a groundhog would have left." Perhaps in the sandy soil where Churchill was supposed to have removed the body from the coffin, returned the now empty coffin to the grave, and filled it in, that is about all that might be expected.

Tom Thomson's body (or at least the metal casket brought by train from Canoe Lake to Owen Sound) was buried at Leith on July 21 following a small family funeral. And that was the end of the story—until 1956.

In the ensuing years, as Thomson's artistic legacy and reputation grew, legends about him developed that have expanded over the years—and continue to do so. Like most legends, the truth about the dead is sometimes distorted by the fantasies of the living. Some examples follow:

Legend: Tom Thomson founded the legendary Group of Seven.

Fact: Although he knew all the members, the group was not formed until 1920, three years after his death. It was disbanded in 1933 and by then ten artists had been included in it.

Legend: Thomson was a prophet of the north.

Fact: When Tom visited his brother in Seattle, he was farther north than he would ever get in Canada. His sketching was all done within 250 miles of Toronto, and his major canvasses were painted within a half mile of Yonge and Bloor, a major intersection in downtown Toronto.

Legend: Thomson was the classic example of the impecunious painter whose work was not recognized until after his death.

Fact: Although not famous, the Toronto newspapers did cover his disappearance and the subsequent discovery of his body. Within a year of beginning serious painting, he had sold a major work for $250—a not inconsiderable sum in 1913. Within two years, his work was hung in the National Gallery of Canada. It must be acknowledged, however, that by 1922 there were still 145 of his sketches stored in the Studio Building, and many went begging for $25 each.

Legend: Tom Thomson was an expert woodsman, swimmer, and canoeist who could not possibly have drowned accidentally while canoeing on a small lake. He must therefore have been murdered, either shot or struck with a paddle across the temple. The "German sympathizer draft dodger" Blecher was the likely suspect.

Fact: Although competent on and in the water, Thomson was neither infallible nor unsinkable. Blecher was an American citizen who was drafted in November 1917 but failed to report.

Legend: The second undertaker, Churchill, never did exhume the body in the dead of night but instead put some sand in the casket, which was then sealed and sent to Leith. Therefore, Canada's most famous artist's remains are still where he would undoubtedly have preferred them to be, on a hillside overlooking Canoe Lake in Algonquin Park.

Fact: Who knows? Read on.

The latter two legends were fueled by the establishment in 1921 by Taylor Statten and his wife of two large children's summer camps on Canoe Lake, Camp Ahmek for boys and Camp Wapomeo for girls. Many generations of campers, including Pierre Trudeau (a future prime minister of Canada), grew up with tales told around the campfire at night by the veteran ranger Mark Robinson. Like vintage red wine, the stories improved with age.

For example, in his diary entry for July 17, 1917, Robinson wrote only that there was a bruise on the left temple "evidently caused by falling on a rock." The note for July 18 says simply that "Mr. Churchill, the undertaker from Huntsville, arrived and took up the body. The body went out on the morning train to Owen Sound." However, by 1930, in the transcript of a lengthy interview now in the National Gallery's archives, Robinson's "facts" had changed only slightly, but a new note was added. The bruise and the exhumation were the same, but now there was a description of Thomson's fishing line mysteriously wrapped several times around his ankle. He added, "Thomson was said to have drowned. It may be quite true, but the mystery remains."

Then, in another interview taped in 1953 two years before his death at age eighty-eight, Robinson's description of the events of July 1917 had changed markedly and, despite the long interval, contained much more detail:

> Tom was found only about 125 feet from shore and the water there is only 35 feet deep. It shouldn't have taken eight days for the body to have surfaced.
> There were 16 or 17 wraps of fishing line on his left ankle.
> Across the left temple, there was a mark as if struck by the edge of a paddle.
> The casket wasn't heavy enough to have had a body in it.
> I still think his body is over there buried just to the north of the other two graves.

Much has been made over the years about the fishing line said to have been wrapped around the ankle. For some, it has been a sinister indicator of a weight attached to the body to hold it down; for others, it was simply how Tom managed his trolling line when fishing in his canoe; and for still others, it was something Tom did to support an injured ankle. I believe there is a simpler explanation.

The body was floating in the lake, and two men in a canoe were asked to get it ashore. How would they do so? They certainly would not attempt to lift it into the canoe; they would probably tow it behind the canoe. What would fishers in a canoe use to tow a body? Their fishing line would be right at hand. How would they attach the tow line to the body? They might wrap it several times around an ankle. How would they attach the body to the shore when they got it there? With the tow line.

One of Lucas's laws is when there is a choice between a simple and a complex scenario, go with the simple one and you will be correct most of the time! There may be nothing sinister in the stories about the fishing line around the ankle if it even was there in the first place.

September–October 1956

On a cold, rainy September 30, 1956, four men who had grown up with all the legends decided to test Mark Robinson's recollections. One of them, William Little, superintendent of a provincial reformatory, described their actions in a book he published in 1970, *The Tom Thomson Mystery*.[3] In the sandy soil a few feet north of the two marked graves on the hill, they dug to a depth of six feet. Nothing. Moving north a few feet, they dug again to no avail. As their energy faded, their doubts rose. About twenty-one feet north of a distinctive birch tree that sheltered the marked graves and appears in the photos they took that day (and was still there in 1996 when Rick Libman and I explored the site), they noticed a slight depression under a spruce tree. One last time, they started to dig and, about five feet down, found pieces of dressed wood, both hard and soft. As their excitement mounted, they found a bone and the immensity of their discovery struck them. They took the bone to Dr. Harry Ebbs, a Toronto doctor who was spending the weekend at his cottage. He confirmed that it was a human tibia.

The discovery was reported to the OPP (which by then had a detachment at nearby Burk's Falls), who arranged for a thorough examination of the site. On October 5, Dr. Ebbs, Corporal Archie Rodger of the OPP, and Dr. Noble Sharpe, medical director of the Attorney General's Laboratory, carefully excavated the grave and sifted the soil. They found fragments of dressed wood (later identified as oak and cedar), some maple coffin handles, and a metal plate engraved "At Rest." No clothing, buttons, boots, boot nails, or any indication of clothing other than a fragment of one sock were found. Almost an entire human skeleton was recovered, with the most exciting finding being a skull with a round hole about ¾ inch in diameter in the left temple. Everyone present (except Dr. Sharpe, who was withholding judgment until he could examine the bones in detail) was convinced that the grave was Thomson's original grave and the skeleton was that of Canada's most famous artist. Dr. Sharpe returned to the laboratory with the bones.

Unfortunately, as is often the case in the real world, the obvious quickly became the obscure.

Forensic anthropology (which involves, among other things, the examination of skeletal remains) did not exist as a unique discipline in 1956. (It did not become a section in the AAFS until 1973.) The few practitioners were employed in museums or universities. Dr. Sharpe freely acknowledged that, in 1956, he had only limited experience in the examination of skeletal remains (although he later becomes much more knowledgeable). For that reason, he consulted with several other specialists as he examined the Canoe Lake skeleton.

No bullet was found in the skull, no mark on the inner table of the skull opposite the ¾-inch hole, and no radiating fractures.[4] The hole was therefore not likely a bullet hole. (Regardless of the confusion about whether the hole was on the left or the right side, it is doubtful that Dr. Howland, a very experienced neurologist, would have described a surface injury to the temple area of a body that resulted in a ¾-inch diameter circular hole in the skull as a "four-inch linear bruise.")

One of Dr. Sharpe's consultants was Dr. J.C.B. Grant, retired professor of anatomy at the University of Toronto and author of one of the most widely

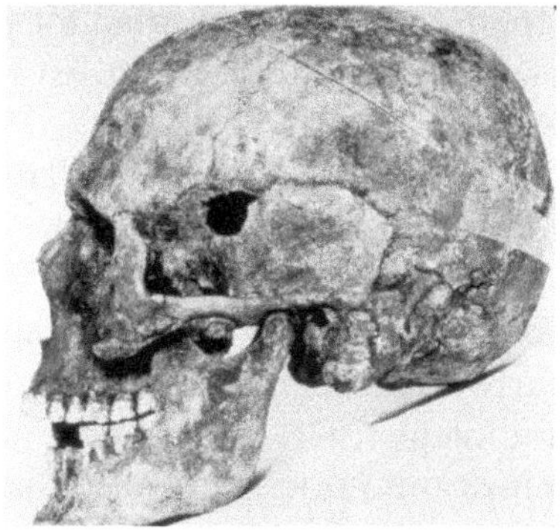

Figure 17.7 The Canoe Lake skull.

respected textbooks on anatomy at the time. In 1956, he was then head of the archeology department at the Royal Ontario Museum (ROM). Dr. Grant concluded that the skull was Mongoloid and, considering the location, probably North American Indian. The length of the femurs indicated a height of five foot eight inches ± two inches. The sacrum and pubic bone identified the bones as male. The epiphyseal lines were not completely consolidated on the upper ends of the humerus, along with the iliac crests and the first two pieces of the sacrum. Along with the well-preserved face of the symphysis pubis, the youthful appearance of the muscle markings and the absence of incipient lipping at the margins of the joints indicated an age of less than thirty years. The absence of caries in the typically Indian "shovel-shaped" teeth supported this estimate. Dr. Sharpe noted that the bones were fairly light from loss of

Figure 17.8 Dr. Noble Sharpe.

calcium and estimated them to have been buried for fifteen to twenty years. Dr. Grant's opinion was that they had been buried for "over ten or fifteen years, but how much longer I cannot say."

Professor Eric Linnell of the Department of Neuropathology examined the hole in the skull and reported that it was "in the classic position for the operation of trephining of the skull for hemorrhage following a head injury. The wound, although not due to a bullet could be caused by a sharp instrument such as a pick, a narrow hammerhead, or an arrow."

X-rays taken by a radiologist, Dr. A. Singleton, after the skull cap was removed established for him and Professor Linnell that the hole "is a surgical trephine opening."

Thus, instead of a thirty-nine-year-old six-foot Caucasian who had been shot in the head, the remains, in a casket and rough box undoubtedly similar to Thomson's (if not the actual originals), in a grave close to Thomson's original grave (if not the actual grave), were those of a younger, shorter, indigenous male who may have had skull surgery shortly before his death. Any record of such a person has never been found.

These findings rapidly cooled the excitement that had been building publicly after the discovery of the skeleton. However, their validity was never accepted by the original search party and others who continued to nurture the legends.

Pressure to open the grave at Leith to confirm Tom's presence there was squelched by the attorney general, who refused an exhumation order on the grounds that the family was satisfied as to the whereabouts of the body. A brother of Thomson's is said to have recalled that there had been a distinct odor about the casket when it arrived at Leith. (Some speculated that Tom's father had opened the casket to establish that it indeed contained Tom's body. That was never confirmed.) An indignant, but unfortunately now senile undertaker, insisted that he had been assisted in the exhumation by four men assigned by Mark Robinson. Of greater interest, the now elderly Winnie Trainor called Dr. Sharpe while he was examining the bones and insisted that she had been engaged to Tom, that she had arranged for the second undertaker, and that her father and brother had helped to exhume the body. When these recollections were described, it was almost forty years since the event.

The bones were returned to Canoe Lake by Corporal Rodger, who marked the grave site with a wooden cross he had made.

A TV Film and Some Books

Although I had been vaguely aware of the Canoe Lake skeleton story from discussions with Dr. Sharpe, my interest was honed in 1968 and 1969 when the Canadian Broadcasting Corporation (CBC) produced a visually magnificent television film about Thomson, his painting, his death, and his body's whereabouts. Almost all of the 1917 participants were dead, and many from the 1956 investigation were either dead or retired. I spent many hours with Hugh Kemp, the talented writer/researcher for this program, going through Dr. Sharpe's case file. During the actual film production, I constantly found myself in the position of trying to introduce some semblance of reality to an overwhelming group of bright young television producers and technicians who unearthed all the old legends and created some new ones. Again, public interest was stimulated, however briefly.

The only new factual material consisted of photographs of Thomson that had not been available in 1956. Dr. Sharpe, although retired and over eighty, was now much more knowledgeable about the examination of skeletal remains. He was able to make a comparison of the bony points on the photos of the skull with those seen on Tom Thomson's head in these new photographs and confirm, in his opinion, that the skull was not Thomson's. At Dr. Sharpe's suggestion, the CBC asked Walter Kenyon of the ROM, one of North America's foremost authorities on aboriginal anthropology and archeology, to examine all the photos, and he agreed with Dr. Sharpe that "the skeleton belonged to an Indian, likely young and male."

Although the CBC film did not present a definite conclusion about the mystery, the title—*Was Tom Thomson Murdered?*—provided a not so subtle hint as to their belief. The film implied that Tom Thomson had been murdered and that his remains were still in the grave at Canoe Lake. This is perhaps not surprising since a major source for their research was a draft of William Little's book. The story cooled again until 1970, when Little's book was published. He was now a judge in the family court in Toronto. According to his book, however, the mystery was solved. Thomson was murdered by Blecher, and the body was never removed from Canoe Lake. Again, the legends were given the weight of fact that goes with publication. I was frequently asked to appear with Little on radio programs promoting his book. Although we disagreed on what was fact and what was speculation, this was always done professionally and with mutual respect.

In 1973, I was speaking to a service club in Toronto, and after I finished, an elderly, distinguished-looking gentleman approached and thanked me for the talk. "By the way," he asked, "do you know anything about the mystery of Tom Thomson's death?" Almost casually I replied, "Yes, a bit." The reader may imagine my reaction when he went on to say, "Well, I was a pallbearer at his funeral!"

Charles Plewman was twenty-seven years old in 1917 and arrived at Mowat Lodge on July 18, the day of the burial. Although Thomson was unknown to him, he was pressed into service to help carry the coffin. By 1973, Mr. Plewman knew all the old legends, but the only new potential fact he offered was a vague recollection that the body was buried inside the fence around the other two graves and not twenty-one feet north where the 1956 grave was found. (Ironically, given my belief that many of the legends were enhanced around campfires at children's summer camps, Mr. Plewman founded such a camp in 1932, Camp Kilcoo, on Gull Lake in the Haliburton Highlands near Minden, Ontario.)

Neither Plewman nor Dr. Sharpe had seen the CBC film, so I borrowed a copy from the CBC and took Mr. Plewman to spend a delightful afternoon watching and discussing it with Dr. Sharpe, who was now living with a daughter near Whitby, Ontario. No new legends emerged.

Before I retired from the Centre of Forensic Sciences (CFS) in 1994, I began having conversations about the story with another author, S. Bernard Shaw. He had started writing a book about the history of the lumber industry in Algonquin Park and particularly the Gilmour log drive from Canoe Lake to Trenton in the 1890s. Of course, one could not go to Canoe Lake and not become interested in the Tom Thomson story, so he added it to his research interests. That led him to CFS and me. His book, *Canoe Lake Algonquin Park, Tom Thomson and Other Mysteries*,[5] was published in 1996. Unfortunately, it did not draw the same attention as had Judge Little's, but it was more thoroughly researched.

Shaw carefully concluded that the skeleton found at Canoe Lake in 1956 was indeed in Thomson's original grave, and it was not Tom Thomson but rather an unknown Indian buried around 1940. Finally, he wrote, "Tom rests at Leith. He was probably stunned by a fall in 1917 and drowned although the possibility remains that he met his death as a result of a blow. In that case, Martin Blecher is the only candidate."

In 2010, Roy MacGregor, a highly respected columnist with the Toronto *Globe and Mail* whose work I always enjoy reading, published *Northern Light, the Enduring Mystery of Tom Thomson and the Woman Who Loved Him*.[6] This book is based on MacGregor's forty years of research on the subject. His interest resulted from having been raised in Huntsville across the street from Winnie Trainor's home (he helped a distant cousin who inherited Winnie's estate to clear out both her Huntsville home and the Canoe Lake cottage after her death). MacGregor's family also had a long association with Algonquin Park because his maternal grandfather had been chief ranger in the park. *Northern Light* was the culmination of MacGregor's research; he had earlier written several magazine articles about the story and, in 1980, had published a novel, *Canoe Lake*, which, although fictionalized, was based on the story and the people involved.

The MacGregor book relies on much of the same material as the others but includes, because of his connection with the area, recollections (forty to fifty years after the fact) of some additional local people. He also had access to a 1975 (nineteen years after the second exhumation) interview of Dr. Ebbs contained in the Algonquin Park archives.

Not content with just the traditional legends, MacGregor also commissioned some new work. He arranged to have a review of photos of the skull made by an archeologist (Dr. R.F. Williamson), a physical anthropologist (Professor Susan Pfeiffer), and a "forensic artist" (Victoria Lywood). In the years since 1956, forensic anthropology had come a very long way, and there had been an enormous amount of research published that was unavailable to Dr. Sharpe and Professor Grant in 1956. The archeologist and anthropologist had the advantage of access to this research data as well as modern computerized photo comparison techniques. Their disadvantage, however, was that they had only photos of the skull to work with and not the actual skeletal remains that Sharpe and Grant had examined.

Both Williamson and Pfeiffer concluded that the skull was Caucasian. Dr. Pfeiffer reported that "the skull appears to be from a north European/British Isles population, based on the shape of vault, jaw, and nose. Based on the complete teeth, he is clearly a mature adult."

She later wrote to MacGregor that "if Grant placed strong emphasis on shovel-shaped incisors, that would have been consistent with scholarly practice in those days, when racial groups were seen as distinct, and certain anatomical features were seen as diagnostic."

Dr. Williamson located a published research paper that found 95 of 622 (about 15%) of Irish Catholics had shovel-shaped incisors. It is not known how much Sharpe's and Grant's opinions about race were based on the teeth and how much on other features; however, the teeth undoubtedly played a part.

Neither Williamson nor Pfeiffer commented on the Sharpe/Grant opinions on stature and age, but it is not clear whether they were given that information or asked to comment on it.

Ms. Lywood provided artistic impressions of what she believed the man whose skull she had a photo of might have looked like. When MacGregor looked at these impressions, he wrote, "I found myself looking at Tom Thomson." There certainly is a resemblance; however, as with all such impressions, some imagination is required to arrive at that conclusion. The resemblance is perhaps not as surprising as one might think because of the information Ms. Lywood was given to work with. She was told that "John Doe would likely be a Caucasian approximately forty years of age. He would have lived in the early twentieth century and worn his straight black hair medium length, parted on the left"—all characteristics that applied to Tom Thomson!

Roy MacGregor clearly believed that the skeletal remains recovered in 1956 were those of Tom Thomson and that his body was therefore never removed from the park. Before the work of Dr. Williamson, Professor Pfeiffer, and Ms. Lywood, his belief was based, at least in part, on the 1975 interview of Dr. Ebbs. In this interview, Dr. Ebbs quoted Dr. Sharpe as remarking at the

1956 exhumation scene that the hole in the left side of the skull was from a .22 caliber bullet. I knew Dr. Sharpe very well, and I cannot imagine him, or anyone with his experience, making such a definitive statement after only a cursory look. Nor can I believe that anyone would look at a ¾-inch hole and opine that it was caused by a .22 caliber bullet. In his interview, Dr. Ebbs also described how, over the years, he had developed a theory about how Martin Blecher Jr. could have shot Thomson and produced the hole in the skull.

One of the things about the hole in the skull that troubled Dr. Ebbs was the suggestion that it was in the classic trephine operation position. He quite correctly insisted that in 1917 such an operation was rarely, if ever, done, and certainly not on an indigenous person. That, of course, presumes that this skull was buried in 1917. However, if Sharpe and Grant were correct, it might not have been buried until around 1940. For me, the hole in the skull is the most compelling evidence that the skull is not Tom Thomson's. Setting aside any confusion about on which side of Thomson's temple the four-inch linear bruise was located, it is impossible to believe that Dr. Howland, or any competent practitioner, would describe an injury that could produce a 3/4-inch circular hole in a skull as a 4-inch linear bruise. Unless Tom Thomson had a very serious injury or some form of skull surgery during his life, of which there is no evidence, the Canoe Lake skull could not be Tom Thomson's.

Dr. Ebbs went on to describe how stunned he was upon hearing of the Sharpe/Grant conclusion. He met with them both, and still unsatisfied with their explanation, he also met with the attorney general and the deputy minister of Lands and Forests. They both said they were satisfied it was an accidental drowning and that they didn't want to have any more fuss over it. Ebbs left, convinced that there was a deliberate and intentional cover-up of a homicide by senior representatives of government.

Given my respect for Roy MacGregor as a writer, I was very disappointed that, by implication, he seemed to have accepted Dr. Ebbs's opinion that there was some government conspiracy to cover up a criminal matter. To believe that such respected scientists as Grant, Sharpe, and others would be part of such a conspiracy is not only disrespectful and insulting, but it also ignores the advice MacGregor received from both Williamson and Pfeiffer that if the opinion that the skull was aboriginal was based on the shovel-shaped teeth, that was the state of the art at the time. It is also difficult for me to believe that such a conspiracy could go unexposed for more than fifty years. It would have to have involved at the very least a minister and deputy minister of the Crown, one or more members of the OPP, and several highly regarded professionals. MacGregor apparently was not aware of (or did not believe) Benjamin Franklin's caution that "three may keep a secret—if two of them are dead!" And that was published in *Poor*

Richard's Almanac in 1734, long before the invention of the Xerox machine in 1959 made secrets a thing of the past.

In his book, MacGregor does include his theory about what happened at Canoe Lake in July 1917. It is interesting that the authors of three books, Little, Shaw, and MacGregor, had access to essentially the same information but came up with three different scenarios. MacGregor's is probably the most creative. It is based in part on information provided to him by Mrs. Daphne Crombie during an interview in 1977, sixty years after the death and second-hand, about something she had been told by Shannon Fraser's wife, Annie, in 1917.

Daphne Crombie and her husband were staying at Mowat Lodge during the winter and spring of 1917 for reasons of Mr. Crombie's health. During their prolonged stay, she became friends with the Frasers and with Tom Thomson. In one of Tom's paintings, *The Artist's Hut*, both Daphne and Annie are a (very tiny) part of the scene.

Mrs. Crombie described to MacGregor how Annie had told her that she had found a letter from Winnie in Tom's room and read it. Annie told Daphne it included "Tom, we must get married because a baby is coming." It also urged Tom to press Shannon Fraser for the money he was owed because he would have to buy a new suit for their wedding. Annie's story to Daphne went on to claim that Tom and Fraser had got into a fight over the money, Fraser knocked Tom down, and he hit his head on a fire grate. He wasn't dead, but Fraser panicked, so he and Annie put Tom into his canoe, towed it out into the lake, and overturned it.

From this recollection (and that of a few others), MacGregor developed his scenario of the events of the week of July 7, 1917. The drunken Saturday night party and Thomson's Sunday noon departure in his canoe are similar to the descriptions of others, but there the similarity ends. In MacGregor's scenario, Thomson returned unnoticed to Mowat Lodge Sunday evening after dark, read the letter from Winnie, and confronted Fraser about repayment of the loan. The fight, injury, and transport out in the lake then occurred as Mrs. Crombie had described. The fishing line around Tom's ankle had been used to attach some weight to ensure the body would sink.

As with all the scenarios, this one also has a potential problem. It ignores Fraser's statement about seeing Tom leave the lodge at 12:50 on Sunday and never returning. However, if Fraser was responsible for the death, then his statements can be easily ignored. A bit more challenging is Mark Robinson's statement some years later that he had seen Tom and Fraser together on the Sunday morning. MacGregor seems to have accepted Daphne Crombie's word that she "didn't believe that Robinson saw Tom that morning."

An indication of the ongoing interest (controversy?) surrounding the death and burial place of Tom Thomson has been provided more recently. As I was writing this chapter in May 2016, another book was published. This one, by Gregory Klages, is titled *The Many Deaths of Tom Thomson—Separating Fact from Fiction*.[7] It is, in my opinion, the best of all the books because the author diligently attempts to, as have I, trace the many stories back to their actual source. When this is done, and there are very few sources, it becomes clear that there is much more fiction than fact.

Klages concluded that "the cause of Thomson's death will remain a mystery forever." Concerning the location of the remains, he similarly opined,

> It is impossible to definitively prove that Thomson's body was indeed moved from one site to the other, or that it remained buried beside Mowat cemetery. However, accounts written immediately following Thomson's death, and the testimony of those who were involved, do provide strong reasons to conclude that the body was exhumed and moved from Canoe Lake to Leith.

Conclusion

We are left then with two mysteries. Was Tom Thomson's death an accident (Shaw), homicide (Little and MacGregor), suicide (one of Shannon Fraser's stories), or by unknown means (Klages), and where are Tom Thomson's remains buried, at Leith or Canoe Lake?

My answer to the first of these is "I don't know; there simply is not enough factual information available to conclude, and probably never will be."

The second mystery is more complicated. If the skeleton exhumed in 1956 at Canoe Lake is not Thomson's, then we have an almost unbelievable situation in which some unknown person(s) at some unknown time between July 1917 and September 1956 buried the body of an unknown male (possibly indigenous) in what may have been Thomson's original casket and grave.

If, on the other hand, the skeletal remains are indeed Thomson's, we have the equally incredible possibility that an undertaker risked his license and reputation by fraudulently claiming to have exhumed and shipped a body without actually having done so (and been paid for his services). The risk of detection of such an act was very high since, although I have never seen any record of the involvement of an undertaker in Owen Sound, there must certainly have been one there to receive the casket, open a grave, and bury it. Would that individual not notice something unusual about a casket filled with sand rather than a body? Would he not be sufficiently concerned to open the casket? Was there not a risk that some member of the family would insist on confirming that this was indeed Tom's body? Also, if Mark Robinson, and perhaps others at Canoe Lake, truly believed in 1917 that Thomson's remains had not been removed from his original grave and were still at Canoe Lake, might they not have placed some form of marker on the grave in memory of their good friend?

Mystery number two is potentially resolvable by opening the grave at Leith. This would require a request from a responsible member of the Thomson family and order by the attorney general of Ontario. Despite suggestions in the past, the family has always been opposed to such an action. Would I like to see this done? As a scientist, of course, I would. That would resolve at least one mystery. However, as a storyteller, I would rather that the mystery remain. It makes for a much better story! For storytellers, there might be the basis for a new story. If Tom's remains are at Leith, then whose bones are buried under that spruce tree at Canoe Lake?

There is, for me, a third mystery that is even more interesting but never part of the stories. It is, "Where would Tom Thomson have gone as an artist if his work had not been aborted in its infancy?" He painted seriously for only about four years, three hundred sketches and twenty-four canvasses, yet his work hangs in the National Gallery of Canada and is highly regarded both in Canada and abroad. His brief life and his mysterious death would not hold their fascination if his art did not display great gifts. As described by another famous Canadian artist, Harold Town, in a 1977 book[2] at the time of Thomson's death, "He was poised on the crevasse between the figurative and non-figurative art. Whether he would have survived the leap is a matter for conjecture; that he would have jumped is a certainty."

I have visited both grave sites. In 1968, on a family trip to the Bruce Peninsula, we stopped at Leith to find Thomson's grave. In September 1996, Rick Libman and I traversed Canoe Lake (by canoe of course) and found our way (with difficulty, as the small trees of 1917 were now much larger and obscured the graves) to the tiny cemetery. By coincidence, that day there were three local gentlemen on site restoring the picket fence that surrounds the two marked graves. The wooden cross under the spruce tree that was left by the CBC in 1969 marking what is believed to be Thomson's original grave site was still there. The locals were quite happy to regale us with all the legends.

At both locations, I quietly asked, "Are you there, Tom?" At neither site did I receive any reply.

Addendum

My interest in Thomson extends beyond that of a storyteller and into the modern-day world of forensic science. As mentioned above, Tom left a large number of sketches, the value of which has multiplied exponentially. After his death in 1917, one of his friends and fellow painters, J.E.H. MacDonald, designed a stamp that he used to brand the front and back of all the known Thomson works. Given their current value, it is not surprising that entrepreneurs have tried to forge this stamp on bogus works. Periodically at CFS, we received these paintings for comparison of suspected fake stamps on them with the authentic one. Another examination we would perform was testing any white areas of the painting for titanium dioxide, a now common pigment that was unknown in 1917.

Figure 17.9 J.E.H. MacDonald stamp used on authentic Thomsons.

Figure 17.10 Counterfeit stamp.

Further Readings

1. Mellen, P. *The Group of Seven*. McLelland and Stewart Ltd., Toronto, 1970.
2. Town, H., and Silcox, D.P. *Tom Thomson, the Silence and the Storm*. McLelland and Stewart Ltd., Toronto, 1977.
3. Little, W.T. *The Tom Thomson Mystery*. McGraw Hill, Toronto, 1970.
4. Sharpe, N.C. The Canoe Lake mystery. *J. Can. Soc. For. Sci.* 3, 34–40, 1970.

5. Shaw, S.B. *Canoe Lake Algonquin Park, Tom Thomson and Other Mysteries*. General Store Publishing House, Burnstown, ON, 1996.
6. MacGregor, R. *Northern Light, the Enduring Mystery of Tom Thomson and the Woman Who Loved Him*. Random House Canada, Toronto, 2010.
7. Klages, G. *The Many Deaths of Tom Thomson—Separating Fact from Fiction*. Dundurn Press, Toronto, 2016.

Last Word Society Stories No. 2 (1983) The Assassination of Thomas D'arcy McGee, "Look for the Tailor with the Red Whiskers"

18

The history of Canada is little known in the rest of the world and, indeed, not that well known even in Canada. Most Canadians would know who Thomas Jefferson was and his place in American history; few, however, would know who Sandfield Macdonald was and what his place in Canadian history might be. All Canadians undoubtedly know of the assassinations of Presidents Abraham Lincoln and John F. Kennedy in the United States; it is doubtful, however, that more than a handful know of the assassinations of D'Arcy McGee and Pierre Laporte in Canada. Each of these had much in common: major national figures in their countries, fanatical opponents, sudden unexpected deaths, allegations of conspiracy, errors of omission and commission in the investigations, and unusual involvement of forensic science. This is a story about one of these cases, the assassination of Thomas D'Arcy McGee in Ottawa on April 7, 1868.

McGee was born in Ireland in 1825. At age 17, he emigrated to Boston, where he became well known as a journalist and militant advocate for Irish nationalism. He returned to Ireland in 1845 to become involved with the Young Ireland movement to free Ireland from British rule, but was forced to flee, with a price on his head, back to the United States in 1848.

Over the next few years, anti-Irish hostility increased in Boston and New York, so in 1857, McGee moved to Montreal. Within a year, he was elected to Parliament. Maturity and responsibility began to temper his militant views, and he began to speak out in favor of forgetting old quarrels and cooperating in building a new nation. In one speech, he said about his youth, "Politically we were a pack of fools. But we were honest in our folly. And no man need blush at forty for the follies of one and twenty."

This transformation earned him the hatred of many Irish immigrants, including a secret society known as the Fenians, founded in New York in 1855; they were sworn to overthrow English rule in Ireland by force. One of their plans was to capture Canada and hold it hostage. In June 1866, 800 Fenians did invade Fort Erie (in what was then known as Upper Canada—now Ontario) from Buffalo and defeated the British at the Battle of Ridgeway. (They withdrew the next day.)

The Civil War in the United States and the Fenian Raids caused many Canadians to appreciate that, as a collection of separate provinces, there was a real risk of annexation by the United States. McGee therefore became one of the first to speak out in favor of a confederation of the Canadian provinces. He made a tour of the maritime provinces in 1863, which led directly to the Charlottetown Conference in 1864, at which the decision to federate Ontario, Quebec, Nova Scotia, and New Brunswick was made. As a result, at the request of these Canadian provinces, the British North America Act was passed by the British Parliament, and on July 1, 1867, Canada became a nation with its capital in Ottawa.

As one of the "Fathers of Confederation," McGee was elected to the new Parliament of Canada and became one of its leading and most respected members. However, his religion and heritage denied him a place in the cabinet of Canada's first prime minister, Sir John A. MacDonald.

Things did not go smoothly for the new country, and discontent developed in some of the provinces. On the night of April 6–7, 1868, the House of Commons sat late, and McGee made an impassioned speech against a motion to dissolve Confederation. Shortly after 02:00, he walked the 400 yards from the Parliament building to his room in the Toronto House (also known as Mrs. Trotter's Boarding House) at 71 Sparks Street. As he inserted his key into the lock, Mrs. Trotter began to open the door from inside. A shot rang out in the dark, and McGee fell dead on the sidewalk.

Police, the coroner, and the prime minister were summoned. The coroner described the body as laying with the head pointed toward the street. There was a glove on the left hand but not on the right, and the latchkey was still in the door. The bullet had passed through McGee's head and exited through his mouth (removing three artificial teeth in the process). It struck the door to the right and just above the keyhole (McGee was only five feet three inches tall), fell out of the door, and was found along with the three teeth on the floor just inside the sill.

Sir John A. MacDonald arrived on the scene and helped to carry the body into the boarding house. The coroner and a physician Member of Parliament (MP), Dr. Donald McGillvray, who also lived at Mrs. Trotter's, performed an autopsy in the attic of the house ten hours later. Eighteen observers attended, including Sir George Etienne Cartier, the leader of the opposition, who was so moved by the death of his colleague that he was described as having left "precipitously."

At the autopsy, Dr. McGillvray described a wound in the back of the neck that smelled strongly of gunpowder and singed hair. The bullet track went through the transverse process of the second and third cervical vertebrae and the pneumogastric nerve on the right side. It exited through the upper lip. Death was due to hemorrhage from the internal carotid artery and the jugular vein.

As the news was released, panic spread across the country. The Fenians were publicly accused, and rumors were rife about a plot to blow up Parliament. About seventy Fenians were arrested and incarcerated indefinitely. (This may sound shockingly familiar to those of us who remember similar roundups after the proclamation of the War Measures Act following the murder in Montreal of Pierre Laporte by the Front de libération du Québec in 1970.)

The city of Ottawa offered a $2,000 reward for "the apprehension and prosecution to conviction of any party or parties in any way implicated in or connected with or privy to the perpetration of this atrocious crime."

A $16,000 reward was offered by the *Montreal Gazette* "to lure the Fenians to inform on their fellow conspirators."

A coroner's jury was convened and concluded that:

> "The Hon. Thomas D'Arcy McGee MP came to his death the morning of the 7th April, 1868 in Sparks St. in the City of Ottawa, by a gunshot wound produced by a bullet, having the appearance of a pistol bullet which entered the back of the neck and passed out of the mouth, the said wound being inflicted by some person or persons unknown."

Lieutenant Edward O'Neill of the new City of Ottawa Police Force was assigned the case, and one of his tips came from Patrick Buckley, a messenger in the House of Commons, to "look for the tailor with the red whiskers." On April 8, Lieutenant O'Neill arrested Patrick James Whelan at Starr's Hotel. Whelan was a red-haired tailor's assistant active in Irish societies and recently relocated to Ottawa from Montreal. He had been seen by Buckley in the Public Gallery during McGee's final speech.

When he was arrested, Whelan had a fully loaded revolver and a box of cartridges in his pocket. Although today this might be considered suspicious, it must be remembered that Ottawa at the time was a rough and tumble logging town, less than two years old as a capital city. Guns were cheap and carrying them not uncommon. The newspapers made much of what was referred to as a "Derringer pistol," similar to that used to murder President Lincoln almost three years to the day earlier (April 14, 1865). Prophetically, at the time of Lincoln's assassination, McGee had written, "A pistol cannot kill the reputation of a virtuous and worthy citizen."

Patrick James Whelan was charged: "On the 7th day of April 1868 in the City of Ottawa, Patrick James Whelan did feloniously and with malice aforethought kill and murder the Hon. Thomas D'Arcy McGee."

Ten others were charged with conspiracy to commit murder. (It is interesting that in almost all political assassinations some conspiracy is suspected. The public appears to be unwilling to believe that a single person could carry out such an act, regardless of the evidence.)

McGee's funeral in Montreal, on what would have been his forty-third birthday, April 13, 1868, was described as the largest ever seen in that city, an indication of his stature as a journalist and statesman.

The prime minister, a longtime member of the Loyal Orange Lodge, was convinced the murder was but a first step in a Fenian conspiracy to take over the country. He wanted Whelan and the others tried by a special commission. However, the administration of justice was then, and still is, a provincial responsibility and the premier of Ontario, Sandfield Macdonald (a political opponent of his namesake), insisted on a normal criminal trial.

The trial began on September 7, 1868, with Mr. James O'Reilly QC (Queen's Counsel) acting as Crown attorney and Mr. Hillyard Cameron QC leading the defense. (Ironically, Cameron was grand master of the Loyal Orange Lodge of British North America and a defeated candidate for the leadership of the Conservative party.)

The evidence was mainly circumstantial, although one witness of doubtful credibility did identify Whelan as the man he had seen shoot McGee. Witnesses testified that they had heard Whelan admit the shooting to other prisoners at the jail. Whelan acknowledged being in the House of Commons gallery that night but said he went straight home from there. Lieutenant O'Neill testified that one of the bullets in Whelan's gun when he was arrested was cleaner and brighter than the others. He also said that in an empty house across from Mrs. Trotter's, he had found a piece of tailor's burlap with the initials P.E. on it. (Whelan worked for the tailor Peter Eagleson.) Evidence was also given about a visit Whelan had made to McGee's home in Montreal on New Year's Eve 1865 to warn him that he had overheard men in a tavern plotting to burn his home. Others testified that in the election of 1867, Whelan had worked for McGee's opponent and had called McGee a traitor who, if elected, would never be allowed to serve.

The trial lasted seven days, with its importance to the budding nation emphasized by the presence on the fifth and sixth days of the prime minister and Lady MacDonald in the courtroom. In fact, to the shock of many, they sat on the dais beside the presiding judge, Chief Justice William B. Richards of the Court of Common Pleas of Ontario. On the seventh day, the jury found Whelan guilty, and he was sentenced to hang.

In December, an appeal was heard by the Court of Queen's Bench based on Judge Richards's ruling on the challenge to a juror. Richards had in the interval been appointed chief justice of the Court of Queen's Bench and, again to the surprise of many, did not recuse himself from the appeal. In fact, he gave the deciding judgment when the other two judges split. Although he agreed his original ruling had been wrong, he concluded that no harm had been done to the accused as a result!

In January 1869, ten judges of the Court of Error and Appeal, including Richards, voted six to four to uphold the conviction. There was no Supreme Court of Canada at that time, and Whelan's request to appeal to the privy council in London was denied. (The Supreme Court of Canada was not established until 1875, with Judge Richards as the first chief justice.)

Before his execution, Whelan is said to have acknowledged that although he was present at the assassination, he did not fire the shot but knew who had. He also exonerated the arrested conspirators, all of whom were subsequently acquitted. One of these was Patrick Buckley. Historians eventually concluded that Whelan was not a Fenian and that no conspiracy had existed.

At 11:00 on a frigid, snowy February 11, 1869, Patrick James Whelan stepped from a second-floor window of the jail on Nicholas Street in Ottawa onto the gallows. There, before an estimated five thousand onlookers, he was hanged in the last public execution in Canada. Because of concern about the emotional impact of a public burial, his body was buried in secret in the jail yard where, so far as I know, it remains. The jail still stands in Ottawa, where it has been converted to a youth hostel, haunted, some claim, by the ghost of Patrick Whelan.

My involvement in this story began 101 years after the murder, by which time some of the physical evidence had "matured" sufficiently to warrant forensic examination. On November 5, 1970, I received a phone call from Timothy P. Slattery QC, a senior member of an old and respected Montreal law firm. He had published a book, *The Assassination of D'Arcy McGee*,[1] in 1968 and, because of his concern about abnormalities in Whelan's trial, was researching a second book about it. Mr. Slattery had learned that the fatal bullet still existed in the Archives of Ontario and asked if we might be interested in examining it in an attempt to identify the type of gun it had been fired from. Because our experience with the examination of 100-year-old homicide bullets was somewhat limited, I quickly agreed to do so.

On November 16, 1970, we received from the archives a small metal box with the initials "JA McD" scratched on the bottom. The initials remain unexplained, but remembering that the prime minister had been sitting beside the judge at the trial and having observed court clerks deal with such exhibits many times previously, I fantasized a scenario in which the court clerk was looking around for a suitable container for the bullet when the prominent spectator seated behind him handed over his snuff box!

Inside the box when we opened it were the bullet and a tooth. The eventual resting place of the other two teeth remains unknown. The bullet exhibited serious deterioration from the ravages of time as the lead was severely oxidized. One of our firearms examiners determined that it weighed 87.3 grains and had only one land and one groove impression suitable for measurement. The land width was 0.095 inches and the groove width was

0.094 inches. The groove diameter was 0.307 inches. The calculated number of lands and grooves was five with a right twist and pitch of 22.5 inches per revolution.

Our firearms examiners researched the literature and concluded that the only handguns available in 1868 that would fit these rifling specifications were the Smith & Wesson Model 1½ and Model 2, .32 caliber revolvers or copies thereof. We had in our collection a Model 2 with serial number 51196, and bullets we fired from it looked similar to the McGee bullet.

Remembering what little I could of the history of the case, I enthusiastically reported to Mr. Slattery on December 22 that the bullet had not been fired from a Derringer but rather from a Smith & Wesson. He seemed somewhat disappointed by our conclusion. By 1970, he had become convinced that he had discovered a real possibility of a miscarriage of justice, and rather dejectedly, he acknowledged to me on January 4, 1971, that the gun found in Whelan's pocket had not been a Derringer but was indeed a Smith & Wesson Model 2, six-shot, .32 caliber revolver with serial number 50847.

The fact that Whelan had a gun of the same caliber as the bullet must undoubtedly have carried great weight with the trial jury. No attempt had been made to relate the bullet to the weapon more specifically since this was twenty years before Professor Lacassagne at the University of Lyon in France first attempted this type of comparison. The jury undoubtedly didn't know, however, that this firearm, made in January or February 1866 and sold by J.W. Storrs of New York for $13.00, was one of 88,699 made between 1861 and 1874. This model had been widely used by both Union and Confederate forces during the Civil War. The Whelan revolver was one of a lot of fifty shipped to a dealer in Montreal in 1866.

Tim Slattery was not one to give up easily, so he now focused on the box of .32 caliber rimfire cartridges found in Whelan's pocket. They had been manufactured by the C.D. Leet Company in Springfield, Massachusetts. If the bullet was not from a Leet cartridge, there was still a possibility that it had not been fired from Whelan's gun. Unfortunately, both the gun and the cartridges had long since disappeared and authentic old Leet cartridges were no longer readily available. Based on photographs we had taken of the bullet, however, several ammunition collectors advised Mr. Slattery that the bullet was probably not a Leet because the nose was more rounded than normal. We, on the other hand, attributed the shape of the nose of the McGee bullet to the insult it had experienced in passing through a body and impacting a wooden door!

There the matter rested for about two years. In 1972, Mr. Slattery's second book about the case, *They Got to Find Me Guilty Yet*[2] (words attributed to Whelan by a cellmate), was published and, unbeknownst to any of us at the time, started a new round of activity.

In early September 1973, Dr. Mary Burns, a historian with the National Capital Commission in Ottawa, called me to ask, "Do you have any interest in the gun that killed D'Arcy McGee?" I quickly seized another opportunity for gaining experience with a century-old homicide. Dr. Burns told me that she had, under somewhat mysterious circumstances, received a revolver alleged to be Whelan's. She had promptly contacted the Royal Canadian Mounted Police in Ottawa, but whoever she spoke with, in true bureaucratic fashion, seemed interested only in whether the gun was registered. I informed her that our interest was quite different, so on September 19, an obviously badly shaken Dr. Burns arrived in my office still suffering the trauma of having tried to carry a firearm, no matter how historically important, on board a commercial flight.

The revolver Dr. Burns produced was a Smith & Wesson Model 2, .32 caliber, six-shot revolver with the serial number 50847 stamped on the butt. There was no indication of any alteration of the serial number, and the impressions of the numerals were similar to those on other contemporaneous Smith & Wessons in our collection. The only "hidden" number was on the upper inner portion of the right grip. This was 50848, just enough to confuse the issue a bit more. An assembly number, 997, was found on the face of the cylinder, on the inner barrel flat, on the left side of the corner of the butt, and on the rear tang. Roy Jinks, the official Smith & Wesson historian, whom we met later, attributed the discrepancy in the grip number to a not uncommon assembly error.

Mr. Jinks provided us with a couple of C.D. Leet cartridges, but they were so old they wouldn't fire. Our firearms examiners therefore pulled the bullets out of the cartridges and reloaded them into CIL .32 cartridge cases. The Leet bullets weighed 93.5 grains compared with the 87.3 grains of the McGee bullet, but it had a small piece missing. After cleaning and oiling, the Whelan revolver fired normally. Bullets fired through a block of modeling clay into a wood board bore a remarkable resemblance to the McGee bullet. There was, unfortunately, no remaining fine detail on the fatal bullet that would permit comparison with the test bullets. The likelihood of it being a Leet bullet was enhanced by the identical spacing of the cannelures on both the test and the McGee bullets.

In October, I flew to Ottawa to meet with Slattery, Jinks, Dr. Burns, and a Mr. Rupert Jeroy. Mr. Jeroy, a longtime employee of a well-known men's clothing shop just a few steps down Sparks Street from where Mrs. Trotter's Boarding House had been, was the source of the gun. It had been given to him in 1963 by a relative, James Kelly, who told him it was the gun that had been used to kill D'Arcy McGee. Mr. Kelly had been given the gun as a young child by his uncle, Lieutenant Edward O'Neill! The detective had apparently kept it as a souvenir following the trial. Kelly had no descendants and so wanted Jeroy to keep the gun for his grandson, Scott Renwick. Like most grandfathers, Mr. Jeroy was certain that Scott would one day become prime minister.

By coincidence, Mr. Jeroy had been given a copy of Tim Slattery's book for his birthday. Upon reading it and discovering that the reported serial number of Whelan's gun was the same as the one in the cedar chest in his basement, he decided that it belonged in a museum. However, he was concerned about what might happen if he admitted to having an unregistered revolver in his possession. He sought the advice of his employer and was advised to contact the National Capital Commission (NCC) and Dr. Burns.

The final entry in the Centre of Forensic Sciences file on the assassination of D'Arcy McGee is a letter dated December 18, 1973, from Dr. Burns in which she speculated, "I wonder what else the good citizens of Ottawa have tucked away in their trunks?" We probably don't want to know!

It seems only fitting that the conclusion to this story is something written by Thomas D'Arcy McGee: "The dead have their rights as the living have; injustice to them is one of the worst forms of all injustice."

Addendum

Periodically after 1973, I would receive calls about the McGee case and the whereabouts of the gun. Dr. Burns had assured me that she would find an appropriate home for it. In 1975, she asked what we thought its value might

Figure 18.1 Thomas D'Arcy McGee.

Figure 18.2 The "snuff" box.

Figure 18.3 The fatal bullet.

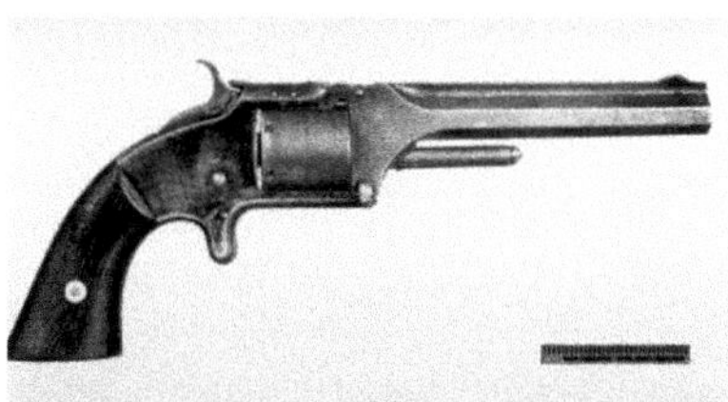

Figure 18.4 Patrick Whelan's Smith & Wesson Model 2, .32 caliber revolver.

be. Our response was, as simply an ordinary old revolver, perhaps $25, but as a significant artifact of Canadian history, who could say? Her question had been prompted by an inquiry from the Rt. Hon. John Diefenbaker, a former prime minister of Canada, who wanted to purchase the gun from Mr. Jeroy and donate it to the Parliamentary Library for display. Unfortunately, nothing came of this.

A few years later, Dr. Burns suffered health problems that caused her to leave the NCC, but she took the gun with her because, as she assured me in one of our telephone conversations in 1980, she was still researching it. At some point, she must have returned it to either Rupert Jeroy or its intended recipient, Scott Renwick, Mr. Jeroy's grandson. In May 2005, Mr. Renwick, by then an auto mechanic, placed it up for auction. It was sold for $105,000 to the Canadian Museum of Civilization, across the Ottawa River from Parliament Hill, where it now resides for all Canadians to see. The municipal Bytown Museum in Ottawa had also been interested in bidding on it. However, it had been unable to raise the necessary funds despite an active campaign, which included a plea to the D'Arcy McGee Pub at 44 Sparks Street!

With the conclusion of one mystery, another developed. At the time of the sale of the gun, a reporter for the *Globe and Mail* was following up on the story and contacted the Archives of Ontario to inquire about the bullet, snuff box, and tooth. He was advised that they "had been temporarily misplaced."

Further Readings

1. Slattery, T.P. *The Assassination of D'Arcy McGee*. Doubleday, Toronto, 1968.
2. Slattery, T.P. *They Got to Find Me Guilty Yet*. Doubleday, Toronto, 1972.

Last Word Society Stories No. 3 (1988)

Arsenic and Old Ice, the Death of Charles Francis Hall

19

During the nineteenth century, Arctic exploration captured public attention in much the same way that exploration of space fascinated us in the second half of the twentieth century. Both had the same elements: uncertainty, vast unknown spaces, beauty, terror, and sometimes death. Newspaper readers hung on every printed word in the same way we clung to the video tube in 1969 when Neil Armstrong stepped onto the moon. A major difference, however, was that while we kept pace with events in real time, our forebears learned of triumph or tragedy only months or years later. Remember the real apprehension we experienced when *Apollo 11* was behind the moon and therefore out of communication for perhaps ninety minutes? Consider then what it must have been like, for both observers and participants, to be out of touch for eighteen months or more.

The analogy between Arctic and space exploration even extends to what we call "technology transfer." We learned of fuel cells, solid fuels, and ablative materials; they learned of iron sheathing for ships, screw propellers, and innovative cabin heating systems. Although the initial motivation for Arctic exploration was the commercial potential of the discovery of a northwest passage to the riches of the Orient, it evolved into the same national prestige and scientific curiosity that drove the space programs.

It can be argued that the challenges and hazards facing Frobisher, Hudson, Baffin, and others were immensely greater than those faced by Gagarin, Glenn, Armstrong, and others. One look at a map of the Arctic indicates the enormous problems of exploration of uncharted mazes of islands, gulfs, capes, inlets, and always the ice in the two-dimensional world of the sailor.

In the summer of 1845, Sir John Franklin and his ships, *Erebus* and *Terror*, were last seen (until 2014 and 2016, respectively) in the Baffin Bay at about 75°N 61°W. By the fall of 1847, when no word had been received from him, the Royal Navy started a search. Over the ensuing years, the mystery of Franklin's disappearance inspired many searchers and fascinated the public in both Europe and North America.

One of those obsessed with the search for Franklin was an obscure, eccentric Cincinnati engraver, Charles Francis Hall. Although devoid of training or experience at sea, let alone in the Arctic, he was compelled by two of man's strongest drives, religion and patriotism, to enter the search. With little more initially than chutzpah, he made three extended trips to what Loomis has called the "Weird and Tragic Shores" of the Arctic.[1]

His first trip was a learning voyage on a whaling ship in 1860–1862 to the area of eastern Baffin Island where he established that Frobisher Bay was, in fact, a bay and not a strait. More importantly, he developed a bond with an Eskimo couple, Ebierbing and Tookoolito, who remained with him for the rest of his life. They taught him how to survive in the Arctic as the Eskimo did, something the earlier English explorers had failed to do with often tragic consequences.

On his return to the United States, Hall was something of a celebrity and, with his two Eskimo friends, hit the lecture circuit in an attempt to raise funds for another voyage. In the middle of the Civil War, however, the government had other priorities.

By 1864, Hall had raised sufficient funds to finance a second expedition. Between 1864 and 1869, he explored Melville Peninsula, Boothia Peninsula, and King William Island. There he found skeletal remains and other relics of the Franklin expedition.

Although this discovery cooled his interest in Franklin, Hall now had another obsession, reaching the North Pole. This would be a true voyage of discovery since existing charts were blank north of 80°N.

The Civil War had ended, and Hall persuaded President Grant and the Navy Department to provide a ship and $50,000. Scientific observations were to be made for the National Academy of Sciences and the Smithsonian Institution. Hall was commissioned "Commander of the U.S. Navy Expedition Toward the North Pole." ("Toward" rather than "To." Bureaucratic precision with language to the point of silliness existed even then.) The ship was a Navy steam tug of 387 tons named *Periwinkle*. With an intuitive sense of public relations, Hall renamed it more dramatically, *Polaris*. (One wonders how much interest *Apollo 11* would have commanded if it had been called *Marigold*.)

Captain Sidney Budington was appointed the sailing master, Captain George Tyson navigator, and Dr. Emil Bessels chief scientist and ship's doctor. All were more experienced in their fields than Hall, and all had no difficulty concealing their respect for him and for each other. Even before they sailed, conflicts of priority, science versus exploration, surfaced.

On July 3, 1871, *Polaris* set sail from New York with a crew of thirty-three equipped for a two-and-half-year voyage. After stops in Newfoundland and southern Greenland, they departed Tasiussaq, Greenland, on August 23, 1871, and quickly lost touch with the rest of the world. The Navy Department heard nothing from its polar expedition during the rest of 1871 and all of 1872 and, as 1873 progressed, began to consider the possibility of disaster. Finally, on May 9, 1873, a terse telegram from St. John's, Newfoundland, reported the discovery of nineteen survivors.

All of what is known about the events between August 1871 and May 1873 comes from the evidence given before a subsequent Navy Board of Inquiry. Hall's journals had disappeared, and the main witnesses were Captains Tyson (no fan of Hall), Budington, and particularly, Dr. Bessels. This reality must temper the appreciation of a good story.

After departing Tasiussaq, *Polaris* had easy sailing for several days, quickly traversing Kane Basin, which was as far as Kane had reached in 1853. On August 30, the ship reached the northern end of Robeson Channel at 82°11'N. Ahead lay only the impenetrable ice of the Lincoln Sea. Although Hall would never know it, no land lay between him and his cherished goal, the North Pole, only 500 miles away. He had, however, found a clear rebuttal of those who believed the polar sea would be open water.

Polaris was struck by an enormous storm and, in fog and ice, was forced southward into what is now called Hall Basin. After four terrifying days, the crew found some open water and took refuge against the shore in a small bay. The mood of the crew can be inferred from the name Hall gave this anchorage, "Thank God Harbor."

A less than unanimous decision was made to winter over there and *Polaris* was banked with snow for insulation. On October 10, Hall and a small party set out by sledge to head north. He reached Newman Bay, where he climbed a mountain to obtain a panoramic view of Robeson Channel and Ellesmere Island. He would never see any farther north.

On his return to *Polaris* on October 24, the crew noted him to be in fine spirits, greatly excited by his trip and with plans for the next season's exploration. On board the ship, he was given a cup of coffee (there is a dispute about who prepared it) and soon became violently ill. Over the next two weeks, his condition deteriorated, although there were intermittent periods of improvement. He had difficulty swallowing, fluctuating temperature, numbness in the tongue, partial left-side paralysis, and periods of dementia. During the latter, he made allegations of attempted murder against many of the crew and particularly against Dr. Bessels. Periodically, he refused Bessels's treatment, but on November 7 he became comatose and at 03:25 on November 8, 1871, Charles Francis Hall died in his fiftieth year. Bessels's diagnosis was "apoplectical insult" (what we would now refer to as a stroke).

The body was cleaned, dressed in a blue uniform, wrapped in a flag, and placed in a pine coffin. On November 10, the coffin was pulled ashore on a sledge and buried in a grave only two feet deep because below that was impenetrable permafrost. Hall might have taken great satisfaction in the fact that if one stands on his grave with a compass in hand, the needle will point southwest. The North Magnetic Pole, one of Canada's more dubious possessions, currently lies in Kane Basin north of Ellesmere Island.

At the Board of Inquiry in 1873, although some evidence about Hall's accusations was presented, based on Dr. Bessels's evidence the conclusion was that death was due to natural causes.[2]

In 1968, Professor Chauncey Loomis of Dartmouth University, who was researching a book on Hall, persuaded the government of Denmark that Hall might have been murdered and received permission to exhume the body and perform an autopsy. He and Dr. Frank Paddock, a pathologist from Pittsfield, Massachusetts, flew from Resolute, Canada to Thank God Harbor and, on August 8, 1968, opened the grave.

The coffin was encased in permafrost, which precluded its removal. Upon opening the upper half, the flag-enshrouded body was identifiable, but the lower half was encased in ice. The face was neither the face of a person nor that of a skull. Flesh, hair, and beard were present, but the eyes were empty sockets and the nose shrunken and discolored. The mouth was drawn into a sort of smile that would eventually become a death's head grin as the body continued its journey from dust toward dust.

An autopsy was performed by Dr. Paddock straddling the coffin in the grave. The flesh had turned to adipocere, and the chest and thoracic cavities were virtually empty. There was only a small amount of amorphous tissue at the base of the skull. Bone, hair, and fingernail samples were collected, and the grave was then restored as closely as possible to its original condition.

Figure 19.1 Charles Francis Hall.

Preliminary tests on a piece of frontal bone by Dr. Arthur McBay in Boston revealed a significant concentration (2 ppm) of arsenic. Early in October 1968, I received a telephone call from Dr. Paddock, who had been referred to me by Dr. McBay, requesting assistance. Since the opportunity to

Figure 19.2 SS *Polaris*.

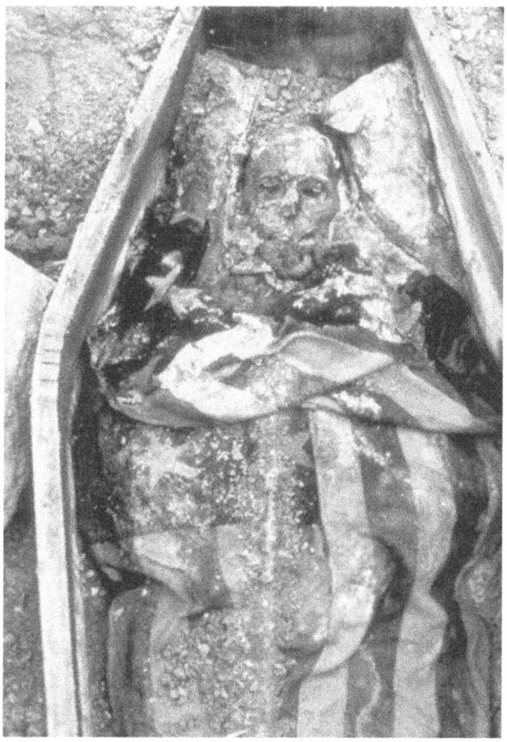

Figure 19.3 The autopsy site.

work on ninety-seven-year-old cases of potential homicide by poison does not often present itself, I readily agreed. Samples of hair and fingernails subsequently arrived at the Centre of Forensic Sciences. They were sectioned (into 2.5 or 5.0 mm lengths of hair and 0.5 or 1 mm of a nail). Together with bone and soil from the grave, these were subjected to neutron activation analysis for arsenic.

The bone contained 10 μg/g of arsenic and the soil 22 μg/g. Of greater interest were the hair, which varied from 10 μg/g at the tip to 30 μg/g at the root, and the fingernail, which varied from 21 μg/g at the tip to 75 μg/g at the root.[3]

The so-called "normal" levels for arsenic in hair and fingernails vary from 1.5 to 2 μg/g and from 4 to 6 μg/g, respectively. Thus, the findings appeared significant. However, the high concentration of arsenic in the soil made interpretation difficult. The same would apply to the flag, which subsequently was tested and found to contain 13 μg/g of arsenic. Migration from the soil or flag into the hair and nails over ninety-seven years was certainly a possibility, but one tempered by the variation in the concentrations between roots and tips. Although embalming fluids of that era contained arsenic, there is no record of the body being embalmed, and it hardly seemed necessary at that latitude. Fowler's solution, a common medicine of the time, which contains arsenic, would certainly have been part of Dr. Bessels's medical kit, and Hall might have treated himself with it.

However, by assuming an average rate of growth of about one centimeter per month for hair and three centimeters per month for fingernails, it was possible to plot the concentrations of arsenic in the sections against the calendar working backward from November 8, starting at the roots. Such a plot revealed a clear inference that Hall might have ingested considerable amounts of arsenic in the last two weeks of his life. Certainly, his symptoms, which began shortly after ingestion of the now suspicious cup of coffee, were consistent with arsenic poisoning. These include difficulty in swallowing, acute pain in the stomach and bowel, vomiting, diarrhea, dehydration, delirium, and skin eruptions, all of which Hall had. These symptoms, however, are nonspecific, and the left-side paralysis was more consistent with Dr. Bessels's diagnosis of apoplectical insult.

Hall's death therefore could have been due to natural causes, as the Navy concluded, but it also could have been accident, suicide, or homicide. Given Hall's reported mood on October 24, 1871, suicide seems unlikely. Dementia made accidental self-overdose a possibility, but for a storyteller, homicide is a much more appealing scenario. Although Captains Budington and Tyson were certainly suspects, they were not as tempting to accuse as Dr. Bessels. He had motive, knowledge, material, and access. Following his return to Washington, Bessels was provided space at the Smithsonian to write his reports. In 1883, the institution decided he had been given sufficient time for this activity, and he was evicted from his office. Bessels returned to Germany, where he died in 1888, from apoplectical insult!

The reader may have noticed at this point that in telling the story of Hall's death, I have avoided describing what happened to the remainder of his crew. Their experiences made an even more fascinating story than a postmortem examination, even one made ninety-seven years after death!

During the winter of 1871–1872, the conflicts between Budington, Bessels, Tyson, and other members of the crew were exacerbated by the isolation and close quarters. Suspicion and fear were the order of the day aboard *Polaris*. Following a half-hearted and unsuccessful attempt at further exploration in the summer of 1872, Budington and Bessels decided in August to abandon the mission and sail for home. After drifting through Smith Sound locked in ice, *Polaris* was struck by an iceberg during a huge storm on October 12 and began to break up. Budington ordered equipment and supplies overboard onto the ice, but during the process, *Polaris* broke free and drifted away, leaving half the supplies and nineteen members of the crew stranded on the ice.

Budington and the remainder of the crew still aboard *Polaris* finally ran aground near Etah, Greenland, where they spent that winter. In the spring, *Polaris* sank, but the crew set sail in two small boats. They were rescued by a Scottish whaler, which took them back to Scotland at the end of the whaling season and returned to Washington in the fall of 1873.

The most incredible adventure of all befell those abandoned on the ice. Captain Tyson took charge (with the support of a pistol). Although they had a store of supplies, they were marooned on an ice floe approximately four miles in circumference. As they drifted slowly southward, their floating refuge steadily became smaller. For almost seven months they fought the ocean, the frigid weather, and starvation. They changed floes several times; as one disappeared, they would transfer to another.

Finally, on May 9, 1873, after covering 1,500 miles on the ice, as they faced death, from each other if not from starvation or the sea, they were rescued off Grady Harbour, Labrador. It was a message from them that informed the world of Hall's death and the fate of the *Polaris* expedition toward the North Pole.

The last word in this story of death, mystery, discovery, and adventure is left to an anonymous member of the crew of the rescue vessel. As the grateful survivors of almost seven months on an ice floe boarded the vessel, they were asked, "And was you on it night and day?"[4] The tension of their ordeal was released by the resultant laughter.

Further Readings

1. Loomis, C.C. *Weird and Tragic Shores*. Alfred A. Knopf, New York, 1971.
2. Butzen, F. Cover story. *J. Am. Med. Assoc.*, December 14, 1979.
3. Paddock, F.K., Loomis, C.C., and Perkons, A.K. An inquest on Charles Francis Hall. *N. Engl. J. Med.* 282, 784–786, 1970.
4. Henderson, B. *Fatal North*. New American Library, New York, 2001.

Miracle of Mississauga "Let's Get the Hell Out of Here" 20

The spectacular fireballs resulting from the derailment of Canadian Pacific (CP) Railway Train 54 in Mississauga, Ontario, just before midnight on Saturday, November 10, 1979, evoked widely different reactions in people with different interests:

The poet: "A fiery orange ball turning midnight into noon and evoking images of Dante's Inferno."
The householder: "Let's get the hell out of here."
The railroad engineer: "Jesus Christ, one of them tankers just blew up."
The firefighter: "There'll be no more movies for us tonight."
The police officer: "I must proceed toward the location of this occurrence to serve and protect."
The forensic scientist: "Wow, there's a lot of chemistry going on there."

Most train wrecks occur on property belonging to the railroad, so there is usually only minimal interest in them on the part of law enforcement and forensic science. Nevertheless, forensic scientists are problem solvers who suffer from an all-consuming desire to learn something about everything. It was therefore inevitable that sooner or later, somewhere, some forensic scientist would become involved in the investigation of a train wreck. Because of the worldwide interest in the events following this derailment, Mississauga was that place when an otherwise "routine" train derailment became a chemical-inspired disaster.

Although some might challenge the use of "disaster" to describe the event, for the 240,000 residents of Mississauga, the entire city, whose living patterns were disrupted, disaster is an understatement.

CP Rail Train 54

This train was born in Chatham, Ontario; its 106 cars included 44 tankers containing propane, butane, toluene, styrene, naphtha, caustic soda, and 1 tank car of chlorine, which, unfortunately, was surrounded by several propane cars.

Propane is a gas at normal temperature and pressure. However, by increasing the pressure, it becomes a liquid, which allows a much larger quantity to be loaded into a tank car. In this condition, any reduction in pressure results in a conversion of liquid back to gas, which increases the volume by a factor of about 270. A significant increase in temperature can also result in a conversion of liquid to gas. In the derailment and subsequent crash, both punctures (causing loss of pressure) and fire (causing increased temperature) occurred.

In 1979, pressure tank cars for compressed gas service had a capacity of about 28,000 gallons (65 tons) of liquid propane (liquefied petroleum gas [LPG]). Each tank had a spring-loaded pressure relief valve that, for LPG service, was set at 280.5 psi. Chlorine cars had a useful capacity of about 12,250 gallons (90 tons). Some pressure cars, including chlorine cars, had additional thermal insulation consisting of a four-inch layer of urethane foam sandwiched between the tank steel and a 1/8-inch-thick outer steel jacket.

Older tank cars had friction bearings for the axles that required lubrication with a film of oil transferred from the "journal box" through a lubricator pad of foam neoprene. "Hot boxes" (overheated axle bearings) were a result of a lubrication failure. Three of the derailed cars had friction bearings. Newer cars, such as those used for LPG and chlorine, had roller bearings that do not require regular lubrication and are much more reliable.

Train 54 was over a mile long as it left its last stop at Woodstock and ran through the night under the control of an engineer and brakeman in the engine and a conductor in the caboose. (Freight trains still had a caboose in 1979.) Its last running inspection was at Guelph Junction, where it received a "highball" sign from the crew of a westbound train.

About twenty miles further on, at Campbellville, witnesses observed smoke rising from the rear wheel of a tank car, and by Derry Road, this had become orange/red flames. At Burnhamthorpe Road (another ten miles), the flames had been replaced by brilliant fireworks. This dramatic change was not surprising since subsequent investigation showed that, just before there, the right rear axle stub of a car loaded with 15,565 gallons of toluene had broken off. The wheel set rolled on for almost a half mile, coming to rest in the backyard of a private residence. The surprised resident found the wheels red hot and used his garden hose to cool them down.

As the train progressed another five miles, witnesses saw a shower of sparks four to five feet high, and by Wolfdale Road, they were rising halfway up the tank car. Just before Mavis Road, the toluene car struck a "frog" (track union) to a siding and started to rock. A man and woman in a southbound car at the Mavis Road crossing saw the tanker coming with the rear wheels off the track and sparks flying. It was swaying violently and, just as it passed them, all the cars started to uncouple and topple over. The driver wildly backed his car north on Mavis until it went into a ditch, forcing them to flee on foot. As they ran, an explosion occurred, knocking them to the ground.

The CP radio recorded the engineer shouting, "Jesus Christ, one of them tankers just blew up!" The engine and its remaining thirty-two cars finally came to a stop about a mile further along the track.

The resultant fireball was observed at the nearby Mississauga Fire Department headquarters and they responded immediately. The enormous fire's glow resulted in alarms to fire departments up to 100 km away.

A Peel Region Police Department (PD) constable on patrol saw the first explosion. After alerting his headquarters and assisting the couple from the ditched car, he heard a tank safety valve start to release and quickly retreated. A second explosion occurred a few minutes after the first, and the engineer radioed: "God, there's another one exploding." Witnesses reported what appeared to be a tank car on fire rocketing northeast through the sky toward the Square One Shopping Centre.

It was sheer good fortune that if a train had to derail, it did so at the Mavis Road crossing, which had only a few small industrial buildings on the south and northwest sides of the tracks and a massive empty field to the northeast. Had it reached the next crossing, which is surrounded by high-rise apartment buildings, the resultant horror would have dwarfed that which occurred in Lac-Mégantic, Quebec, in July 2013, which resulted in forty-seven deaths. That was perhaps the real "Miracle of Mississauga."

During the next hour, frantic but futile efforts were made to determine how many and which cars had derailed. Although the conductor had a copy of the "consist list," the extreme heat and fear of additional explosions prevented any close approach to the derailment area. Finally, by identifying the last cars still attached to the engine and to the caboose, it was determined that twenty-four cars had derailed, starting with the toluene car, the thirty-third car from the engine. These included three cars of toluene, three of styrene, four containing 50% caustic soda, two boxcars loaded with insulation, eleven LPG cars, and unfortunately, the sole chlorine car.

Although the fire and explosions represented major hazards, they were manageable; the fire, although intense, was confined to the immediate area of the Mavis Road crossing. However, the presence of potentially ninety tons of chlorine at an unidentified location in the pileup added an entirely different dimension. Specialized transportation and chlorine emergency personnel were alerted and dispatched from Dow Chemical at Sarnia, arriving on site early Sunday morning.

The Evacuation

From a command post south of the crossing, the fire and police chiefs agreed that there was a significant risk to people in the immediate area and, at 01:30 Sunday, ordered an evacuation affecting about 6,000 people. Because of the existing light winds from the north, the evacuation area was gradually extended south and west, and by 04:00, about 20,000 people had been evacuated to the Square One Shopping Centre.

About 06:00, a greenish cloud was observed rising from one of the tank cars, and the acrid odor was sufficient that the police command post had to be evacuated and relocated to a building about one mile north of the crossing.

At 09:00, the solicitor general (who was also attorney general) arrived at the site and, because of the uncertainty about the condition of the chlorine car and the isolated reports of "chlorine odor" being detected, extended the evacuation area to include the Mississauga General Hospital and two nursing homes. At 12:30, the Square One Shopping Centre had to be evacuated and the International Centre near Pearson International Airport, about eight miles away, became the evacuation center.

By 13:30, four propane cars were still burning, and the Ministry of the Environment started to monitor the area with two mobile mass spectrometer air monitoring systems. By crisscrossing Mississauga, they found small amounts of chlorine in a swath about a mile and a half wide and three miles long downwind from the site. The highest chlorine concentration detected, 0.13 ppm, was around midnight on Sunday at a point about 400 yards southeast of the crash site. Most readings were less than 0.04 ppm, and by Wednesday, only occasional traces were detected. Traces of xylene, toluene, acetophenone, methyl styrene, chlorostyrene, styrene, glycol, hydroxyacetophenone, methyl acetophenone, and chloroacetophenone were also detected. (There was indeed a lot of chemistry going on!)

Although the Ministry of the Environment was developing masses of sophisticated data, its value was limited by the lack of information about the amount of chlorine remaining in the tank car and by uncertainty about the effect of the thermal plume generated by the fires.

Decisions about evacuations had to be made by the solicitor general using very conservative guidelines (0.01 ppm, some discomfort; 1.0 ppm, allowable maximum average occupational exposure over an eight-hour period; and 3.0 ppm, short-term health effects). These were used with an assumption of a possible sudden ground-level release of ninety tons of chlorine. Seven additional evacuations were ordered, and by 21:00 on Sunday night, 240,000 people, essentially the entire city, had been evacuated. This included three hospitals and six nursing homes in an area of forty square miles.

Managing such a massive evacuation and then maintaining security for the empty city presented a major challenge. Both the Ontario Provincial Police (OPP) and the Toronto PD volunteered assistance. Initially, a majority of the citizens treated the evacuation as an adventure, but as time went on, they understandably became frustrated. Police were very reluctant to allow anyone back into their neighborhoods; however, they understood critical situations, such as pets left unattended, and did make exceptions. One woman insisted that she be allowed back in her home because she had forgotten her birth control pills.

By Monday morning, only two propane cars were still burning, and it was considered safe enough to approach and identify the exact location of the chlorine car. The emergency response team determined that there was about three feet of something remaining in the tank with a solid layer of ice or chlorine hydrate (formed by the reaction of chlorine with water) on the surface. The hole in the tank was about three feet in diameter. On the strength of this, they advised the solicitor general that there could still be twenty tons of chlorine in the tank.

Removal of the chlorine tanker's contents could not begin until the hole was sealed, and that could not happen until all the fires had burned themselves out. While waiting, the team used a photograph of the hole to design a steel patch that was fabricated by one of North America's largest tank car manufacturers, Procor Ltd., which fortuitously was located only a few miles away in Oakville.

About 02:30 on Tuesday, all the fires had burned themselves out, and repair work began at daybreak. The steel patch was put in place with a rubber gasket, but it didn't fit tightly enough because of irregularities around the hole. (A tight fit was necessary to allow the tank to be pressurized sufficiently to force the contents out into tank trucks.) Although a perfect seal had not been obtained, it was considered safe enough to reduce the evacuation area, and to their great relief, 110,000 people were allowed to return to their homes. By Friday evening, the entire evacuation was lifted. What was labeled the "miracle of Mississauga" concluded with no fatalities or serious injuries.

Figure 20.1 The Mississauga derailment.

Figure 20.2 The hole in the chlorine car.

After many attempts, patching the hole was abandoned and a reverse approach was applied. A septic tank cleaning truck was brought in to suck out the contents of the tanker and transfer them to another tank car. This process continued until November 19, when it was finally confirmed that the chlorine car was empty. The transfer car was returned to Dow Chemical at Sarnia but was never weighed, and we shall therefore never know how much chlorine was left in the chlorine car after the initial explosions. Dow estimated a maximum of ten tons.

Until Thursday, November 15, although much science had been involved in the monitoring of gases and the estimation of the extent of the potential chlorine plume, forensic scientists had been involved in this event only to the extent that several Centre of Forensic Sciences staff who lived in Mississauga were among the evacuees. That day, Peel Regional PD received unconfirmed intelligence that CP Rail Train #54 had been the victim of a sabotage attempt. (It was claimed that someone had put grit in the journal box at the last stop and then left by air for South America.) Although within a few days this report was confirmed as a hoax, it was sufficient to prompt the solicitor general to order a police investigation into all the circumstances of the crash and the possibility of sabotage of any kind, including with explosives.

He also appointed Mr. Justice Samuel Grange of the Ontario Court of Appeal as commissioner of an inquiry into all the circumstances of the event. The commission counsel, Robert Armstrong, requested my participation in the investigation.

Thus, early on Friday morning, I joined Vic Henderson (who had retired from Toronto PD and been recruited by Peel Regional PD to establish its Explosives Unit) and Detective Fred Lemieux at the scene of an event that was to occupy a considerable portion of our time for the next seven months!

The Investigation

Investigating the scene of an accident six days after it occurred, particularly one involving unfamiliar vehicles, at a site not under the control of the investigators, where salvage activities involving large crews and heavy equipment are underway, is a less than ideal situation. Nevertheless, it was possible to locate and identify all the tank cars and determine their contents from the train consist list. Of the twenty-four derailed cars (which we numbered from front to back), only the last two (#23 [propane] and #24 [toluene]) were relatively undamaged. Five cars had obviously exploded, one toluene (#1), three propane (#8, #12, and #13), and one boxcar (#16). None of these showed any signs of a detonation, and high explosives were eliminated as a possible cause.

Together with the commission counsel, we drew up a list of questions likely to require our input to the inquiry:

What caused the journal box and axle to fail?
What caused the extensive fires?
Which cars exploded, why, and in what sequence?
Why did some propane cars not explode?
What caused the hole in the chlorine car and when?
And, of greatest interest, how much chlorine was left in the tank Sunday morning and where did the rest go?

What Caused the Journal Box and Axle to Fail?

The first challenge was finding all the pieces that were scattered along several miles of track and into backyards. CP Rail staff did an excellent job searching for, finding, and identifying the parts belonging to car no. 1, the toluene car. We were fortunate that one of Canada's leading metallurgical labs was located at the Ontario Research Foundation (ORF) in, of all places, Mississauga. (It, in fact, had been closed during the evacuation.) Exhaustive chemical and metallurgical tests were conducted on these parts with the conclusion that there were no inherent defects.

Why the lubrication failed was not determined. The car had received its last major service in July 1979. The only possible hint of irregularity was that some of the lubricator pads removed from the other journal boxes were the wrong size.

What Caused the Extensive Fires?

Given the presence of 1,100 tons of flammable liquids and gases spilling from ruptured and punctured tank cars crashing together, this was a simple question to answer.

The bottom outlet on the no. 1 (toluene) car was knocked off as it struck the crossing, so it was spilling toluene along the track until it came to rest on its side in a field about 100 yards from the crossing. At that point, it emptied most of the rest of its contents, creating a large burning pool. Another toluene car (no. 15) and three styrene cars (nos. 9, 10, and 11) all suffered punctures and damage to their bottom outlets, thus spilling their contents into the same general area.

One of the propane cars exploded within the first minute, spreading fire over a large area from the east edge of Mavis Road to about sixty yards west of the crossing. This fire ignited propane leaking from at least six of the other punctured cars.

Which Cars Exploded, Why, and in What Sequence?

The first part of this question was quickly established at the site. Three propane tankers (nos. 8, 12, and 13) exploded in the first twenty minutes, and pieces were scattered in several directions. The first was no. 8. Its A head was found 230 yards to the northeast and the B head at the site near car nos. 3 and 4. (The ends of tank cars are labeled A and B, with B being the end with the brake handwheel.)

Car no. 12 was the second to explode. A police officer described a large section of a tank rolling westward down the tracks after this explosion, and its B head was found on the tracks 180 yards west of the site. The A head was found 400 yards to the east. The remainder landed on a building thirty-five yards south of the tracks, setting it on fire.

Firefighters agreed that the third explosion was the most spectacular because it sent a large part of a flaming tank car rocketing toward Square One. This was car no. 13; a thirty-eight-foot-long section of the A end was found about a half mile northeast of the crossing. The B end remained at the crash site.

The toluene car (no. 1) was seen by firefighters to explode on Sunday morning. A large hole in its right side was the result of this explosion, which was undoubtedly due to a toluene vapor/air mixture.

Pieces of boxcar no. 16 were found up to 800 feet north of the site and could only be accounted for by toluene or propane having leaked into the car and being ignited. The major portion of this car remained at the site sandwiched between nos. 15 and 18.

Explanation of the why for the propane cars was much more challenging. It was necessary to determine their location and orientation immediately following the derailment and before they exploded. This required detailed study of the pieces of them as well as those of closely adjoined tank cars. Since, to clear the tracks for regular service, these had all been placed in gondola cars and moved to the Agincourt rail yards, many chilly hours were spent scrambling up, over, and under tanks and other debris at that location. Our home at the time was in Agincourt, so at the end of many of these days, Vic, Fred, and I would warm up in our rec room while discussing, speculating about, and sometimes arguing over our observations and interpretations. Fred had an uncanny ability to mentally unbend the twisted wreckage of some of the cars and sketch what it would have looked like originally. This allowed us to piece together the fractured cars like an enormous jigsaw puzzle. Eventually, our conclusions about what, why, and when filled a two-inch-thick file that I testified about at the Grange Inquiry.

The evidence we used included the location and nature of punctures or ruptures, final locations of the pieces and the intact cars, impact damage, fire damage, patterns of remaining paint (which indicated where liquid remained in the tanks), location and pattern of welds (different tank manufacturers used different weld patterns), and knowledge about the type of explosions involved. We were fortunate to locate an engineering professor at Queen's University in Kingston, Ontario, whose research specialty was the design of railroad tank cars. He gave us a crash course on terminology, function, and design variables.

The three major explosions in propane car nos. 8, 12, and 13 were neither detonations nor deflagrations. Explosions result in tank cars of liquefied flammable gases in accidents when the damage and the fire are such that the increased pressure cannot be adequately relieved or the tank shell is significantly weakened by impact or heat. A special name had evolved to describe these explosions: BLEVE (boiling liquid expanding vapor explosion). We also found a professor at McGill University in Montreal who was a world authority on BLEVEs and who was very cooperative in educating us about his specialty.

If a puncture is sufficiently large to allow a large volume of gas to escape rapidly, the pressure in the tank will not rise to the burst pressure, and no explosion will result. The released gas will of course burn if there is a source of ignition nearby. If the input of heat is not too great, the increase in pressure can be maintained at the "start-to-discharge" pressure of the pressure relief valve and the increased volume of gas will be released to the atmosphere. The relief valves are, however, intended to release vapor rather than liquid, so if the tank is overturned, as many were, the valve is in contact with liquid rather than vapor and thus not as effective.

A typical sequence of events in this type of incident is the temperature of the shell in contact with vapor, and the temperature of the vapor will rise rapidly as the tank is heated, while the temperature of the shell in contact with liquid and of the liquid will rise relatively slowly. The liquid will expand due to the heat, and the resultant increased pressure will raise the boiling point of the liquid, causing some of the vapor to condense back to liquid. If the tank becomes liquid full, a small amount of additional heat will then result in a very large and rapid increase in pressure and the tank will fail.

Another possibility is that an intensely localized flame impingement may heat a section of the shell so rapidly that it fails before the safety relief valve reaches its start-to-discharge setting. The weakening of the tank by mechanical impact in the derailment or from missiles created by other explosions may compound these situations. For example, expansion of the tank shell may result in longitudinal fractures in the hotter section of the tank. These may branch into circumferential shears, which, if they progress completely around the tank, create two "tubs" that can "rocket" for considerable distances. Rocketing of tub-shaped missiles can occur regardless of the state of fill of the tank at the moment of rupture as long as it contains some liquid. Since there would not be sufficient air in the tank for combustion, the thrust is not a result of combustion but rather from the violent expansion of the contents. Combustion of fuel after it escapes may create a spectacular plume but does not contribute to the thrust. This is what happened with car no. 13.

BLEVEs can have three distinct damage-producing effects:

- A blast wave due to internal pressure relief
- Fireballs due to the burning of the released vapor in air
- Missiles

The blast wave damage is usually minor because the bursting pressures are of the order of 225–500 psi and only a portion of the tank contains vapor at this pressure. Fireball damage is probably the most serious effect of this type of explosion. Theoretically, if all the contents of one of the propane cars were to be instantly released and ignited, a fireball up to 450 feet in diameter with a duration of about eleven seconds could develop. Practically, fireballs of 150-feet diameter occur. Missiles from exploding tank cars can be very hot and very large and travel considerable distances. The resultant damage will, of course, depend on where they land. For example, only one of the missiles in the Mississauga derailment (from tanker no. 12) did any significant damage off-site.

The three major explosions occurred in three separate propane cars. The speed with which the first tank (no. 8) exploded was unusual, particularly since it was an insulated tank. Although much of this car was found in the area of car nos. 4 and 23, it would have been expected to be near car nos. 7 and 9. The flattened appearance of nos. 10 and 15 suggested that a car had exploded on top of them. Placing no. 8 in this position also placed it in contact with the exploded boxcar no. 16 and explained the direction of flight of no. 8's A end toward the northeast. Paint remaining on all but the left side of this end indicated that this tank had been lying on its right side with the dome in the three o'clock position. A tear in the right side, which would have spilled propane, must have contributed to the intense fire already present from the burning toluene. This intense heat and the mechanical damage accounted for the rapid explosion.

The second, and most violent, explosion involved tank car no. 12. Witnesses described the sound of a safety relief valve venting immediately before this explosion. This car would be expected to be found near nos. 11 and 13. Since no. 13 had also exploded, only nos. 11 and 14 were available as possible reference points. Tankers no. 9 and 11 were side by side and were flattened from an explosion on top of them. A large flattened section of tank remained on these cars, which we initially believed to be part of no. 13 but later identified as part of no. 12 by its weld pattern. Placing a car on top of these two tanks also explained the trajectories of the two heads of no. 12.

Witnesses also described the sound of a safety relief valve venting immediately before the third propane explosion. Car no. 13 would be expected to be found near nos. 12 and 14. In fact, the B head was found at the site between where no. 12 had been and no. 14. The trajectory of almost three-fourths of this tank indicated that the A head was pointing in a northeasterly direction. The only paint burning was to the right side of this head, indicating that this car was lying on its left side with the dome at the ten o'clock position and the head raised slightly when it exploded. Some soot on this tank also helped to place it near the styrene fires. This tank was heated by the styrene fires, the fireballs from the two previous explosions, liquid propane escaping from its relief valve, and perhaps by the fire around no. 14. Its long flight was due to the amount of fuel it still contained when it exploded, the launch angle, the fact that it suffered a rather clean circumferential break, and the fact that its open end was squeezed in to create a "nozzle."

Why Did Some Propane Cars Not Explode?

Although perhaps not as important as the previous question, it does help to increase confidence in the explanation of why some tanks exploded if a rational explanation can be given for why others did not. They also may serve as real-world test beds for improvements in design or construction.

Eight propane cars (nos. 14, 17, 18, 19, 20, 21, 22, and 23) did not explode. Examinations similar to those described above permitted us to develop explanations for each of them. For example, no. 14 suffered a thirty-inch puncture in its top left side but was lying with the dome at about seven o'clock. The liquid escaping caused a severe fire, but this was an insulated car. It was also the closest to Mavis Road, and the fire department had three hoses keeping it cool at a very early stage.

What Caused the Hole in the Chlorine Tank?

The hole was near the junction of the tank and the A head at about the ten o'clock position, and there were globules of molten steel on the lower left side. Much of the insulation had been burned away from the entire right side of the tank. There was a large dent in the tank jacket and shell at and below the hole. There was another large dent in this head of the tank at about the four o'clock position. The dent around the hole probably resulted from impact with the coupling unit of car no. 9, which was found in direct contact with the dent. This damage could have occurred during the derailment or as a result of the subsequent explosions.

On the inner surface of the tank, in the area surrounding the hole, there was a large area covered with small craters and several areas of the inside of the tank car were covered with an unknown black material. The pressure relief valve was examined and found to have been capable of functioning but had not functioned. The lead seals in this valve would have melted around 306°C but had not melted.

Two possible explanations for the hole were considered:

- A puncture at the time the dent was made
- A rupture from within as a result of increased pressure and weakening of the shell material (Theoretically, a BLEVE is possible in a chlorine tank.)

The major piece of evidence suggesting a puncture was the obvious impact shown by the dent in the area of the hole. A puncture of the tank would expose the contents to atmospheric pressure, and it would be predicted that 20%–25% of the chlorine would have been rapidly released as chlorine gas. An additional unknown amount of chlorine liquid would also have been released in aerosol form.

Since the pressure relief valve apparently did not function, a rupture from within could only have occurred if the tank shell material was weakened. The thinning of the tank around the hole was the major evidence supporting the possibility of a rupture. Since the jacket was torn away from a large area below the hole, the tank shell material in this area would have been exposed directly to heat from the fire in car no. 12, which would have been pointing at it. If, during this fire, the chlorine car was oriented as it was when it was found, the hole would have been in the vapor space area of the tank. The heat from the fire would rapidly have increased the temperature of the steel, thereby weakening it.

While dry chlorine does not react with steel, moist chlorine will, and as the temperature increases to about 150°C, this corrosion can be significant. There were obvious signs of heat in the melted steel globules, and there were obvious signs of corrosion around the inside of the hole.

Exhaustive chemical and metallurgical tests of the material from this tank at ORF showed that there were no inherent defects and the area around the hole had been exposed to high temperatures. Ferric chloride and ferric oxide were detected in the black sludge from the inside of the tank.

Regardless of the method of the creation of the hole, it must have occurred at a time close to the times of the three explosions. Since a large amount of chlorine would have been released when it occurred, it would have been carried aloft by the fireball from one of the three explosions. The dozens of photographs taken the night of the derailment showed no fires near the chlorine car after the first hour following the explosions.

The question of how the hole was made remained without an unequivocal answer.

How Much Chlorine Was Left in the Tank on Sunday Morning?

This question also remained unanswered, although it is clear that there must have been some. The frost on the tank on Friday and the suction lines during the suction process indicated that something very cold was inside.

If the Dow estimate of 20,000 pounds remaining when they started to pump out the tank is accepted, then almost 160,000 pounds had to have been released into the atmosphere between midnight Saturday and 16:00 on Tuesday without producing any significant chlorine concentration in the air over Mississauga.

Our McGill professor made some very sophisticated calculations (which I did not even pretend to understand) and concluded that, of the original ninety tons of chlorine, eighty tons could have been released through the twenty-seven-inch hole in thirty-eight minutes following its creation. Making assumptions for the thermal plumes from the intense fires and fireballs that existed early Sunday morning, this vapor would have risen rapidly to a maximum height of 375–2,000 feet at a distance of 400–2,500 feet downwind and been dispersed without achieving maximum ground-level concentrations greater than 52 ppm, which would have been located at distances one to twenty-eight miles downwind. Thus, the maximum chlorine concentration probably occurred somewhere out over Lake Ontario.

If these estimates were valid, and they were the best available, then most of the chlorine was gone before the evacuation was ordered. That, however, is based on hindsight; the calculations were made several months after the event. The people responsible for ordering the evacuation had no way of knowing this and had to act on the assumption that there was a significant threat to the safety of the citizens of Mississauga during the hours and days following the derailment of CP Rail Train 54.

Conclusion

Forensic science can be defined as "the application of all aspects of science to the problems of the law." Since estimates of the losses in the Miracle of Mississauga ranged upward of $100 million, it was inevitable that there would be problems of the law. Some of the possible complications were as follows.

The initial cause of the crash was a hot box in a tank car owned by one company, leased to another, serviced by another, and carried by another. The major loss was not directly related to the derailment but rather to the evacuation. The evacuation was because of chlorine owned by one company and carried in a car owned by another.

The chlorine wouldn't have been as big of a problem if the fires and explosions hadn't occurred in propane cars owned by two different companies and leased to several other companies.

If the hole in the chlorine tank were made during the derailment, different companies would have some liability than if it was made during the fires and explosions.

If the evacuation was unnecessary, perhaps those making that decision had some liability.

All these can be described without even hinting at complications due to different insurance companies and policies. Given these kinds of problems, was it any wonder that the citizens who suffered the loss had worried looks, the scientists who had to help answer the questions had puzzled expressions, and the lawyers couldn't stop smiling.

The Grange Inquiry into the Mississauga derailment and evacuation began in February 1980 and ran until October of that year. I presented our findings over a couple of days and was questioned by twenty-two lawyers representing the different parties. My concern was that I might have to spend the rest of my life testifying in subsequent civil suits brought by the various parties against the others. Fortunately, Mr. Justice Grange did such a thorough job that the parties must have all accepted his findings and settled financial issues among themselves, as I never heard from any of the lawyers again. Judge Grange agreed with our findings for the questions we had initially formulated. For example, with respect to the hole in the chlorine car and whether it was a puncture or a rupture, being the very down-to-earth, commonsense person he was, he asked me very simply, "How would you bet if you had to bet?" and I replied, "I would bet on a puncture."

And I learned a lot about chlorine, propane, BLEVEs, and the design of railway tank cars, most of which I never used again.

21 The Baby Deaths at Sick Kids Hospital
"George the Moose Was Still Standing"

The cases and items that forensic scientists work on are usually, almost by definition, unpleasant. To compensate for this, we develop an ability to think of the items, for example, bloodstained clothing, ashes from a house fire, and panties from sexual assaults, simply as "things" without any connection to real people. We rarely come into personal contact with victims or suspects. While this helps us to remove emotion from our examinations and conclusions, which is a good thing, there is a risk that we may come to treat the items we work on as just that, another thing we have to work on, and not consider their potential critical importance. I made a point of occasionally reminding our staff that these things, and our results from them, are always of vital importance to someone, a victim, a suspect, a relative, or a friend, and can have a very major impact on those people's lives.

This case is one that put that advice to a test, for me. It is difficult, if not impossible, to avoid some emotion in a case involving the deaths of small babies. The work placed the greatest scientific/technical demands on two of our staff of any case we ever dealt with, and near its end created one of the most stressful meetings of my career.

The case began on March 22, 1981, with a telephone call from the chief coroner saying that there had been a death of a child at the Hospital for Sick Kids (commonly referred to as "Sick Kids") in Toronto, possibly as a result of digoxin toxicity. The circumstances were suspicious, and he had asked the Toronto Police Homicide Squad to conduct the investigation with our support. Matters became even more urgent that night when a second death occurred at the hospital under similar circumstances. However, this second baby had not had digoxin prescribed for him!

At a meeting with the chief coroner and the investigators on March 23, George Cimbura, the head of the Centre of Forensic Sciences (CFS) Toxicology Section, and I expressed considerable reluctance to undertake the required analyses because we had no experience with analysis for digoxin in postmortem samples, nor did any other forensic science laboratory. A hasty review of the literature revealed that while there was considerable knowledge about digoxin as a therapeutic agent, very little was known about its use as a toxic agent. There was virtually nothing about the analysis of digoxin in postmortem samples. The therapeutic concentrations in blood are very low (2–3 ng/mL), so any analytical method would have to be extremely sensitive. Another problem was that after death, the blood concentrations could change and might increase by as much as five times.

Digoxin analysis for clinical purposes is quite routine in hospitals where it is performed on samples from patients receiving it as part of their treatment. The analysis is simply to determine the concentration in the blood; identification of it is not an issue. For forensic purposes, however, determining both the concentration and a specific identification would be required. To develop an analytical method with the required sensitivity and specificity would require a major developmental project on our part.

At the meeting, it became apparent that it would be inappropriate to use the hospital laboratory for the analyses because of the suspicion that something untoward was going on in the hospital. For this reason, we agreed to undertake the analyses, but with the caveat that it would take us some time to develop the procedures and the quality assurance protocols required.

Within a few days, the police investigation began to focus on one nursing team that had been on duty in four similar deaths between January and March. In all four, the hospital lab had found very high digoxin concentrations; instead of the 2–3 ng/mL expected in a baby that had been prescribed the drug, they found concentrations up to 70 ng/mL. In the case of the child who died on March 22, the investigation found that one of the nurses on this team, Susan Nelles, had been assigned to what was referred to as "constant care." The investigating officers understood this to mean that she was with this child constantly. She was with him at the time he died, and digoxin acts quite quickly, fifteen to thirty minutes from dosage to effects.

They therefore focused on Miss Nelles and within a couple of days were quite satisfied that they had reasonable and probable grounds to believe that she had caused the deaths of these babies. After consulting with the Crown attorney, they went to interview Miss Nelles; however, she refused to answer any questions until she had consulted with a lawyer. The investigators then arrested her and charged her with four murders.

In the months following our decision to perform these analyses, George Cimbura and Eva Koves, his chief technician, worked virtually full-time developing and validating a procedure for digoxin analysis that could be applied to postmortem samples. The common technique in clinical labs for this purpose was radioimmunoassay (RIA) because of its great sensitivity. Its limitation, however, is that it is not specific for digoxin. There were other substances that could give a positive RIA result. In a clinical setting, lack of specificity is not a serious problem, but in a forensic setting, the presence of the specific drug has to be proven, and lack of specificity would be a major weakness.

There were several commercial RIA kits available, and the first task was to test all of them to determine which had the greatest specificity. Once they had settled on a particular kit, George and Eva had to develop a method to extract digoxin from postmortem samples and separate it from other materials in the extract. For this function, they focused on a relatively new (at that time) process, high-pressure liquid chromatography (HPLC).

The protocol eventually settled on involved extracting and purifying (as much as possible) the digoxin and testing the resultant extract with the RIA kit. If the result was negative, that was the end of it. But if the RIA was positive, they would process the extract with HPLC to separate the digoxin from other extractants, and then determine the amount of digoxin using RIA. This was a time-consuming process, but it proved to be the best possible way of doing these analyses.

Miss Nelles's preliminary hearing began in January 1982 and went on for about forty days. During it, evidence was presented that constant care meant only that Miss Nelles was with the baby most of the time, but she would be relieved for coffee breaks or lunch. It also became clear that although she had been on the nursing team that cared for all four of these babies, when the first one died in January, she had not been on duty.

Near the end of the hearing, George Cimbura testified to the results of his analyses; he had found very high concentrations of digoxin in all four babies. These results were, however, complicated by the fact that three of the babies had had it prescribed for them. Nevertheless, the concentrations found were much higher than would be expected from clinical use. There was thus quite clear evidence that digoxin was somehow involved, particularly in the case of the last of the deaths because that baby had not been prescribed any digoxin. It must be remembered, of course, that all these babies were quite sick; they had not, however, been expected to die.

During the preliminary hearing, an additional suspicious case was identified involving another baby who had not been prescribed digoxin and had died in December 1980. No autopsy had been performed, and thus no samples were available. That baby's body had to be exhumed, a serious emotional challenge for the family and some of the hospital staff.

We received tissue from the exhumation, never the best samples to work with, and George Cimbura found very high digoxin concentrations in it. There was, in fact, so much extracted that George and Eva were able not only to use the HPLC/RIA process but also to make an unequivocal identification of digoxin by mean of mass spectroscopy (MS).

Throughout this entire period, most of the clinical staff at the hospital, and particularly those in the laboratory, did not believe that there had been any digoxin overdose deaths. They were, perhaps understandably, extremely reluctant to accept that there was anything untoward occurring in the hospital. They challenged our results and kept coming up with possible alternative explanations. This added to the pressure on George and Eva to make sure that every i was dotted twice and every t was crossed multiple times in all their results.

At the conclusion of the preliminary hearing, the judge discharged Miss Nelles.

As might be expected, there was enormous media interest in this case and criticism of the police for their "rush to judgment." A new investigative team was assigned to delve even deeper into the case. During the ensuing months, some outside epidemiologists were retained to review the events at the hospital, and they produced some startling information. There had been thirty-six deaths on cardiac wards A and B in the period between June 30, 1980, and March 22, 1981. This was very unusual because in the four equivalent previous time periods reviewed, the number of deaths on these wards had ranged from just one to seven. Something unusual was happening between June 1980 and March 1981.

Perhaps even more startling was that of the thirty-six deaths, twenty-four occurred in one very short period of the day, between 01:00 and 06:00. In the four previous periods, only one death had occurred in that same interval. Still more unusual was that in all the cases except one, one or more members of a single nursing team (of the four teams) had been on duty.

The reopened investigation also found that the nurses themselves had become very concerned about the increased number of deaths on the cardiac wards and, as early as the summer of 1980, had been voicing those concerns. Susan Nelles was one of the more vociferous. They were frustrated because they had been unable to persuade other clinical staff, the doctors in particular, of their concern until the rapid increase in deaths began in early 1981. However, by the critical weekend of March 21–22, the doctors had taken the unusual step of placing digoxin under close control. It had to be locked up and administered only when two people were present. They also decided after the death on March 22 to relieve this one nursing team from duty because of concern about stress on the members due to this very unfortunate number of deaths on their watch.

In April 1983, as a result of all the publicity and public concern about the suspicious nature of deaths in such a highly respected institution, Mr. Justice Grange of the Court of Appeal (who had conducted the Mississauga train derailment inquiry in 1980) was appointed as a royal commissioner to investigate these events. He conducted an extremely wide-ranging inquiry, retaining experts and calling evidence, and had Ontario Provincial Police investigators assist him. In addition to epidemiologists, he also had expert clinicians and pharmacologists testify about each baby's course of treatment and their final symptoms. The inquiry went on from April 1983 until Justice Grange issued his report in December 1984.

Throughout this time, additional samples from some of the babies were being found in the hospital and, in the end, we received samples from twenty-two of the thirty-six babies. George Cimbura identified digoxin in fifteen of the twenty-two. In five of the others, his results were inconclusive, and in two they were negative. Only four of the twenty-two babies had not had digoxin prescribed for them. The finding of what was digoxin in these samples was significant; however, the quantitative results were of limited value because of the nature of the samples, from either exhumed bodies or fixed tissue that had been retained in the hospital.

During testimony at the inquiry, all the experts, except one, agreed that our finding of digoxin in those babies who had not had it prescribed for them was indeed significant. They also agreed that the quantitative levels, which were very high in some of the babies who had been prescribed the drug, were probably not significant for a variety of reasons.

The one expert who disagreed did so because he believed that the possibility that digoxin was somehow created in these bodies after death could not be ruled out. Although he acknowledged that it would be an extremely difficult piece of research to do, he testified that the only way the inquiry could be sure of this was to exhume babies' bodies and take samples to see if there was digoxin present or not. In his final report, Mr. Justice Grange acknowledged this testimony but decided not to accept it.

Shortly before the inquiry started, another issue had arisen. A paper published in the *New England Journal of Medicine* reported something that was referred to as "Substance X" that, by RIA analysis, appeared to be digoxin but was not. This created quite a furor and called our analytical results into question. George Cimbura had to spend a lot of time reviewing this paper and explaining its significance (or lack thereof) to his results.

The paper's authors had used a different immunoassay kit from the one George used, and its specificity was much less than that which he had established in the one we used. Also, those authors had not done the extractions/purifications or the HPLC separation that George had. As a result, the findings reported in that paper were not relevant to the results presented to Mr. Justice Grange.

The paper did, however, prompt another piece of research for George and the Pathology Department at the hospital. With their cooperation, he obtained postmortem blood samples from twenty-four children and heart tissue from another twenty, none of whom had had digoxin prescribed for them. The highest apparent digoxin concentration that he found in any of these samples using our procedure was 1 ng/mL, essentially a negative result. This data pretty well ruled out the suggestion that the extremely high concentrations that George had found were simply something that happened with postmortem samples.

Some of the hospital staff were still not convinced about the validity of our results, and in March 1984, they convened a two-day meeting of experts on laboratory procedures for the identification of digoxin. They expected this meeting to produce support for their position that digoxin had not been identified in these cases. This peer group reviewed all the data that George

Cimbura had developed, by then a voluminous amount. After the first day, the meeting unanimously concluded that the procedures George had developed were the best that could be used, that they gave reliable results, and that all the criteria for the identification of digoxin had been met. They also agreed that there was no evidence that digoxin was produced in the body either pre- or postmortem. The members of the group decided they didn't need the second day and went home, much to the chagrin of a couple of people in the hospital.

George testified to all his data at the Grange Inquiry; it was carefully scrutinized and, in the end, Mr. Justice Grange accepted it. An amusing sidelight in this major tragedy was contained in a book about these events written by Maggie Siggins. She described George in the witness box as "George the Moose" because he testified in a rather slow, plodding, and extremely thorough manner. However, she went on to describe all the challenges that were put to him by the various lawyers and concluded with "and at the end of all this, George the Moose, was still standing."

In his final report, Judge Grange concluded that there were, in fact, eight babies who died from digoxin poisoning in the hospital during this period. He based this on both the clinical evidence provided by expert clinicians and the toxicological confirmation that there was digoxin present in high concentrations. There were an additional five deaths that he considered highly suspicious of digoxin overdose, but for one reason or another, there was no toxicological data available, and his conclusion was limited to the clinical evidence. Ten additional cases were considered suspicious in the sense that he just couldn't call them natural; the evidence in these cases was equivocal, but the babies had not been expected to die, even though they were very sick. There were six deaths that he deemed natural, and an additional seven that he was unable to reach any conclusion on.

The baby deaths at Sick Kids required more demanding effort on the part of CFS staff, particularly George Cimbura and Eva Koves, who worked virtually full-time on it for more than two years, than any other case we had ever worked. It required developing groundbreaking procedures and applying them to samples of varying or dubious quality. But the results stood up and allowed Mr. Justice Grange to reach valid conclusions. In his report he wrote,

> I think it is safe to say that more has been discovered about digoxin, methods of testing for it and the interpretation of levels obtained, over the past three years than was discovered in the almost three hundred years that it has been with us as a therapeutic drug.

In spite of the fact that digoxin had been widely used in clinical practice for many decades, until the development of the immunoassay procedure in the early 1970s, there was no procedure for its analysis. Even in the pharmaceutical industry, where they had the pure drug to work with, there was no chemical analysis for it. I remember in the 1950s visiting a pharmaceutical plant where digoxin was produced, and the only analytical procedure they had was what was referred to as a "biological assay." This involved administering the digoxin-containing product to pigeons and then seeing how many of them vomited (a side effect of digoxin ingestion) and how much. In one laboratory, there was a pigeon coop across one wall with trays underneath the birds to collect the vomit. Technicians then measured the amount of vomit, and that determined the concentration of the drug in the product.

Despite periodic reports in the literature and the media suggesting that our data was faulty, to this day there has never been anything that casts significant scientific doubt on it. (George succeeded me as director of CFS in 1994 and retired in 1996. Sadly, he died within a few years.)

An indication of the importance of the pioneering work that George and Eva had done in the early 1980s was provided in 1996 during one of my reviews of the FBI Laboratory described in Chapter 25. I was interviewing the head of their Toxicology Section, who was in the process of developing an analytical procedure for digoxin to deal with a series of deaths that had occurred in a hospital in the United States. He told me that this had never been done before. Much to his surprise, I referred him to Mr. Justice Grange's report and the process we had developed at CFS in 1982–1983.

The stressful meeting I referred to at the beginning of this chapter occurred after the investigations were complete and Judge Grange's report issued. Despite all the work, there were still some deaths of babies that could not be unequivocally established as digoxin deaths. The parents of some of these babies remained very upset by this uncertainty. They wanted closure and to know definitely, "Was their baby poisoned or not?" The investigating officers asked if we would meet with these parents to explain all that we had done and why, in some cases, we could not reach any conclusion. That was one of the very rare times in my career where I had to sit down across the table from a group of people who were so directly affected and emotionally involved with something we had done (or tried to do).

I found that to be a very stressful meeting, and it gave me an even greater appreciation of the stress that police officers have to face when dealing with victims' relatives. George and I explained to them as best we could all the work that had been done but, in the end, had to acknowledge that we could not definitively answer their question. All we could say was that something very unusual was happening in cardiac wards A and B at the Hospital for Sick Children in 1980 and 1981.

Figure 21.1 George Cimbura.

Introduction of DNA Profiling
"If You Are Going to Do It, Do It Right!"

22

One of the most common examinations requested of all forensic science labs is the comparison of stains of blood (or other body fluids) with known samples of blood from victims or suspects. Until the mid-1960s, the only tool we had to attempt this was ABO blood grouping, a tool of limited discrimination value since about 45% of the population are group O and about 40% are group A.

Gradually in the late 1960s and 1970s, other genetic markers became available that permitted additional discrimination and which could be applied to dried stains. Nevertheless, there were still limitations in the degree of discrimination possible. It was like trying to recognize people in the audience in a darkened theatre. In the almost total darkness, they are all simply silhouettes. As the lights are gradually turned up, additional features become visible and it is possible to tell increasing numbers of the audience apart. However, even when the lights are fully on, there are still some at the back of the hall who appear indistinguishable. This was the situation with body fluid comparisons before DNA profiling became available.

The genetic markers we were using were manifestations of an individual's DNA, surrogates in other words. Why not look at the DNA itself? There was no way to do so, until November 1984, when Alec Jeffreys (now Professor Sir Alec), a thirty-four-year-old assistant professor at the University of Leicester, described a new observation at a meeting in London. His subsequent publication in *Nature* in March 1985 described regions along the length of the DNA molecule that are highly variable. In the conclusion of the paper, he wrote, in a massive understatement, "we anticipate that these DNA 'fingerprints' can be used in forensic applications." Forensic science would never be quite the same again.

As with many discoveries, there was an element of serendipity in this finding. Jeffreys, a molecular biologist, was not trying to revolutionize forensic science; he was looking for a human copy of the myoglobin gene in grey seals. One Monday morning, he noticed large variations in patterns on an autorad and almost immediately recognized their potential for what was for him a foreign field, forensic science.

The first forensic application of DNA profiling came in 1986 when a police officer in nearby Leicester asked Jeffreys if his procedure could be used to confirm that a young man who had confessed to a double rape/murder had done it. After his analysis, Jeffreys informed the officer that yes, both girls had been raped by the same man, but no, it was not the young man in custody. The first forensic DNA case was therefore like so many since, an exoneration. After a massive investigation that became known as "the blooding" (in which all the males in the community were asked to provide "voluntary" blood samples), Colin Pitchfork was charged and convicted of the crime. (Although DNA received credit for Pitchfork's confession, it was his wife's fiercely expressed outrage at him that led to it after she learned that he had avoided providing a sample during the blooding by having a friend show up in his stead.)

The obvious potential of this new technique excited interest in forensic labs all over the world, led by the Home Office Forensic Science Service (FSS) in the United Kingdom and the FBI Lab in the United States. They had the "deep pockets" required to transition the process from the research lab to the working forensic lab.

In 1986, I decided that the Centre of Forensic Sciences (CFS) had to become actively involved in developing a capability with this new system. Pamela Newall, the research scientist in our Biology Section, was assigned to lead this activity. We obtained the $100,000 worth of equipment necessary and, because Jeffreys' process was very labor-intensive, Pam had to devote all of her time over the next couple of years learning the basic manipulations required, establishing that she could, in fact, obtain valid results, and building a population database of the frequency of occurrence of various combinations of loci (positions) on the DNA molecule.

While we, and other forensic labs, were going through this process, two commercial clinical laboratories in the United States jumped right in because the police and prosecutors were not prepared to wait two years until the FBI, the Royal Canadian Mounted Police (RCMP), or the CFS were ready to apply it to casework. We all believed the commercial labs were premature in offering the service because they did not appreciate the problems that real-world forensic science samples, as opposed to clinical samples, can present. Several of their cases went through the courts in the United States and got a lot of publicity, which in turn increased the demand from the law enforcement community for us to get with it!

Unfortunately, although predictably, a major case came along in which one of the commercial labs got it wrong. In New York City, there was a landmark case, *People v. Castro*, in which the defense mounted a very significant challenge to the evidence and demonstrated that the DNA work had been poorly done. As a result, the evidence was rejected. This resulted in much publicity, some of which suggested a problem with the basic concept of forensic DNA analysis, not at all what the case represented. A few weeks later at an American Society of Crime Laboratory Directors (ASCLD) meeting, I attended a talk by the judge in the Castro case and was very impressed with the knowledge about DNA that he had gained during the trial. His message to the forensic science community was simply, "Don't read too much into my decision. All that it stands for is if you are going to do it, do it right."

By mid-1988, the FBI Lab had validated the process and was ready to start accepting cases. Later that year, the RCMP Lab in Ottawa also began accepting cases. The first trial in the United States was in 1987 in Florida. In Canada, the first was in New Brunswick in 1989. When I was satisfied that CFS was ready to accept our first case, I began looking for a low-profile one so that we could dip our feet into the water gently. "Best laid plans ..."

In early July 1990, a case came along that I decided we had to accept in spite of the fact that it was going to become a very high-profile case. It involved the disappearance and suspected murder on June 19, 1990, of a young woman in Scarborough, Elizabeth Bain, whose body has never been found. Her boyfriend was a suspect.

In the absence of a body, a major issue was whether Elizabeth was in fact dead. Her car had been found filled with so much blood that the pathologist opined that the person the blood had come from could no longer be alive. We were asked if it was possible to establish whether this was Elizabeth Bain's blood, in spite of there being no known sample available from her. We knew that DNA analysis might allow us to do this, so the decision was made that despite our original plan, we would have to introduce DNA to Ontario in this case.

One of the many advantages of DNA, because it is inherited from one's parents, is that in the absence of a known sample from a missing person, samples of the DNA from the natural parents can be analyzed and the results used to predict the DNA profile of their offspring. Pam Newall examined samples from Miss Bain's mother and father and was able to conclude that the blood in the car was from a female child of Mr. and Mrs. Bain. They had two daughters, one of whom was known to be alive, so this had to be Elizabeth's blood.

A complicating factor in this analysis was the fact that most of the blood had been recovered from a large pool in the footwell of the car. It hadn't dried and had been exposed to the heat of the day for several days. Moisture and heat destroy DNA quite rapidly, and thus although there was a lot of blood, there was very little usable DNA. Fortunately, a small amount of blood had dried on the seat fabric, and that was what was used to develop the profile.

In November 1990, Elizabeth's boyfriend was charged with her murder. He was tried and convicted in March 1992. The conviction went through several appeals, and in April 2008, he was acquitted at a new trial when the Crown decided to present no evidence. There was considerable speculation that Paul Bernardo (see below) might have been Elizabeth's killer since he was known to have been active in Scarborough around the time she disappeared. DNA later played a significant role in the trials of Bernardo and his wife, Karla Homolka.

Once we had introduced DNA profiling and the evidence had been accepted, we were overwhelmed with demand for the service. The process we used at that time, restriction fragment length polymorphism (RFLP), was very time-consuming and labor-intensive. Initially, only Pam Newall, with the help of a technician, was qualified to perform the analysis, and they could do only about thirty cases a year. Typically, we would receive about 1,000–1,200 cases a year involving body fluids. Training our existing Biology Section staff in DNA analysis was going to take up to one year per individual, so we had to establish criteria for cases on which we would use DNA. Identification of an individual had to be a major issue in the case; appropriate samples, including known samples from the parties involved, had to be available; it would have to be a crime of violence and/or part of a serial crime situation; and there had to be time before any trial to actually perform the analyses, that is, a court date ten weeks or longer away.

Because the potential significance of the results of DNA analysis was so much greater than it had been with conventional genetic markers, we also had to develop wording for reporting this information. It was important to establish that this was far more significant than what police and courts were used to receiving from us, but it was also essential, given the enormous publicity that DNA had received, that its significance not be overstated. We were developing DNA profiles for which the chance of a random occurrence of the same profile in two people in the population was, for example, one in fourteen billion, i.e., greater than the total population of the world.

The difficulty with numbers that large, although they are statistically valid, is that it is a challenge for people to truly appreciate what they mean. It is like trying to understand the size of the universe. It was these population frequency numbers that generated the major challenges in the courtroom. Many arguments were made, and in the first two DNA cases in Canada, the courts did not allow the frequency of occurrence data to be presented. The DNA analyst was allowed to say, "This is extremely rare" or "I would not expect to find this very commonly," but they were not permitted to use numbers. Finally, in a case in Woodstock, Ontario, a judge made the commonsense ruling that the numbers were there and they meant more than words like "very rare" or "extremely uncommon." The statistics might not be entirely comprehensible, but they did give the jury a better sense of the significance of the results. Subsequently, the Supreme Court of Canada agreed with that opinion.

A major value of DNA evidence has been its ability to eliminate possible sources of a body fluid stain. Typically, our experience was that about 20% of the samples received, particularly in sexual assault cases, excluded the suspected source. One of the things that happened in the early years of DNA evidence was that people who had been convicted before it became available and were serving (or had served) time in prison were subsequently exonerated by DNA evidence. The only forensic evidence available in those cases had been from conventional genetic markers that, as described above, had limited discriminating power. As a result, they often could not be ruled out as the source of the semen in a sexual assault case and had been convicted by that and whatever other evidence was presented. Once DNA analysis was performed, their chances of being ruled out were vastly increased.

In Ontario, the most notorious wrongful conviction case was that of Guy Paul Morin, who was serving time for the murder of a young girl who had been his neighbor. Eventually, the DNA found in a semen stain on her panties was shown to be different from his, and he was exonerated. (See Chapter 23.)

Another major advantage of DNA profiling is its ability to provide investigative leads to the police. One of the values of fingerprints, for example, is that large databases of fingerprints of known persons have been created against which an unknown crime scene fingerprint can be searched and the source of that fingerprint possibly identified. That can also be done with DNA profiles, and most countries, including Canada, have developed large DNA databases against which suspect profiles can be searched and investigative leads provided.

In the early 1990s, newer techniques replaced the very sample demanding and labor-intensive RFLP process. Beginning in 1986, Kary Mullis, a molecular biologist in California, developed a technique called polymerase chain reaction (PCR), which allowed him to, in effect, make copies of tiny bits of DNA until there was a sufficient amount for DNA analysis. This made the analysis even more valuable because very often we just didn't have a sufficient sample in good enough condition that we could use the RFLP technique. The PCR technique was much less labor-intensive and much quicker; results could be obtained virtually overnight. The number of loci on the DNA molecule to which PCR can be applied had also expanded. Thus, in 1992, we began applying the PCR technique. Initially, the discriminating power was not as great as it was with RFLP, but gradually PCR was applied to short tandem repeats (STRs) on the DNA molecule, and match probabilities similar to those from RFLP became the norm. RFLP was phased out, the number of our staff qualified to perform DNA analysis increased, and by the time I retired in 1994, we had stopped using conventional genetic markers and DNA was used in all body fluid stain cases.

DNA has become a model for the introduction of new forensic science evidence because it originated in academia with a solid basic scientific background. The forensic science profession decided that all the background science had to be evaluated and validated before ever going near a court and that this work would best be done cooperatively within the profession.

I had always given enormous credit to Roger Castonguay, director of the FBI Laboratory in 1987–1988 when this started. Roger had no background in science; he was an investigator who had risen through the ranks in the FBI to become the assistant director in charge of the laboratory. He decided that the FBI would do the work in cooperation with other forensic science laboratories around the United States and Canada and established an organization called TWGDAM (Technical Working Group for DNA Analysis Methods), funded by the FBI. TWGDAM consisted of about twenty forensic (and other) scientists from around the United States, Canada (including Pam Newall from CFS), and the United Kingdom. They cooperatively performed and shared an enormous amount of validation work and standards development. Thus, when forensic science laboratories started to report DNA cases, they had the benefit of analytical protocols, quality assurance procedures, and population statistics procedures that were all based soundly on science.

That approach was very different from other traditional processes in forensic science labs. Previously, when something new came along, everyone said, "We can do this" and started doing it. Most of the time that worked. What we have seen since DNA was introduced is challenges being made to traditional techniques in forensic science that have long been assumed to be based on validated data but which may not have been. For example, with firearms identification, the basic premise is that bullets fired through different barrels will have different markings. That premise is probably valid, but there was only minimal properly documented literature to support it. As a result, since the introduction of DNA, forensic scientists have been performing, and documenting, the basic science of such things as firearms, fingerprints, and handwriting identification, and the entire profession has been significantly improved.

A less positive effect of DNA has been on some of the other common types of evidence, such as glass, paint, soil, hairs, and fibers, which are commonly referred to as "trace evidence." With these, the premise is that valid examinations can reliably show whether two samples have the same characteristics or composition. However, these are common materials, and there are undoubtedly many other samples of them that have the same properties. For example, we can show that the paint found on the clothing of a hit-and-run victim has the same properties as the paint from a suspect automobile, but we know there are other vehicles that have the same paint. That is simply the nature of the auto production process. We could never therefore say, "This paint came from that vehicle to the exclusion of all others." Yes, the vast majority of cars will have different paint, but there certainly are some that are the same. Police and courts that have become used to receiving DNA results showing that the chances of another source of DNA having the same properties as a questioned sample are only, for example, one in fifteen billion may not be prepared to accept evidence that "the paint on this clothing could have come from the suspect car." Frequency data are just not available and probably never will be.

I believe juries can bring common sense to such questions and recognize that the issue is not whether this paint could have come from any car in the entire world but rather from one painted in the same assembly plant around the same time and which was in the same location as the victim at the same time, an infinitely smaller number!

The Bernardo Case

I referred earlier to the use of DNA in the Bernardo case, another very high-profile event. It was perceived in the media, and by many law enforcement officers, lawyers, and judges, as a case in which the law enforcement system, including the CFS, essentially screwed up and took far too long to identify someone who should have been identified as a suspect much sooner. Certainly, before he and his wife killed two teenaged girls, Leslie Mahaffy and Kristen French, in June 1991 and April 1992, respectively.

Between August 1985 and August 1991, CFS received sixteen "no suspect" sexual assault cases for which Paul Bernardo eventually, although not at the time, became a suspect. Three different police agencies were involved; two cases were submitted by Peel Regional Police, one by Niagara Regional Police, and the remainder by the Toronto Police. Not all of them were ever confirmed as Bernardo cases.

Because almost all these cases were received before CFS began reporting DNA analysis, the conventional genetic markers in use did not lend themselves to developing information that would be of much investigative value. Therefore, the items were preserved until a suspect could be developed or it became a reasonable possibility that the case was one of a series. By December 1987, the Scarborough cases began to be suspected to be linked and so were treated as a series. (The Niagara Regional Police case was not linked to the others until after Bernardo's arrest. Before that, the investigation was focused on a different suspect.) One CFS examiner was assigned to all these cases.

Examinations for semen/saliva were made on appropriate items, and grouping in the ABO and phosphoglucomutase (PGM) systems was attempted when the amount or condition of the samples allowed. Because of the intense interest of the investigators in these cases, they were assigned priority status, and results were provided verbally to the investigators as they were developed. One of the suspects from whom known samples were received in November 1990 was Paul Bernardo. His ABO and PGM analyses were completed in early December, and he remained one of the many suspects. In January 1989, as a result of the examinations in one of these cases, it had become apparent that the source of the semen was a nonsecretor (of their ABO type; 20% of the male population), and this information became useful for screening suspects. By October 1991, 194 of a total of 279 suspects had been eliminated as possible sources by their secretor status.

By this time, we had started reporting DNA analyses on a very limited number of cases. However, Pam Newall was already overwhelmed by the demand. The examiner who had been doing the conventional serology in these cases was close to finishing her DNA training, and so I decided that she should be the one to also do the DNA.

In April 1992, samples from five of the seventy-nine nonexcluded suspects (including Bernardo) and three of the cases were resubmitted by the Toronto Police Department for DNA analysis. This was still in the RFLP era, and the typical turnaround time for DNA cases was four to six months. Additional samples were needed, but these were not all received until November. Finally, after we were advised that no additional samples were available, on February 1, 1993, the first RFLP autorad was examined; there was a possible match to Bernardo but a nonmatch to the other two suspects from whom adequate samples had been provided. The police were immediately advised but were cautioned that this was only the first DNA probe and additional work had yet to be done. Between February 4 and April 29, 1993, the second through the ninth probes were run, and all confirmed the match between Paul Bernardo and three of the Scarborough cases. Bernardo was arrested on February 17.

After February 17, 1993, hundreds of items from the Bernardo residence were received and processed, with DNA analysis (both RFLP and PCR) done on sixty of these. The results of all this work essentially established the presence of traces of the blood of Leslie Mahaffy and Kristen French in the Bernardo residence on Bayview Drive in St. Catherines.

Trace evidence examinations were made on more than 390 items. Hairs from the church parking lot where Kristen had been abducted and hair clippings from the bedroom carpet in the Bernardo residence were determined to be similar to hers. A few fibers recovered from Kristen's body were consistent with fibers from the carpets in the dining room and master bedroom of the residence.

Concerning timing, had these cases occurred in the mid-eighties rather than the late eighties, not only would CFS's work have represented state-of-the-art practices, but also the results would have been considered quite timely. The serology examinations were reported very quickly once the cases were identified as a series, and some results were useful for screening suspects. Alternatively, had the cases occurred in the early nineties, the resources for DNA analysis would have permitted a more expeditious start to the analyses, and the newer, faster PCR techniques would have resulted in quicker results for the investigators. Unfortunately, these cases occurred during the transition period when the process was new to the CFS, trained staff were limited in number, and the technology was changing rapidly.

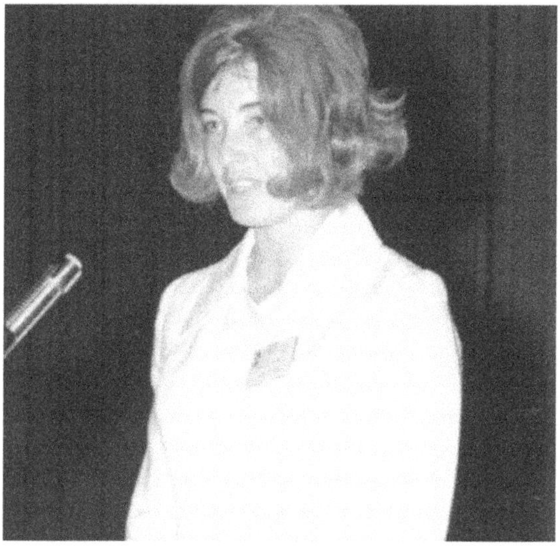

Figure 22.1 Pamela Newall.

23 The Guy Paul Morin Case, a "Tragedy of Errors"

On January 23, 1995, an appeal by Guy Paul Morin against his conviction for murder in July 1992 was allowed by the Ontario Court of Appeal, and a verdict of acquittal was entered. His name has since become synonymous in Ontario with the phrase "wrongful conviction." Forensic science played a role in his conviction and, later, in establishing his factual innocence. Along the way, there were many serendipitous events; mistakes by police, prosecutors, and forensic scientists; bad luck; embarrassments; two marathon trials; several appeals; and a Judicial Commission of Inquiry. There were many, including myself, who were astounded that he was ever convicted in the first place. It was indeed a "tragedy of errors."

The Crime

On October 3, 1984, a nine-year-old girl, Christine Jessup, who lived with her parents and fourteen-year-old brother in Queensville, a small village in the northern part of York Region, disappeared after returning home from school. She was last seen between 15:30 and 16:00 by a nearby variety store owner who sold her some bubble gum. When her mother and brother arrived home around 16:30, they began calling Christine's friends to try to locate her. About 19:00, Mrs. Jessup reported her daughter missing to York Regional Police. (The York Regional Police Force [PF] had been formed in 1971 through the amalgamation of nine small town and rural police agencies.)

Members of the York Region PF immediately began an extensive search that included interviews with the Jessups's next-door neighbors, the Morin family. Guy Paul Morin was twenty-five years old at the time and lived at home with his parents. He told police that he had arrived home from work between 17:00 and 17:30, a timing that later became a matter of major dispute at his trials.

The search and investigation continued fruitlessly until December 31, 1984, when a resident of Durham Region out for a walk in a rural area discovered a partially decomposed body in an isolated area off Ravenshoe Road, thirty-five miles east of Queensville. This was in the jurisdiction of the Durham Regional PF, which had been formed in 1974 through the amalgamation of seven smaller forces, and they took charge of the investigation.

Communication between the two forces was not as effective as it should have been, nor as it would be today.

Durham PF members searched the immediate area; however, it was New Year's Eve, and that search was not as thorough as it might have been on any other day. (For example, in May 1985, the Jessup family found additional bones at the site that were subsequently identified as Christine's.) The remains were transferred to the Chief Coroner's Office in Toronto, where they were examined by the then chief forensic pathologist and identified through dental records as Christine's. She had been stabbed multiple times in the chest.

The Investigation

Many items collected at the scene, including a necklace and panties, were taken initially by a Durham PF identification officer back to his crowded work and storage area and eventually to the Centre of Forensic Sciences (CFS). Because there was an incomplete hair tangled in the necklace, the case was assigned to a hair and fiber examiner. Unfortunately, at that time, as a result of retirements and the dismissal of a trainee who had been unsuccessful during his training program, we had only two qualified hair and fiber examiners. One of these was the Biology Section head, Norman Erickson, who also had to manage a busy section. The other had only recently completed her training program and had limited experience dealing with investigators. The case was assigned to her, which, as it later turned out, was a serious mistake on my part.

As the Durham PF investigation proceeded through the winter months of 1985, Guy Paul Morin was interviewed several times. The investigators found him to be what they referred to as a "weird guy" because of his diverse interests (e.g., music and beekeeping) and some of his ambiguous comments about the case. Despite his alibi, which they believed was concocted by his family, the investigators began to focus on him as a suspect, and on April 22, following a six-hour interrogation, he was arrested and charged with Christine's murder. During his pretrial detention, two "jailhouse informants" told police that he had confessed to them. Eventually, this "evidence" became extremely dubious.

Extensive searches were made of the Morin house, property, and vehicles, as a result of which 141 items were taken to the Durham Police Identification Office and subsequently to CFS. (It was later revealed that some items were lost by the identification officer, and he tried to conceal this by creating a second set of notes. He was subsequently charged with perjury, but this charge was eventually stayed by the Crown because of his ill health.)

Small spots of semen were found on Christine's panties, but this was in the pre-DNA era, so only ABO typing was attempted, and it was unsuccessful.

Most of the lab work focused on the very labor-intensive microscopic examination of hundreds of hairs and fibers that were collected. The hair found in the necklace was found to be different from Christine's but could not be distinguished from Guy's known hairs (which, however, had not been collected until about six months after Christine's disappearance). It was an incomplete hair (missing the root and tip) and therefore had very limited evidential value. Three incomplete hairs found in Guy's car (which was very dirty and cluttered inside when it was searched at CFS) were different from his hairs but had similar microscopic characteristics to Christine's.

Of the fibers examined, there was a reddish-pink angora wool fiber from the car that was similar to a fiber on one of Christine's socks and to one from her right shoe, two purple-pink animal hairs from the car that were similar to hairs on her pants and sweatshirt, a pink polyester fiber from the car that was similar to one on her recorder pouch, and a dark grey animal hair from the Morin living room that was similar to two hairs on Christine's sweater. Of these, the angora hairs were the ones of potentially greatest interest because they were less common than the others.

Until well into the DNA era in the 1990s, the "state of the art" for comparison of hairs was a microscopic examination of the many features visible under the microscope. The most that could be said of a "match" (a word we avoided when testifying about hair but which was commonly used by police and attorneys during informal discussions) was that a known and unknown hair had similar characteristics and "could have come" from the same source, or they had different features and could not have come from the same source. The former conclusion could only be made after examination of a complete (root-to-tip) hair and comparison of it with a sample of up to fifty complete known hairs. Hair could never be used for identification of a source.

Even though we had stressed the limited value of the necklace hair, the police placed considerable evidential value on it. In an attempt to strengthen this, they had collected hair from all thirty-two of Christine's schoolmates and asked that these be compared with the necklace hair in the hope of showing that it had not come from any of them. We resisted this request as being of no value, because of the limited characteristics visible in the necklace hair, and were prepared to acknowledge that there probably would be hairs from at least one of the students that could not be distinguished from it. In the end, we finally did agree to make these examinations before the second trial, and as we had predicted, there were hairs from two of the students that "matched" the necklace hair.

More could be done with fibers both microscopically and analytically. The chemical type, construction, and color could all be used for comparison. Although an enormous amount of effort was devoted by the police and our examiner to trying to locate a known source for any of the fibers, none was ever located. This further limited their evidential value.

Since the Jessups and Morins were neighbors, the possibility of accidental transfer of hairs or fibers between the two families and their homes in the course of normal activities was considered. The police were convinced, however, that there was virtually no interchange between the families and that Christine had never been in the Morin home nor in Guy's car. Otherwise, the hair and fiber comparisons would have been of even less evidential value and the effort to locate a source for the fibers would not have been so extensive.

As all this work progressed, there was constant interaction and discussion between the investigators and our examiner. As was common for us at that time, she made no detailed record of what was said during these discussions, but the investigators did. They became convinced that when she told them the hair from the necklace had similar characteristics to Guy's, that meant it came from him. She denied ever saying this (because it was not a complete hair and even complete hairs did not permit such a conclusion), but she had no documentary record to support this, and they did. (We later changed our practice and required detailed notes to be made of all such conversations.)

The First Trial and Appeals

Guy Paul Morin went to trial in London, Ontario (a change of venue had been granted), in January 1986. He was represented by prominent Toronto lawyer Clayton Ruby, and the trial lasted four weeks. Evidence was presented on all the issues mentioned above, including the hair and fiber evidence, and many more. (The possibility of the fibers having been found in both locations as a result of accidental transfer because both families used the same laundromat was suggested by Mr. Ruby to our hair and fiber examiner, who replied that it was unlikely that an angora wool garment would be put through a wash and dry process. Nevertheless, the police did do a test that showed that fibers could be accidentally transferred in a laundromat.)

Mr. Ruby's interesting defense strategy was twofold. The first was that, based on the timing in his alibi, Guy could not have killed Christine. Alternatively, if Guy's alibi was not accepted and the jury believed he had killed her, he was not guilty by reason of insanity. (There was psychiatric evidence that he suffered from schizophrenia.) On February 7, 1986, after deliberating for thirteen hours, the jury acquitted Guy Paul Morin and he was released from custody.

In a very unusual move, the Crown appealed the verdict of the jury on the basis that the judge had misdirected the jury on the doctrine of "reasonable doubt" and the psychiatric testimony. In June 1987, the Ontario Court of Appeal allowed the appeal and ordered a new trial. Guy was returned to custody. He appealed to the Supreme Court of Canada (SCC) and, pending the hearing of his appeal, Guy was released from custody. In November 1988, the SCC dismissed this appeal and affirmed the order for a new trial. In April 1990, another appeal to the SCC was filed, but it was dismissed in March 1991.

Over the next eight months, many pretrial motions were heard and the second trial began in London on November 13, 1991. During the interim, as discussed in Chapter 22, CFS had begun using the restriction fragment length polymorphism (RFLP) technique for DNA analysis. Attempts were made to obtain useful profiles from the blood and semen stains on Christine's blouse and panties, but RFLP was not sufficiently sensitive to produce meaningful results. We did not begin using the more sensitive polymerase chain reaction (PCR) technique until 1992, i.e., after the second trial. Also, during this period our examiner was seriously injured in an automobile accident and had to retire on long-term disability. Despite this, she had to return to testify during the second trial.

The Second Trial and Appeals

Both the lead Crown and defense attorneys were different at the second trial. The defense was led by a very competent and meticulous lawyer, Jack Pinkovsky, who prepared much more thoroughly than most and worked exceptionally hard for his client. His courtroom style, however, was extremely aggressive, to the point of being described as "abusive" both in his questions of witnesses and in his arguments before the judge. Some trial observers noted that his style might have antagonized the jurors against both him and his client. Mr. Pinkovsky was well matched by senior Crown attorney Leo McGuigan, who was equally competent and hardworking and whose style was much more along the lines of an American prosecutor than the traditional Canadian Crown attorney.

Largely as a result of the two lead attorneys' style, the second trial went on for about ten months, four months of pretrial motions and six months of testimony from 120 witnesses. Much of the evidence was the same as at the first trial, but all was much more severely challenged by Guy's lawyer. Because the CFS hair and fiber examiner had left the center almost five years previously due to her accident, Norm Erickson had to review all of her earlier examinations, and both had to testify.

It quickly became clear that the Crown attorneys were placing much more weight on the hair and fiber evidence, particularly that of the necklace hair, than we believed it warranted. After several discussions with them, I took the very unusual step of having Norm Erickson write a formal letter to them emphasizing our belief in the limited value of the necklace hair. A letter to the defense made the same point, and in his testimony at the trial, Norm stated that although the hair could have come from Mr. Morin, it could also have come from any number of other people, male or female, or even from two of Christine's classmates. The value of this hair was "extremely limited," he testified. Much the same testimony was given about the three hairs from Guy's car that had characteristics similar to Christine's.

Most of the CFS staff, including myself, were convinced that although Guy Paul was a legitimate suspect in Christine's murder, there was not sufficient evidence to make him anything more than a suspect. We believed he would be acquitted, as he had been at the first trial. Much to our surprise, on July 30, 1992, after seven days of deliberation, the jury returned a verdict of guilty. This was one of those events that leave a lasting memory of where one was when it happened. Marie and I were on holiday on our boat and had stopped in Picton for supplies. As we walked down the main street, we met Jack Evans, a retired Toronto Police homicide investigator and then the executive officer for the chief forensic pathologist, who had a summer cottage in the area. He had a copy of the *Toronto Star* in his hand, which bore a large headline: "Morin Guilty." Both of us were astonished.

We were not alone in our thoughts about the result. When Guy was sent to the penitentiary in Kingston, he was placed in the general population rather than in segregation, as would normally be the case for someone convicted of the rape/murder of a child. After his appeal was filed in November, he applied in February 1993 for bail pending the appeal. Bail was granted, and he was released from custody, another unusual decision.

In late 1994, PCR analysis of DNA was becoming more common, and the court ordered three scientists from the United States and Canada who had experience with the technique to again attempt DNA analysis. They were successful, and on January 22, 1995, they reported to the Court of Appeal that the DNA in the semen spots on Christine's panties could not have originated from Guy Paul Morin. The next day, Guy's appeal was allowed, his conviction was set aside, and a verdict of acquittal was entered. He eventually received $1.25 million in compensation from the provincial government.

The Inquiry

Because Guy Paul Morin had been wrongfully arrested, charged, and convicted of a heinous crime, in June 1996 the Ontario attorney general appointed a Commission of Inquiry under Mr. Justice Fred Kaufman into all the proceedings related to Guy Paul Morin. This massive inquiry went on for almost two years and heard evidence from many witnesses (including myself, even though I had retired in 1994 and had no time for preparation as I had spent the week before my testimony in Washington as part of the FBI inquiry described in Chapter 25). Cross-examination and arguments were presented by many lawyers representing interested parties. The final 1,400-page report was issued in two volumes in March 1998.

The report included, among many findings, serious criticism of the hair and fiber evidence provided by the CFS and made multiple recommendations about the structure, policies, and practices of CFS. Some of these were useful.

During the inquiry, we learned for the first time that at least some of the fiber evidence had been contaminated, probably at CFS, and that our hair and fiber examiner and the section head had become aware of this before the first trial. I was stunned by this revelation, which produced what was probably the lowest moment in my professional career! What was particularly shocking was that they had never told anyone at any time about this problem. They reasoned that they did not believe the contamination had any impact on their findings. It is difficult to understand how anyone could believe that any contamination could not impact on the findings, and even if they believed this, they were still obliged to advise me and the attorneys for both sides about it.

The potential for contamination, particularly with trace evidence such as hairs and fibers, is always a major concern in forensic science laboratories, in part because we have little control over the handling of the items before they arrive in the lab and also in part because the very nature of such items makes the possibility of random incidental transfer very real. Ray Prime, who had succeeded George Cimbura as CFS director, immediately did the correct thing and launched an investigation into the source of the contamination, but as a result of the passage of about ten years since the incident likely occurred, a definite cause was never established. One possibility was that during the search of Guy's car, our examiner had used a student intern to assist her. One afternoon, the intern had been observed wearing a red sweater without the protective covering of a lab coat. Attempts to locate that sweater to obtain known fibers from it were unsuccessful.

A major challenge for managers of any large busy operation is keeping well informed about the activities within the organization. They can never know (or need to know) everything and must establish guidelines for their staff about what they should be informed of. Whenever I was asked by my staff about how much I knew about the activities within CFS, my response was always "about half as much as I would like to know and twice as much as you think I know." The contamination issue in the Morin case was clearly in the first half.

The Morin case and the results of the inquiry were enormously embarrassing for CFS and significantly damaged its excellent reputation. Following the inquiry, it was a great credit to Ray Prime and his staff that they worked very hard at, and eventually succeeded in, reestablishing that reputation.

The Morin case had another significant impact on the CFS for a reason other than might be expected. I was once asked by a frustrated lab director in California about how to raise the profile of his laboratory so it would be funded properly. My semi-facetious response to him was, "That's easy. Screw up big time and you will raise your profile." That, in fact, works, at least in government. The Morin case (together with the contemporaneous Bernardo case) had that effect on CFS. It received the major additional necessary funding that I and my successors had been unable to successfully sell to the bureaucracy previously. Approval was received to hire twenty-three additional staff members. No one ever wants to screw up, but sadly it is an effective fund-raiser.

The Steven Truscott Case Wrongful Conviction or Factual Innocence?

24

I have left the description of this historic case to the end of my discussion of some of the Centre of Forensic Sciences (CFS) cases I was involved with. It began in 1959, just two years after I started in the Attorney General's Laboratory and has been a frequent subject of discussions about forensic science, both domestically and internationally, throughout my entire career. The final (presumably) disposition of it did not occur until 2007, thirteen years after I had retired from CFS. Over those forty-eight years, controversy surrounding this case generated more books, media articles, television documentaries, and articles in scientific, medical, and legal journals than probably any other Canadian homicide case.

Having said that, as one looks at the case from purely investigative, forensic science, and legal points of view, there wasn't anything very unusual about it. One certainly could wonder how it developed the international significance that it did if one ignored the fact that the accused person was only fourteen years old at the time of the crime, and the fact that after his conviction he was sentenced to hang!

The Crime

The case involved the rape/murder of a twelve-year-old girl, Lynne Harper. The principals were all members of families stationed at the Royal Canadian Air Force (RCAF) Station near Clinton in southwestern Ontario, a training base for telecommunications, radar, and electronic navigation systems personnel.

(I had a peripheral contact with this station during my first summer with the RCAF in 1950. While stationed at RCAF Station Crumlin near London, the station softball team played several interstation games at Clinton, and I was a member of that team.) Although RCAF Station Clinton was closed in the early 1960s, the area today still looks very much as it did in 1959. Some of the Air Force buildings are now part of a village named "Vanastra," derived from the RCAF motto "per ardua ad astra," which translates as "through adversity to the stars." The farms in the area are still much the same—at least they were in 2001, the last time I was in the area—and the bush that featured in this case was still there and was still known as "Lawson's bush."

The case began on June 9, 1959, when Lynne Harper had dinner with her family sometime between 17:30 and 17:45; the time later became a significant issue. Her mother subsequently described exactly what Lynne had eaten because that also became important. Lynne left home and walked toward the school, where she was seen by people at a Brownie meeting. Sometime around 19:00 she met a schoolmate, Steven Truscott, in the schoolyard. (See Figure 24.3a sketch of the general area.) One of the few bits of evidence that was reasonably certain came from the two adult Brownie leaders, who said that they saw Lynne and Steven leave the schoolyard together about 19:00–19:10. (Most of the other witnesses were children, the oldest being sixteen, and their estimates of time, which became very critical to the case, were not very reliable. Thus, 19:00–19:10 was the last time any known adult saw Lynne alive, and she was in the company of Steven.)

Although their timing was not clear, some of the child witnesses mentioned seeing Steven riding with Lynne on the handlebar of his bike heading north on the County Road toward Lawson's bush and Highway #8. There was no reliable evidence of anyone seeing them north of the bush. It is about one mile from the schoolyard north to Highway #8. Lawson's bush is about halfway between the school and the highway, and the bridge over the Bayfield River is about halfway between the bush and the highway.

Steven returned to the schoolyard where he met other people shortly after 20:00 and was home by 20:30. There was therefore a gap of about an hour, between 19:00 and 20:00, when his location was unknown.

Later that evening, Lynne's father reported her missing to the station police, but only a limited search was made that night. The next day, the Ontario Provincial Police (OPP) was advised of Lynne's disappearance and, as the last person known to have been with her, Steven was interviewed. He told police that he gave her a ride to Highway #8, where he left her to hitch a ride (hitchhiking was not uncommon with the youth in the area). On his way back, as he crossed the bridge over the Bayfield River, where many of his schoolmates were swimming in a local swimming hole, he looked back toward the highway and saw Lynne getting into a late-model Chevrolet that had yellow license plates.

A well-organized search for Lynne began on June 11, and, shortly after 13:00 her body was found in Lawson's bush. The clothing had been removed except for her undershirt, which was pushed up. She had been strangled with her sleeveless blouse, which had been ripped up the entire left side and twisted around her neck with a knot just to the left of her chin. This subsequently became a matter of great interest.

There was a suggestion of an attempt to conceal the body because several small saplings had been broken off and placed over it. The OPP and the coroner, in what was an unusual practice in those days, called for Dr. John Penistan, the pathologist at Stratford General Hospital, who was also the regional pathologist for the attorney general, to attend the scene. He arrived and examined the body about 16:45. The body was then removed to a funeral home in Clinton, where under what we would today consider poor conditions, particularly with respect to the lighting, Dr. Penistan began the autopsy at about 19:15.

Following the autopsy, Dr. Penistan concluded that the cause of death was strangulation and gave a preliminary opinion about the time of death. This opinion was based to a considerable extent on the contents of the stomach, which he described as being "about a pint of material, poorly chewed." Based on those observations, he believed that the food could not have been in the stomach longer than about two hours. This opinion was formed partly from his own experience but also from one of the classic textbooks of forensic medicine, *The Essentials of Forensic Medicine*, published by Professor C.J. Polson in England in 1955. Concerning stomach contents, Professor Polson wrote, "It is permissible with gastric contents half to one pint in volume, and obviously undigested food, to say that a meal has been eaten perhaps less than two hours before death."

Thus, if Lynne had finished her meal about 17:45, she had probably died sometime before 19:45 on June 9. During at least part of this period, Steven was known to have been with her.

The Investigation

The OPP assigned Criminal Investigation Branch (CIB) Inspector Harold Graham, a very experienced homicide investigator, to the case. He immediately focused on Steven, simply because he was the last person seen with Lynne. On the evening of June 12, Steven was taken into custody and early on June 13, Steven Truscott was charged with murder.

The Attorney General's Laboratory quickly became involved in the investigation, as was the case with almost all homicides in the province. Our staff, particularly Elgin Brown and John Funk, did an enormous amount of work but, partly because of the limitations of science at the time, produced only a small amount of significant information for the trial.

One of the questions of interest was whether sex was involved. At the crime scene, it appeared that this was a sexual homicide because the body was lying on its back, the clothes had been removed and were in the immediate area, and in the ground below her feet, in a position that one would expect to find them if this were indeed a sexual assault, there were two shoe prints. An examination for semen was done on swabs from the vagina and on the clothing, but none was confirmed. There was a high level of seminal acid phosphatase (SAP); however, the SAP test is only indicative not positive evidence of semen. There were no spermatozoa identified. This wasn't surprising because that part of the body was covered with maggots and had started to decompose. In 1959, the only blood grouping that could be done was ABO, and both Lynne and Steven were group A, so it was of limited value.

Another issue was whether Lynne had been killed in the bush or somewhere else and her body dumped there. The evidence against her being killed somewhere else included the two footprints in the ground by the body, her removed clothing at the site, and a button found underneath the body that appeared similar to the buttons on her blouse, one of which was missing. To try to confirm that this button was from the blouse, I analyzed it and one remaining on the blouse and found that both were made of the same material. This button provided additional evidence that the blouse had been ripped and used as a ligature at the scene in Lawson's bush.

The clothing Steven had been wearing on June 9 was seized by the OPP on June 12. It was found either in the laundry basket or hanging on the Truscott clothesline. All had been washed. His mother said that she had washed them on June 10. There was nothing unusual about a mother washing a fourteen-year-old boy's clothing in the summer, but it did seem a bit unusual that his shoes had also been washed and were hanging on the line. Even though the clothing had been washed, Elgin Brown found traces of blood in the crotch area of the trousers. Also, there were traces of chlorophyll on both knees of the trousers. Grass stains on the trousers of a fourteen-year-old boy are not unusual, but given the circumstances and the suspicions in the case, the fact that they were on both knees had possible significance.

During his examinations, Dr. Penistan took the unusual step of collecting samples of insect maggots and eggs from different areas of the body, both at the scene and later during the autopsy. He had a vague recollection of having read somewhere that these might be used to assist in estimating the time of death (some insects lay eggs on bodies immediately following death). Fortuitously, Elgin Brown had taken courses in entomology as an undergraduate at the Ontario Agricultural College in Guelph. He reared the larva samples and was able to identify both flesh flies and blowflies. On this subject, Penistan and Brown were well ahead of their time since the now well-recognized science of forensic entomology would not become well established for another twenty-five years. Therefore, nothing more was done with this information, until almost fifty years later!

Without a doubt, the most significant work that the lab did in this case, at least at the time of the investigation and trial, was on the stomach contents. The primary interest was whether they represented the food from the last meal that Lynne was known to have eaten. If she had been somewhere else for a day or two before being brought back to Lawson's bush and strangled, it might be expected that she would have had something else to eat. John Funk made a very detailed examination of the approximately 250 mL of stomach contents he had received from Dr. Penistan. He was able to identify pineapple, celery, pickled cucumber and cauliflower, peas (probably canned), onion, potatoes, two types of meat (probably fowl and ham), and spices, both leaflike and seedlike. Mrs. Harper described the food on the table that evening as ham, white turkey meat, brown turkey skin, a dressing containing spices, potatoes, peas, celery, onion, pickles, two kinds of pie, and pineapple upside-down cake. Lynne also had a purple lollipop for dessert. It appeared quite clear that the stomach contents were from Lynne's last supper at home.

Concerning what the stomach contents might indicate about the time of death, John decided that we should perform an experiment—we had all learned from Professor Rogers! So, John, two female members of the staff, and I went to lunch at the Town and Country Dining Room in the old Westminster Hotel on Jarvis Street. We chose it because it served a very substantial buffet and we could pick and choose items that were similar to Lynne's supper. John also found some purple lollipops. Each of us consumed a meal of white and dark turkey meat with dressing and gravy, sliced cold ham, boiled potatoes, canned peas, sliced tomatoes, celery, and sweet mixed pickles, with pineapple, cake, and a purple lollipop for dessert.

We finished our meal about 13:30 and returned to the lab. Beginning about 14:30 and continuing for another hour, each of us went into a washroom and attempted to regurgitate and collect our stomach contents (not an experiment I would want to repeat or would recommend to anyone else). John examined these contents and was able to identify the components.

I would like to be able to say that, by that experiment, we found that the time of death could be established from stomach contents, but we couldn't. There was a significant variation in the extent of the digestion by each of us. All that could be said was that within two hours of finishing our meal, John could identify food in a condition similar to what he had seen in Lynne's stomach contents. (I could also identify the purple dye from the lollipops, a lot of work that produced no information of any significance.)

The Trial

Because of the ages of the victim and the accused, the case developed a very high profile in the area. The Crown attorney, Glen Hayes, went to the juvenile court and obtained an order for Steven to be tried as an adult. This order meant that in the event of a conviction, a death sentence was mandatory.

Steven's family retained as his lawyer Frank Donnelly, who was highly regarded in the area and subsequently was appointed to the Ontario High Court of Justice. In fact, at the time of the trial, Donnelly knew of this appointment but had asked that it be deferred until after the trial.

By today's standards, the case proceeded very quickly. The preliminary hearing in July lasted only two days. The trial before Mr. Justice Ferguson, a very experienced, very firm, and somewhat crusty judge, and a jury began in the High Court in Goderich on September 16.

The central issue at the trial was the time of death because of what was believed to be the narrow one-hour window of opportunity. If death occurred later than 20:00 on June 9, Steven Truscott could not have been the person responsible. Dr. Penistan, who I later came to know very well, was a very articulate, cultured individual and a highly experienced clinical pathologist (although less so as a forensic pathologist). He was quite firm in his opinion about the cause of death but less so about the time of death. The latter was based primarily on the stomach contents but also on the fact that rigor mortis was almost completely gone from the body at the time of his examination, and on the extent of the decomposition.

None of John Funk's work was introduced at the trial because of an oversight on the part of the Crown attorney. There was a rule in the Canada Evidence Act that required that a party could not call more than five expert witnesses without prior permission from the court. Mr. Hayes had not asked for such permission because he did not think he had more than five experts. Unfortunately, Mr. Justice Ferguson ruled that the two OPP identification officers who had done the crime scene search and had attempted to compare the shoe impressions taken there with the soles of Steven's shoes were in fact experts but hadn't been counted. One of these officers concluded that there was insufficient detail in the shoe impressions to reach any conclusion, and the other thought that there was enough to conclude that they could have been made by Steven's shoes. The Crown therefore had Dr. Penistan, Dr. Brooks, the base doctor who had examined Steven when he was arrested, the two identification officers, and Elgin Brown as expert witnesses. As a result, John Funk could not be called to testify about his work with the stomach contents.

The trial lasted twelve days, an unusually short time by today's standards. Dr. Penistan testified about his findings and opinions, and a very well-qualified professor from the University of Western Ontario Medical School testified for the defense. The latter had experience in gastroenterology, and his evidence was to the effect that the stomach would not be empty until 3½–4 hours after a meal. This was interpreted by some as conflicting with what Dr. Penistan had said, but actually it was not because the stomach wasn't empty. If it had been, Dr. Penistan wouldn't have found the eight or nine ounces of contents of "poorly digested food" in it. So, there wasn't that much conflict between these two experts. Both testified in a very professional and proper manner.

I cannot say the same about the testimony of Dr. Brooks, the RCAF Station doctor. He had observed a small lesion on the side of Steven's penis and expressed the opinion that this was consistent with Steven having been involved in sex with a young girl. I don't believe that opinion had any merit. Dr. Brooks was not a forensic scientist and had no experience with police investigations or the courts; he was simply a general practitioner. I have seen many other people who have never been involved with the police or with the courts try to become too involved in a case and extend their role to that of an investigator rather than remaining simply a witness.

Based on all the evidence they heard (Steven did not testify), on September 30, the jury returned a verdict of guilty as charged, with a recommendation for mercy. As mandated by the law of the day, Judge Ferguson had the awesome responsibility of pronouncing the sentence of death on a fourteen-year-old boy. Even the extremely remote prospect of hanging such a youth was very disturbing to most people and prompted an enormous amount of critical comment.

After the trial, Mr. Donnelly accepted his appointment to the court, and the appeal was handled by John O'Driscoll, who himself was later appointed to the same court. On January 21, 1960, the Ontario Court of Appeal dismissed the appeal and, almost immediately, the minister of justice commuted Steven's sentence to life imprisonment. Leave to appeal to the Supreme Court of Canada (SCC) was requested, but that court rejected it on February 24. Steven was transferred from the Huron County Jail in Goderich to Kingston Penitentiary, where he was assessed and then sent to the Ontario Reformatory at Guelph. In January 1963, when he turned eighteen, he was transferred to Collins Bay Penitentiary. By all accounts, he was a model prisoner.

The Supreme Court of Canada Reference

In the early 1960s, the Steven Truscott case had developed considerable notoriety in Canada, but not so much internationally. The notoriety was primarily due to the age of the person involved rather than any specific legal or scientific issues. One freelance journalist/author, Mrs. Isabel LeBourdais, was, however, so upset by any thought that a fourteen-year-old could be responsible for such a crime that she began researching the case and writing a book, *The Trial of Steven Truscott*, which was published in Canada and the United Kingdom in 1966.[1]

The book, which was essentially a defense brief, hit like a bombshell and turned the case into a cause célèbre internationally. Certainly, anyone whose knowledge of the case was based solely on this book could not help but be convinced that Steven Truscott had been wrongfully convicted.

Mrs. LeBourdais was extremely critical of both the investigative and the trial processes and of much of the evidence that was given. She emphasized inconsistencies in the eyewitness testimony, and there certainly were some, as there are in many homicide cases. More problematic were her distortions of what some of the evidence was. For example, about the saplings that covered the body and which were twisted, bent, and broken off about seven feet above the ground, she insisted that a fourteen-year-old boy could not possibly have done this. She completely ignored the fact that such saplings can bend and be pulled down to break them off well above their base.

Not surprisingly, her greatest criticism (and distortion) was of Dr. Penistan's evidence about the time of death. It was Mrs. LeBourdais's comments about this evidence that stimulated so much interest in this case in the international forensic science community. She wrote that, based on an autopsy done two days later, Dr. Penistan set the time of death at between 19:15 and 19:45 on June 9. If he had done that, he would certainly have deserved her criticism. Anyone with any knowledge of the challenge in establishing time of death would know that in such circumstances and with such autopsy findings, one simply couldn't be that precise.

What Dr. Penistan said, however, was, "Given the limited degree of digestion and the large quantity of food in the stomach, I find it difficult to believe that this food could have been in the stomach for as long as two hours, unless some complicating factor was present, of which I have no information."

That was a perfectly reasonable and professional statement for him to make based on his experience and the medical literature available at the time. He recognized the possibility of other unknown factors affecting this opinion. His testimony continued: "If the last meal was finished at 5:45 p.m., I would therefore conclude that death occurred prior to 7:45 pm. This finding would be compatible with death as early as 7:15."

He didn't set the parameter of the narrow time window; it was set by the evidence that Lynne had finished her supper sometime between 17:30 and 17:45.

Another source of distortion was Dr. Penistan's opinion that the extent of rigor mortis, which had almost passed off, and of decomposition was entirely compatible with death approximately "forty-five hours prior to identification." Mrs. LeBourdais picked up on that but assumed that the identification of the body referred to the time of the autopsy around 19:15. Forty-five hours before the autopsy would have put the time of death around 22:15 and ruled Steven out as the murderer. The identification time that Dr. Penistan referred to, however, was not the time of the autopsy but rather the time he examined the body in Lawson's bush around 16:15. Forty-five hours before that time was completely compatible with the 19:15 to 19:45 time frame.

One unusual item emphasized in the book was a triangular piece of the blouse that was missing when Elgin Brown examined it. Mrs. LeBourdais interpreted the missing piece as being a "trophy" taken by a killer who was a sexual deviant, i.e., someone other than Steven. The mystery of the cloth triangle was subsequently resolved in front of the SCC and will be described later.

The international extent of the controversy developed by Mrs. LeBourdais's book is indicated by the fact that Dr. Keith Simpson, an outstanding forensic pathologist and a professor of forensic pathology at Guys Hospital in London, England, was asked to write a review of the book for the British Medico-Legal Society journal. Dr. Simpson was a person who used words precisely and never left any doubt with his readers about his position on any topic. (At the time of his review, Dr. Simpson was unaware that he would soon become directly embroiled in the Truscott case.)

Dr. Simpson wrote about the book:[2]

> This critical review of a Canadian case in which a fourteen-year-old boy was found guilty upon a trial of the sex murder of a twelve-year-old RCAF family's daughter, is so biased with the outraged feelings of the authoress that it is difficult to weigh the facts.

He also commented on some of the principals in the trial:

> Truscott it seemed lacked evidence in support of the rather colorless defence put up by Frank Donnelly, a virtually unknown lawyer who was briefed by the family.

About the medical evidence, he opined that

> No figure appeared on either side, the case was, except for the youth of the parties concerned, just like so many others, and one wonders why it was selected for such a meticulous scientific discussion.

Having known Keith Simpson, I do not doubt that by "figure" he meant someone of his stature as a pathologist.

Mrs. LeBourdais, he wrote,

> unfortunately relies upon extracts verbatim from, and repeatedly invokes the aid of, two historic Scottish textbooks of forensic medicine of 1938 and 1939. The latter still, of course, bearing the misleading title 'Recent Advances in Forensic Medicine,' this hardly adds substance to her argument. The medical and scientific evidence given seemed to us surprisingly sound, coming as it did from quite moderate experts and we do not subscribe to the feelings of outrage that were repeatedly called for in this account of the Truscott case.

Notwithstanding Professor Simpson's review, Mrs. LeBourdais's book created so much comment and criticism of the trial of Steven Truscott that the attorney general of Canada, in keeping with the principle that justice must not only be done but also be seen to be done, took the very unusual step of referring the case directly to the Supreme Court of Canada. In effect, he asked the court to consider the evidence presented at the trial together with any new evidence that might be available and advise what they might have decided had they heard the evidence at the time of Steven's request for leave to appeal.

For this reference, the Crown was represented by Mr. William Bowman, the Ontario director of public prosecutions, and Mr. Donald Scott, the Crown attorney for Welland County. Mr. G. Arthur Martin, probably the most highly respected defense lawyer in Ontario, if not all of Canada, at the time, represented Steven Truscott. Thus, both sides had extremely professional and very capable people to review and present the case to the SCC.

Again, the time of death was a major focus. Both sides retained outstanding experts in forensic pathology. For the Crown, these were Dr. Keith Simpson from London; Dr. Milton Helpern, the chief medical examiner for New York City and dean of forensic pathologists in the United States; Dr. Samuel Gerber, longtime chief coroner for Cuyahoga County, Cleveland, Ohio; and Dr. Noble Sharpe, the medical director of the Centre of Forensic Sciences. Not to be outdone, Mr. Martin retained Dr. Francis Camps, professor of forensic pathology at the London University Medical School (and a rival of Dr. Simpson for recognition as the leading forensic pathologist in the United Kingdom); Dr. Charles Petty, at that time assistant chief medical examiner for the state of Maryland and later chief medical examiner for the city and county of Dallas; and Dr. Fred Jaffe from Toronto, who would later succeed Dr. Sharpe as medical director of CFS.

The dynamics of these groups was fascinating to watch, particularly that between Drs. Simpson and Camps. Both were very prolific writers, both highly regarded, but two very different individuals. Simpson was very austere, while Camps was more of a social animal. Their relationship was not excessively harmonious even though both had similar positions in the same city and both were highly respected. As an example of their relationship, when I was organizing the International Meeting of the Forensic Sciences in Toronto in 1969, I would have considered it a coup to have both Simpson and Camps attend. Professor Camps agreed to come because he had hosted the meeting in London in 1963. When I called Professor Simpson to invite him, his response was, "Will Camps be there?" When I answered, "Yes, he will be," he immediately reacted with, "Well, I won't!" I have always believed that both were competing for the knighthood that had traditionally been bestowed on the leading forensic pathologist in the United Kingdom. Neither was ever tapped on the shoulder by the queen's sword.

Both consultant groups worked quite collegially in reviewing the evidence. They spent quite a bit of time in our lab going through all our notes and were very complimentary about the detail with which the items had been examined and the findings recorded. Nevertheless, when they got into the court, they had quite different views.

The SCC heard testimony in October 1966 from twenty-five witnesses, including Steven Truscott. (Because this was a reference and not an appeal, it was the first time the court had ever actually heard live testimony from witnesses. An initial problem that apparently no one had thought of was that there was no witness box in the courtroom and one quickly had to be jury-rigged to accommodate this process.)

The Crown called Helpern, Simpson, and Sharpe, each of whom essentially said they agreed with Dr. Penistan's evidence. They were thoroughly cross-examined by Mr. Martin and quite properly acknowledged the variables but concluded that, based on the evidence that Dr. Penistan had and on his observations, they would have said much the same thing.

The defense pathologists took a different tack. Dr. Petty was the leader of that group, and he concluded that Dr. Penistan had not allowed for all the variables that could affect the emptying of the stomach. One of these was drug use, even though there was no evidence of that. He concluded that death had probably occurred sometime between twenty-four and forty-eight hours before recovery of the body, which would put it sometime on the morning of June 10. He also thought that he saw more evidence of rigor mortis than Dr. Penistan had, although all he ever viewed was photographs. Dr. Petty's conclusion was that she had not been murdered at that scene but had been murdered somewhere else, brought there, and dumped. Dr. Camps essentially agreed with him, as did Dr. Jaffe.

All the consultant pathologists at the reference had to operate under the handicap of not having seen the body or the autopsy and of being limited to their review of photographs and Dr. Penistan's notes. The gist of all their evidence about stomach contents was that stomach contents by themselves are not a good indicator of the time of death. The fact is, however, that there is nothing that is a good indicator of time of death unless you happen to have a witness with a chronometer and a stethoscope in their hands standing and watching. Stomach contents were essentially all they and Dr. Penistan had to go on.

The missing triangular piece of blouse Mrs. LeBourdais had described as a "trophy" was thoroughly reviewed. Dr. Penistan believed and freely acknowledged that it might have been lost during the autopsy because of the poor lighting conditions under which he had to work. As described above, the blouse had been ripped up one side, twisted around the neck, and tied in a knot. Dr. Penistan had removed it by cutting through the blouse just below the knot. He then packaged the blouse without paying much attention to it and sent it to the lab. That a piece was missing was not noticed until Elgin Brown examined the blouse some days later.

Because of Mrs. LeBourdais's insistence that there was something sinister about this missing piece, Elgin Brown worked for several days (and went through many sleeveless blouses) trying to determine how it might have been lost. Eventually, he came up with the answer. Elgin then had the unique experience of not only testifying but also performing a demonstration in front of the court, another first for the SCC. He stood in front of the nine judges and behind one of our female staff who was about the same size as Lynne Harper and was wearing a similar blouse. He reached down, gripped the blouse along the bottom, yanked it up, and knotted it into a ligature around his model's neck. The judges watched with rapt attention. Elgin then took a pair of surgical scissors and cut the ligature just below the knot, as Dr. Penistan had done. As he did so, a triangular piece of the cloth floated free and slowly drifted to the courtroom floor accompanied by an audible gasp from the judges and spectators. So much for the trophy theory!

Steven's testimony was essentially the same as what he had told the police during their investigation. He and Lynne left the schoolyard around 19:30 (in spite of the evidence of the Brownie pack leaders that it was closer to 19:00). She asked him to give her a ride down to the intersection of the County Road and Highway #8 because she wanted to go to a farm east of that intersection to see some ponies. He rode her on the handlebar of his bike to the intersection, left her off, and rode back toward the school. As he got to the bridge across Bayfield River, he looked back and saw her getting into a 1959 Chevrolet that had yellow license plates. That was the last he saw of her.

One of the issues that was explored in detail was whether he could have identified this car and the yellow license plates from that distance, about a quarter of a mile. The conclusion was that he could if he was looking for a yellow license plate and if the car was in a specific position at that time of day with the sun striking it.

On May 4, 1967, the SCC in an eight-to-one decision held that if Truscott's appeal had been heard by the court, it would have been dismissed.[3] Among other reasons, they found that "there were many incredibilites [*sic*] inherent in the evidence given by Truscott before us, and we do not believe his testimony."

Concerning Dr. Penistan's evidence, the court wrote,

> The effect of the sum total of the testimony of the expert witnesses is, in our opinion, to add strength to the opinion expressed by Dr. Penistan at the trial that the murdered girl was dead by 7:45 p.m. The effect of the fresh evidence which we heard on the Reference, considered in its entirety, is to strengthen that view.

Finally,

> the verdict of the jury, read in the light of the charge of the trial judge, makes it clear that they were satisfied beyond a reasonable doubt that the facts, which they found to be established by the evidence which they accepted, were not only consistent with the guilt of Truscott but were inconsistent with any rational conclusion other than that Steven Truscott was the guilty person.

Steven was returned to Collins Bay, where he continued to maintain an unblemished institutional record. On October 21, 1969, he was released on parole. After living in Kingston with his parole officer for a while, he moved under an assumed name to Guelph, Ontario, where he got a job as a millwright, married, and raised three children. On November 12, 1974, Steven was released from the terms and conditions of his parole, and he continued to be gainfully employed and free from any criminal involvement. The case, however, was not yet put to bed.

The Ontario Court of Appeal Reference

Steven Truscott maintained a low profile in Guelph until 2000, when a production on CBC Television's *The Fifth Estate* revived interest in his case. As with Mrs. LeBourdais's book thirty-four years earlier, the program suggested that significant evidence in favor of Steven's innocence had been ignored at the original trial. In November 2001, the Association in Defence of the Wrongly Convicted (AIDWIC), led by prominent Toronto lawyer James Lockyer, who had represented Guy Paul Morin at the judicial inquiry into his wrongful conviction, filed an appeal with the federal minister of justice to have the case reopened. In October 2004, following a judicial investigation, the minister directed that another reference be held, this time in the Ontario Court of Appeal, to review whether the new evidence might have changed the 1959 verdict.

A five-judge panel of the court, led by Chief Justice Roy McMurtry, heard three weeks of testimony, including new evidence, from twenty-five witnesses in June 2006, followed by ten days of legal argument in January 2007. Not only was it a first for this court to receive oral testimony, but it also was the first time that its proceedings were televised. The court, with the assistance of experienced counsel, particularly Mr. Lockyer, conducted an exhaustive review of all the evidence presented at the trial and the SCC reference. As might be expected, again the focus was primarily on the time of death.

Concerning Dr. Penistan's conclusions, two forensic pathologists and a gastroenterologist testified that much more was known in 2006 about digestion and stomach-emptying times than was the case in 1959. Essentially, their evidence was that while Dr. Penistan's opinion about a possible period of up to two hours since the time of the last meal might be possible, it would not be a reliable indicator of the time of death. One of the pathologists concluded that "overall, the time of Lynne Harper's death cannot be precisely ascertained from the autopsy findings, and it certainly cannot be specified to between 7:00 p.m. and 7:45 p.m. on June 9, 1959."

Undoubtedly, the most significant new evidence about the time of death was based on Elgin Brown's almost fifty-year-old observations about the maggots collected from the body. Although Elgin was now in his mid-eighties and had been retired for almost a quarter century, he again had the rare experience of testifying before an appeal court about work he had done many years before. He was more than equal to the challenge and proved to be one of the more credible witnesses the court heard. (One of the media reports about Elgin's testimony described him as "a fastidious government scientist." A "fastidious" individual is defined as someone who is "very attentive to and concerned about accuracy and detail," a perfect description of Elgin Brown as a forensic scientist.)

In 1959, there was no such discipline as "forensic entomology." Over the ensuing decades, however, it had become a recognized specialty. A small number of university professors had it as their primary area of research and had developed mountains of data, including research in locations referred to as "body farms." Three of these professors testified before the court; there was a bit of "battle of the experts" between them, but all relied on the same basic data that Elgin had serendipitously developed almost half a century earlier.

Elgin had reported the maggots as being between 1/16 and 1/4 inches in length (their size was critical to the opinions of the forensic entomologists), and after he had reared them to adult status, he had identified two families of flies, flesh flies and blowflies. Flesh flies arrive after death and deposit first instar larvae. Blowflies arrive after death and deposit eggs. Blowflies lay hundreds of eggs at a time, while flesh flies deposit much fewer live larvae. There are several genera or tribes of flesh flies and blowflies and many species within the tribes, which develop at different rates.

Entomologists cannot pinpoint with absolute precision the postmortem interval (PMI), but they can provide a range of times during which the insects likely deposited their eggs or larvae. If the PMI range extends from several hours of darkness and into early daylight hours, the reasonable inference is that the eggs or larvae were deposited in the daylight hours, i.e., after sunrise. Similarly, if the PMI covers a period from the late afternoon or evening and into the night, it is likely the eggs or larvae were deposited before sunset.

Although there was some disagreement between the three entomologists, there was a consensus that the eggs probably were deposited in the daylight hours sometime after 11:00 on June 10. (No one apparently explored the matter of what the condition of the stomach contents might be expected to have been if death had occurred seventeen or eighteen hours following completion of the last meal rather than two hours.) They also agreed, however, that they could not exclude the possibility that the eggs were deposited before sunset on June 9 because a slight increase in size, about one millimeter, would increase the likelihood that the eggs were deposited before sunset on June 9. So, much depended on the reliability of the observations of length recorded by Dr. Penistan and Elgin Brown almost fifty years earlier. Dr. Penistan was no longer alive, and Elgin could not remember if he had actually measured the length or merely estimated it!

On August 28, 2007, the court issued its findings. In a normal appeal, if the court concluded that the appeal should be allowed, it would order a new trial. This was not, however, a normal appeal, but rather was a "reference." Also, clearly, given the almost fifty years that had passed since the trial, a new trial was not a viable option. The court therefore went further to its conclusion and wrote,

> Based on evidence that qualifies as fresh evidence in these proceedings, we are satisfied that Mr. Truscott's conviction was a miscarriage of justice and must be quashed. We are further satisfied upon a review of the entirety of the evidentiary record and the additional material available to this court and not previously judicially considered, that if a new trial were possible, an acquittal would clearly be the likely result. The interests of justice dictate that we make that order. Mr. Truscott should stand acquitted of the murder of Lynne Harper.[4]

It added,

> The appellant has not demonstrated his factual innocence [as had Guy Paul Morin]. To do so would be a most daunting task absent definitive forensic evidence such as DNA. Despite the appellant's best efforts, that kind of evidence is not available. The task of demonstrating innocence is particularly difficult in this case where in addition to the passage of almost a half-century since the crime, certain immutable facts cast some suspicion on the appellant. He was the last known person to see the victim alive and was with her at a location very close to where she was murdered. At this time, and on the totality of the record, we are in no position to make a declaration of innocence. Indeed, we are not satisfied that an acquittal would be the only reasonable verdict.

In July 2008, the Ontario government announced that "given the unique circumstances of Mr. Truscott's case," it had awarded him $6.5 million in compensation for his wrongful conviction.

The prolonged history of Steven Truscott's case, the eventual result, and his exemplary conduct as a prisoner, parolee, productive citizen, husband, and father should be instructive to those "tough on crime" zealots who support mandatory minimum penalties and, in murder cases, life without any chance of parole or perhaps even the death penalty.

In conclusion, was it a wrongful conviction? By the standards of the twenty-first century, clearly. But was it factual innocence? That is not so clear. Does it achieve finality? One can only hope so.

Further Reading

1. Lebourdais, Isabel; The trial of Steven Truscott: McClelland and Stewart, Toronto; 1966.

2. Simpson, Keith: Medico-Legal Journal; Review: The Trial of Steven Truscott. Vol. 34 No. 2, pp 82-83, 1966.
3. Supreme Court of Canada; Reference Re: Steven Murray Truscott (1967) S.C.R 309, 1967-05-04
4. Court of Appeal for Ontario; Re Truscott, ONCA 575, Docket C42726, 2007-08-28.

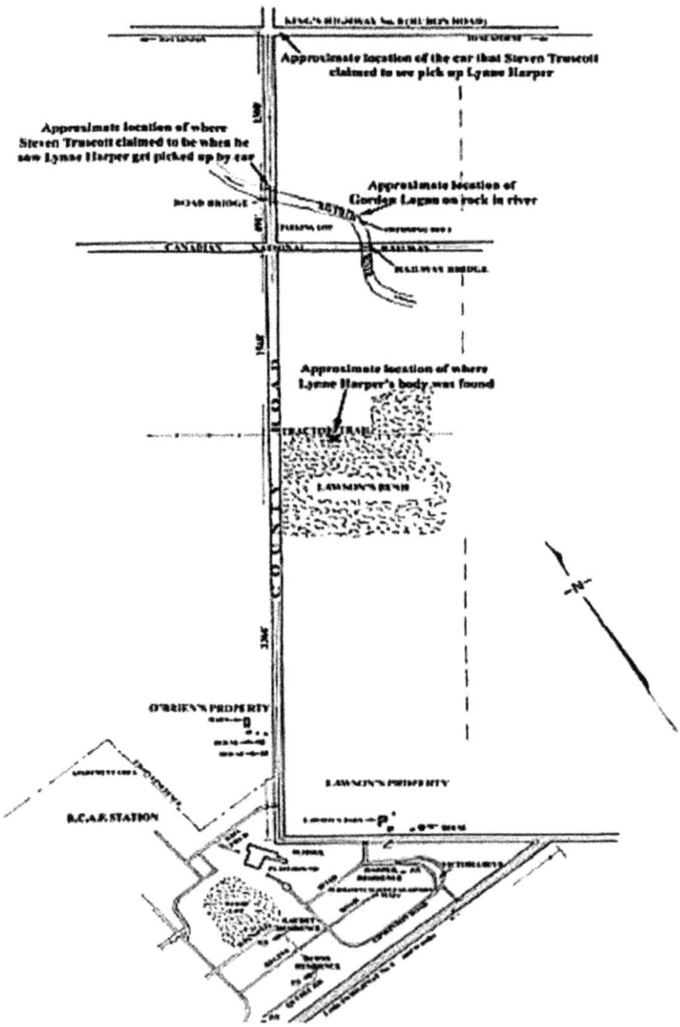

Figure 24.1 The area of the Truscott case.

Figure 24.2 Dr. John Penistan.

Figure 24.3 Elgin Brown.

Retirement, Part 1 "So, What Do I Do Now?" 25

In May 1994, I reached the Ontario government employee mandatory retirement age of sixty-five. Although mandatory retirement is sometimes controversial, for me it was a good thing; otherwise, I would have probably stayed on at the Centre of Forensic Sciences (CFS) until I was carried out the door. That would not have been a good thing—either for the organization or for me. For me, it would have meant that I would miss many challenging new experiences, and for CFS it would have resulted in comfortable stagnation, good but static. By 1994, as director, I had "been there, done that, seen that" for just about anything that could present itself. Nothing surprised or particularly disturbed me. I was comfortable, and so were most of the staff. For CFS to continue to progress, a fresh sense of challenge was required, by both leadership and staff. It was time for me to go!

My departure was made a bit easier because during my final eighteen months, in addition to being CFS director, I was also acting assistant deputy minister (ADM) in charge of the Public Safety Division (CFS, Chief Coroner's Office, Fire Marshal's Office, Emergency Measures Organization, and Animal Protection) of the ministry. I was my own boss! Domenic Alfieri, our wonderful ADM, had been seconded to another ministry to establish a lottery control agency, and I was to fill in for him for six months. In fact, Domenic never did return to the Ministry of the Solicitor General, and his permanent replacement was not appointed until after I had retired.

I did not enjoy the ADM work because it was primarily administrative and a little too close to the political side of the ministry. I was quite happy to leave it. Friends often used to ask me about the pressures associated with my work at CFS, and I didn't know how to answer them because I wasn't conscious of work-associated pressure until it was no longer there. "Did I really do that?" was a frequent intrusion into my retirement comfort zone.

On that final Friday, May 27, 1994, I was particularly proud of the last document I signed as CFS director, an agreement with the University of Toronto at Mississauga for CFS to provide support, advice, and adjunct faculty to a new undergraduate forensic science program, the first such academic program in Canada. It has since gone on to considerable success.

As I closed the office door behind me that day, I wondered what on earth I was going to do with myself Monday morning. (Marie probably had even greater apprehension!) I had done none of the things that one is supposed to do in preparation for retirement—new hobbies, community interests, volunteer commitments, and so forth. The only thing I was certain of was that I would somehow continue to be involved with forensic science. I was not interested in doing court work or becoming a full-time "consultant" for casework in either defense or civil cases (even though I had seen that become quite lucrative for some of my retired staff).

I did know that I was going to continue with the proficiency testing program that I had been supporting for more than fifteen years and which had grown enormously, in both the number of labs participating and the countries they represented (more than 400 labs in almost seventy countries on every continent except Antarctica). I had agreed to a request from Charles Leete, the president of Collaborative Testing Services Inc. (CTS), which manages that program, to provide CTS with advice and quality assurance support on a volunteer basis. CTS, in turn, would pay my expenses to attend the annual American Academy of Forensic Sciences (AAFS) and American Society of Crime Laboratory Directors (ASCLD) meetings.

Also, as mentioned in Chapter 16, Bud Keaton, the executive director of ASCLD/LAB (Laboratory Accreditation Board), had asked me to continue to occasionally lead teams in the inspection of some very large laboratories or laboratories he believed might present a challenge. But that was it. As things turned out, the move from a very active position to "retirement" was the easiest transition I ever made.

Forensic Science Consultant

As my new career progressed, the nature of the work could be classified into three categories: reviews of specific quality issues in individual laboratories, reviews of the progress of labs in their preparation for accreditation, and reviews of cases where there was believed to have been a wrongful conviction. A few examples of each are described below.

Laboratory Quality Reviews

Vancouver City Analyst Laboratory

On that first Monday morning of retirement, I received a phone call from the chief of police in Vancouver asking if I would assist him by making a review of the capabilities of the Vancouver City Analyst Laboratory (CAL). Although the CAL was in the Department of Health (DOH), it had for many years also provided forensic science support to the Vancouver Police Department (VPD). The DOH had decided that it no longer wished to fund the CAL and suggested to the chief that he take it over. He wisely realized that before he took on that responsibility, he should find out whether it was something he wanted. During our conversation, he also asked what I would charge for my services, something I had never previously thought about. When I pulled a number out of thin air, he immediately agreed, which suggested to me that my number was probably too low. (This was to be a continuing issue for me throughout my consulting career.)

Thus, in June 1994, I found myself in Vancouver for a week making a detailed review of the CAL. This involved examining the facility and equipment, interviewing the staff, and reviewing dozens of case files. As the week progressed, I realized that I also needed to interview some of the lab's "clients," police investigators, and Crown attorneys. From those interviews, it became apparent that they were not at all satisfied with the quality of the service they were receiving. This begged the question of why they were using CAL when they could, at no cost, have used the excellent Royal Canadian Mounted Police (RCMP) Laboratory just a mile or two up the street?

The reason they gave was a firmly held belief that the RCMP Laboratory would give priority to RCMP cases and city cases would always go to the end of the queue. I didn't believe this was correct, so I gathered data from the RCMP Lab that showed that there was no distinction in priority between RCMP cases and municipal police cases. The belief of the investigators was a myth that had grown over the years because no one had ever bothered to check. While police are often skeptical about the information they receive from non-police sources, some will blindly accept anything they are told by other police officers.

As a result of my review, I found that the CAL was essentially a mess. The facility was antiquated, the equipment was inadequate (some of it having been discarded by the RCMP Lab), the analytical protocols were seriously lacking, the staff was poorly trained, and the clients were dissatisfied with the product they were receiving. A major reason for this was the very serious underfunding by the city. The financial managers were interested only in reducing costs. My final recommendation to the VPD chief was that he could spend several million dollars and at least two years to upgrade the facility, equipment, and protocols, and to train the staff to appropriate standards, or he could refuse the offer and let the city close the lab down. As a result, the lab was closed in March 1995, and VPD began using the RCMP Lab. That has since worked out very well.

One valuable lesson from this first experience in private consulting was that I no longer had to be bound by silly and unrealistic government rules on such things as travel and other expenses. Clients, including, ironically, other government agencies, would pay whatever was requested, usually without question. For example, I decided that if someone wanted me to cross an ocean at their request, they would have to provide business class flights. No one ever questioned that.

An unusual postscript to this first experience with private consulting was my final job as a consultant, long after I thought I had retired from that activity.

In October 2013, I was contacted by a lawyer for the city of Vancouver who was defending the city in a civil case that involved the VPD and the former CAL. The suit was brought by a man named Ivan Henry, who in 1983 had been convicted of a series of sexual assaults in the 1980–1982 period. These assaults were investigated by VPD, and in some, the CAL had received items for examination. Mr. Henry served twenty-seven years in prison before the British Columbia Court of Appeal quashed his convictions, and he was released in 2010.

Mr. Henry's allegation was that if the VPD and CAL had done a proper investigation, he would never have been convicted in the first place. The lawyer had found a copy of my 1994 report on the CAL and wanted my assessment of the work CAL had done in these cases. I reviewed the files from all the cases and found that the CAL had not done much, if anything, with the items they received (which, given the capability I had seen in 1994, was probably just as well). The civil trial took place in late 2015, but to my relief, the city lawyer wisely decided that my testimony would not likely be helpful to him. As is often the case in civil matters, after hearing three months of testimony, the parties settled for an undisclosed sum, which undoubtedly contained at least seven figures.

San Francisco Police Department Lab

In May 1995, the director of the San Francisco Police Department (PD) lab, Shoji Horikoshi, asked me and Susan Johns, a manager in the Illinois State Police (ISP) Lab System, to review a problem in his lab. Because the district attorney had established an unrealistic requirement that drug cases be reported within twelve hours of submission seven days a week, all lab staff, regardless of their primary assignment, had to be trained to do drug cases in rotation on weekends.

One of the DNA staff was so upset about finding herself alone in the lab doing drug cases on Saturdays and Sundays in San Francisco that she decided to get even with management by doing something that would adversely impact the reputation of the lab. She completely ignored the fact that it would also impact her! On her working weekends, she decided that she would write reports on the drug cases without bothering to make any analyses. (Since almost all the plant material was marijuana and the white powder was most often cocaine, her reported identifications were usually correct, even though completely unsupported by any analytical data.)

After several weeks of this, another member of the staff advised Shoji that she thought it odd that on the weekends that the DNA analyst worked, no analytical reagents appeared to have been used up. A hidden camera was installed to observe the analyst's weekend work, and confirmation of the suspicion was produced. She was dismissed.

Our review of the operations revealed an old (built in 1960), poorly maintained, inadequately staffed (the same number that it had in 1979) operation.

More significantly, we identified serious weaknesses in the lab protocols for evidence security and peer review of analytical reports. These resulted in significant changes to the lab following our report. The obvious recommendation, to end the unwise reporting policy, was not accepted. Elected district attorneys do not take kindly to criticism from forensic scientists.

Baltimore County Police Department Lab

In November 1995, I was requested by the Baltimore County PD to do a review of their laboratory. They had two members of the staff who the new lab director, Karen Irish, did not believe were competent, and she wanted an independent opinion. After several days in Baltimore, I concluded that the director's assessment was correct and recommended that the two be terminated because I was not convinced that their limitations could be corrected through any amount of retraining. (Having now recommended closing a lab and firing three people, I began to worry that I was becoming a bit of a hatchet man!)

My ventures into professional consultations provided several surprises for me:

- Sometimes people ask for advice about what they think they need, when in fact they need something entirely different.
- Staff and lab managers generally know what the problems are and have ideas for solutions; they just need an outsider to confirm their thoughts.
- Clients are unaware of the quality of the service they are receiving; they simply assume it is OK.
- Financial managers have no concept of how expensive good-quality forensic science work can be.

FBI Laboratory

In September 1995, I received a telephone call from Michael Bromwich, the inspector general (IG) for the U.S. Department of Justice. He invited me to serve on a five-member international "Blue Ribbon Panel" to assist his office with an investigation of serious allegations made by Dr. Frederic Whitehurst (a member of the FBI Laboratory staff) about wrongdoing and improper practices by a few other staff members and units within the lab. The other members of the panel were Nic Cartwright from the Ottawa RCMP Lab; Gerry Murray of the Northern Ireland forensic science lab; Paul Ferrara, director of the Virginia State Lab System; and Richard Schwoebel from the Sandia National Laboratory in the United States.

That invitation resulted in the next eighteen months being spent traveling regularly to Washington, D.C., reviewing hundreds of pages of documents and court transcripts, interviewing FBI Lab staff, and examining lab facilities, equipment, and procedures used in some of the most significant investigations in recent FBI history. These included the first World Trade Center bombing, the Oklahoma City bombing, the murder of a U.S. circuit court judge with a mail bomb, two international commercial aircraft bombings, an international terrorism case, and the homicide case in Los Angeles for which O.J. Simpson was accused, tried, and acquitted.

In addition to his investigators, Mr. Bromwich also brought in four very experienced assistant U.S. attorneys from around the United States who I enjoyed working with immensely. Their attention to detail and ability to pick up on scientific/technical issues quickly was remarkable. One of them, Scott Bales, with whom I have kept in touch, later became a judge on the Arizona Court of Appeal.

Most of the allegations were against the staff of the Explosives Unit. Dr. Whitehurst submitted thousands of pages of allegations, including circumvention of proper procedures, falsification of lab reports, flawed results, fabrication of evidence, perjury, and obstruction of justice. The FBI had conducted internal investigations of these allegations, but the IG's investigation found that these were not as rigorous as they might have been.

In April 1997, the IG produced a 500-page report detailing his findings. Although the vast majority of Whitehurst's allegations were unsubstantiated, a few were in fact confirmed. Ironically, we found some of these same flaws in Dr. Whitehurst's own work.

One example of wrongdoing was in an international terrorism case. An FBI examiner testified that he had identified the explosive PETN on a significant item of evidence. His identification was based on a single gas chromatography run. When challenged in court about the absence of any confirmatory analysis, he testified that his confirmation came from an FBI field agent who told him that he knew it was PETN because some detonating cord wrapper had been found in the defendant's garbage. (PETN is the explosive component in detonating cord.) The judge recognized the fallacy in this and rejected the evidence, the charge was dismissed, and an accused terrorist went free.

Another example was in the first New York World Trade Center attack in 1993; a different FBI examiner testified that the bomb consisted of 1200 pounds of urea nitrate. He had no scientific data with which to identify urea nitrate, and his estimate of the amount was much more precise than the enormous damage would permit anyone to make. During our interview, he acknowledged this but claimed he could testify as he did because he knew that field agents had found receipts showing that the defendants had purchased sufficient chemicals to make 1,200 pounds of urea nitrate. His circular reasoning was that the defendants could manufacture 1,200 pounds of urea nitrate and the defendants had planted the bomb. Therefore, the bomb had to consist of 1,200 pounds of urea nitrate. This conclusion may well have been correct, but it was not based on any valid scientific data and was therefore a breach of his scientific responsibility. This examiner did the same thing in the Oklahoma City bombing in April 1995.

We concluded that there was a fundamental systemic reason for these problems, a failure by lab management to adequately supervise their senior examiners, who were, at that time, all FBI special agents. The culture in the lab was simply because they were the FBI, it was a given that all their results were the best possible. Nobody ever really checked them, including in the courts, where their testimony was rarely challenged. During our interviews with some of the examiners, it was apparent that they had difficulty coping with our questions because it was the first time they had ever been challenged.

One of the lessons I learned from this experience was that although instilling pride in an organization should be a positive thing, the transition from pride to arrogance can be a very slippery slope that can have highly negative consequences. Some of the FBI examiners had made that transition. Unfortunately, because a few examiners behaved improperly in a relatively small number of cases, more than 3,000 major criminal cases were cast into doubt, and the otherwise well-deserved excellent reputation of a fine forensic science laboratory was seriously tarnished.

I also found that government bureaucrat bean counters are the same everywhere. During our many days in Washington, our team would find the traditional coffee and doughnuts in the meeting room each morning. It was not until the end of the project that we learned that $3 per day was being deducted from our meager per diem to pay for these.

Forensic Science Center at Chicago

The Illinois State Police has operated an excellent eight-laboratory forensic science laboratory system for many years. The Chicago Police Department (CPD) had also operated a laboratory since 1938, one of the first "crime laboratories" to be established in the United States. In 1994, an agreement was reached for the ISP to absorb the CPD lab into a new facility to be constructed and known as the ISP Forensic Science Center at Chicago (FSC-C).

About eighty-five new staff were recruited and trained, the necessity for so many explaining the reason why the city had agreed to the "merger" (aka "takeover"). This had the effect of virtually doubling the size of the entire ISP Lab System. In the summer of 1996, these new staff, together with a few senior members of other ISP labs and forty-five former staff of the CPD, moved into a new 80,000-square-foot laboratory facility. Accomplishing all this in such a short time was a major achievement, but not surprisingly, integrating the staff from two separate agencies with different cultures proved to be a challenge.

The other ISP labs were much smaller, more structured, and more centrally controlled than had been the CPD lab. Also, a few of the CPD lab staff brought with them some interpersonal conflicts that had existed in their former organization. Of the three senior managers of the new FSC-C, the director had been director of the CPD lab for only a brief period, one deputy director had a long background as a laboratory director in the ISP, and the other deputy director had only very recently joined the ISP after a distinguished career in the FBI Lab. Within a few months, the director was replaced with an ISP manager who, although highly qualified as a police manager, had no forensic science experience.

In June 1997, the FSC-C was preparing for an accreditation inspection and requested an external audit of its DNA units, which were part of the Biochemistry Section. The supervisors and analysts in these units were relatively inexperienced, and their workload was overwhelming. Given that situation, it wasn't surprising that the audit identified some weaknesses. This was followed in March 1998 by the discovery of a contamination problem in one of the DNA units, and during the investigation of that issue, other deficiencies in the units' quality control/quality assurance (QA/QC) protocols were uncovered.

Based on his concern about these issues and the response to them, in April 1998 the commander of the ISP Lab System, Bruce Vander Kolk, asked me to perform a management review of the Biochemistry Section. This involved examination of many documents and interviews with senior managers, supervisors, and analysts. I found both systemic and personnel issues in the section. As expected, the former were easier to deal with than the latter.

The Biochemistry Section chief had been the assistant director of the CPD lab and was a highly experienced serologist. However, she had no hands-on DNA casework experience. The DNA analytical staff, almost all of whom had less than two years of experience in forensic science, had been trained in different locations, and there were differences in their approach to casework that required resolution. Such a situation would present a substantial challenge to even the most experienced supervisors, but one of these had been an analyst in the CPD with only brief experience in DNA casework, and the other had come directly from academia. Neither had received any management/supervisory training.

Many of the issues were the result of trying to impose a management structure appropriate to the small labs of the ISP onto a very large new lab. For example, during my interviews, it became clear that there was great uncertainty about who was responsible for what in QA/QC. Often, the response to my question "Who is responsible for quality control functions?" was, "We all are" or "It's shared" or "We rotate it." A situation in which responsibility is seen as belonging to everyone is tantamount to it belonging to no one.

While it might normally be expected that the section chief would deal with this issue, the organizational and working environment was not conducive to this. She believed that this responsibility belonged to the DNA technical leader, who in turn believed that it belonged to the DNA unit supervisors.

Because of their inexperience, most of the analysts in the DNA groups required close supervision, ready access to their supervisors, and constant mentoring. They were not receiving this. The section chief was highly respected for her case management skills and her intimate knowledge of the workings of the CPD, the major client, but not for her knowledge of DNA analysis. Both supervisors lacked in confidence, were hesitant to make decisions, and were sometimes inconsistent in their decisions. Both had a strong need, and desire, for mentoring but were not getting this from the section chief or the DNA technical leader. Their relationship with the technical leader was less than collegial. By default, they turned to one of the deputy directors for advice and mentoring.

In the end, I made fifteen specific recommendations. These included a realignment of the responsibilities of both deputy directors and transfer of the Biochemistry Section chief. Her problem was a classic example of a good person being in the wrong job. I therefore recommended creating a badly needed evidence management coordinator position that would make much better use of her skills and knowledge. She could be replaced as section chief with someone with greater practical DNA experience from one of the other ISP labs. Most of these suggestions were implemented, and FSC-C went on to achieve accreditation and great success.

Houston Police Department Laboratory

During the FBI Lab review, Mike Bromwich and I had become good friends. In 1999, he left the Office of the Inspector General to join a large law firm in Washington to head their Internal Investigations Group. Mike would call me periodically when he had a forensic science question or just to keep in touch. In December 2004, during one of these calls, he asked if I would accompany him to Houston to assist with the presentation of a proposal he was making to the city for a review of scientific and administrative problems in the Houston Police Department (HPD) lab. I agreed to the challenge because I had developed great respect for Mike as a brilliant, hands-on leader.

The HPD lab was established in 1953 under the direction of a scientist who was also a sworn police officer. Like other forensic science labs of that era, it gradually expanded its range of services and was state of the art for that time. During the late 1970s, the department found that it could recruit civilians at a much lower cost than uniform personnel, and the lab gradually developed a mixed civilian/police staff, a recipe for serious morale problems. In 1983, the original lab director retired, and his successors were unable to maintain the same stature within the senior ranks of the PD that he had. By 1995, the then lab director had lost interest in managing the lab. His practice was to arrive at his office around 07:00, shut the door, and then emerge at

15:00 to go to what he considered his real job, managing a photography store. There was a complete absence of scientific or administrative leadership.

The serious, and predictable, problems that developed during this time finally became public in 2001 when a Houston TV station presented a series of in-depth reports detailing major problems in cases examined by the lab, particularly in the Serology/DNA Section. Not surprisingly, the lab director assured his superiors that there was nothing to these reports and agreed to have the Texas Department of Public Safety (DPS) lab review the cases described in the TV shows. After only two days on site, the DPS review team was so appalled by what they were finding that they advised the police chief to immediately shut down the Serology/DNA Section. In the aftermath, the entire lab was subjected to a constant stream of critical media reports questioning the integrity of every section within the lab.

During 2003, several investigations were undertaken by the HPD Internal Affairs Unit, which seriously upset the civilian staff members. The lab director remained in denial and retired. In December 2003, the PD recruited a new lab director, Irma Rios, from the DPS Lab System (she had been one of the two who made the initial recommendation to suspend the Serology/DNA activities). Ms. Rios, who was the perfect person for this challenge, received commitments of increased support from the chief and began working toward preparing the lab for accreditation, a process she viewed as the path to correction of the lab's multiple weaknesses.

During 2004, despite the progress Ms. Rios was making, the stream of media criticism continued (the *Houston Chronicle* alone published more than 200 articles) until the mayor decided that an independent outside review was required. In March 2005, Mike Bromwich's proposal was accepted. He selected a team of eight lawyers and paralegals from his firm, and I helped assemble a group of thirteen forensic scientists from around the United States to perform the scientific/technical reviews. Another two years of my "retirement" found an active outlet!

The Bromwich Review covered twenty-five years of cases and included more than 100 interviews and detailed examination of over 3,500 case files. Contrary to the impression created by the media reports, we found that most of the work produced in the Toxicology, Trace Evidence, Firearms, and Questioned Documents Sections was, with a few exceptions, of quite good quality. Most of the work of the Controlled Substances Section, primarily cannabis and cocaine cases, was satisfactory, but there were problems with other types of drug cases. We were, however, shocked to find that two of the controlled substances analysts had been caught "dry labbing" (reporting cases without doing any analyses), not once but twice, and yet were still employed in the lab.

In stark contrast, we found significant and pervasive problems in the work of the Serology/DNA Section. Major issues were identified in a third of the more than 3,500 cases reviewed, including 4 death penalty cases. Some of these issues were systematic failure to examine critical evidence, perform potentially probative examinations, or report potentially exculpatory results, and the routine misreporting of the statistical significance of DNA profiles. For example, in a sexual assault case, they would report the population frequency of the suspect's DNA profile rather than that of the profile found in the semen recovered from the complainant. In other words, they simply assumed the suspect was the semen donor. The potential for these errors producing miscarriages of justice was enormous.

Although only one wrongful conviction directly attributed to faulty work by the lab was identified, the real possibility of others, including death penalty cases, could not be dismissed. The District Attorney's Office was provided with a list of 180 cases in which there were critical scientific/technical errors that, depending on the other evidence in the cases, might have contributed to wrongful convictions. Because of the extreme length of sentences in the U.S. justice system, most of these individuals were still incarcerated.

As the causes of these problems were examined, we identified two that I had found common in other problem labs: inadequate support/resources and ineffective or nonexistent scientific leadership. As a support function populated largely with civilian staff in a police agency, the HPD lab was seriously marginalized. As one member described it, "We were treated like red-headed stepchildren." Salaries of civilian analysts were significantly lower than those at other public labs in the state, resulting in the loss of trained staff and inability to recruit good-quality new staff. The absence of scientific/technical leadership resulted in improper or inadequate training and, in some cases, incompetent supervision of those who were recruited and trained.

The supervisor of the Serology/DNA Section was self-trained and only held his position by default. In contrast to normal forensic science practice, he saw his job as providing the answers the detectives wanted rather than those a proper examination developed. He and his staff effectively served simply as technicians for the detectives.

Another serious lab-wide problem was the absence of a functional quality assurance system. One of the rare decisions made by the former director had been to appoint a QA manager; however, he did so only to create a "dumping spot" for a problem employee who had been found to be incompetent.

During the two years of the review, we were also able to monitor the progress Ms. Rios was making, and I was impressed with how quickly a change in leadership could achieve positive results. By 2007, the lab bore little resemblance to the dysfunctional entity that had previously existed. The budget had more than doubled. Staff pay scales had significantly increased, permitting the recruitment and retention of capable managers, supervisors, and analytical staff. A rigorous training program for new staff had been implemented, and outside development opportunities for all staff were provided. The QA program was now performing its proper function, ensuring that the results delivered were of good quality. Before our work in Houston was finished in 2007, the lab received full ASCLD/LAB accreditation, an accomplishment that had been unthinkable just four years earlier. The city and the HPD had invested heavily, in both resources and attention, in salvaging and rebuilding the lab. They had learned the lesson I constantly preached to other agencies' management: "You can pay now or you will pay later!"

One evening in June 2010, Marie and I were watching a speech by President Obama on TV about the major disaster in the Gulf of Mexico resulting from the BP Deepwater Horizon drilling accident. Suddenly, a photo of Mike Bromwich appeared on the screen, and the president announced that he had appointed Mike to reform the regulation and oversight of all offshore drilling. I called Mike the next day to congratulate him and, in the course of our conversation, asked how he had learned of the appointment. He had been at home on a Saturday afternoon when a call came that his caller ID did not identify, so he didn't answer. Over the next two hours, two similar calls were ignored. He finally answered the fourth call to silence whoever it was when the voice said, "This is the White House calling; the President would like to speak with you." Mike must be one of the very few people who ever declined to answer a phone call from the president of the United States!

I was not yet finished with Mike Bromwich or the HPD lab. In 2012, an HPD assistant chief, with the support of Irma Rios, had written a series of detailed papers making the bold recommendation that the lab be removed from the control of the PD and placed under a civilian agency. The mayor agreed, and a plan was developed to create a private, local government-owned corporation called the Houston Forensic Science Center reporting to a board of directors appointed by the mayor. During 2013, this board developed a plan that included taking over all the staff and equipment of the lab from the PD, together with parts of the Identification Bureau and the Crime Scene Unit.

Before this transaction was implemented, the board, which included some very experienced business people and lawyers, realized that they should know much more about what they were getting. They therefore contacted Mike Bromwich, who had finished his work with the government in 2012 and had established his own law firm in Washington. He was retained to make a review of the current status of the HPD lab and advise the board as to whether it was a viable entity producing good work. Again, Mike asked me to put together a small team, and over the next couple of months, we examined the lab's current status and operations. This was a much easier task than the earlier one, and we were delighted to find that Irma and her staff were still progressing and turning out a valid quality product. In April 2014, the HPD lab became the Houston Forensic Science Center, a private local government corporation owned by the city, an interesting new concept for a forensic science laboratory administrative structure.

Preaccreditation Reviews

In October 1994, the director of the Hong Kong Government Analyst's Laboratory was interested in applying for ASCLD/LAB accreditation and asked for my assessment of how far the lab was from being ready for that process. That was a very interesting experience because it was so unusual to go into a government operation where money was not an issue. For everything I recommended as needed, the response was, "No problem. We can have that tomorrow," and they could.

One of the hazards of such international work that I quickly became aware of is the time change. The thirteen-hour difference between Burlington and Hong Kong meant that the lab's workday began just as I was ready for bed, and when their workday ended, I was wide awake. I got very little sleep that week!

Other labs realized that this sort of review could be very helpful, and I was asked to do the same thing for the New York City PD lab in 1996; the Suffolk County, New York, crime lab in 1997; the Hong Kong Police Force Identification Bureau Advanced Testing Unit in 1998; and the Contra Costa County, California, sheriff/coroner lab in 1999. These all eventually achieved accreditation, although some took longer than others, and I learned something from each.

NYPD Laboratory

Of the labs I assisted with preparing for accreditation, the most challenging, and eventually the most satisfying, was the New York City Police Department (NYPD) lab. It is a very large laboratory that had been allowed to deteriorate over the years as a result of insufficient funding, neglect by the city, and inadequate scientific leadership. The lab is a unit within the department's Forensic Science Division, which also includes the Crime Scene Unit, the Bomb Squad, and the Identification (Fingerprint) Bureau. The division was traditionally commanded by a career police officer holding the rank of inspector for whom this was a temporary stopping point on his (they had all been male) advance through the ranks. The nominal director of the laboratory was a civilian scientist who had very little authority and who was essentially simply a scientific advisor to the division commander.

Predictably, this leadership arrangement led to serious problems, which were finally acknowledged in 1996 when New York State mandated that all forensic science labs in the state had to become accredited. The initial reaction of some senior managers in the NYPD was to ignore this mandate. Their attitude was that because the NYPD lab handled such a huge volume of cases, the state "would not have the b--ls to shut it down." Fortunately, wiser heads prevailed, and the department assigned Inspector Phil Pulaski to prepare the lab for accreditation. He had not only exceptional experience as an investigator but also degrees in engineering and law and had proven himself to be a dynamic leader and agent of change.

As Pulaski began his task, he very quickly realized that he had inherited serious problems and that he would need considerable assistance. An excellent scientist, Dr. Richard Wilks, was recruited from academia to be the lab director, and I was invited to put a small team of experienced lab directors together to assess the problems and provide advice and recommendations for their correction. I was fortunate to persuade three other retired lab directors, Barry Fisher from the Los Angeles County Sheriff's labs, Richard Frank from the Drug Enforcement Agency Lab System, and Bruce Vander Kolk from the Illinois State Police Lab System, to share this challenge. On our first visit to the lab in November 1996, we were appalled by what we found.

The existing facility was located within the police academy building in Lower Manhattan. It had been designed in 1963 for a staff of forty, but there were now more than 200 members in it. Essentially, no renovation had been done over those thirty-three years and, it appeared, very little maintenance. The lab had one cleaner for a half day per week, and the windows were so dirty we could not see out of them. I asked one of the serologists, "When was the last time the floor in your lab was cleaned?" and her response was, "Not in my time." She had been there for eighteen years! Conditions were so bad that the staff seemed to take vicarious pride in them; they did, however, try to keep their immediate work areas as clean as possible considering their surroundings.

Fortunately, the physical space issues were slated to be resolved in 1998 when the laboratory was to relocate to newly renovated space in a building in suburban Queens. We toured the new facility and agreed that it had the potential to be adequate if the existing maintenance service was substantially upgraded.

Unfortunately, the physical plant was not the most serious of the lab's problems. Most of the staff were demoralized because of the neglect they had experienced. While some appeared quite competent, many others were poorly trained and devoid of any semblance of competence or interest! To make the best use of the inadequate space, staff were divided into two shifts. Because New York City is such an expensive place to live, many staff had to hold two jobs to make ends meet, and for some, most of whom were schoolteachers, this shift arrangement meant that the lab was their secondary job!

All the supervisors were sworn police officers, some with no technical or scientific background, and since they worked only one shift, they were unable to adequately monitor half of their staff. There were no written analytical protocols, no quality assurance system, minimal proficiency testing, inadequate health and safety procedures, and a complicated and unfair staff classification and pay system for the civilian scientists. After a week of reviewing the lab, we concluded that it could meet fewer than half of the criteria for accreditation, and those only after relocation to the new facility. Our review team left Inspector Pulaski and Dr. Wilks with a long series of recommendations for necessary improvements.

Since most of our recommendations required a significant increase in funding, Inspector Pulaski invited me to join him in a meeting with senior budget staff in the mayor's office, where we outlined these requirements. During this discussion, one of the budget people remarked, "It sounds to me like this good-quality work that you describe is very expensive." Hallelujah! A bean counter finally got it! My immediate response was, "Exactly. The only thing more expensive than high-quality work is poor-quality work. Sooner or later you will pay!"

Over the ensuing ten months, I spent many hours on the phone with Inspector Pulaski, and we got to know each other very well. (Because of his unique NYPD accent and vocabulary, Marie got to recognize his voice whenever he called, and they also became friends.)

In September 1997, we returned to the lab and were dumbfounded by what the management and staff had accomplished. Approval had been received for an additional 110 civilian positions. In a breakthrough, the laboratory director was now actively involved in the interview process for these positions; previously, they had to accept whomever the City Personnel Department assigned to the lab. We were particularly pleased to note the establishment of a Quality Assurance Unit with three positions and the addition of a position for a full-time safety officer.

Although the facility was still old and crowded, they had confirmed what we had written in our 1996 report: "An old and crowded facility does not preclude a neat and clean facility." The maintenance staff had been increased from one person a half day per week to seven full-time "Lucas memorial cleaners." The entire lab had been cleaned and painted; we could even see out through the windows!

Manuals and procedural documents had been prepared and put into service, security enhanced, and staff training improved. Most significantly, staff morale had undergone a virtual 180-degree turnaround, and there was a positive sense of confidence among them, as contrasted with the defeatist attitude of the previous year. There was a clear commitment to meet the accreditation standards and to abide by them.

Our concern about some supervisors not being present during the duty tours of some of their subordinates had been corrected by scheduling overlapping shifts. Although a few of the supervisors were still not technically qualified, they had access to qualified "technical managers," and the longer-term plan was to have all supervisor positions occupied by civilian scientists.

Although I had previously considered Phil Pulaski to be a wonderful, capable person to work with, I had also thought I would not want to work for him. He could be very demanding. What I learned was that the staff credited him for all the positive changes that had occurred and were grateful for them. One member explained to me the reason for this: "Inspector Pulaski cares about us and what we do!" An essential quality for any leader!

In spite of the remarkable progress, there were still accreditation criteria that had as yet not been met, many of them related to the physical plant, and we again made recommendations to Inspector Pulaski and Dr. Wilks.

To no one's surprise, the move to the new facility was delayed, and in April 1998, we performed another review on site. Major improvements had occurred in the instrumentation available and in the capability of the staff to use it. Relocation did not occur until June 1998, and in April 1999, we made our final preaccreditation review. (During these additional reviews, Bob Horn, retired from the New York State Police labs; Cliff Vander Ark of the Arizona State labs; and Ed Hueske from Fort Worth filled in if one of the other team members wasn't available.) The laboratory was now housed in an excellent facility, and once again, we were impressed with the progress and found that the staff was now comfortable with the new space, equipment, and procedures. We concluded that if the ASCLD/LAB inspection team and board agreed with our observations, accreditation of the laboratory should result. They did agree, and in the fall of 1999, the NYPD laboratory became fully accredited.

Inspector Pulaski, Dr. Wilks, and the entire staff were justifiably elated by this recognition of their accomplishments. I was equally pleased with what our team had been able to contribute and derived almost as much satisfaction as I had when the CFS and its Northern Regional Laboratory were accredited in 1994 and 1995, respectively. Ours were two good labs that had become even better, but the NYPD lab had been a poor lab that had become very good!

During this process, Inspector Pulaski had asked me to make several presentations, including one on professional ethics, to his staff. When I visited the lab following their accreditation, I was surprised and delighted to find that they had taken some quotes from those presentations and had them printed, framed, and mounted in several locations throughout the lab. My favorite dealt with ethics:

- Be selfish about your personal and professional reputation.
- Don't make ethics more difficult than they are.
- It is easier to tell the truth than it is to lie.
- Trust discomfort, and if still in doubt, ask yourself what your mother would want you to do.

The NYPD management recognized the excellent job that Inspector Pulaski had done with the lab and promoted and reassigned him to other units within the department that needed improvement, but we kept in close touch. On 9/11, he was chief of detectives for Manhattan South, and when Marie and I heard the tragic news of that day, we both reacted with, "Phil will be the first one up the stairs!" Three nights later he called to let us know he was fine, but three of his men had been killed, and he was on his way to wakes for them. Phil Pulaski finished his career as chief of detectives for the entire NYPD, the job he had always aspired to. He retired in 2014.

As a postscript to my association with the NYPD lab, they were due for a reaccreditation inspection in 2004, and the new lab director, Mark Dale, former director of the New York State Police laboratories, asked me to assemble a team for another review, which I did in May of that year. This was a much easier task, and the lab was still doing very well.

Wrongful Conviction Reviews

Since the introduction of DNA analysis to North America in 1987, it has been used not only to support investigations that result in convictions or acquittals but also to establish factual innocence for persons who have previously been wrongfully convicted. Unfortunately, there have been too many of the latter, more than 350 in the United States and a handful in Canada. Some of them involved forensic science, as a result of either analytical errors, misinterpretations, faulty testimony, or in a few cases, ethical transgressions by forensic scientists. The testimony in some of these latter cases was quite shocking.

As might be expected, these cases have primarily been sexual assaults and homicides from the pre-DNA era. Most involved ABO and phosphoglucomutase (PGM) results or microscopic hair comparisons; i.e., they were the types of examinations that had limited evidential value but also had the physical evidence remaining, which permitted the DNA analysis that led to the exoneration.

I have been asked to review documents in a few such cases, for purposes of either civil suits the exoneree filed against the state or, in one case in Canada, a judicial inquiry. This work typically involved examining hundreds of pages of documents, including laboratory reports, bench notes, testimony transcripts, declarations, correspondence, and expert reports. These cases all had several things in common:

- None of the labs involved was accredited at the time. Had they been, the conduct involved would have been much less likely to occur or would have been detected before the case ever went to trial.
- Most of the labs had weak or nonexistent scientific leadership.
- The cases occurred before the advent of DNA analysis.
- Zealous or overzealous prosecutors.

Some of the wrongfully convicted individuals were not nice people, one of the reasons they became suspects in the first place. That, of course, is irrelevant.

Montana State Forensic Laboratory

In 2006, I was retained to examine the forensic science work that had contributed to the wrongful conviction of Jimmy Ray Bromgard, who was suing the state of Montana, the attorney general of Montana, and the former director of the State Crime Laboratory, Arnold Melnikoff.

In December 1987, Mr. Bromgard was convicted of the rape of an eight-year-old girl in her bed and was sentenced to serve forty years in prison. His conviction was based largely on a composite sketch prepared from the little girl's description of her attacker, her identification of him in a police lineup (which surprisingly went unchallenged by his lawyer at trial), and testimony about hair comparisons by Mr. Melnikoff. In 2002, DNA results from semen in a stain on the girl's panties excluded Mr. Bromgard as the source of the semen. As a result, his conviction was vacated and he was released from prison. In 2015, another man was shown by DNA analysis to have been the source of the semen, and he was convicted of the crime.

Mr. Melnikoff was hired in June 1970 to be the director and, at the time, the only staff member of a new forensic laboratory established by the state of Montana in Missoula. He had just received an MS degree in organic chemistry from the University of Montana, had no prior training in forensic science, and had no mentor following his recruitment. He initially performed only drug analysis, for which his academic background was appropriate. As the lab expanded from one person to nine between 1970 and 1989, he also became responsible for drug, arson, toxicology, serology, DUI, trace evidence (including hair), and firearms examinations.

The training of a forensic scientist is obviously critical to their subsequent performance. Most learn the basic science aspects in university, but the forensic application of that knowledge is normally developed through working as an "understudy" to experienced forensic scientists in an operational forensic laboratory. Short (one or two week) evidence-specific courses can be valuable adjuncts to such training but are quite insufficient in themselves to qualify a journeyman examiner. There is no adequate substitute for the skills and knowledge that derive from long-term guidance by a fully experienced forensic scientist serving as a mentor.

At Mr. Bromgard's trial, Mr. Melnikoff testified about his microscopic examination of a scalp hair and a pubic hair removed from the victim's bedding. (At the time of the Bromgard case, Mr. Melnikoff was the only person performing microscopic hair comparisons in the laboratory. There was therefore no peer review of his work.)

Mr. Melnikoff's report was fairly typical of those issued by competent hair examiners at the time (e.g., "The questioned head hair had the same range of microscopic characteristics as the suspect's known head hair"). In its early stages, his trial testimony was also similar to that which would have been given by most other hair examiners (e.g., "Head and pubic hairs of the same microscopic characteristics as Jimmy Bromgard's were present on the blue blanket.")

Unfortunately, as his testimony progressed, he expanded it to "So, if you find both head and pubic hair there, you have one chance in a hundred for the head hair matching a particular individual and one chance in a hundred for the pubic hair. If you find both, it's a multiplying effect, it would be one chance in 10,000."

This testimony was unfounded and made the significance of the hair comparisons sound much stronger than it merited. In depositions before the civil case in 2006, Mr. Melnikoff acknowledged that the "one chance in a hundred" number was based simply on his experience. In fact, he examined only 244 hair cases during his entire career in Montana and had never actually done a statistical analysis of them. The number was essentially just pulled out of the air.

Of greater concern than his questionable numbers was Mr. Melnikoff's use of "a multiplying effect" to obtain the "one chance in 10,000." Multiplying frequencies of occurrence is a well-established statistical technique that is commonly used in forensic science when frequencies of occurrence are known for two or more characteristics that are independently variable. The very large numbers seen in DNA cases result from the multiplication of the population frequencies of multiple alleles in any DNA profile because they are each independently inherited. If, for example, four alleles each had a frequency of 10% in the population, their combined frequency would be 10% of 10% of 10% of 10%, or 0.0001%, i.e., one person in 10,000 in the population. Population frequencies for the various microscopic characteristics of the scalp and pubic hairs have not been established, however, and it was thus improper for Mr. Melnikoff to multiply his stated frequencies.

There are two steps to a forensic microscopic comparison of hair. The first involves determining whether a questioned hair is microscopically similar to a known standard sample. The second is articulating the evidential significance of that similarity. Hair examiners are very competent at the first step; they do it regularly in the laboratory. The second step is much more challenging because there is no—and it is unlikely that there ever will be—recognized database of population distributions for hair as there is, for example, with conventional blood groups or DNA. As a result, most examiners resorted to phrases such as "could have come from" or "consistent with" to try to express their conclusions. Some have tried to formulate a frequency of occurrence based on their experience with the discrimination of known hair standards. Many of these, however, confused their ability to discriminate between known standard hair samples from an individual (which consist of up to fifty known hairs) with their ability to relate a single hair to a particular source, particularly when, as in the Bromgard case, the number of potential sources is unknown. Mr. Melnikoff appears to have been one of these examiners.

Mr. Bromgard, who was just eighteen years old when he was arrested, settled his lawsuit with the state in 2008 for $3.5 million. Another example of you can pay now, or you will pay later.

Oklahoma City Police Department Laboratory

In 2006 and 2008, I reviewed two very similar cases involving the Oklahoma City PD laboratory and one of its staff members, Joyce Gilchrist. One case related to Jeffrey Todd Pierce and the other to David Johns Bryson.

Mr. Bryson, 28 years old, was convicted of sexual assault in 1983 and was sentenced to 105 years in prison. The victim told police that she had bit the rapist's penis during the assault, and Mr. Bryson was arrested that night when he attended a hospital emergency room for treatment of an injured penis (as it turned out, a very unusual and unfortunate coincidence). The victim subsequently identified him as her assailant during a police lineup. Ms. Gilchrist presented damning serological and microscopic hair comparison testimony at his trial. In 1997, DNA analysis showed that Mr. Bryson could not have been the source of the semen found on items from the case. Despite this, the prosecutor continued to accuse him of the crime based on Ms. Gilchrist's hair comparisons, but in 1999, a court ordered his release from prison. Finally, in 2003, mitochondrial DNA analysis of the questioned hairs showed that none could have originated from Mr. Bryson, and an order was issued dismissing the case against him. He received $16.5 million in compensation.

Mr. Pierce was convicted of sexual assault in 1986 and was sentenced to sixty-five years in prison. He was twenty-three years old at the time. The assault occurred at the victim's apartment, and Mr. Pierce had been working as a landscaper at the building that day. Her initial description did not match him, and she could not pick him out of a lineup. However, the police later showed her a photo lineup with a picture of Mr. Pierce wearing the clothes he had been wearing the day of the assault, and she identified him. Ms. Gilchrist was a principal witness at his trial, testifying about her findings and conclusions from serological and microscopic examinations of items collected during the investigation. In May 2001, the district court vacated the conviction based on the results of DNA tests that demonstrated that Mr. Pierce was not the source of the semen that Ms. Gilchrist said she had detected. Another man, then in prison, was identified as the source, and Mr. Pierce settled a lawsuit with the city for $4.0 million.

Suffice it to say that in both cases there were serious errors in the serological analyses and the microscopic hair examinations that Ms. Gilchrist performed, as well as in the testimony she provided about her findings. All tended to point toward the involvement of each man.

Indeed, there was such a litany of issues described in the documents I reviewed that covered Ms. Gilchrist's entire career in the OCPD laboratory that it is difficult to understand why they were not identified and dealt with much sooner. Criticism of her work became public, in the media and court decisions, within four years of her initial employment in 1980. Nevertheless, OCPD ignored such criticism as evidenced by the fact that, even after major criticism by judges of the Oklahoma Court of Appeals in 1988 and 1989, the department promoted Ms. Gilchrist to senior forensic chemist in 1990.

Some of the problems could be attributed directly to her incompetence as a forensic scientist and her ethical irresponsibility. Other issues reflected systemic problems in the supervision and management of the OCPD laboratory.

The lab was commanded by sworn police officers who typically rotated through this position as one assignment in their career progression. None had a scientific background or experience in forensic science. Ms. Gilchrist had eight lab commanders during her twenty-one years with OCPD, and there was no real scientific leadership of the lab, a recipe for disaster.

One problem with the sworn police lab manager system is the risk that the civilian forensic scientists may adopt a more prosecution-oriented attitude and approach to their work than is appropriate for them. Some of the criticism of Ms. Gilchrist suggested that she had succumbed to this risk. The police investigate; forensic scientists examine—quite a significant difference. As scientists, we strive to achieve the right answer from our examinations. For the police investigator, the right answer is usually the one that points toward the culpability of the accused person. Scientific validity is, for them, not an issue unless the evidence fails to meet a challenge in court. As long as Ms. Gilchrist kept providing these "right" answers, the investigators and prosecutors were content. They all loved her. She was rarely challenged and reveled in the nickname "Black Magic" (Ms. Gilchrist was African American) given to her by investigators because she seemed to have the ability to see things no one else could see.

When Ms. Gilchrist joined the OCPD laboratory in 1980, she had only the very basic academic qualification for a forensic scientist recruit, a 1980 BS degree with a major in forensic science (with modest grades) from Central Oklahoma State University. Her training in microscopic hair examination began with a two-week course in hair and fiber examination (of which only one week was devoted to hair) at the FBI Laboratory in early 1981, followed by six or seven months of understudy training with her supervisor in the OCPD lab. Her serology training was similar. Once she started reporting cases on her own, she was essentially unsupervised since her domineering personality was intimidating to her supervisor and the lab commanders were not technically competent to review her work.

In 2001, after much criticism of Ms. Gilchrist by the courts, the OCPD finally asked the Oklahoma State Bureau of Investigation (OSBI) laboratory to review 566 of Ms. Gilchrist's cases. They found at least one discrepancy in 159 (28%) of these cases and concluded,

> Some of the findings in our review are in direct conflict with testimony provided by Ms. Gilchrist and the contents of the case files. Some of the findings are poor laboratory practice based on training provided during the period these cases were completed. Some of the findings are due to inadequate or incomplete documentation of testing results or questions concerning the interpretation of testing results.

Also in 2001, a member of the FBI Laboratory reviewed transcripts, case notes, and evidence slides in eight of Ms. Gilchrist's hair and fiber cases. In the five cases in which microscope slides were still available for reexamination, he reported all "had either errors in identification or interpretation." In the only fiber case available, the "questioned fibers did not exhibit the same microscopic characteristics as the known fibers."

Two serologists from a private lab reviewed her work in the Pierce case and concluded that

> while her lab notes appeared to be in order, her testimony at various places was misleading at best, erroneous, lacking in foundation and self-contradictory. In fact, as her testimony progressed, she exhibited a tendency towards increasing prejudice to the defendant.

Also, in the Pierce case Ms. Gilchrist reported the identification of spermatozoa on seven microscope slides, but in 2001, three other examiners in the OCPD lab and one in the OSBI lab could detect sperm on only one of these slides.

In Mr. Bryson's case, her notes indicated serological results that, if properly interpreted, excluded him as a possible source of the semen. They also record a telephone call by her to the FBI Lab asking how the result she obtained might be rationalized. Then, without performing the tests the FBI recommended, she included in her report their suggested wording, if the additional tests had indicated a possible explanation for her results. The inescapable impression was that Ms. Gilchrist was convinced that Mr. Bryson was the source of the semen and she was prepared to ignore any data that might suggest otherwise.

She also found one pubic hair and four scalp hairs in Mr. Bryson's case that she described as having "the same range of microscopic characteristics as the suspect's known head hair." However, in 2001 an FBI Lab hair examiner found that these hairs "do not exhibit the same microscopic characteristics as the known head hairs from the suspect." Two OCPD examiners and one from the OSBI said that they could not see the characteristics that Ms. Gilchrist said she had seen. In 2003, mtDNA of these hairs proved that they were not from Mr. Bryson.

In another case, she testified before a jury about hair comparisons: "I can include people. I can positively exclude a person. But I cannot positively identify a person based on hair," which is quite correct. However, she then went on:

> I can promise you I can take hairs, hairs taken from each one of you and I can pull known samples from each one of you and make my comparisons. And I would be able to make an ID or match or whatever you want to call it because I can say these hairs could have come from you or could not have come from you based on the pigmentation.

Such a claim could well have left the impression with the jury that she could "positively identify" a person.

All these issues were a clear indication that Ms. Gilchrist was a somewhat less than competent forensic scientist and was, in part at least, a result of inadequate training and supervision. It was also clear that she did not distinguish between an expert opinion, which a forensic scientist can express in testimony, and a personal opinion, which is not allowed. For example, in one case she did not limit her testimony to describing the fibers on the sole of a suspect's shoe as being similar to those from a rug at a crime scene, which would have been appropriate, but instead testified that they proved that the person wearing that shoe "had to have been at the crime scene either during the crime or after the crime had occurred," which was well beyond her expertise and very prejudicial.

This may have been a result of the influence of one of her chiefs and the district attorney. The former testified at one of her hearings that "what chemists do all over the country, FBI Lab, OCPD lab, every lab you will find is their testimony is tailored to the most incriminating result. That's what they do."

He also said, "And the DA even said publicly that he didn't want an expert witness over there that wouldn't give their opinions. I mean, he wanted his experts to testify as aggressively as possible."

Two very disturbing, and hopefully rare, opinions!

Based on my review of Ms. Gilchrist's analyses and testimony, there was no doubt that some were at best ambiguous, some were misleading or distorted, and some was simply incorrect. Whether this was due to incompetence or was deliberate on her part might be debated. However, the frequency with which it occurred and its common thread suggested the latter. Also, I reluctantly concluded that some must also be attributed to her interpretation of what constitutes professional integrity.

There were two egregious examples of this in the Pierce and Bryson cases. In 1990 in the Bryson case, when Mr. Bryson's lawyer asked for items from the case to have DNA analysis performed, Ms. Gilchrist advised him that they had all been destroyed in 1983. In fact, they still existed.

In the Pierce case, she testified that when she first examined the hairs from the scene (before Mr. Pierce became a suspect), she observed a uniform change in pigmentation from root to tip and concluded that they were from someone who wore something on his head that shaded the hair from the sun. Her hair examination notes did not describe anything like this. By the time she testified, however, she knew there was a photograph of Mr. Pierce wearing a headband. She also testified that all of Mr. Pierce's known hairs had this same pattern, despite the fact that the sexual assault had occurred in May 1985, but the known hairs from Mr. Pierce were not collected until March and July 1986. It is highly unlikely that, even in Oklahoma, exposure to the sun would be so consistent over a ten- to fourteen-month period.

Joyce Gilchrist was dismissed from the OCPD lab in 2001. She died in 2015.

Chicago Police Department Laboratory

Larry Gillard was convicted of the rape and armed robbery of a twenty-five-year-old woman in her Chicago apartment on May 19, 1981. He had been arrested a week after the crime four blocks from the crime scene by a police officer who saw him run from a home that the officer thought might have been burglarized. Due to the proximity of the rape victim's apartment, Gillard was put into a police lineup from which the rape victim identified him as her assailant. (Ironically, he was never charged with the burglary that had led to his arrest.)

At his trial for the rape in January 1982, the only evidence linking him to the crime was the victim's identification and the testimony of a CPD lab analyst, who claimed that Mr. Gillard was among only 4.4% of the African American population who could have been the source of semen recovered from the victim. The jury deliberated only an hour before returning a guilty verdict, and he was sentenced to twenty-four years in prison. His appeals were denied.

In 2008, the Exoneration Project at the University of Chicago Law School obtained DNA analysis that excluded Mr. Gillard as the source of the semen and identified the actual rapist. The conviction was dismissed, and he was released on May 26, 2009. He filed a lawsuit against the city of Chicago, and in January 2014, the city agreed to pay $6.375 million to settle the lawsuit.

As part of Mr. Gillard's lawsuit against the city, two forensic scientists from a private laboratory in California provided lengthy reports on their reviews of the CPD lab's work in Mr. Gillard's case and the work done by members of that lab in ten other cases between 1985 and 1995. These reports were highly critical not only of the serology work and testimony in these cases but also about what they referred to as the "culture of scientific and ethical unaccountability" in the CPD lab. Another highly respected forensic scientist, Lucy Davis, who I knew well through our involvement with AAFS, dealt with the scientific/technical aspects of those reports and the serology work in those cases. She found much of the criticism to be either trivial or based on the application of twenty-first-century standards to work done in the 1980s.

The purpose of my review was to determine if there were any significant ethical issues or indications of a "culture of scientific and ethical unaccountability" revealed in any of the hundreds of documents I reviewed.

Following the St. Valentine's Day Massacre in 1929, private funding was used to establish the Scientific Crime Laboratory of Chicago in the Law School at Northwestern University in 1930. This was the second crime laboratory established in the United States. In 1938, this laboratory was purchased by the CPD, where it remained until 1996 when, as described earlier, it was transferred to the Illinois State Police and relocated to the newly constructed Forensic Science Center at Chicago.

As part of its due diligence before the transfer, the ISP commissioned audits of the CPD lab in 1993 and 1995, and reports of these audits were available for my review. These reports were quite typical of such preaccreditation reports and indicated many deficiencies, ranging from the physical plant, through some procedures, supervision, staff competence, and lack of an adequate QA program, to the lack of conclusions in the lab reports. The CPD lab had done little, if any, of the enormous amount of work required to prepare a lab for accreditation. For most of the period under review, the lab director had been a career police officer, the staff was primarily trained in-house, and most had little opportunity for interchange with other labs. The facility was quite inadequate, as was the funding.

Of the eleven cases reviewed, there were two, including Mr. Gillard's, that displayed what I considered to be potential ethical deficiencies by two members of the CPD lab staff. In one of these, possible exculpatory analytical results were not presented at the trial. During her testimony, one of the examiners had been confronted with a classic dilemma for a witness when she was not asked a question that would have allowed her to provide the exculpatory results. In such situations, a scientist has to try to find a way to "volunteer" the information, something that witnesses are typically instructed not to do. Alternatively, after finishing their testimony, they can advise the attorney who called them (prosecutor or defense) of the oversight in the hope of being recalled to present the evidence. If a recall is denied, they can, as a last resort, ask to speak with the presiding judge to explain their dilemma. There was insufficient information available for me to determine whether appropriate attempts had been made by the examiner in this case to correct the situation. She was no longer employed as a forensic scientist and not available for me to interview. Thus, a definite conclusion about ethical performance could not be made.

In Mr. Gillard's case, another CPD lab witness had testified that the semen was from a nonsecretor and that she had established through ABH testing of Mr. Gillard's saliva that he was a nonsecretor. She also had tested his blood in the Lewis system and found it to be Lewis a–b–. Nonsecretors make up about 20% of the population and Lewis a–b– occurs in about 22% of the African American population. She therefore multiplied these two frequencies to conclude that Mr. Gillard's blood groups could be found in only 4.4% of the population.

There were three problems with this testimony. The first was her multiplication of the two frequencies, which was not justified because secretor status and Lewis blood groups are not independent genetic events and therefore the population frequencies cannot be multiplied. The second was that the frequencies used were for the characteristics of the known samples from Mr. Gillard when the only relevant evidence would have been the frequencies of the characteristics of the questioned semen, on which no Lewis testing had been done. The third was that there was no mention in the lab report of any Lewis testing, and it was not discussed during the witness' pretrial interview with Mr. Gillard's lawyer. It was therefore clear to me that the CPD lab member had failed in her ethical responsibility by presenting improper testimony and by not disclosing all of her analytical results before trial.

At the time of my review, the former CPD lab member was no longer working in forensic science.

RCMP Laboratory

In 1984 (and until 2014), the RCMP Laboratory system consisted of six operational laboratories in Vancouver, Edmonton, Regina, Winnipeg, Ottawa, and Halifax. This case involved only the Winnipeg lab. (The system now consists of just three labs, in Vancouver, Edmonton, and Ottawa.)

James Driskell and Perry Harder were involved in a variety of criminal activities, including a "chop shop" in Winnipeg, in which they cut up stolen cars and sold the parts. They were arrested in November 1989 and charged with a variety of offenses. Harder negotiated a plea bargain in exchange for agreeing to testify against Driskell. When the trial was scheduled to begin on June 21, 1990, Harder failed to appear and was never seen alive again. Mr. Driskell was therefore discharged.

On September 30, 1990, Harder's badly decomposed body was found in a shallow grave near some railroad tracks in Winnipeg. He had died from two gunshots to his chest. Police considered Driskell to be a suspect because he had become aware of Harder's plea bargain. In October, another criminal associate of Driskell's gave a statement to the police as a result of which Driskell was arrested and charged with Harder's murder.

Known hairs of Harder from the grave site and items from a van that had been owned by Mr. Driskell (which he had since sold to another associate) were submitted to the Winnipeg lab. Because the investigators believed the van had been used to transport Harder's body, the lab was requested to examine the vacuumed debris, the cargo area carpet, and a single hair collected from the van for any hairs similar to those from the grave. They were also asked to examine clothing from the body for any fibers similar to those of the carpet.

Twenty-five fibers were recovered from the clothing, but none were similar to the carpet. Twenty-four scalp hairs were examined, and the lab examiner concluded that three of these were "consistent with having originated from the same person as the known scalp hair samples purportedly from the deceased."

Mr. Driskell's trial began on June 3, 1991. The prosecution case relied primarily on the testimony of two career criminals, who said that Driskell had confessed the crime to them, and of the RCMP Lab examiner. The latter testified according to the wording of his report, but when asked what he meant by "consistent with," he explained, "So if the hair is consistent, that means it either came from the same person as that known sample or from somebody else who has hair exactly like that." Also, "the chances were small that the hairs came from someone other than Mr. Harder."

On June 14, the jury found Driskell guilty of first-degree murder, and he was sentenced to life imprisonment. His appeals were denied. He eventually made contact with the Association in Defence of the Wrongly Convicted (AIDWYC) and convinced one of its founders, James Lockyer, to take up his case. In December 2001, Mr. Lockyer persuaded the attorney general of Manitoba that mitochondrial DNA analysis (which had not been available at the time of the trial) should be done on the hairs, and in June 2002 they were submitted to the UK Home Office Forensic Science Service (FSS). Their report in December 2002 stated,

> The mitochondrial DNA findings do not support the proposition that the hairs found in the van originated from Perry Harder. The findings provide extremely strong support for the proposition that the hairs from the van originated from three individuals, none of whom was Perry Harder.

Given this finding, AIDWYC was granted access to the Crown and police case files. These revealed even more shocking information. The two criminals who testified at the trial had been paid significant sums of money in exchange for their testimony. Moreover, one of them had also been granted immunity from an arson charge. None of this information had ever been disclosed to Mr. Driskell's trial lawyer.

Based on this new information, Mr. Lockyer applied for Ministerial Review of the conviction and, while the application was being reviewed, Driskell was released on bail in November 2003. Finally, on March 3, 2005, the federal minister of justice quashed Driskell's murder conviction. Rather than launch a new trial, the Crown chose to stay the proceedings, meaning that he would not be prosecuted again but also that he would never have a jury formally exonerate him. In December 2005, the government of Manitoba called a public commission of inquiry into the causes of Mr. Driskell's wrongful conviction and the Honorable Patrick LeSage, QC, retired chief justice of the Ontario Superior Court, was appointed commissioner. One of his terms of reference was to inquire into "the role of the RCMP Laboratory in the prosecution of James Driskell, and to review any systemic issues that may arise out of its role."

On May 1, 2006, I was invited by the commission counsel, Michael Code, to review and report on the forensic science aspects of the commission's mandate. This required reviewing a great many documents, including the relevant RCMP Lab training manuals and method manuals, work notes, the report and transcript of testimony of the hair and fiber examiner, and a lengthy interview of him and his supervisors in the Winnipeg lab; inspecting the relevant portions of the lab; organizing and chairing a panel discussion at the inquiry consisting of two prominent lawyers from the United States (Michael Bromwich and Peter Neufeld) and three highly respected forensic scientists from the United States and Canada (Peter DeForest, William Tilstone, and Joel Mayer); and testifying myself at the inquiry in Winnipeg.

My conclusions included findings that the RCMP Lab hair and fiber examiner was well trained and fully qualified to perform the examinations, and that the methods used were well documented and, with minor exceptions, accepted in forensic science. The work notes, although consistent with general practice in the field at the time, were less detailed than what would be expected in an accredited lab in 2006 and thus severely limited a supervisor's ability to validate the results and report. The conclusions provided in the laboratory report were expressed in terms that were generally accepted conclusions for hair comparison at the time.

The examiner's testimony was quite straightforward and similar to what most forensic hair and fiber examiners would have provided. He acknowledged that microscopic hair examination does not provide a positive identification of a source and that he could not provide population distribution numbers. The only testimony that I, and many hair examiners, might not agree with was his statement that the chances of a random match between hairs from two different sources are "very small."

Since microscopic hair comparison and mtDNA analysis are based on totally different parameters, it is not unexpected that they will sometimes produce different conclusions. It was, however, quite surprising that the three hairs that were considered microscopically "consistent with" the known sample were found by the mtDNA analyst to be not only different from the known sample but also different from each other; i.e., they were from three different sources. Thus, either the RCMP examiner's observations were incorrect, the mtDNA results were incorrect, or the microscopic similarity of the questioned hairs to the known sample was a chance occurrence. Since no other qualified person ever examined the hairs microscopically and they were no longer available for examination, the first possibility could not be assessed. The nature of mtDNA analysis and the reputation of the FSS made the second possibility highly unlikely. That left the possibility of a random match of the microscopic characteristics of three hairs from different individuals, however remote, as the more likely possibility.

Concerning the issue of the examiner's results being influenced by the fact that he was employed in a laboratory operated by a police agency, there was nothing apparent in any of the material reviewed to suggest this. The RCMP Labs were managed and staffed entirely by civilians, and the Winnipeg lab was housed in a separate building remote from any police building. The panel in its discussion at the inquiry agreed that while there may be a perception of potential bias in a "police laboratory," it is just that, a perception, and not necessarily a reality.

In his report in January 2007, the commissioner accepted the conclusions in my report and found that the three hairs did not come from Mr. Harder. This raised questions about the reliability of hair microscopy evidence, but he agreed with the views expressed by the panelists that if hair microscopy evidence is to remain admissible, any conclusions should be expressed in "exclusionary" rather than "inclusionary" terms (i.e., framed as a statement that the source of the known hairs cannot be excluded as the source of the questioned hairs).

Concerning the laboratory being part of a police agency, the commissioner decided that

> it would not be appropriate for me to make a recommendation, on the evidence before me, on this difficult question. The forensic science panelists agreed that in their experience, formal affiliations between a forensic laboratory and a police force are not always a cause for concern.

Insofar as the RCMP Labs, and most other forensic science labs, are concerned, the matter of microscopic hair comparisons is now moot because it is a technique that is no longer used other than perhaps for preliminary screening purposes. Hair comparisons are now done by DNA analysis, either nuclear or mitochondrial.

In 2008, Mr. Driskell was compensated by the city and province in the amount of $4 million.

The "Troubles" in Northern Ireland

Although the conflict between Protestants and Catholics in Northern Ireland goes back to at least the time of Henry VIII, the more modern civil unrest and violence, including bombings, which is referred to as the Troubles, began in the mid to late 1960s. It reached a climax on "Bloody Sunday" in Londonderry on January 30, 1972, and then again on August 15, 1998, with a tragic car bombing, which killed twenty-nine people and wounded many others, in Omagh. The former resulted in the Bloody Sunday Inquiry (BSI) and the latter in a prolonged investigation by Police Service Northern Ireland (PSNI). I became involved with both investigations.

The Bloody Sunday Inquiry On the morning of Sunday, January 30, 1972, some 10,000 people gathered in Londonderry for a civil rights march to protest against the British government policy of internment without trial for members of the Irish Republican Army (IRA). The active participants at the time in Northern Ireland were a militant split-off group known as the Provisional IRA (PIRA). British troops had been sent into Derry (Republican supporters never refer to it as "Londonderry") as a peacekeeping force in August 1969, but by the early 1970s they were considered by the predominantly Roman Catholic community to be just as discriminatory as the mainly Protestant Royal Ulster Constabulary. The residents of the Catholic Bogside area of the city had therefore declared it to be "Free Derry" and had set up barriers creating a "no go" zone for the army and the police.

The army assigned two companies of the First Parachute Regiment, the most aggressive element of the army, to control the demonstration, and they blocked off the planned route, which would have led the demonstrators to the Guildhall in the city center. The leaders of the march therefore led most of the marchers toward "Free Derry Corner" in the Bogside. In protest, a number of them, predominantly young males, ignored the leaders and continued on the original route toward an army barricade. There they began throwing stones and epithets at the soldiers, who responded with a water cannon, tear gas, and rubber bullets.

As this riot began to disperse, the paratroopers were ordered to move in and arrest as many of the young rioters as possible. In the minutes that followed, some of the troops opened fire, killing thirteen and wounding thirteen others, one of whom died later.

While the army maintained that the troops had only reacted after coming under fire themselves, the people of the Bogside saw the killings as blatant murders. Concern was so serious that the British home secretary announced the following day an official inquiry into the circumstances of the shootings. This tribunal was quickly set up and led by British Lord Chief Justice Lord Widgery. His report, produced within just a few weeks of a somewhat cursory inquiry, served only to further polarize the community because it exonerated the army and cast suspicion on many of the victims, suggesting that they had been handling bombs and guns.

The Widgery Report served as a "burr under the saddle" for the relatives of the dead and the wider Catholic community, who vigorously campaigned over the ensuing twenty-five years for a fresh public inquiry. Finally, as part of the peace process leading to the "Good Friday Accord" of 1998, their demand was met by then prime minister Tony Blair. The Bloody Sunday Inquiry (BSI) was announced on April 3, 1998, under Lord Saville of Newdigate, a law lord, supported by two other senior judges from Canada and Australia.

In December 1998, I was invited by counsel to the BSI, to serve as a member of a "Peer Review Panel" (PRP), which would review the original forensic science work from 1972, suggest potential new avenues of examination that might be explored, and review the work that resulted from any such new examinations. The other members of the panel were Professor Peter DeForest of the John Jay College of Criminal Justice in New York and Professor Pierre Margot of L'Institut de Police Scientifique et de Criminologie in the University of Lausanne in Lausanne, Switzerland. Our work was coordinated by David Barclay, formerly of the Home Office Forensic Science Service and then a member of the National Crime Faculty at Bramshill in England.

Little did any of us appreciate the commitment of time that would be required over the next two years. While much of our work was performed using email and the Internet, we also attended several meetings with inquiry experts and staff at the BSI offices in London. In March 1999, we also spent a day touring the Bloody Sunday site in Londonderry. Although this was twenty-seven years after the event, we could sense the tension that still existed within the community, and each of us had the feeling that we were being closely watched while we were in Derry. After we returned to London, Dave Barclay had a call from a friend in the Intelligence Division at Scotland Yard asking what we had been doing in Londonderry that day? We were relieved to learn that we had not just been paranoid.

The PRP reviewed hundreds of pages of documents, reports, statements, charts, and maps, including the reports and laboratory notes of the original Widgery experts, transcripts of those experts' testimony at the Widgery Inquiry, and their 1999 formal statements to BSI staff. We also examined copies of hundreds of contemporary news photographs, videos and audio tapes, curricula vitae, and reports of the experts retained by the BSI, and had many discussions with them.

The autopsies on the victims had been conducted in a hospital in Letterkenny in the Republic of Ireland, just across the border from Londonderry. They confirmed that the victims had all died from gunshots and described the bullet tracks through the bodies. In at least eight of the cases, the pathologists concluded that they saw "nothing to indicate that the weapon had been fired at close range." This was of considerable importance since some of the relatives and many of the demonstrators insisted that some of the victims had essentially been "executed" with shots at close range as they lay on the ground.

The BSI experts who reviewed all the original autopsy reports, photos, and testimony in 1999 concluded that "with the exception of G. McKinney, the apparent absence of a visible deposit from a muzzle discharge on the deceased's clothing or skin indicates that the shots were fired from distances of probably no less than a meter." We agreed with that conclusion.

Another gunshot-related issue was the directionality of some of the gunshots. Although in most of the victims it was clear that the shots had been fired by paratroopers at street level, the demonstrators insisted that three of the victims had been killed by shots fired by other troops stationed on the city walls, high above street level. They based this belief on the angles of the bullet tracks through the bodies.

Intuitively, it might seem reasonable to believe that shots fired from the elevation of the city walls would strike bodies on the street at significantly different angles from shots fired at street level. However, the considerable horizontal distance from the walls to where these victims were shot was such that the difference in the angle of declination between a shot from the walls and one from the street was only about five degrees, easily within the range of movement of a body. The possible activities of the victims at the time they were shot (standing, bending, kneeling, etc.) could readily account for the angles of the wound tracks through the bodies. Thus, we concluded that the shots could have been fired from either the street or the city walls.

A more significant firearms-related issue was the conclusion in 1972 by a member of the staff of the Northern Ireland forensic science laboratory that he had "detected particles of lead on some of the samples that had been collected from the hands and clothing of the deceased" and that at least some of these "would have been firearms-derived." This implied that at least five of the victims had either fired a gun or been very close to one when it was fired, something that outraged the citizens of the Bogside.

Although there were several techniques for gunshot residue (GSR) analysis used in forensic science in 1972, the only one available to the lab in Northern Ireland was a simple color test for lead. Using it, the examiner found varying numbers of lead particles on the items he examined. However, it was apparent to us that there was a tendency for the numbers of particles to increase rather than decrease as the distance from the hands increased, which conflicted with the examiner's testimony that his results showed the hands were nearer the source of the particles than the clothing. Also, there were larger numbers of particles on trousers than on jackets and on left hands than on the right.

More importantly, because of the considerable likelihood of lead contamination, both at the scene and in the process of recovery and transport of the bodies in army vehicles, we did not believe that the lead particles were informative or that there would be any value in attempting to reexamine any items that might remain using modern more sensitive and specific techniques for GSR.

During the original investigation, GSR was also used by the examiner to estimate the muzzle-to-target distance (range determination). In some of the garments, he referred to the bullet holes as having been made from ranges "greater than 30 feet." This was surprising to us because, although quite accurate estimates of range can be made for shots at fairly close distances, the accuracy decreases dramatically as the distance increases, to the point that most firearms examiners will not attempt a range estimate at distances exceeding about one meter.

The lab examiner stated at the Widgery Inquiry that "the British Army SLR [self-loading rifle] can on occasion throw it [lead particles] up to 30 ft. This is the basis of the range test. It consistently throws it with direction to 12 ft. Between 12 ft. and 30 ft. it is subject to drift and air currents."

We were unable to determine his basis for this statement, which was completely at odds with all the literature and our experience. We postulated that the examiner had misinterpreted the presence of isolated lead particles (which can be found randomly downrange from a gunshot), rather than looking for the pattern of GSR that can be found around close-range bullet holes. Our conclusion from the results available was simply that at least twelve of the thirteen victims had been shot at ranges of greater than one meter.

The lab also made examinations for explosive residues on clothing from some of the victims. The only positive finding was a "nitrate ester consistent with nitroglycerine" in the right pocket of one victim's jacket. This was not surprising since an army bomb disposal officer had removed a nail bomb from this pocket. The real question was not whether at some point there was a nail bomb in this pocket, but rather when and how it got there. The demonstrators insisted that it (and three others found in the other pockets of the jacket) had been put there by the army after the victim had been shot. The fatal bullet had gone through the pocket and, if it had struck the bomb, would have been expected to detonate it. The lab examiner had tried placing the bomb in the pocket and found that if it were placed deep into the pocket, the bullet would have missed it. Unfortunately, the value of this test was limited because the pocket had been cut open during the removal process and the explosive filler of the bomb had been removed before the lab received it.

We were unable to reach any conclusion about how or when these bombs got into the victim's pockets.

Our review of materials was not limited to traditional forensic science examinations but extended to trying to derive additional information from contemporary news photographs, films, and audio recordings. An enormous amount of this material was acquired by BSI staff, and we searched through it to select any that might contain useful information. A good example of the type of thing we were searching for was a photo that showed a man holding an unidentified object in his left hand: Could it be a gun or a nail bomb? It was not clear in the photo available, which, like most of this material, was a copy of uncertain generation. Another example was trying to determine from audio tapes on which gunshots could be heard whether there were guns other than the paratroopers' SLRs being fired. A commercial digital media firm was retained to try to enhance the information available from such items, but because it was not actual original material (i.e., negatives, positive transparencies, cine film, or audio tapes), success was very limited.

Our work for the BSI was essentially completed by late 2000, although we continued to monitor the hearings for anything of a previously unknown scientific nature. The actual hearings began in Londonderry's Guildhall in March 2000 and went on until January 2005. More than nine hundred witnesses were heard. Lord Saville's final report was not published until June 15, 2010, making it one of the longest and most expensive (£400 million) inquiries in British legal history. The report established that although the first shot was probably fired by a PIRA supporter, none of the victims had fired a shot, and it laid responsibility for what happened that Sunday squarely on the army. Perhaps the BSI's most important contribution was giving everyone who wanted to say something an opportunity to be heard. Those words were perhaps the most expensive ever uttered!

Omagh Bombing

By the 1990s, many people on both sides in Northern Ireland had had enough of the Troubles and talks began to try to find the basis for a settlement. As part of these discussions, the PIRA agreed to a cease-fire. Not all members accepted this, however, and a splinter group of the more militant members broke away to form the Real IRA (RIRA) to continue their campaign of violence.

During 1998, some explosives-related incidents for which the RIRA claimed responsibility occurred in communities across Northern Ireland. These consisted of either mortar attacks with homemade mortars, or car bombs. The targets were typically Royal Ulster Constabulary (RUC) or army establishments and government buildings such as courthouses. Some of the car bombs and mortars were detected and disarmed before they functioned, and none of the events before August resulted in any serious injuries.

However, on August 15, 1998, at 15:04, a large car bomb detonated on Market Street, the main business thoroughfare, in the town of Omagh. Twenty-nine people and two unborn babies were killed as a result, and 220 were injured. This represented the largest loss of life in a single incident in Northern Ireland during the Troubles. The RIRA had telephoned a warning to the police that a car bomb would explode outside the courthouse in forty minutes and officers had begun directing people away from that area south down Market Street. Unfortunately, it was a busy Saturday afternoon, and the car bombers delivering the bomb car could not find a parking place near the courthouse. The closest spot they could find was two blocks to the south, exactly where the police were directing people to "safety"!

This event turned the vast majority of citizens of Omagh and Northern Ireland, including Republicans, against the violence and the RIRA.

Initially, each of the 1998 incidents was investigated as a separate event by the RUC, and later by its renamed successor, Police Service Northern Ireland (PSNI), but as the Omagh investigation progressed, a decision was made to search for possible linkages between them. Eventually, the number of incidents considered to be linked became thirteen. A critical factor in establishing the linkages was information derived from the forensic science examinations performed by Forensic Science Northern Ireland (FSNI) and the UK Forensic Science Service. Ultimately, in September 2003, Sean Gerard Hoey, an RIRA member, was arrested and charged with fifty-eight offenses related to the thirteen incidents.

In December 2003, PSNI invited the Peer Review Panel from the Bloody Sunday Inquiry to perform a similar role in this investigation. Again, we found ourselves deeply committed to this task for the next almost six years. Although much of our work was again accomplished using the Internet, we did have five face-to-face meetings in Enniskillen (including a visit to the scene in Omagh), Belfast (with a visit to the FSNI laboratory in Carrickfergus), Toronto/Burlington, and New York (Peter DeForest and I had complained about having to do all the traveling).

Two events gave us personal reason to understand the concern of the people of Northern Ireland about the Troubles. Our first meeting in Belfast was interrupted just as it began by a bomb scare causing an evacuation of our hotel: "Welcome to Belfast!" The FSNI lab was located in Carrickfergus because the original lab in Belfast had been destroyed by a bomb in 1992. The lab had then relocated to "temporary quarters" in a former cigarette factory in Carrickfergus, a suburb of Belfast. As is typical of government planning, it was still in those temporary quarters twelve years later.

Sadly, incidents involving bombings and mortar attacks in Northern Ireland were not uncommon. With minimal damage and few if any injuries, the investigations were conducted as matters of relative routine. The crime scene examinations by the police were therefore not pursued with the intensity and thoroughness that might have been expected in jurisdictions where such events were less common. No useful fingerprints had been found on vehicles or other objects. Some items had been returned to their owners, and others were not retained or were not stored under proper conditions, thus limiting potential reconsideration and reprocessing later.

The laboratory examinations that were performed were competent, but due to other casework pressures, not everything that might have been done was in fact done and the priorities assigned were not high. Because of the tragic effects of the Omagh bombing, however, FSNI staff members led the examination of that scene from the beginning. Dennis McAuley, an explosives expert in the lab, took charge of the crime scene search, which lasted for five days. Very early in the process, he recognized an electrical toggle switch found near the remains of the front end of the bomb vehicle as being typical of those previously observed in other recent bombing cases and was able to show the searchers the other types of components they should be looking for. "Routine" examinations for fingerprints, tool marks, fibers, and so forth, were undertaken, but with a greater sense of urgency than for the earlier incidents.

Sufficient items, many of them quite small, were recovered to permit Dennis to make a good description of the explosive device. These included some of the timer power unit (TPU) components, fragments of the booster assembly, and traces of the explosives. Also, he examined the crater left by the bomb and determined that it was about 3 m in diameter and about 0.8 m deep. From these dimensions, and the damage to the vehicle and its surroundings, he estimated that "a charge of approximately 150–200 kg of improvised explosive had functioned in the boot of the Vauxhall Cavalier."

All the devices were similar. The mortars consisted of steel fabricated launch tubes and firing frames, black powder propellant, TPU "triggers," and improvised mortar bombs with percussion cap impact initiators and improvised detonating cord. The car bombs consisted of a TPU, usually placed on the passenger seat; a power source in the form of dry cell batteries; twin-flex wires connecting the TPU to an electric detonator; an improvised detonating cord; an improvised booster tube filled with the same explosive as the main charge; and the main charge, which was typically a crushed ammonium nitrate fertilizer/sugar improvised explosive placed in the trunk of the vehicle.

The TPU became a critical contributor to the linkages because it was a new design that had first been encountered in Northern Ireland in January 1998. As of the time of the Omagh bombing, it had been identified in sixteen incidents in Northern Ireland, three in the Republic and one in London. It was so different from earlier units that FSNI had given it its own designation: "TPU Mark 19." It consisted of a circuit made up of two toggle switches, a two-hour electromechanical timer, a 390-ohm resistor, a red LED function light, and connecting wires. In all the Mark 19 TPUs, the components were fixed in place in the same configuration with thermoplastic glue within plastic lunch boxes. The timer spindle, the switch toggles, and the LED protruded through holes in the bottom of the boxes.

Dennis McAuley noted that all the timers in the TPUs bore the same manufacturer's part number and date code. From this, it was learned that the timers had been made in France as a single lot on March 4, 1997, to fill an order for 480 such timers placed and paid for with cash by what proved to be a fictitious entity in the Republic. This information could best be explained by a linkage of the timers to a common illicit purpose, although not necessarily exclusive to this series of incidents.

Another linkage of these devices was provided by some idiosyncrasies in the construction of the TPUs. An example was the use of a three-way connection of the resistor with two wires, one of which was redundant and required an unnecessary soldered joint. This was significant because this wire was found in eleven of the Northern Ireland devices but not in those in the Republic and London. There were several other such idiosyncrasies that led us to conclude that the Northern Ireland devices were probably put together by a single individual.

Linkage of at least three of the devices was supported by the observation that three of the plastic lunch boxes had coincident holes for the switches and LED to pass through, indicating that they were produced simultaneously, while the boxes were "nested." These three devices were all used within eleven days.

There were other examinations done on the devices. The thermoplastic glue was found to be different both between and within devices. This was not surprising because multiple sticks of glue were required for each device. Most of the connections in the TPUs were soldered, and the soldered connections were neatly trimmed with a twin-bladed implement. The quality of the soldering was much different from that in the London and Republic devices.

The hand-printed markings ("ON," "OFF," "A," "B," and "C") on the plastic lunch boxes, made with thick-point black marker pen(s), were examined, but the very limited amount of hand printing on each box, although similar, was insufficient to conclude that it was produced by only one person. The ink in the printing was also compared, and although it was found that the inks on four of the devices were the same, those on the others were different.

All the recovered TPUs in the series had plastic adhesive tape used in various positions. Five different colors were used, but there did not appear to be any pattern for particular colors. An attempt to "match" the ends of the tape pieces, including those from even a single unit, was unsuccessful.

An impressive effort was made by Dr. Ruth Griffin of FSNI to compare almost 1,500 fibers recovered from the thermoplastic glue in the TPUs or adhering to the sticky surfaces of the plastic tapes. Three populations shared by two or more TPUs were identified, grey-green bilobal acrylic fibers, grey bilobal acrylics, and a larger population of dark blue-green round acrylic fibers. The latter is often seen in black knitted gloves. The experience in Northern Ireland was that fingerprints were rarely if ever detected on explosive devices, indicating that gloves were worn during their construction and delivery. We asked Dennis McAuley to try to make a similar TPU while wearing gloves, and somewhat to our surprise, he had no difficulty assembling a device in as little as two and a quarter hours.

Dr. Griffin concluded that the finding of the matching blue-green round acrylic fibers "would support the proposition that the fibers from" five of the devices, including Omagh, "have originated from the same source or the same combination of sources, that is from two or more sources/pairs of gloves or mismatched pairs of gloves."

Unfortunately, no gloves of the type were ever found in any relevant location. While we recognized that the lack of a specific source would normally weaken the significance of a fiber comparison that attempted to associate an individual with another individual or object, in this instance this was less of a concern because the objective was simply to determine if there was evidence of a linkage of similar devices.

A substantial effort was devoted to the search for an examination of potential tool marks, but no significant associative information was derived.

Although, as noted above, fingerprints were rarely developed from bombing events, nevertheless, some fingerprints were developed from telephone handsets, cars, and documents. These were searched against available records without success.

Audio tapes of some of the warning calls were submitted for comparison with the known recorded speech of Mr. Hoey, but the results were of very limited value.

Several telephones, both mobile and fixed, registered to persons of interest (including Mr. Hoey) were identified by FSNI, and some very impressive cell site and call log analysis was done by PSNI. Cell site analysis located the approximate position of the mobile phones at significant times relevant to incidents at Lisburn, Newry Courthouse, Banbridge, and Omagh. While such information was helpful, it applied only to the phone and its location; the identity of the user could only be inferred.

At the time of the Omagh bombing, DNA analytical techniques were not sufficiently sensitive to be useful for the amounts of DNA that might be present on the physical evidence. In 1999, a new specialized technique, low-copy-number (LCN) DNA, with greatly enhanced sensitivity (so much so that it is now sometimes referred to as "touch DNA") was developed at the FSS, and it began to be used on a few items from the series in 2000. Increased sensitivity is, of course, accompanied by an increased risk of obtaining a DNA profile from contamination on the item. "Mixed profiles" (from more than one individual) are quite common. The application of LCN DNA must therefore be made with extreme caution, and the results require particularly careful interpretation.

Profiles that could be interpreted were obtained from items in five of the incidents, including Omagh, and were searched against the UK and Northern Ireland databases. They also were compared with "elimination" profiles obtained from all PSNI and FSNI personnel who may have had contact with the items.

Initially, the profiles were attributed to unknown persons "Male A," "Male B," and "Female C." The Male A profile was detected on brown tape on the battery housing and blue tape from the detonator in a car bomb in Lisburn, and on tape on the detonator from a car bomb in Armagh. Partial profiles that could relate to Male A were detected on red-brown tape from the detonating cord from Lisburn, and on tape from the detonator from a trailer bomb, also in Armagh. These profiles thus provided evidence that Male A was associated with these cases, thus linking them. Following Sean Hoey's arrest in 2003 and the profiling of a reference buccal swab from him, the Male A DNA was attributed to him with the chance of that DNA being from some other person being only about one in one billion.

In our final report in November 2005, we concluded that significant linkages had been identified: the general design of the Mark 19 TPUs, the use of a specific brand of plastic lunch boxes with the brand name erased (three of which had coincident holes) to contain the components of the TPUs, the specific manufacturing batch of the timers, the consistent choice of timer knobs out of the many that would have been available, the floating T junction in the TPU circuit, the color sequences of the wiring, the location and general style of the hand printing on ten of the lunch boxes, the common population of fibers in six of the devices, the finding of DNA alleles attributable to a specific person in three of the devices, and the design, construction, and components of the detonating cords and booster tubes. The fact that this DNA was detected on parts of the TPUs normally inaccessible to anyone other than the fabricator and before a known sample was obtained from Mr. Hoey was significant to negating any possible suggestion of tampering with the evidence. This information was reinforced by the multiple differences in these characteristics that appeared in the London and Republic devices.

Information derived from the telephone inquiries indicated that contacts were made between a small group of telephones at locations and times that corresponded to at least four of the incidents: Lisburn, Newry Courthouse, Banbridge, and Omagh.

The fiber evidence contributed to the linkage of six of the incidents: Lisburn, Finaghy Halt in Belfast, Newry Courthouse, Blackwater Road in Armagh, Corry Square RUC station in Newry, and Omagh.

We concluded that

> if the conclusion is reached that all of the incidents in the series are linked (as is supported by the physical evidence) and that each of the TPUs in this series was produced by one person (as is also supported by the physical evidence), then Mr. Hoey is logically linked to all of them.

Mr. Hoey's trial before a judge without a jury (unbiased jurors were almost impossible to be found in Northern Ireland during these times) took place between September 2006 and January 2007. The judgment was delivered on December 12, 2007, and Mr. Hoey was acquitted of all charges.

After the acquittal, reviews of various aspects of the investigation and trial were conducted by PSNI, the Northern Ireland Police Board, the police ombudsman of Northern Ireland, and the UK forensic science regulator. The PRP was also asked by PSNI to comment on relevant aspects of the judgment and to review the forensic science results in light of some of the testimony and judgment in Mr. Hoey's trial and the results of some of the reviews. We were not finished yet!

When we read the judgment, we were astounded at the harsh criticism of some of the police officers and the judge's obvious misunderstanding of some of the forensic science evidence. One egregious example was his naming two detectives for lying about wearing protective clothing at the crime scene when there was a media photo showing them not so dressed. He wrote about them:

> The explanation as to how their untruths came to be told and the deliberate attempts, as I am satisfied they were, to conceal what the Defence not unfairly characterized as the 'beefing up' of the initial statement of (the SOCO) are deeply disquieting. I am left in the position that I do not know what if anything I can believe of the evidence of these two and I am satisfied that, had photographs not been available to gainsay their lies, they would have persisted in seeking to and very possibly have succeeded in convincing me that, being at that time (somewhat unusually if the evidence of others is correct) alive to the possibility of DNA contamination, they were wearing suitable protective clothing to obviate such risk.

He formally referred this criticism to the police ombudsman, whose investigation found that the photo referred to had been taken after all the crime scene search and handling of the evidence had been completed.

The judge also wrote about Dennis McAuley: "I am not satisfied beyond a reasonable doubt or indeed to any acceptable standard that Mr. McAuley's painstaking work establishes common authorship of any of the Mark 19 TPUs."

While it was the judge's right and responsibility to be satisfied beyond a reasonable doubt, we could not agree with his finding that Mr. McAuley's conclusions did not meet "any acceptable standard." Dennis simply provided his observations about what were technical facts. These were well documented and were capable of being checked by other observers and, in our view, clearly met acceptable standards in forensic science.

Specifically, the judge found that "his [McAuley's] conclusions as to similarity of solder joints, based as he readily conceded upon an absence of any prior science, expertise in soldering or soldered joints, are, when examined, in reality no more than speculation."

We disagreed with the judge's description of these conclusions as "speculation." They were reasonable conclusions based on many detailed observations. While for obvious reasons there may not have been "any prior science," that does not preclude drawing reasonable conclusions. While Mr. McAuley's "expertise" in soldering may not have been great, he did indeed have more than most forensic scientists and had produced test exemplars of the TPUs. He also had, unfortunately, because of the nature of his work in Northern

Ireland, experience from a detailed examination of a very substantial number of soldered joints in a great many explosive devices.

It is clear from the judgment that the judge was not impressed with the testimony of the DNA expert from the FSS. For example, "I found him inappropriately combative as an expert witness and his unwillingness to debate constructively the various matters put to him was unhelpful in the extreme."

Based on our review of the transcripts, we could not agree with this description. Most of the "unwillingness" referred to was simply an expert witness quite properly and correctly defending statements and opinions that he considered valid.

The LCN DNA evidence was challenged by two experts for the defense, both of whom, although very knowledgeable about DNA evidence, acknowledged that they had no personal experience with LCN DNA analysis. One testified that he had "no peer-reviewed publications" on DNA and that he "would emphasize again that I am not an expert in the interpretation of these," and the other testified that he had "not specifically" been trained in the interpretation of LCN results. Nevertheless, the judge rejected the DNA evidence.

Following the release of the judgment, the UK forensic science regulator appointed an expert panel to review the science of "low-template" DNA (LTDNA), a generic term that would include LCN DNA analysis. They concluded that "this technique is fit for purpose."

Although no DNA was found on the Omagh device, our conclusion based on Mr. Hoey's DNA on three devices that were linked to the other devices, including the one in Omagh, was that "the inescapable impression we are left with is of such internal consistency that one person must have been responsible for the assembly of all the TPUs in the defined series."

Our involvement in the investigation of the Omagh bombing finally ended in July 2009.

Two Incredible Surprises

Early in 2001 and late in 2003, I received two unexpected telephone calls from people I did not know. Each occurred just as Marie and I were in the middle of lunch and almost caused me to choke on my food. In 2001, it was the president of the John Jay College of Criminal Justice in the City University of New York (CUNY), and in 2003 it was the president of the University of Toronto. They each advised that their university senates had voted to honor me with a doctor of science degree, honoris causa (DSc Hon). In New York, it was in recognition of being "one of the world's leading forensic scientists who has been a major influence in the professionalization of the field nationally and internationally," and in Toronto because my "years of tireless work have helped to develop professional standards for the field of forensic sciences and transformed the nature of criminal investigations."

If that wasn't enough of a shock, they each also asked if I would accept the honor! Who would ever refuse? The degrees were conferred at convocations in May 2001 in Madison Square Garden in New York and in June 2004 at Convocation Hall in Toronto. All quite overwhelming! At each ceremony, I was invited to address the graduating students.

Figure 25.1 Londonderry, January 30, 1972.

Figure 25.2 Londonderry, January 30, 1972.

Figure 25.3 The BSI Peer Review Panel, left to right: Barclay, Margot, DeForest, and Lucas.

Figure 25.4 Londonderry, August 30, 2009.

Figure 25.5 Londonderry, August 30, 2009.

Figure 25.6 Dr. Lucas #1 (with Professor Peter DeForest).

Figure 25.7 Dr. Lucas #2.

Retirement, Part 2
My Final Presentation 26

In 2013, I decided it was time to cease accepting consultancies as I was getting further and further away from feeling competent to deal with some of the issues I was being asked to examine. I did, however, continue to accept invitations to participate in panel discussions or to present lectures on something I was familiar with, the history and development of the forensic sciences! During this period, I became increasingly frustrated by the constant references in the media to the science that most forensic scientists practice as "junk science." I decided to make this the subject of my "swan song" presentation, which was at the Twenty-First Triennial Meeting of the International Association of Forensic Sciences (IAFS) meeting in Toronto in August, 2017. What follows is the text of that presentation.

Scientific Evidence or Junk Science?

Following the 2009 publication of the National Research Council (NRC) report "Strengthening Forensic Science in the United States, a Path Forward," we have seen constant reference in the media to forensic science, or at least some of its disciplines, as "junk science." Then, the release of a report by the President's Council of Advisors on Science and Technology (PCAST), "Forensic Science in Criminal Courts: Ensuring Scientific Validity of Feature-Comparison Methods" in September 2016, stimulated a renewal of these types of articles.

Some examples:

- "Junk Science at the FBI," *New York Times*, April 2, 2015
- "A Wake-Up Call on the Junk Science Infesting Our Courtrooms," *Washington Post*, September 20, 2016
- "Jeff Sessions Is Keeping Junk Science in America's Courts," *Rolling Stone*, May 9, 2016
- "Is Forensic Ballistics 'Junk Science'?" *Weapon Man*, May 9, 2016

Both the NRC and PCAST reports focused on methods for comparing bite marks, latent fingerprints, firearms/tool marks, footwear impressions, hair, and handwriting. It is important to understand that neither report concluded that these disciplines were invalid, but rather that they simply had not been adequately validated, quite a different thing and a distinction not always recognized by the authors of these media articles.

Not surprisingly, neither report contained the term *junk science*, which was first coined by Peter Huber in his 1991 book *Galileo's Revenge, Junk Science in the Courtroom*, in which he described it thus:

> Junk science is the mirror image of real science, with much of the same form but none of the same substance.
>
> It is a hodgepodge of biased data, spurious inferences, and logical legerdemain, patched together by researchers whose enthusiasm for discovery and diagnosis far outstrips their skill. It is a catalog of every conceivable kind of error: data dredging, wishful thinking, truculent dogmatism, and, now and again, outright fraud.

A damning indictment indeed; but does that sound like the forensic science we are familiar with?

The PCAST report described validation as requiring that the methods "be shown, based on empirical studies, to be repeatable, reproducible, and accurate, at levels that have been measured and are appropriate to the *intended application*" (my emphasis, p. 5).

So, what is the "intended application" of forensic science? In criminal cases, it is usually to assist in resolving some issue "beyond a reasonable doubt." Thus, validation would require that these methods be shown to be capable of producing results, not beyond any doubt but, rather, beyond a reasonable doubt, sometimes described as "an honest doubt of a reasonable person." So, when a latent print is compared with a known print, or a fired bullet with one known to be from a specific firearm, or a questioned item of trace evidence with a known source sample, the purpose is not to determine whether they came from the same source to the exclusion of all other such sources in the world, but rather whether they could have come from a population that might reasonably be expected to have been at that location during a time frame relevant to the incident. The comparison population for a questioned glass sample from a burglar's glove is not all the windows in town but only the broken windows. A bullet from a shooting in Toronto is not reasonably expected to have been fired from a rifle carried by a goat herder in the mountains of Nepal.

Thus, validation for the intended application in forensic science need not be as challenging as some might believe. None of us, however, would dispute that there are limitations in the number of "peer-reviewed, published studies establishing the scientific bases" of some of our disciplines, or that more research to enhance knowledge about their validity and reliability is desirable. Of course it is! Actually, for most of our disciplines, mountains of potential validation data do exist; unfortunately, they are not readily available for external peer review or publication because they are in the training files of all the examiners who have gone through good training programs. Those examiners had to convince themselves and their supervisors through "empirical studies" that the methods they used do indeed produce results of the required reliability before they were ever allowed to apply them to a real case. The toughest test a result has to pass is not the one in the courtroom but rather the one it has to pass before it leaves the laboratory. Junk science, I don't think so!

Something we learn from working with the law is the importance of definitions to any attempt to bring understanding to an issue. There are many definitions of *science*, but all consist of something like

> Science: Knowledge of general facts, laws, and relationships that is obtained through systematic observation and experiment, especially as applied to the physical world and the phenomena associated with it. (McLelland and Stewart, *The Canadian Encyclopedia*, Toronto, 1996)

One definition of junk is

> Junk: Old or discarded articles that are considered useless or of little value. (www.dictionary.com)

If we accept such definitions, information obtained through "systematic observation and experiment" can hardly be considered "useless or of little value." Science and junk are thus mutually exclusive; if something is science, it cannot be junk! There can, therefore, be no such thing as junk science.

In most of the media articles referred to, it is not junk science that is the concern of the writers; it is "junk testimony." For example, there is the testimony by some latent print examiners that their conclusions have "zero error rates" or by some firearms examiners that a bullet was fired from a specific weapon "to the exclusion of all other firearms in the world." Such unnecessarily improper testimony is not limited to these disciplines nor the familiar names, such as Fred Zain, Joyce Gilchrist, or Arnold Melnikoff. It is much more widespread, as shown in a study by Brandon Garrett and Peter Neufeld published in the *Virginia Law Review* in March 2009 titled "Invalid Forensic Science Testimony and Wrongful Convictions."

These authors examined trial transcripts from 137 of 156 DNA exoneration cases, and in 82 (60%) of these, there was forensic science testimony that they described as "invalid testimony." An important feature of this paper, which is the reason I cite it, is that it includes relevant portions of those transcripts so we can evaluate the testimony for ourselves. While I might argue that some of the testimony is not forensic science at all and challenge their categorization of some of it as invalid, the fact is that in many of the cases, it was quite shocking and was presented by seventy-two examiners from fifty-two labs in twenty-five states.

As might be expected, the majority of these cases were sexual assaults from the 1980s and early 1990s, and many involved ABO/PGM [phosphoglucomutase] results or microscopic hair comparisons; i.e., they were the types of cases that had the potential DNA evidence that eventually led to the exoneration. The most common transgressions were a failure to present potentially exculpatory evidence, presenting improper population frequency numbers, and overstating the significance of hair comparisons.

For example, some hair examiners overstated the significance of their observations with statements such as

> Out of all the pubic hairs that I have examined, I have never found two known samples to match in their microscopic characteristics. (*Florida v. Dredge*)

or:

> I have in fact looked at thousands of hair standards and haven't seen two that matched exactly. (*New York v. Richardson and Wise*)

Note that both refer to "known" or "standard" samples that consist of large numbers of hairs rather than to the one or two hairs of a typical questioned sample—quite a different challenge!

There also were tortuous attempts to rationalize results that did not support the prosecution's case. In one case in which the evidence sample was ABO group B, but the defendant was an A, the examiner testified:

> There is a possibility that a bacteria could have worked on these antigens or that they could have broken down so that I could no longer detect that they were there. Given sufficient time for those bacteria to act, it would be possible to convert a group A substance to a B or a B substance to an A. (*Pennsylvania v. Laughman*)

In conclusion, to counter those media articles we must continue to establish that the methods we use are indeed valid and ensure that the testimony offered by forensic scientists is proper and appropriate. Inadequate validation of procedures can be dealt with by additional research and publication. Indeed, much has been done and continues to be done since the release of the NAS [National Academy of Sciences] report in 2009.

Junk testimony, however, is more challenging because it often takes a random event for such a problem with an individual examiner or a particular laboratory to become public. A correction may require the challenging alteration of an institutional culture or an individual's attitude.

I believe there are fewer examples of junk testimony today than there were in the 1980s and 1990s. Accreditation and certification, with their requirements for enhanced training, improved documentation, and careful monitoring, deserve much credit for this. Greater emphasis on professional ethics is also a contributor. Nevertheless, such testimony still occurs. The transmutation of junk (testimony) into gold is difficult, but it can be done, and it is worth doing! We must continue to strive to do so.

Epilogue: A Sense of Pride

During my final interview with Rick Libman in October 1996, he asked a question that I had never seriously thought about: "Having had the good fortune to observe forensic science practices in many countries around the world, have you found that there are many things in common or are things really quite different?" As I considered the question, I began to realize that although there are many different ways to deliver forensic science services, for example, individual practitioners, large or small laboratories staffed with civilian or police specialists, law enforcement agencies, other government entities, university departments, or coroner/medical examiner offices, the methods they use and the items to which these are applied are pretty much the same everywhere. Regardless of the justice system, adversarial as in North America, inquisitorial as in much of Europe, or some unique systems such as in China, forensic science is used to aid in the investigation of the same sorts of cases, with the same types of evidence items, and using the same kinds of equipment and techniques. In the international proficiency testing program described in Chapter 16, there are participants from all corners of the world. Charles Leete, the founder of CTS Inc., and I once examined the results of some tests to see if we could identify significant national differences, and the remarkable thing was that there was nothing remarkable. The volume and distribution of types of cases may differ between countries, states, and provinces, but the practitioners, with very few exceptions, perform their examinations in much the same way and present their results with objectivity and competence.

Rick's final question to me was, "Which of your career achievements gives you the greatest sense of pride?" While I am proud of many of the things accomplished during my more than half-century career in forensic science, I will mention just three.

The first relates to my initial involvement in forensic science, the development of a scientifically sound program of breath testing for alcohol in Ontario. This represented an enormous change in the way in which drinking/driving cases were investigated and made possible large-scale enforcement programs that have saved large, but unknown, numbers of lives. Successfully transitioning from relatively small numbers of blood samples analyzed by university professors or hospital pathologists to large numbers of breath samples analyzed by scientifically unsophisticated police officers, and having their results accepted by the courts in the face of hundreds of legal and scientific challenges, was a remarkable achievement. I am very proud that Ontario has one of the best breath testing programs anywhere in the world. In many jurisdictions, breath testing was considered to be just another technique in law enforcement and was managed by police agencies. In Ontario (and the rest of Canada), it was science based and managed by forensic scientists from the beginning, because it is forensic science! In fact, it is one of the more important of the forensic sciences because of the large impact it has on society. In Ontario, there are something in the order of 40,000 people who are subjected to breath tests each year. For every one of those people, it is a critical event. By comparison, in the rest of the operations of the Centre of Forensic Sciences (CFS), we would typically deal with perhaps a total of 15,000 other cases.

The second pride-inducing achievement was the successful introduction of DNA profiling in Ontario. Not only has this had a major impact on the judicial resolution of serious crimes against persons, but also it is providing valuable support at the investigative stage of the law enforcement process by developing leads to potential suspects from the national DNA databases. Before the establishment of computerized databases of DNA profiles (as well as firearms and fingerprint databases), most of what we did in forensic science did not have a great impact at the investigative stage. We were very good at comparing things and saying, "This sample from the crime scene relates to this sample from this suspect," but that didn't occur until after a suspect had been developed using conventional police procedures. Now, with the DNA (and other) databases, we can provide investigative leads to the investigators in cases where body materials such as blood, semen, saliva, or hairs are found, i.e., the most serious cases, crimes against persons.

As described in Chapter 22, CFS began preparing to introduce DNA analysis within a year of the technique appearing in the scientific literature. It was an enormously complicated process, and under the leadership of Pamela Newall, we moved very slowly and carefully, which resulted in some conflict with police investigators who were "hot to trot" with this new tool. We needed to be certain of everything we did because we were aware of the enormous impact DNA analysis was going to have. As a result, in Ontario we had virtually no significant problems with the introduction of DNA—we had done our homework thoroughly; the staff who were doing the work were well qualified; the validation data was complete; we provided a lot of instruction to Crown attorneys, defense attorneys, and judges; and we introduced it slowly but soundly.

Parenthetically, it is important to understand that although DNA analysis has achieved so much publicity that many people seem to believe that it is all that is done in forensic science laboratories nowadays, the fact is that it is used in only about 20% of the cases examined in most labs.

The third matter of which I am most proud is the quality of the staff that was developed at CFS during my tenure. Although most have now retired, they set the high standards for competence, integrity, and objectivity that are being maintained by their successors. They did so in the face of enormous challenges regarding resources and workload. At one time, I had a real concern that when staff saw a huge backlog of cases constantly waiting for their attention, they might eventually think, "What's the use, we're not making any progress. The heck with it." To their great credit, they never did. Forensic scientists tend not to be very interested in politics; they focus on their science. As a result, we do ourselves a disservice by trying to make the best of what we have and doing a pretty good job with it. This means that we don't have a very high profile, which in government means we don't get the funding required. In spite of this, the staff persevered.

Those three accomplishments are what I take the greatest pride in from my career. If Rick's question had, however, been "What are you proudest of in your life?" my answer would have been easier to provide and quite different: "Our family!" Marie and I have been so fortunate to be blessed with five offspring who have all developed into fine productive members of society, and who have now produced their own families of which we are equally proud. While we share the pride, I have to say that the bulk of the credit for the success of our family must go to Marie. It was she who found all of our residences and developed them into homes. She ensured that there was always food on the table, clothes on everyone's backs, books on the shelves, and love in the air. I have been so fortunate!

Figure E.1 Dr. Lucas and family.

Appendix: Curriculum Vitae of Douglas M. Lucas, DSc (Hon)

Education/Degrees

Primary and Secondary School, Windsor, Ontario
BSc (Pharmacy), University of Toronto, 1953
MSc (Pharmaceutical Chemistry), University of Toronto, 1957
DSc (Honorary), John Jay College of Criminal Justice, City University of New York, 2001
DSc (Honorary), The University of Toronto, 2004

Employment

University of Toronto Faculty of Pharmacy, Instructor, 1953–1957
Attorney General's Laboratory (Centre of Forensic Sciences), Ministry of the Solicitor General Province of Ontario
  Chemist, 1957–1960
  Section Head, Organic Chemistry, 1960–1967
  Director, 1967–1994

Professional Affiliations

Canadian Society of Forensic Science (CSFS)

Member, 1958–1995
Emeritus Member, 1995–present
President, 1968–1969
Alcohol Test Committee
  Member, 1967–2000
  Chairman, 1980–1984

American Academy of Forensic Sciences (AAFS)

Member/Fellow, 1960–1990
Distinguished Fellow, 1990–1994
Retired Fellow, 1994–present
President, 1972–1973
Criminalistics Section
  Secretary, 1961–1962
  Chairman, 1962–1963
  Section Award, 1981
  Outstanding Service Award, 1996
Ad Hoc Committee on Code of Ethics and Bylaws, Co-Chair, 1976
Ethics Committee
  Member, 1977–1994
  Chairman, 1982–1994
Last Word Society, Chairman, 1980–1983
History Committee, Member, 1990–1998
Strategic Planning Committee, Member, 1989–1998
Long Term Planning Committee, Member, 1998–2009
Oversight Task Force, Member, 1995–1997
Golden Anniversary Planning Committee, Chairman 1995–1998
Forensic Sciences Foundation Inc., Chairman, 1986–1991
Gradwohl Medal Recipient, 1995
Douglas M. Lucas Medal for Outstanding International Contributions to Forensic Science—Established, 1999
Code of Ethics Review Committee, Co-Chair, 2007–2008

American Society of Crime Laboratory Directors (ASCLD)

Member, 1974–1994
Emeritus Member, 1994–present
President, 1977–1978
Membership Committee, Chairman, 1982–1985
Proficiency Advisory Committee, Member, 1978–2000
  Chairman, 1981–1991
Briggs J. White Award for Leadership Excellence, 1999

ASCLD/Laboratory Accreditation Board (ASCLD/LAB)

Inspector, 1981–2003
First Recipient of the ASCLD/LAB Douglas M. Lucas Distinguished Service Award, 1993

Forensic Science Society (UK)

Member, 1971–1994
Retired Member, 1994–2009

International Association of Forensic Sciences (IAFS)

President, 1968–1969
Member of Council, 1969–present
First Recipient of the Adelaide Medal, 1990

National Safety Council (US) Committee on Alcohol and Other Drugs

Member, 1960–1994
Emeritus Member, 1994–present
Chairman, 1977–1979
Robert F. Borkenstein Award, 1997

International Committee on Alcohol, Drugs and Traffic Safety

Vice President, 1983–1986

Canadian Association of Fire Investigators

Honorary Member, 1994–present

International Association of Arson Investigators

Member, 1970–1995

Editorial Boards

Journal of the Canadian Society of Forensic Science, 1975–1995
Journal of Forensic Sciences, 1972–1995
Forensic Science International, 1972–1999
Journal of the Forensic Science Society, 1983–1990
Forensic Science Review, 1986–present

Other Honors

Canada Centennial Medal, 1967
Queen Elizabeth Silver Anniversary Medal, 1977

U.S. Department of Justice, Office of the Inspector General Award, 1997
Department of Justice (Canada) Special Award for Service, 1999

Consultation Practice

Postretirement consultation has been restricted primarily to assisting forensic laboratories with solutions to management and/or quality assurance issues, including preparation for accreditation. This has involved laboratories in Australia, Canada, Hong Kong, and the United States. It has also involved serving on a five-member international "Blue Ribbon Scientific Panel" in support of an eighteen-month investigation by the Office of the Inspector General in the U.S. Department of Justice of allegations of misconduct and improper practices by staff of the FBI Laboratory in Washington, DC.

From December 1998 to December 2003, a major activity involved serving as a member of a three-person international "Peer Review Panel" advising the judicial tribunal for the "Bloody Sunday Inquiry" regarding the tragic events of January 30, 1972, in Londonderry, Northern Ireland, in which thirteen civilians were killed and fourteen seriously wounded by gunshots during a confrontation with the British Army. During the period 2003–2006, a similar activity has been associated with a major investigation by the Northern Ireland Police Service, the Omagh bombing in August 1998, in which twenty-nine people were killed by an IRA bomb.

Between January 2005 and June 2006, another important activity involved serving as a scientific advisor to the independent investigator investigating serious problems in the Houston Police Department Crime Laboratory and Property Room. There has also been involvement as a consultant and advisor on generally accepted policies and practices in forensic science laboratories during the 1970s, 1980s, and 1990s in connection with formal reviews of several wrongful conviction cases that occurred during these periods in Canada and the United States.

Lecturing activities since retirement have been restricted primarily to topics on the history of forensic science and on ethics in forensic science.

Publications

Basu, PK, M Avaria, R. Jankie, BM Kapur and DM Lucas, "Effect of Prolonged Immersion on the Ethanol Concentration of Vitreous Humor," *J. Can. Soc. Forensic Sci.*, 16, 2 (1983).

Cimbura, G, DM Lucas, RC Bennett and AC Donelson, "Incidence and Toxicological Aspects of Cannabis and Ethanol Detected in 1,394 Fatally Injured Drivers and Pedestrians in Ontario (1982–1984)," *J. Forensic Sci.*, 35, 1035 (1990).

Cimbura, G, DM Lucas, RC Bennett, RA Warren and HM Simpson, "Incidence and Toxicological Aspects of Drugs Detected in 484 Fatally Injured Drivers and Pedestrians in Ontario," *J. Forensic Sci.*, 27, 855 (1982).

Cimbura, G, RA Warren, RC Bennett, DM Lucas and HM Simpson, "Drugs Detected in Fatally Injured Drivers and Pedestrians in the Province of Ontario," TIRF Report, March (1980).

Field, KS and DM Lucas, "Coming of Age: The American Academy of Forensic Sciences and the Forensic Science Profession—1948 to 1998," *Forensic Sci. Rev.*, 11, 121 (1999).

Howes, JR, RA Hallett and DM Lucas, "A Study of the Accuracy of the Breathalyzer as Operated by Police Personnel," *J. Forensic Sci.*, 12, 444 (1967).

Jones, AW, RH Liu and DM Lucas, "Obituary—Professor RF Borkenstein (1912–2002)," *Accident Anal. Prev.*, 35, 1 (2003).

Lucas, DM, "The Identification of Petroleum Products in Forensic Science by Gas Chromatography," *J. Forensic Sci.*, 5, 336 (1960).

Lucas, DM, "Some New Equipment for the Handling and Transportation of Explosive Devices," *J. Forensic Sci. Soc.*, 7, 204 (1967).

Lucas, DM, "Optics and Instrumentation in Forensic Science," *Appl. Optics*, 8, 15 (1969).

Lucas, DM, "What's New in Forensic Chemistry—1972," *Am. Acad. Forensic Sci. Newsl.*, 2, (1973).

Lucas, DM, "Drugs and Driving," *Crowns Newsl.*, 2, (1985).

Lucas, DM, "Nitroglycerine and Its Neutralization," *Can. Forces Explosive Ordnance Info. Bull.*, September (1985).

Lucas, DM, "Approved Screening Devices—How They Work," in *Breathalyzer Law in Canada*, RM McLeod, JD Takach and MD Segal, Eds., Carswell, Toronto (1986), Chapter 25.

Lucas, DM, "The Breathalyzer—How It Works," in *Breathalyzer Law in Canada*, RM McLeod, JD Takach and MD Segal, Eds., Carswell, Toronto (1986), Chapter 24.

Lucas, DM, "Assessing Breath Test Estimation of Blood Alcohol Concentration," *J. Anal. Toxicol.*, 13, 241 (1989).

Lucas, DM, "Gas Chromatography: Principles and Forensic Applications," in *Advances in Forensic Science*, Vol. 2, HC Lee and RE Gaensslen, Eds., Year Book Medical Publishers, Chicago (1989), Chapter 5.

Lucas, DM, "Production of Breathalyzer Material," *J. Motor Veh. Law*, 1, 103 (1989).

Lucas, DM, "The Ethical Responsibilities of the Forensic Scientist: Exploring the Limits," *J. Forensic Sci.*, 34, 719 (1989).

Lucas, DM, "North of 49—The Development of Forensic Science in Canada," *Sci. Justice*, 37, 47 (1997).

Lucas, DM, "Professor Robert F. Borkenstein—An Appreciation of His Life and Work," *Forensic Sci. Rev.*, 12, 1 (2000).

Lucas, DM, "In Memoriam—Robert F. Borkenstein," *Forensic Sci. Rev.*, 15(1), 2003.

Lucas, DM, "Alcohol and Driving: The Development of Law Enforcement Countermeasures in Canada," *Can. Soc. Forensic. Sci. J.*, 42, 237 (2009).

Lucas, DM, "H. Ward Smith: A Canadian Leader in the Forensic Sciences," *Can. Soc. Forensic. Sci. J.*, 42, 228 (2009).

Lucas, DM, "Professor L. Joslyn Rogers: A Tribute to a Canadian Pioneer in Forensic Science," *Can. Soc. Forensic Sci. J.*, 42, 223 (2009).

Lucas, DM, "Review of: Georgia's Crime Doctor, the Story of Herman Jones and the First 20 Years of the Georgia Crime Laboratory" by J. Jarvis (Book Review), *J. Forensic Sci.*, 55, 277 (2010).
Lucas, DM, "Foreword," in *Wigmore on Alcohol: Courtroom Alcohol Toxicology for the Medicolegal Professional*," JG Wigmore, Irwin Law, Toronto, Ontario (2011).
Lucas, DM, "Global Forensic Science Collaboration: Standards and Research," *Forensic Sci. Policy Manag. Int. J.*, 2, 148 (2012).
Lucas, DM, "The Forensic Sciences: Ideally, How Might They Be Delivered?" *Forensic Sci. Policy Manag. Int. J.*, 4, 7 (2013).
Lucas, DM, "Forensic Science in the Nineteenth and Twentieth Centruries," in *Encyclopedia of Criminology and Criminal Justice*, G Bruinsma and D Weisburd, Eds., Springer Science + Business Media, New York (2014), 1805–1819.
Lucas, DM, "Laboratory Excellence and Ethics, an Essential Association," in *Forensic Laboratory Management: Applying Business Principles*, WM Dale and WS Becker, Eds., Taylor & Francis, New York (2014), 250.
Lucas, DM and G. Eijgelaar, "An Evaluation of a Technique for the Examination of Lipstick Stains," *J. Forensic. Sci.*, 6, 354 (1961).
Lucas, DM and WJ Hayman, "The Determination of Telephone Numbers from the Dial Sounds on a Tape Recording," *Proc. Can. Soc. Forensic Sci.*, (1962).
Lucas, DM, CG Leete and KS Field, "An American Proficiency Testing Program," *Forensic Sci. Int.*, 27, 71 (1985).
Lucas, DM, PJ Newall and DG Sidenberg, "DNA Profiling—A Primer for Crown Attorneys," *Crowns Newsl.*, 4 (1988).
Lucas, DM and NC Sharpe, "The Development of Forensic Science in Ontario," *J. Can. Soc. Forensic Sci.*, 2, 30 (1969).
Lucas, DM and JG Wigmore, "The Broken Telephone Effect," *J. Can. Soc. Forensic Sci.*, 22, 225 (1989).
Salem, H, GWH Lucas and DM Lucas, "Saran Plastic Bags as Containers for Breath Samples," *Can. Med. Assoc. J.*, 82, 682 (1960).
Smith, HW and DM Lucas, "Breath Tests for Alcohol," *Criminal Law Q.*, 1, 1 (1958).
Smith, HW and DM Lucas, "The Development of a Large Scale Breath Testing Program in Ontario," *Proc. 3rd Int. Conf. on Alcohol and Road Traffic*, (1962).
Wigmore, JG and DM Lucas, "The Scientific Validity of the Decision in *Regina v. Phillips*," *J. Motor Veh. Law*, 2, 43 (1990).
Wigmore, JG and DM Lucas, "The Intoxilyzer 5000C—A Computerized Infrared Evidentiary Breath Alcohol Instrument," *J. Motor Veh. Law*, 5, 119 (1993).
Wigmore, JG, DM Lucas and RM Langille, "Blood Alcohol Testing," in *Breathalyzer Law in Canada*, RM McLeod, JD Takach and MD Segal, Eds., Carswell, Toronto (2008), Chapter 20.
Yip, HL and DM Lucas, "A Gas Chromatographic Method for the Comparison of Candle Waxes in Arson Cases," *Proc. Can. Soc. Forensic Sci.*, (1965).

Index

For Product Safety Concerns and Information please contact our EU
representative GPSR@taylorandfrancis.com
Taylor & Francis Verlag GmbH, Kaufingerstraße 24, 80331 München, Germany

www.ingramcontent.com/pod-product-compliance
Ingram Content Group UK Ltd.
Pitfield, Milton Keynes, MK11 3LW, UK
UKHW020021200926
475702UK00014B/1991
9780367787523